United States History:

TO 1877
Fifth Edition

Nelson Klose
Professor Emeritus, American History
San Jose State University

Robert F. Jones
Associate Professor, Department of History
Fordham University, New York

BARRON'S

All inquiries should be addressed to:
Barron's Educational Series, Inc.
250 Wireless Boulevard
Hauppauge, New York 11788

International Standard Book No. 0-8120-1834-6

Library of Congress Catalog Card No. 94-2572

Library of Congress Cataloging-in-Publication Data

Klose, Nelson, 1914–
  United States history to 1877 / Nelson Klose, Robert F.
Jones. — 5th ed.
  p.   cm.
  Rev. ed. of: United States history. 4th ed. ©1972.
  Includes bibliographical references (p.) and index.
  ISBN 0-8120-1834-6
  1.   United   States—History—Colonial   period,   ca.
1600–1775.   2. United   States—History—Revolution,
1775–1783.   3. United States—History—1783–1865.   4.
United States—History—1865–1877.   I. Jones, Robert
Francis, 1935– . II. Klose, Nelson, 1914–   United States
history.   III. Title.
E188.K57   1972
973—dc20   94-2572
                                                  CIP

PRINTED IN THE UNITED STATES OF AMERICA

4567   9770   98765432

TO THE STUDENT

This book has been written to simplify and present the essentials of American history in unified topics to help college students understand and remember subject-matter. The authors have taught college classes in history for many years. A controlling aim has been to avoid personal, original interpretations which are unavoidably controversial and confusing to students. Such originality of treatment reflecting individual interpretations and choice of subject-matter and emphasis limits the usefulness of the usual study aid. The author has avoided the enlargement of his favorite subjects; he has sought to explain American history rather than "reinterpret" it. A student aid should not attempt to be encyclopedic; accordingly, the selective approach used here has avoided the fault of citing unimportant persons and a multitude of official names of agencies and of less significant legislation.

How To Use This Book—Special features have been provided to make this book especially helpful. The topical treatment of subject-matter arranges significant facts and the explanation of each topic in a unified discussion that is easy to follow. This avoids the choppiness and fragmentation of "outlines" and makes it unnecessary to artificially force bits of information under headings where they may not belong. The relative importance of subjects, as determined by the consensus of leading history textbooks, is indicated at the beginning of each topic by stars (✪). This more significant information is likely to be emphasized in well-balanced college examinations; some examination questions, however will probe, quite properly, the thoroughness of the student's preparation by questions over less significant material.

Dates carried at the top of each page guide the student in locating events by chronology; attention to chronological arrangement of topics has made this possible. Anachronistic organization of topics under large-subject headings in stylized writing confuse history students who think chronologically as they should. A chronological arrangement is more likely to parallel any given textbook than an arrangement of subject-matter under broad headings.

Students may underline for themselves important names, dates, and facts as indicated by the instructor in the classroom; this underscoring is an important learning exercise in itself. It is assumed the student will probably be assigned a traditional textbook with its detailed treatment. Bibliographies are provided here to guide the student in selecting additional reading and sources for doing assigned written projects. A large number of review questions have been provided after each chapter and essay questions for midterm and final examination review are given in the back of the book.

Use of Stars—This guide offers a useful feature to assist the student and teacher in concentrating attention on the relatively more significant subjects in the great mass of materials presented in American history courses and textbooks. The author has inserted stars (✪) before headings to indicate the importance of each topic. The determination of the relative importance of topics represents a consensus based upon a study of widely used textbooks, books of selected readings and documents, and subjects covered by prepared examination questions offered for the use of students and teachers.

Three stars (✪✪✪) indicate topics of great significance, two stars (✪✪) indicate important topics, one star (✪) indicates topics of secondary importance, and topics not marked are of least relative significance but too important to omit. This use of stars should help the student gain perspective, but, since opinions vary, students should be alert to the individual instructor's judgment of the significance of topics covered in his lectures. To be well prepared for examinations, students may "overlearn" the more important topics and study the others as time permits.

How to Use the Review Questions—Review questions of several types follow each chapter. These questions have been carefully prepared to give the types of questions at the level of difficulty the student is likely to encounter in college objective examinations. They have been prepared for use as study exercises and by themselves will give the student a substantial review of important subject matter. College teachers much prefer to use the multiple-choice items in examinations; therefore, more space has been given to this type of question. The name "best-answer" is actually a better description of this type of question. If these questions are ideally framed the student will often find that there are two or more alternate responses that seem to be correct; therefore, the student needs to consider each response carefully and select the response that seems to be the "best answer"—rather than marking the first answer that appears to be satisfactory. In using these exercises for review, remember that it is just as helpful to understand why a statement is untrue as to know that it is true.

Dictionary of Important and Difficult Terms—A full dictionary and glossary has been added to provide definitions conveniently for difficult, confusing, and more important terms. It is suggested the student mark those he has difficulty with and concentrate his study upon them. If a term is not found here, use the index to locate it in the main body of this study aid.

TO THE INSTRUCTOR

The instructor who wishes to replace the traditional textbook with supplementary, selected readings of sources, documents, and interpretative articles should find this ample summary sufficient to supply the basic, factual subject-matter of his course. Classroom time can then be used for lectures on special subjects, discussion, and the use of other teaching devices instead of dictating essential subject-matter to students. This condensed treatment could be used also in conjunction with an inexpensive paperback United States history (not necessarily a standard textbook) with literary and interpretive features. This plan would still leave the student enough time and textbook budget to afford a book of "readings" or documents. Or, still better, a selection of fine paperback histories, of which so many are now available, could be substituted for the traditional textbook. Lists of currently available paperbacks are provided here after each chapter, but many new titles are constantly being issued. For these see Bowker's guide to *Paperbound Books in Print*.

The *Chronology* at the beginning of each chapter is intended to give the student a summary of leading events and to satisfy his queries regarding important dates. The *Review Questions* following each chapter and essay questions in the Appendix may be used by the student in lieu of a workbook or other guide to provide study exercises. They also might be suggested for the student's use as review exercises for examinations and to illustrate the type of questions to be expected in both objective and essay examinations.

The emphasis in this concise guide has been placed upon the traditional subject-matter of political, diplomatic, military, and economic history. Cultural and intellectual developments are selected mainly when there is a consensus of opinion as to their significance and to their relevance to traditional subjects.

CONTENTS

(Stars are used to indicate the relative importance of topics. See instructions "To the Student"
for "Use of Stars.")

THE EARLY REPUBLIC, 1789–1861   107

8. THE FEDERALIST PERIOD, 1789–1801   110

THE COLONIAL PERIOD
1492–1763

CHRONOLOGY / CHAPTER 1

1000   Leif Ericson discovered Vinland in North America.
1095   The Crusades began; ended in 1291.
1460   Prince Henry of Portugal died.
1487   Bartholomeu Dias rounded Cape of Good Hope.
1492   Columbus made voyage of discovery to America.
1493   Treaty of Tordesillas revised Line of Demarcation.
1498   Vasco da Gama sailed to India.
1500   Cabral explored Brazil on voyage to India.
1513   Balboa claimed the Pacific for Spain.
        Ponce de Leon explored Florida.
1519   Cortes began conquest of Mexico.
        Magellan began circumnavigation of the globe, completed in 1522.
1524   Verazzano sent by France to explore North America.
1531   Pizarro began conquest of Peru.
1533   Cartier began several exploring expeditions in St. Lawrence Valley.
1539   De Soto began exploration of Mississippi Valley.
1540   Coronado began expedition that explored the Southwest until 1542.
1565   St. Augustine, Florida, founded by Spanish.
1608   Champlain founded Quebec.
1609   Henry Hudson explored North American coast for the Dutch.
        Santa Fe, New Mexico, founded.
1624   Dutch West India Company founded New Amsterdam (New York).
1638   Swedes settled Delaware.
1682   La Salle claimed the Mississippi Valley for France.
1718   San Antonio, Texas, founded.
1769   Colonization of California begun by Spanish Franciscans.

Chapter

1

AMERICA AND EUROPE: THE FIRST ENCOUNTER, 1492–1700

> Columbus's voyages to the land he thought were the Indies were the result of the medieval and early modern expansion of Europe. Since at least the year 1000, Europe had been steadily expanding its political influence and commerce. Recent advances in science and geography had made the times ripe for Columbus's effort and if he had not done so, someone else certainly would have sailed west from Europe, thus encountering the hitherto largely unknown American continent. To properly understand this, the European background to the age of discovery and exploration should be studied. One would then realize that Columbus was not an isolated adventurer, but rather part of the expansion of Europe. The Spanish were the first to introduce European culture to the Americas; the Portuguese, French, Dutch, and English would come later.

MAJOR DEVELOPMENTS IN THE EUROPEAN BACKGROUND OF THE DISCOVERY OF AMERICA

These significant developments and events in Europe explain why and how America came to be discovered.

✪ **The Crusades**—From 1095 to 1291 the Christians of Europe waged a series of religious wars in the eastern Mediterranean against the Moslems. Their object was to capture the Holy lands, including Jerusalem, associated with the life of Christ; their leaders were interested in carving out small principalities for themselves.

The effects of the Crusades upon Europe were significant. 1) These military campaigns brought Europeans in contact with a different, more advanced people and thereby stimulated their curiosity and broadened their intellectual outlook. 2) As they learned more about the Mediterranean

4

area to the east and south, their knowledge of geography increased. 3) Europeans learned to appreciate many of the commodities of Asia. At this time the East was far ahead of Europe in achievements in medicine and science, in the culture and glamour of its cities, and in the enjoyment of a wide variety of food, cloths, and other goods.

Europeans came to appreciate many of the goods of Asia which they had not previously known. Among them were textiles such as silks, damasks, oriental rugs, tapestries, and fine cotton goods. They developed a taste for Asiatic spices—cloves, allspice, ginger, nutmeg, cinnamon, mace, and pepper; these spices proved useful in preserving and making more palatable their stale foods and monotonous diet. A large volume of trade sprang up between Europe and Asia.

○ **The Difficulty of Obtaining Asiatic Goods**—It proved difficult and expensive for Europe to obtain Asiatic goods. Merchants became interested in finding better ways to obtain them. There were about three obstacles to be overcome in conducting commerce with the East: 1) The goods were expensive after being transported over long, hazardous routes. These goods originated in distant China, India, the East Indies, and Persia. Other goods came from Mediterranean areas. Some goods were transported by long caravan routes overland or by a combination of sea and land travel. They were picked up by the Italian merchants at ports in Asia Minor, in the region of Palestine, and in Egypt. 2) The shortage of gold in Europe and the absence of demand in the East for European goods made it difficult for Europe to pay for Asiatic imports or exchange goods for them. 3) Another problem was the monopoly of the Asiatic trade by the Italian merchants. This monopoly made goods more expensive. Other countries in Europe wished to overcome these barriers to commerce.

○ **Rise of the National States**—Before the discovery of America, feudal holdings in the nations of Europe, in particular Portugal, Spain, England, and France, were being steadily consolidated into unified states under the dominance of monarchical dynasties. The increase in trade since the Crusades had given rise to a strong middle class, including rich merchants. Since the kings protected domestic and foreign commerce, the merchants lent money and willingly paid taxes to them and thereby enabled the monarchs to gain power at the expense of the fractious nobility. The introduction and use of gunpowder enabled the kings to win victories over the forces of the feudal nobles and gain territory from them or deprive them of governmental powers they had been exercising. The powerful monarchical states thus created had command of sufficient resources to finance voyages of exploration. As these nation-states became strong, their kings tried to gain advantages for their own nations over the others in a contest to dominate territory and trade.

The Commercial and Geographic Revolutions—All of the changes accompanying the rise of commerce in Europe are usually referred to as the Commercial Revolution. This term denotes the rise of modern business methods such as banking and the use of borrowed capital at interest, the use of money as a medium of exchange, large scale merchandising, and the great increase in the volume and variety of goods traded. These long-developing changes were soon followed by a shift in the main trade routes of Europe from the Mediterranean to the Atlantic Ocean and the eventual commercial supremacy of western Europe over Italy. The expansion of commerce was an essential element in the background of discovery.

The Geographic Revolution increased interest in other lands as more information was gathered concerning them. Marco Polo and other members of this family of merchants visited in the imperial court of China; Marco Polo wrote an interesting account of his stay of over 17 years in China; this account helped arouse a desire for trade with Asia. Missionaries who traveled in Persia, India, China, and still later in Japan added to this knowledge and interest in the Far East.

Pre-Columbian Explorers—Columbus, a thorough student of geography as well as of navigation, had more than an inkling of the possibility of finding new lands (which he thought would be Asia) to the west across the Atlantic. The Norsemen, or Vikings, skilled and daring navigators from Scandinavia, had explored Iceland, Greenland, and Labrador before A.D. 1000. In that year Leif Ericson discovered Vinland, probably present New England, and founded a colony there but it did not become permanent. The Basques made distant fishing voyages in the Atlantic. There were numerous legends and accounts of others who had visited lands far to the west.

✪✪ **Advances in Navigation**—Twelfth century Europe witnessed a number of new inventions. Such technological advances as navigational instruments and better ships made it possible for navigators to venture far outside the Mediterranean Sea. The compass was introduced; the astrolabe, forerunner of today's sextant, was improved so that navigators could determine their location by the stars, in the absence of any landmarks. Larger and better ships were built and sailing methods improved. More and better maps and charts aided navigators in locating their position, in taking advantage of winds and sea currents, and in avoiding dangers.

✪ **Prince Henry *the Navigator* and the Portuguese**—Henry, Prince of Portugal (1394–1460), led his country in the advancement of navigation and exploration. He established a school of navigation for purposes of studying the arts of seamanship. Many famous navigators, students at Prince Henry's school, explored the coast of Africa, discovered new lands for Portugal, and opened trade in ivory, gold, and slaves. These explorations reached farther and farther down the coast of Africa until the Cape of Good Hope was rounded in 1487 by Bartholomeu Dias.

In 1498 Vasco da Gama sailed to India and started a profitable trade between Portugal and the Far East; in doing so he first achieved the goal pursued by Columbus.

THE WORK OF COLUMBUS

Christopher Columbus's birth in a family of merchants in Genoa, Italy, gave him a strong interest in navigation and trade. This ambitious, persistent, aggressive Italian, an able student of geography and navigation, conceived and promoted the idea that a direct, all-water route to the Indies might be found by sailing due west. There were stories among sailors of lands to the west. Columbus believed, like other well-informed men of his time, that the world was round. Thus Columbus reasoned that the Indies might be reached by sailing either east or west, and by his calculations he convinced himself that the route to the west was the shorter one. As early as 1482 Columbus sought the support of the King of Portugal, was refused, but called in vain on other monarchs for support.

❂❂❂ **The Voyages of Columbus**—Columbus, with the aid of a friendly scholar in the Spanish court, finally convinced King Ferdinand and Queen Isabella of the feasibility and importance of his project for locating a direct trade route to the Indies. With the backing of the Spanish crown he sailed, in August 1492, in three small ships and in October reached the Bahamas. On this first voyage he also discovered Cuba and Haiti. He believed the new lands he had discovered to be outlying parts of the Indies and called the natives "Indians." He left a garrison on Haiti (Hispaniola) but all these men had been killed by the Native Americans when Columbus returned on his second voyage to America.

❂❂ **Later Voyages of Columbus and Other Sea Voyages of the Spanish**—Columbus made three later voyages, exploring in the West Indies and along the coast of Central America. Since he was not able to live up to his promises to tap into the spice trade or discover the golden cities of which Marco Polo had written, he died discredited.

Other Spanish voyages brought more information about America. Americus Vespucius made voyages of exploration in South America and proved America to be a continent. A German geographer named the new world for Americus. In 1513 the explorer Balboa led several hundred men across Panama to the continental divide; viewing the Pacific from the mountains, he named it the South Seas and claimed all the lands washed by its waters for Spain. Ferdinand Magellan, sailing for Spain (1519–1522), first circumnavigated the globe. Magellan himself was killed by the natives of the Philippines but one of his vessels completed the voyage.

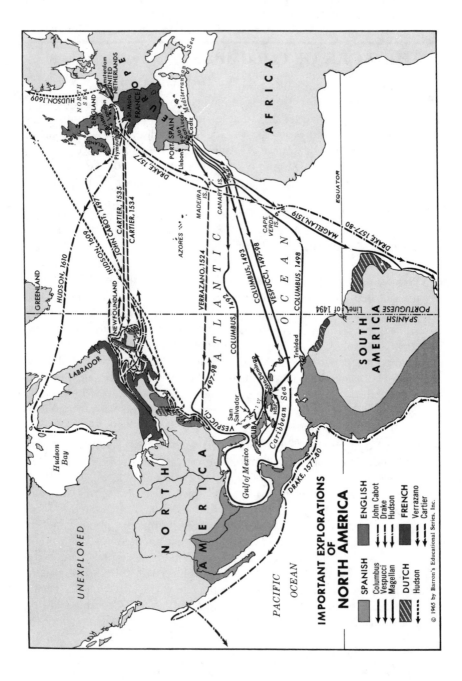

IMPORTANT EXPLORATIONS OF NORTH AMERICA

SPANISH
Columbus
Vespucci
Magellan

ENGLISH
John Cabot
Drake
Hudson

FRENCH
Verrazano
Cartier

DUTCH
Hudson

© 1965 by Barron's Educational Series, Inc.

✪✪✪ **The Line of Demarcation**—As a result of the conflicting claims of Spain and Portugal for title to the land their explorers were traversing, the Pope drew a Line of Demarcation to divide the American continent into two equal parts. The first line was drawn 100 leagues west of the Cape Verde Islands. In 1493 the Treaty of Tordesillas changed the line to run still farther to the west of the Cape Verde Islands and through the eastern part of South America. The Demarcation Line and the accidental voyage of Pedro Cabral to the coast of Brazil in 1500 explain how Brazil came to be settled by the Portuguese. The Demarcation Line reserved most of America for Spain and reserved Asia for Portugal. Europe's later division into Catholic and Protestant as a result of the Reformation meant that other nations ignored the Pope's authority and Line of Demarcation and explored and colonized America, some for religious reasons, but mostly because they wanted to establish colonies.

THE NATIVE AMERICANS

Most scientists agree that the Native Americans are descendants of migrants coming from Asia by way of the Aleutian Islands. By 1492 their numbers had multiplied to probably several million and they had spread over both North and South America. Relatively advanced civilizations were developed by the several Native American cultures in Central and South America.

Among the Native Americans in the present United States the basic political unit was the clan. Chiefs served as military leaders and sachems as political leaders and judges. The land belonged to the tribe and clan; private ownership was not known and never understood even when Europeans sought to enforce it. European trade rivalry added a new motive to the usual wars of the Native American tribes.

Native American contributions to the continent's life and culture have been mainly in utilitarian areas. 1) Their greatest contribution was in the agricultural plants they had developed. Native Americans taught the Europeans how to cultivate and use these crops. Leading crops of Native American origin are corn, white and sweet potatoes, cotton, tobacco, tomatoes, and many varieties of beans and squash. Native Americans did not have the benefit of any of our familiar domesticated animals except the dog. 2) Native Americans in our population are now about equal in number to the population in America at the time of Columbus. Native American blood has been perpetuated purely and partly by intermarriage with whites and African Americans. 3) A conspicuous contribution was made in place names; many American states, rivers, and cities have names of Native American origin. Some words in our vocabulary are of Native American origin, such as *caucas, moccasin,* and *succotash.* 4) Native Americans taught the first Europeans how to live from the abundance of nature by hunting, trapping, and woodcraft and thus gave geographical information to early explorers and settlers.

SPANISH SETTLEMENT OF THE MAINLAND

Settlers brought to Haiti on the second voyage of Columbus in 1493 founded the first permanent Spanish colony in America. By 1515 the Spaniards had also occupied Puerto Rico, Jamaica, and Cuba. These colonies served as bases for the extension of Spanish conquest to the mainland of America where the centers of Spanish control were established.

○○ **Early Exploration and Conquest**—The two greatest conquests of the Spanish were the overthrow of the two Native American empires, the Aztecs and the Incas. Hernan Cortes (1519–1521) with a small band of soldiers overthrew Montezuma and conquered his Aztec subjects of central Mexico. Francisco Pizarro in a similar adventure beginning in 1531, conquered the Incas of Peru. Cortes and Pizarro both looted fabulous hoards of gold and silver and whetted the Spanish appetite for more such treasures.

Spanish incursions into the present mainland of the United States began in 1513 when Ponce de Leon explored Florida. Panfilo de Narvaez with 600 men also landed in Florida, in 1528; of this expedition only Cabeza de Vaca and three others survived, after wandering over the vast territory north of Mexico. Next, Hernando de Soto led 600 men into Florida in 1539; marching as far to the west as Oklahoma, they discovered the Mississippi River where De Soto was buried. In the Southwest, Francisco Coronado (1540–1542) marched up from Mexico, crossed the Rio Grande, and explored the high plains of New Mexico, Texas, Oklahoma, and Kansas. These explorations gave the Spanish territorial claims that were later followed by colonization.

Colonization by the Spanish—Failing to find precious metals or wealthy Native American civilizations in the regions of the present United States, the Spanish neglected to colonize until they felt forced to do so by the intrusions of the French, English, or Russians. To prevent the French from occupying the east coast of Florida, the Spanish established a post at St. Augustine in 1565; this was the first white settlement within the present United States.

New Mexico was the next such region to be settled; in 1598 Juan de Onate occupied the upper Rio Grande valley. The settlement of Santa Fe, founded in 1609, came to be the capital of New Mexico. In 1769 Upper California's settlement was begun when San Diego was founded. Several missions were begun in the early eighteenth century to check French expansion from Louisiana into Texas; of these San Antonio, founded in 1718, came to be the main center of Spanish influence in Texas.

○ **The Spanish Colonial System**—At first the Spanish King entrusted the conquest of new lands to the conquistadors such as Cortez. Military leaders were given permission to establish economic and political control over the native populations by grants of encomiendas (huge landed estates). Later missions and military posts, or presidios, became the instrument for the extension of Spanish rule on the American frontiers. In many places towns, ranches, and mines were opened by private enterprise.

Everywhere the authority of the Spanish King was supreme. A strict and highly regulated mercantilistic policy—to develop the colonies for the benefit of Spain—was enforced. Foreigners were excluded from trade with the colonies and trade with Spain was under strict government control. For the government of the colonies a Council of the Indies was created in Spain and the colonies placed under two viceroys in America, one in Mexico, the other in Peru. The crown appointed all officials and governed autocratically.

EARLY EXPLORATION AND SETTLEMENT IN NORTH AMERICA BY THE FRENCH AND THE DUTCH

The papal division of the world between Spain and Portugal did little to deter other nations from exploring and colonizing America when they chose to do so.

○○ **The French in America**—At first the French came to the Canadian coasts and to Newfoundland organized as small fishing and fur trading expeditions, beginning about 1504. In 1524 the French government sent its first explorer, Giovanni Verazzano, to the American Atlantic coast to search for the Northwest Passage through America to the Pacific. Jacques Cartier, in three different expeditions from 1533 to 1541, explored the lower reaches of the St. Lawrence and gave France a claim to Canada. The growing French interest in the profitable fur trade brought the founding of Quebec in 1608 by Samuel de Champlain. This beginning of permanent settlement by the French in Canada was extended by traders and missionaries far into the interior by way of the Great Lakes and the Mississippi River system.

The French first moved into the Mississippi Valley in 1673 with the voyages of Jacques Marquette, a Jesuit missionary and explorer, and Louis Jolliet, a fur trader and explorer. Later, Sieur Robert de La Salle traveled the Mississippi to the Gulf of Mexico and claimed it for France in 1682. La Salle was exploring to the southwest of the Mississippi in Texas when he was killed by his men in 1687. On the Gulf of Mexico the French, from 1699 to 1718, founded Biloxi, Mobile, and New Orleans.

Over the vast area explored and claimed by the French, widely scattered missions, trading posts, and agricultural settlements were founded. The French traded with the Native Americans and maintained friendly relations with them. However, an important powerful Native American confederacy was converted into fierce enemies of the French when Champlain aided some Algonquins in an attack on the Iroquois in 1609. The Iroquois became allies of the Dutch and English and helped prevent French expansion south of Montreal.

○ **Dutch Exploration and Settlement**—The search of the American east coast for a Northwest Passage led the Dutch West Indian Company to send Henry Hudson, an Englishman employed by them, to explore the coast from Virginia to Newfoundland in 1609. The next year the Dutch began fur trade with the Native Americans on the Hudson River. In 1624 the Dutch West Indian Company founded the settlement of New Amsterdam (New York) on the Hudson River and the colony of New Netherland.

The Dutch used the patroon system to secure the settlement of the colony; patroons were granted large blocks of land in return for settling families. The fur trade was the most important business of the colony. The Dutch expanded to the east as far as the Connecticut River and in the south captured settlements on the Delaware that Sweden had founded in 1638.

CHAPTER BOOK LIST

Bakeless, John, *Eyes of Discovery: America as Seen by the First Explorers* (Dover). Observations of Native Americans and plant and animal life by early explorers in the present United States.

Bourne, E.G., *Spain in America* (Barnes and Noble). Best concise work on Spanish colonization in America.

Cheyney, E.P., *European Background of American History: 1300–1600* (Collier). Social influences upon the colonies.

Crosby, Alfred W., Jr., *The Columbian Voyages, the Columbian Exchange, and their Historians* (1987). Ecological impact of exploration on America and Europe.

Davis, Ralph, *The Rise of Atlantic Economies* (1973). Economic transformation of early modern Europe.

Fagan, Brian, *Kingdoms of Gold, Kingdoms of Jade: The Americas before Columbus* (1991). Pre-Columbian civilizations.

Lockhart, James, and Schwartz, Stuart B., *Early Latin America: A History of Colonial Latin America and Brazil.* (1983). Complete and competent survey.

Mahn-Lot, Marianne, *Columbus* (Evergreen). Gives background of the age of exploration and uses original sources to describe explorations of Columbus.

Morgan, Edmund S., *American Slavery, American Freedom: The Ordeal of Colonial Virginia* (1975).

Morison, E.E., *Admiral of the Ocean Sea* (1942). Authoritative, reads like an adventure story. The author retraced the voyages of Columbus personally.

Morison, S.E., *Christopher Columbus* (Mentor). Brief, fascinating account by the leading authority on Columbus.

Morison, Samuel Eliot, *The European Discovery of America: The Northern Voyages, 500–1600* (1971); The European Discovery of America: The Southern Voyages, 1492–1616. (1974).

Packard, L.B., *The Commercial Revolution* (1927). Brief study stressing mercantilism.

Parkman, Francis, *Discovery of the Great West: La Salle* (Holt). Classic biography of the great discoverer.

Parry, J.H., *The Discovery of the Sea* (1981). European expansion.

Prescott, W.H, *Conquest of Peru* (Dolphin). Lengthy, standard work; authoritative and reads like an adventure story.

Wissler, Clark, *Indians of the United States: Four Centuries of Their History and Culture* (1946). Anthropological approach.

Wright, Louis B., *Religion and Empire: The Alliance Between Piety and Commerce in English Expansion 1558–1625* (1943).

REVIEW QUESTIONS

MULTIPLE CHOICE

1. The section of the North American coast called Vinland by Leif Ericson was probably present day (1) Greenland (2) Virginia (3) New England (4) Iceland.

2. The growth of the commerce and wealth of the cities of Italy resulted from (1) the failure of Spain to open an all-water route to the Far East (2) contacts made during the Crusades (3) Columbus's discovery of an all-water route to the East (4) Turkish conquests in the region of the Far East.

3. The rise of the nation-states of the late Middle Ages is due mostly to (1) the church (2) the nobility (3) the serfs (4) the middle class.

4. The exploration for new sea routes to the Far East was begun by (1) Italian seamen (2) Portuguese navigators (3) English merchants (4) Spanish conquistadors.

5. The opening of an all-water route to India (1) came after Columbus's first voyage (2) prevented Dutch exploitation of the Far East (3) ended the Italian monopoly of trade with Asia (4) gave the English an immediate monopoly in India.

6. Cities dominating the commerce between Europe and the East were (1) Cherbourg and Marseilles (2) Venice and Genoa (3) Cadiz and Oporto (4) Bristol and London.

7. Columbus made his first landfall in (1) the Bahama Islands (2) Cuba (3) Puerto Rico (4) Haiti.

8. The Papal Line of Demarcation (1) allowed Portugal to claim Brazil, (2) gave the Philippines to Spain (3) permitted France to claim Canada (4) recognized the Italian domination of trade with Asia.

9. What was the Native Americans' greatest contribution to American civilization? (1) Corn, tobacco, white potatoes (2) several kinds of domesticated animals (3) many geographic names (4) methods of warfare.

10. Columbus (1) never discovered any of mainland America (2) thought he had found lands adjacent to China (3) was of Venetian origin (4) made two voyages to America.

11. In America the Spanish first occupied (1) Panama (2) Mexico (3) Florida (4) Hispaniola.

12. Which of these men founded Quebec? (1) Verazzano (2) Champlain (3) La Salle (4) Cartier.

13. The relationship of the Iroquois to the French proved significant because the Iroquois (1) kept the French from colonizing South Carolina (2) helped the French against the New Englanders (3) allied themselves with the English and checked French expansion south of Montreal (4) were the most energetic fur gathering Native Americans.

14. Which of these colonizing nations occupied the largest area in North America during the colonial period? (1) English (2) French (3) Dutch (4) Swedes.

TRUE-FALSE

15. America was discovered accidentally within ten years after the discovery by Columbus.

16. The Crusades caused a great increase in trade between Europe and Asia because Asia wished to enjoy the luxuries of Europe's more advanced civilization.

17. Imports from Asia were expensive mainly because they were transported by land.

18. The term "Commercial Revolution" refers partly to the introduction of modern business methods, including the use of money.

19. There is little reason to believe any Europeans other than the Norsemen visited America before Columbus.

20. The astrolabe was invented by Italian navigators a few years before Columbus made his voyage.

21. Bartholomeu Dias opened the all-water trade route between Portugal and India.

22. During Columbus's time educated men believed the world to be round.

23. In his voyages to America Columbus never realized he had discovered new lands not a part of Asia.

24. In drawing the Line of Demarcation the Pope was seeking to pre vent a quarrel between Spain and Portugal.

25. Private ownership of land was not recognized by Native Americans.

26. Spanish colonization north of Mexico into the Southwest was motivated by the opportunity to loot Native American treasures there.

27. A single viceroy ruled the Spanish colonies in America.

28. The profitable fur trade caused the French to spread rapidly over the area they came to control.

29. The Dutch settled in America to gain control of land for speculative purposes.

MATCHING

30. Prince Henry
31. Pizarro
32. Balboa
33. Narvaez
34. Magellan
35. De Leon
36. Marquette
37. Coronado
38. Champlain
39. Hudson

a. Cabeza de Vaca survived his expedition

b. Encouraged exploration of African coast

c. His ships first circumnavigated the globe

d. Explored in New Mexico and Kansas

e. First to sight the Pacific

f. Explored in New York for the Dutch

g. Founder of Quebec

h. Conqueror of Peru

i. Discoverer of Brazil

j. Missionary explorer of the Mississippi Valley

k. First to explore Florida

CHRONOLOGY / CHAPTER 2

1497 John Cabot's exploration along the North American coast gave England a claim to American soil.

1534 Separation of the English Church from Rome led to English leadership of Protestant nations in the Religious Wars.

1558 Elizabeth I (1558–1603) became Queen of England.

1577 Drake began voyage of circumnavigation of the globe; completed in 1580.

1587 Raleigh's colony at Roanoke Island begun.

1588 English defeat of the Spanish Armada.

1603 James I (1603–1625) ascended English throne.

1607 Jamestown colony founded.

1620 Pilgrims settled Plymouth colony.

1624 Jamestown made a royal colony.

1634 St. Mary's, Maryland, settled.

1636 Roger Williams began settlement of Rhode Island.

1640 English Civil War and Cromwellian period until 1660.

1649 Maryland Act of Toleration passed.

1660 Charles I (1660–1685) ascended English throne.

1664 New Netherland taken by the English.

1670 Settlement of Charles Towne, Carolina, begun.

1676 Bacon's Rebellion.

1681 Pennsylvania granted to William Penn.

1685 James II (1685–1688) ascended English throne.

1689 Glorious Revolution brought William and Mary to the English throne.

1733 Savannah, Georgia, settled.

Chapter

2

THE FOUNDING OF THE BRITISH AMERICAN COLONIES, 1607–1733

English colonization of America was long delayed. The Tudor kings busied themselves in consolidating their claims to the throne and in centralizing government in the crown. In 1497 John Cabot touched the North American coast and gave England her first claim to American soil but no settlement was attempted. Throughout most of the sixteenth century, England was distracted by the Protestant Reformation and the accompanying wars of religion in Europe. In addition, the contest with Catholic Spain was especially sharp, partly the result of the Spanish King, Phillip II's marriage to the short-lived Queen Mary of England, and partly owing to the usual imperial considerations. After England's defeat of the Spanish Armada in 1588, Spain could not effectively oppose her entry into America.

BEGINNINGS OF ENGLISH COLONIZATION IN AMERICA

As with other European nations, England's exploration of North America was partly motivated by a search for a water passage through to the Pacific—the Northwest Passage. After Elizabeth, the Protestant daughter of Henry VIII, became Queen, England, as head of the European Protestant nations, began a long period of rivalry and warfare with Spain. At first this rivalry, on the part of England, took the form of piratical sea raids against Spanish colonies and shipping.

○○ **The "Sea Dogs"**—In the 1560s John Hawkins, the leader of the "sea dogs," began raiding Spanish treasure ships and ports in the Caribbean—with the secret support of Elizabeth. Hawkins also engaged in illicit trade, particularly in slaves from Africa. In the 1570s Sir Francis Drake began making raids in the Spanish West Indies. On his most famous voyage he sailed into the Pacific Ocean to raid unguarded Spanish shipping on the Pacific coast as far north as San Francisco. From California he crossed the Pacific to return to England and thereby completed the second circumnavigation of the globe. He was knighted by Elizabeth for his daring exploits against Spain. Subsequently open warfare broke out with Spain. The defeat of the Spanish Armada in 1588 gave Britain naval supremacy over Spain and made possible the planting of the first colonies in America.

✪ **Early English Failures in Founding Colonies**—Sir Humphrey Gilbert in 1583 attempted to found a colony in Newfoundland, but these plans ended when Gilbert died in a sea storm. His half-brother, Sir Walter Raleigh, was responsible for sending three expeditions to Roanoke Island in North Carolina from 1585 to 1587. The first two attempts failed completely. The third expedition planted a colony in 1587. When a relief vessel arrived in 1590, only the buildings built by the colonists were found; the settlers had disappeared and their fate has never been determined.

ENGLISH MOTIVES FOR COLONIZATION

English leaders for a long time and for various reasons had advocated the founding of colonies in America. The defeat of the Spanish Armada and experience gained from the failure of Raleigh paved the way for success.

✪✪✪ **Economic Motives**—Economic considerations were undoubtedly the most effective in promoting colonization. 1) Among these was the accumulation of surplus capital and the profit motive. Wealthy businessmen sought opportunities to invest their money. Joint-stock companies sold shares of stock to venturers and enabled them to share the great expense and risk of founding colonies as business enterprises. 2) The prevailing economic theory of mercantilism stressed the need of a nation to accumulate the precious metals—the English hoped to find gold in the colonies. 3) Thus, England wished to secure vital raw materials from her own colonies instead of paying precious coin to other countries. 4) The need for markets for England's surplus of manufactures argued for the establishment of captive markets in the form of colonies. 5) Among individual colonists the simple desire to own land and enjoy a better living motivated emigration.

✪✪✪ **Religious Motives**—The Protestant Reformation gave rise to dissenting sects who aggressively sought to worship according to their own ideas instead of conforming to the religious uniformity required by the Anglican Church. Since religious conformity was identified with political conformity, the kings sought to enforce obedience to the practices of the established church. The nonconforming sects were persecuted in the attempts to enforce the religious law of the land. The persecuted sought to escape to America where vacant land offered them an opportunity to settle and follow their own consciences in religious matters. Among these religious groups were the Catholics, Puritans, and Quakers. Unlike the French and Spanish, relatively few of the English colonizers wished to convert the natives to Christianity.

✪✪✪ **Social and Political Motives**—1) The enclosure movement, taking land out of cultivation and converting it into pastureland for sheep, was creating an apparent surplus population. Sheep raising, although profitable for the realm, required many fewer laborers than agriculture. The social and political pressures created by the dispossessed tenants caused some to propose colonization as a way of employing the "sturdy beggars," (unemployed persons) who roamed the country looking for work. 2) The desire for adventure—opportunity and new experiences—moved others to go to America. 3) Related to a desire for religious freedom was the wish of some for a greater degree of political freedom than they had in England. 4) The government also wanted to weaken Spain by establishing military and naval outposts in America.

THE COLONY OF VIRGINIA

King James I in 1606 chartered the Virginia Company. This company was composed of two subsidiary groups, the London Company and the Plymouth Company. The London Company succeeded in settling the first permanent English settlement in what was to become the United States when, in 1607, the colony at Jamestown was founded in Virginia.

✪✪ **Early Difficulties at Jamestown**—In the spring of 1607 three vessels brought 105 colonists to establish the Jamestown colony on a low peninsula in the James River. The ultimate success of the colony was not assured for several years; disease and starvation brought death to a large majority of the settlers of the first few years but new colonists replaced the losses.

The great sufferings of the colony were due to: 1) the choice of a swampy malarial location, 2) a lack of incentive to individual industriousness since all members shared the company profits regardless of how hard they worked, 3) simple ignorance of how to cope with their environment and how to use the abundance it offered, 4) unsuitability of the colonists for the labor required of them—many were gentlemen or were unambitious, 5) poor management by council members, 6) wasting time searching for gold and a route to the Indies, and 7) hostility of the Native Americans. Only the forceful leadership and common sense of the adventurer, Captain John Smith, who was soon made "president" of the colony, saved it from complete failure.

⊙ **Leading Events in Early Virginia**—The ultimate success of the colony was assured in 1612 when John Rolfe introduced the cultivation of a superior variety of tobacco for which there was a large and profitable market in Europe. In 1616 the joint-stock system was terminated and land was granted to private owners to give the colonists a greater incentive to produce. The labor supply of the colony increased as indentured servants were imported.

Several changes in the government of the colony were made during the early years. In 1609 a new charter placed supreme authority in a governor but the council was retained to advise him; both governor and council were appointed by the company. In 1619 the first legislature was established; each plantation was permitted to send two elected representatives to meet with the governor and his council to legislate for the colony.

In 1624 the crown dissolved the Virginia Company and Virginia became a royal colony. An increase in the death rate and a Native American massacre in 1622, in which 357 colonists were killed, gave James I the excuse to force the company to surrender its charter.

⊙⊙ **Virginia After 1624**—As a royal colony, Virginia was ruled by a governor and council appointed by the king but the assembly was elected by the limited number of settlers who qualified to vote. Actually the colony enjoyed a considerable degree of self-government.

In 1676 Bacon's Rebellion occurred. Sir William Berkeley, who served as governor from 1642 to 1677, favored the strong monarchy under Charles II beginning in 1660. Berkeley showed strong favoritism for the planters of eastern Virginia while he neglected the interests of the settlers on the frontier to the west. The western farmers became so infuriated at the failure of the government to stop the continual Native American attacks on white settlers that they formed an expedition, without the governor's authority, to punish the Native Americans. Nathaniel Bacon, a well-educated, recent emigrant from England, placed himself at the head of the expedition. Berkeley did not dare to punish Bacon but instead called a long overdue election to choose delegates for a new meeting of the assembly. The assembly voted many needed reforms against Berkeley's wishes and sent Bacon on another expedition against the Native Americans. While Bacon was away, Governor Berkeley organized an army against him. Bacon responded by marching against Jamestown, burning the city, and forcing the governor to flee. At this moment Bacon died of fever. Berkeley regained control of the colony and hanged so many of the rebels that Charles II in 1677 recalled him to England in disgrace. Bacon's Rebellion foreshadowed later disturbances in that it came out of the resentment of backcountry settlers at the lack of services and protection from a government dominated by those living in the safe areas of the colony.

ESTABLISHMENT OF THE NEW ENGLAND COLONIES

The religious motive is often emphasized as the predominant one in the migration of the early English colonizers to New England, but economic motives were equally strong.

OO The Plymouth Colony—The Pilgrims who settled at Plymouth were a group of Separatists from the town of Scrooby. The Separatists believed in complete independence of each congregation and strongly opposed the authority of the Anglican Church. They first migrated to Holland but, not wanting their children to become Dutch, secured a patent from the Virginia Company to settle in Virginia. They secured the financial support of a joint-stock company of London merchants. Aboard the *Mayflower* the Pilgrims reached Cape Cod in November, 1620.

When storms blew the *Mayflower* off its course and the Pilgrims found themselves about to land outside the bounds of the Virginia Company, they drew up The Mayflower Compact to pledge the colonists to abide by a system of government under the rule of the majority. In 1621 they secured possession of the land in a patent from the Council for New England, successor to the Virginia Company. In 1623 the colony divided its lands among the settlers. Besides farming, the colonists engaged in a profitable fur trade. The governor and the assistants met with the people to legislate until the population became too large and widespread. Later, outlying towns chose representatives to attend the General Court (legislature). William Bradford, the first governor, served for thirty years. In 1686 Plymouth was made a part of the Dominion of New England and in 1691 was absorbed by Massachusetts.

OOO The Massachusetts Bay Colony—The Bay Colony was much larger and of more importance in the founding of New England than Plymouth. It originated as a commercial (fishing) venture but was later populated by thousands of Puritan refugees who settled the land to become farmers. In 1629 the merchant founders of the colony secured a new self-governing charter for the Massachusetts Bay Company. The founding of the Bay Colony is usually dated from 1630 when John Winthrop, who was chosen governor, settled at Boston with a thousand followers. Other towns quickly sprang up around Boston from 1630 to 1640 during the "Great Migration" when about 25,000 Puritans came to Massachusetts to escape the persecution of Bishop Laud and the High Church Anglicans during the rule of Charles I.

Although the Massachusetts government was heavily influenced by the Puritan clergy, it was not a theocracy, as the clergy were not elected to civil office and a careful (for the seventeenth century) line was drawn between civil and religious matters. Only members of the church were permitted to vote and participate in government. According to the colony's charter the "freemen"—of whom there were only 12 in 1630—were to choose the court of assistants to the governor. The base of the government was broadened in the fall of 1630 when 109 members of the church won the right to become "freemen."

When, in 1634, the General Court sought to levy taxes against outlying towns, these towns demanded the right to send deputies to the General Court. This right was granted. After 1644 the deputies and assistants began to meet separately and thus originated a two-house legislature, which not only levied taxes but passed laws. The government was still far from democratic as only members of the church, those who were convinced and had satisfied the minister and elders that they were among the elect, chosen by God to be saved, were allowed to vote. Anyone who disagreed substantially with the ruling group either left the colony voluntarily or was expelled. The outstanding leader among the Boston Puritans was John Winthrop; he served as governor during most of the years of the two decades from 1630 to 1650.

✪ Rhode Island—This colony south of Boston resulted from the religious intolerance of Massachusetts. The leader in the founding of Rhode Island was Roger Williams. Williams advocated separation of church and state because he feared that the church, composed only of the elect, would be contaminated by even the slightest involvement in civil affairs. Thus, the state could not enforce attendance at services nor could it support the church financially from tax revenues. He also believed that land could be acquired only by honest purchase from the Native Americans.

When his expulsion from the Bay Colony was voted in 1635, Williams fled to the Narragansett Native Americans and in 1636 began the settlement of Providence. Another disputatious individual, Mrs. Anne Hutchinson, after creating great dissension in Boston, was banished. With some of her followers, she founded Portsmouth (1638) near Williams' town of Providence. Newport (1639) was founded when a group led by William Coddington was expelled from Portsmouth. A heretical refugee from Boston named Samuel Gorton, unacceptable even to Roger Williams, founded Warwick (1643), the fourth of the Rhode Island settlements. In 1644 Williams secured from Parliament a charter for the four communities and in 1663 a permanent charter was granted. Complete religious liberty was assured by the latter charter.

✪ Connecticut—The fertile lands along the Connecticut River and the profits of the fur trade operated as the primary motives in the founding of Connecticut. Controversies over religious and political matters were of secondary importance. Thomas Hooker in 1636 led the first group of migrants westward from the vicinity of Boston to found Hartford. In the same year other towns were established by settlers from Massachusetts. In 1639 the Fundamental Orders of Connecticut were drawn up to provide government for the Connecticut towns. This became the first constitution written in America. It provided a representative government through a General Court that combined legislative, judicial, and administrative powers as did the same body in Massachusetts.

A colony at New Haven was founded by London Puritans in 1637 under the Reverend John Davenport and a merchant, Theophilus Eaton. This strict Puritan colony suffered from various weaknesses and in 1662 reluctantly joined Connecticut under a new charter that combined the two colonies.

New Hampshire and Maine—In 1623 two English gentlemen, Sir Ferdinando Gorges and Captain John Mason, were granted a patent to the regions north of Massachusetts. Later Mason took the western part and named it New Hampshire and Gorges took the region next to the coast which became Maine. The colonizers had little success and the colonies were settled by immigrants from Massachusetts instead. Since these settlers looked to Massachusetts for their government, they were taken over by the Bay Colony. In 1679 Charles II made New Hampshire a separate royal colony. Maine remained a part of Massachusetts until it entered the Union as a separate state under the Compromise of 1820.

The region known as Vermont never existed as a separate colony. During the colonial period, its area was disputed between New York and New Hampshire and it had no definite boundaries until it was admitted as the fourteenth state in 1791.

✪✪✪ **The New England Confederation (1643)**—The first move to combine the colonies in any common effort was made in 1643 in the face of military danger from the Native American tribes of New England, the Dutch to the southwest, and the French to the north. The Confederation, composed of four members, Massachusetts, Plymouth, Connecticut, and New Haven, endured until 1684 but was somewhat ineffective after 1665. The detested Rhode Islanders were never admitted. The colony members each sent annually two representatives to determine Native American policy, deal with foreign powers, and settle differences among themselves. Lack of cooperation from Massachusetts led to its disintegration.

ESTABLISHMENT OF THE SOUTHERN COLONIES

The Southern Colonies all originated under proprietary charters except Virginia and Delaware which were founded as trading companies.

✪✪ **Maryland**—Sir George Calvert (Lord Baltimore) in 1632 obtained a grant of land between the Potomac River and the 49th parallel in order to establish a refuge for Catholics and others who were persecuted religiously, as well as to improve his family's fortunes. When George Calvert died in 1632, his son Cecilius Calvert received the charter. In 1634 the first settlement was made at St. Mary's. The colony prospered from the very beginning as an agricultural colony and benefited from the experiences of Virginia as well as material aid from her southern neighbor.

The colony set a pattern for proprietary colonies. The manor lords held estates of 1,000 to 3,000 acres as tenants directly from Cecilius Calvert and in turn rented the land directly to small tenants. Thus was transplanted the relics of the English feudal system. The tenants owed no obligation to the landlord except a small tax called a quit-rent. In effect, the tenants were owners of their land. In government, the colony was headed by a governor and council appointed by the proprietor but the assembly was chosen by the voters.

Under the circumstances of vacant land and a heterogeneity of people in Maryland, both democracy and religious toleration made headway. In 1649 the Maryland Assembly passed her famous Toleration Act. The Act was made necessary by the large number of Protestant immigrants, including Puritan refugees from Virginia. When the Catholics were outnumbered by the Protestant majority it became necessary to protect Catholic freedom by providing freedom of worship for all who believed in the divinity of Christ. This Act was ineffective and the Catholic minority later suffered from a variety of civil and religious disabilities, especially after the Glorious Revolution of 1688 in England removed James II, the last Catholic King of England. In 1650 the freemen won the right to initiate legislation and began meeting as a separate body. Their privileges were increased further after Bacon's Rebellion in Virginia.

❍ Settlement of the Carolinas—North and South Carolina originally were included in the same large grant of territory south of Virginia. The region was granted in 1663 by Charles II to the eight Lords Proprietors, friends of the King. The systematic and successful settlement of the Carolinas began in 1670 when an expedition founded Charles Towne (later Charleston) at Albemarle Point. The proprietors asked John Locke, the famous philosopher, to write a framework of government, known as the Fundamental Constitutions of Carolina. The document set up a model feudal system but proved so unpopular and unworkable under the frontier conditions of America that it had to be abandoned. Over a period of time a representative system of government developed.

The colony of Carolina was slow in establishing an agricultural staple but a profitable trade in deerskins sprang up with the Native Americans to the southwest. By 1700 the cultivation of rice brought a profitable export staple. African slaves were imported to work the rice fields and a plantation type of economy developed.

North Carolina was established as a completely separate colony in 1729 when the proprietors sold out their interest in Carolina to the crown. The original center of settlement in North Carolina was in the region of the Albemarle Sound. There, widely separated from Charleston, a democratic society of small farmers sprang up to offer contrast with the plantation aristocracies of Virginia and South Carolina on either side.

✪ **Georgia**—Georgia was the last English colony to be founded on the North American mainland. James Oglethorpe, philanthropist, headed a group of trustees who secured title to the grant in 1732. In 1733 the first colonists arrived and founded Savannah. In origin the colonists varied; there were Salzburgers, Highland Scots, Scotch-Irish, and Welsh, in addition to the English.

The motivation in establishing Georgia was 1) to create a buffer colony between South Carolina and Spanish Florida, 2) to provide a refuge for the "poor debtors" in the jails of England, 3) to provide a haven for persecuted Protestants from Europe, and 4) to convert the Native Americans to Christianity. An economy based on the production of silk and wine on small landholdings was planned, but Georgia did not prosper until ineffectual regulations against liquor, slavery, and large landholdings were removed. This allowed the open development of a plantation economy similar to that of South Carolina. In 1751 Georgia became a royal colony according to the terms of its charter.

THE MIDDLE COLONIES

The Middle Colonies were settled by the English only after the Stuart King, Charles II, was restored to his throne in 1660. His brother, the Duke of York, and William Penn figured prominently in the development of New York, New Jersey, Pennsylvania, and Delaware. Although Delaware was southern in geography and economy, it was part of Pennsylvania until 1776.

✪✪ **New York**—This Dutch colony of New Netherland was captured by the English in the course of their three seventeenth century commercial wars with Holland. The English resented Dutch rivalry in the fur trade and the separation by the Dutch of English colonies to the north and the south. In 1664 Charles II granted the lands between the Connecticut and Delaware rivers to his brother, the Duke of York, and supplied him with a fleet for their conquest. Easily captured in 1664, the colony was renamed New York. The almost absolute rule of the colony by the Duke of York made it the least democratic of all the colonies.

New Jersey—This proprietary colony originated when the Duke of York transferred part of his holdings to Lord John Berkeley and Sir George Carteret. Dutch settlements were already established in the region and liberal terms for acquiring land attracted many emigrants from New England and from the British Isles. In 1674 a part of New Jersey to the west was purchased by the Quakers. Later East New Jersey was acquired by a group of Quakers. In 1702 New Jersey was reunited as a royal colony.

○○ **Pennsylvania**—William Penn, like Oglethorpe in Georgia, founded his colony as a philanthropic experiment, but like Calvert in Maryland, he also wished to make a profit. He did both. In 1681 Pennsylvania received the grant from Charles II in return for cancelling a debt owed to Penn's father. The "Holy Experiment," as Penn called his colony, provided complete freedom of worship and established democratic government. Settlement was carried out by Quaker associates and German immigrants to whom he sold land. The colony benefited from settlers already living in this fertile region with its mild climate. Trouble with Native Americans was avoided by treating them fairly. The "Frame of Government" provided for a one-house legislature. Even Penn's wise and liberal government was not entirely satisfactory to settlers under the conditions of opportunity offered by boundless vacant lands. Settlers disliked paying the small quit-rents to the proprietor.

The liberal nature of the Quaker colony attracted immigrants and Pennsylvania grew and prospered from the beginning. In Germany Penn advertised the generous terms for acquiring land, his liberal government and policy of religious toleration and attracted various radical religious sects. The colony attracted a more heterogeneous lot of settlers than any other in America.

Delaware—This colony was originally founded by the Swedes, captured by the Dutch, and later awarded to the Duke of York as a part of his grant. In 1682 William Penn bought Delaware to assure free access to the sea for Pennsylvania. In 1702 Delaware was given the right to select its own assembly but the Penn family remained proprietors and chose the governors of Delaware.

West Indian Colonies—All of the English colonies in America were not located on the mainland. Sir George Somers founded a colony in Bermuda in 1612 for the purpose of growing tobacco. In the West Indies, St. Christopher (1823) and Barbados (1625) were colonized and sugar cane became their leading production. Jamaica, acquired during a war with Spain in 1655, also became a very prosperous "sugar island" where large numbers of African slaves worked on plantations. The sugar islands proved much more profitable to England than did the Atlantic seaboard colonies.

CHAPTER BOOK LIST

Andrews, C.M., *The Colonial Period in American History* (four vols., 1934–1938). Most lengthy recent history.

Beer, G.L., *Origins of the British Colonial System* (1908). Older history of mother country control of the colonies.

Bradford, William, *Of Plymouth Plantation* (Capricorn).

Condon, Thomas J., *New York Beginnings: The Commercial Origins of New Netherlands* (1968).

Crane, V.W., *Southern Frontier, 1670–1732* (University of Michigan) Describes work of Charleston Native American traders among Southern tribes.

Foster, Stephen, *The Long Argument: English Puritanism and the Shaping of New England Culture, 1570–1700* (1991).

Hunt, George T., *The Wars of the Iroquois* (University of Wisconsin).

Lang, James, *Conquest and Commerce: Spain and England in the Americas* (1975). A comparison of English and Spanish colonization processes.

Morgan, Edmund S., *The Puritan Dilemma: The Story of John Winthrop* (1958). Good, popular treatment of important figure.

Morison, S.E., *Builders of the Bay Colony* (1930). Favorable viewpoint of the early Puritans.

Notestein, Wallace, *England on the Eve of Colonization* (1954).

Osgood, Herbert Levi, *The American Colonies in the Seventeenth Century* (three vols., 1957).

Vaughn, Alden T., *American Genesis: Captain John Smith and the Founding of Virginia* (1975). Good treatment of an important figure.

Ver Steeg, C.L., *The Formative Years* (1964).

Wish, Harvey, *Society and Thought in Early America* (1950). Brief and clear.

Wright, Louis B., *The Atlantic Frontier* (Great Seal Books). Social and economic development in the colonies.

REVIEW QUESTIONS

MULTIPLE CHOICE

1. An important motive of English and other voyages of exploration in the sixteenth century was (1) the need for more geographic information (2) the search for better agricultural lands (3) scientific curiosity (4) the desire for a direct water route westward from Europe to Asia.

2. Early attempts of the English to colonize in America failed because (1) of war with Spain and a lack of experience (2) early colonies were destroyed by Spain (3) most colonizing expeditions were lost at sea (4) recruits for the colonies could not be found.

3. The two most important motives of English colonization of America were (1) the love of adventure and religious rivalry with Spain (2) the need to establish religious freedom and military bases against Spain (3) the desire for religious freedom and economic opportunity (4) the love of adventure and need to achieve a favorable balance of trade.

4. English colonization differed from that of other colonizing nations in America because (1) the English colonists enjoyed a greater degree of neglect and freedom from mother country interference (2) more attention was given to developing fishing and lumbering enterprises (3) more aid was given by the mother country (4) salutary regulation and helpful paternalism provided sound foundations.

5. Virginia's early difficulties as a colony were due to all of the following *except* (1) the poor choice of location for the settlement of Jamestown (2) the poor choice of colonists for such an enterprise (3) loss of time due to Spanish interference (4) loss of time due to searching for gold and a water passage leading to the Indies.

6. When the economic success of the Jamestown settlement was finally won it was due to (1) the opening of fur trade with the Native Americans (2) subsidies by the British government (3) the introduction of a more marketable variety of tobacco (4) the finding of gold.

7. Bacon's Rebellion is significant chiefly because (1) it was caused by some of the same conflicts of interests that are associated with the American Revolution (2) it showed that Westerners would fight Native Americans on the slightest provocation (3) it was planned to overthrow British rule (4) its success encouraged other rebellions.

8. The Mayflower Compact (1) provided a detailed framework of government (2) was disallowed by the Privy Council (3) went into effect in Boston in 1630 (4) provided for rule by the majority at Plymouth.

9. Massachusetts Bay Colony was founded because (1) the Mayflower was blown off course by a storm (2) its founders sought religious freedom and opportunities for economic betterment (3) the English Separatists were being persecuted by Bishop Laud (4) the English King sought to banish all Puritans and Catholics.

10. Which is the correct statement of the leaders in the founding of Rhode Island? (1) Roger Williams, Anne Hutchinson, Thomas Hooker, John Davenport (2) Roger Williams, Anne Hutchinson, Samuel Gorton, William Coddington (3) Roger Williams, Samuel Gorton, Thomas Hooker, William Coddington (4) Roger Williams, Thomas Hooker, Theophilus Eaton, and John Davenport.

11. The Fundamental Orders of Connecticut were (1) only an agreement to abide by the will of the majority (2) the first instrument for self-government in the colonies (3) the first written constitution in America (4) merely an agreement to combine the towns of Connecticut under a single government.

12. The Confederation of New England was organized (1) for joint measures of defense against common enemies (2) but never went into operation because of disapproval of legislatures of the separated colonies (3) in spite of the disapproval of the English King (4) in 1686.

13. The Toleration Act in Maryland was passed (1) to encourage immigration (2) because of imminent danger of a religious uprising (3) because Catholic settlers had become a minority in danger of losing religious freedom (4) after James II was overthrown in England.

14. The largest number of proprietary colonies were founded under (1) James I (2) Charles II (3) Charles I (4) George I.

15. John Locke's "Fundamental Constitutions of Carolina" were never put in effect because (1) North Carolina's settlement was delayed too long (2) the philosopher was too far ahead of the times in his political thinking (3) the king substituted a charter for the colony (4) the provisions were feudal, artificial, and unsuited to conditions in the American wilderness.

16. The name Oglethorpe is associated with the founding of which of these colonies? (1) Maryland (2) North Carolina (3) New York (4) Georgia.

17. New York was similar to South Carolina in its beginnings since (1) both were founded as joint-stock companies (2) religion was not a major motive in the founding of either colony (3) aristocracy never dominated either colony (4) both were grants made by James II.

18. Which colony was outstanding in its deliberate attempts to attract colonists from Europe? (1) Georgia (2) New York (3) North Carolina (4) Pennsylvania.

19. In which of these colonies was its founder most interested in the advanced humanitarian and social reforms that strongly influenced later attitudes in America? (1) Massachusetts (2) Pennsylvania (3) Georgia (4) New Jersey.

TRUE-FALSE

20. After Elizabeth became Queen, the rivalry over religion and empire began in earnest between England and Spain.

21. First attempts at founding English colonies in America were begun by Sir Humphrey Gilbert and his half-brother Sir Walter Raleigh.

22. Wealthy businessmen in England avoided investing in the American colony-founding ventures as being too risky.

23. Religion was only a minor motive in the migration of colonists to America.

24. Under the English agricultural system in effect in the seventeenth century, England suffered from overpopulation.

25. John Smith in reality contributed little to save the Jamestown colony.

26. The first representative legislature in the colonies was held in Virginia.

27. The leading cause of Bacon's Rebellion was extortionate tax levies by the Jamestown ruling clique.

28. By 1700 the colonies of Rhode Island, Connecticut, and Massachusetts all were formed by mergers of previously separate colonies or settlements.

29. During the "Great Migration" about 25,000 Puritans settled in the Massachusetts Bay Colony.

30. In Massachusetts representative government began when outlying towns demanded the right to send deputies to the General Court before paying taxes.

31. Puritanism assured uniformity of opinion and prevented disagreement among the settlers who came to Boston.

32. Almost nowhere in New England did the fur trade assume much economic significance.

33. Neither New Hampshire nor Vermont were separate colonies among the original thirteen.

34. Maryland is a prominent example of a proprietary colony.

35. Rhode Island was never admitted to the New England Confederation.

36. South Carolina quickly became a rich and successful agricultural colony after her founding.

37. Pennsylvania did more to attract non-English immigrants than any other colony.

COMPLETION

38. The name of the great Spanish fleet sent to England in 1588 was the _____ .

39. The English raiders against Spanish treasure ships and Caribbean towns were known as the _____ .

40. The ejection of tenants in England from their holdings to make land available for sheep grazing was known as the _____ movement.

41. Virginia was colonized by a business investment group known as a _____ company.

42. The notable rebellion in Virginia in 1676 against Governor Berkeley was led by _____ .

43. The settlers at the Plymouth colony were known as the _____ .

44. The Puritans at Boston were followers of the doctrine of the great religious leader _____ .

45. Those citizens who were qualified to vote in Massachusetts were known as the _____ .

46. The best known leader in the founding of Rhode Island belonged to what religious denomination? _____

47. The first migrant and best known leader in the founding of Connecticut was _____ .

48. The least cooperative member of the New England Confederation was _____ .

59. _____ was the first settlement in the colony of Maryland.

50. A small payment made by tenants in the proprietary colonies was known as a _____ .

51. The noblemen who were granted the Carolinas were known as the _____ .

52. William Penn referred to his colony as the _____ .

53. Two religious groups prominent in the settlement of New Jersey were the _____ and the Puritans.

54. Delaware was originally settled by the _____ .

MATCHING

55. John Cabot	a. Wrote the plan of government for the Carolinas
56. Henry VIII	b. Gave England a claim to North America
57. John Rolfe	c. Settled South Carolina
58. Cecilius Calvert	d. A name associated with proprietary colonies
59. John Locke	e. Started profitable tobacco growing in Virginia
60. James Oglethorpe	f. Made England Protestant
61. Charles II	g. Unsuccessful colonizer at Roanoke Island
62. William Bradford	h. Settled Maryland
63. Humphrey Gilbert	i. Philanthropist who settled Georgia
64. Francis Drake	j. Circumnavigated the globe
	k. Famous governor at Plymouth colony

MATCHING

65. Massachusetts   a. First proprietary colony

66. Plymouth   b. Second joint stock colony

67. Georgia   c. First self-governing charter

68. Maryland   d. First to become a royal colony

69. Delaware   e. Founded by the Swedes

70. Virginia   f. Founded by the Dutch

     g. Last colony chartered

CHRONOLOGY / CHAPTER 3

1612   Tobacco culture begun in Virginia.
1619   First slaves sold in Jamestown.
1639   Fundamental Orders of Connecticut drafted.
1643   New England Confederation organized.
1651   First navigation act passed.
1660   Navigation Act of 1660 enumerated articles to be shipped to England.
1663   Navigation Act of 1663 required that imports from Europe go through English customs.
1685   James I became King of England.
          Dominion of New England begun.
1689   William and Mary became English sovereigns in Glorious Revolution.
          Bill of Rights confirmed.
1696   Navigation Act of 1696 provided stricter enforcement of previous navigation acts.
1697   Triangular trade begun.
1699   Woolens Act.
1721   Beginning of the time of "salutary neglect" under Prime Minister Walpole, gave colonies much freedom until 1763.
1733   Molasses Act passed.
1750   Iron Act.

Chapter

3

THE GOVERNMENT AND ECONOMY OF THE COLONIES, 1607–1763

Many of the political institutions of England were transmitted to the United States through their establishment during the colonial period. In America, England gained her first experience in developing machinery for control of colonies. Her controls were never as stringent as those of the other colonial powers in America. The geography of the Atlantic coast determined the natural resources of the different colonies; resources in turn strongly influenced the economy of the New England, Middle, and Southern Colonies.

GOVERNMENT IN THE COLONIES

Privileges of self-government granted by the colonial charters and neglect by England permitted the colonials to enjoy a relatively large degree of freedom.

❂❂❂ **Types of Colonies**—There were three types of colonies. 1) The proprietary colonies were founded either by joint-stock companies or by individuals; ten of the colonies were founded as some form of proprietorship, but only Pennsylvania and Maryland endured under that form. 2) The corporate (or colonial colonies), Rhode Island and Connecticut, were founded by settlers who had moved from other colonies, and secured charters from the crown that gave them control over their own political and fiscal affairs. 3) Royal colonies, the form of government England most preferred, were ruled directly by a representative of the king; most of them became royal when a colony was deprived of its original charter, as Massachusetts did in 1691. In 1776 nine of the thirteen colonies were royal.

The charters served as constitutions for the colonies. The English colonists retained in America the ancient rights and privileges of the king's subjects at home. This contrasted with the countries of the continent of Europe whose subjects were not equal in rights and privileges to those at home.

34

OO The Governor, Council, and Assembly—The governments of all the colonies were similar. The office of the governor originated as the executive head of a joint-stock business corporation but was transformed into a political position. The governor in the proprietary colonies was chosen by the proprietor; in the corporate colonies, he was elected by the assembly; in the royal colonies, he was appointed by the king. Closely associated with the governor in his functions was his council whose members were chosen in the same way as the governor (except in Massachusetts where the council was chosen by the General Court). The governor exercised the traditional executive powers, enforcing the laws, appointing officials, heading the colony's armed forces, and vetoing objectionable acts of the assembly. The governor's position was a difficult one since he had to carry out orders from those who appointed him but received his salary and appropriations from the assemblies.

There was no clear cut separation of powers among the three branches of government. The governor and his council sat as the highest court. The council also served as the upper house of the legislature. The assembly or lower house consisted of members elected by the eligible voters. It was clearly separated from the executive. The assemblies engaged in frequent quarrels with the governors and used their power of voting appropriations for the various expenses of government to force concessions from the governors; this was true even in the corporate colonies. The assemblies came to regard the power of taxation and appropriation of revenues as powers belonging to them alone.

Voting and Office Holding—Qualifications for voting and office holding seem restrictive when contrasted with those of today, but they actually excluded few white adult males, the only group thought capable of participating in government. Religious qualifications, originally restrictive, were relaxed in the eighteenth century. The high incidence of land holding allowed many to vote, especially in New England and the Middle Colonies. In the South, the suffrage was somewhat more restrictive. Office holders were usually required to own more property than voters, and custom held them to residence in their district. Although there were no political parties in the modern sense, political divisions did occur over land and defense policy, economic development, and sectional interests, especially the frontier against the more settled areas, as in Bacon's Rebellion.

O Local Government—In the South the county was transplanted from England as the basic unit of local government, the county sheriff and the justices of peace being the leading local officials. Usually these officials were appointed by the governor. The parish was a subdivision of county government. In New England the township with its "town meeting" and the selectmen became the local unit of government. It also named the representatives to the assemblies. In the Middle Colonies local government included both the county and township. As for the courts, judges were everywhere appointed by the governor.

The basic law was the common (or customary) law of England and the teachings of the Bible. Punishments in America were less severe than in England. The whipping post, the branding iron, the stocks, and the ducking stool often took the place of the gallows and the prisons of England.

IMPERIAL CONTROL AND MERCANTILISM

In theory the colonies existed for the benefit of the mother country and were chartered by England for the economic benefits it was hoped they would bring.

✪✪✪ **British Mercantilism**—The prevailing European economic theory of mercantilism was applied in the British colonies but much less rigidly than applied by other colonial powers. Mercantilism was a policy of national economic self-sufficiency that grew out of a desire for power and the wars of the seventeenth and eighteenth centuries. In practice the overriding aim of mercantilist measures was to achieve a favorable balance of trade by selling more outside the empire than was bought; the difference would be accumulated as a gold reserve that could be used to many advantages in case of war. By producing goods within the empire a nation could avoid paying out gold to foreigners and at the same time achieve a greater degree of self-sufficiency. Colonies fitted into this economic system of European nations by producing commodities such as sugar, lumber, naval stores, and fish. Britain, therefore, used bounties to encourage the production of indigo and silk and enacted laws against certain manufactures in the colonies. Extensive controls over trade and shipping were employed by Britain.

✪ **Britain's Colonial Administration**—Britain was slow in developing machinery for the control of the colonies. Since the American colonies were practically the first she had, England lacked experience in establishing machinery for governing them. The struggles between king and Parliament and the civil war left the colonies relatively free in their early years. Distance and the usual ignorance of conditions in the colonies always made it difficult to govern them. With the restoration of the Stuarts in 1660, colonial administration was brought under control of the king and his Privy Council. A subordinate committee of the Privy Council that came to be known as the Board of Trade evolved. The Board of Trade proceeded to make recommendations to effectuate the policies of mercantilism and Parliament enacted the necessary legislation. The Privy Council, the admiralty, and other English courts heard cases arising under the Navigation Acts. The Privy Council could cancel colonial laws if it chose. The colonists developed great skill in the evasion of British laws they found harmful and often showed an independent spirit toward English domination.

○○ **The Navigation Acts**—These Acts of Trade and Navigation controlled colonial overseas commerce and shipping in the interests of the whole empire.

The Navigation Act of 1660, intended to promote English shipping, required 1) that goods shipped within the empire be carried on ships owned and operated by British subjects (which included the colonists). 2) Certain enumerated articles could be sold only to England or to another colony: sugar, tobacco, cotton, indigo, ginger, and dyewoods. Later other commodities were added to the enumerated list: rice, naval stores, furs, iron, and lumber. To benefit the colonies the act forbade the production of tobacco in England and its importation from foreign countries.

The Navigation Act of 1663 provided that imports to the colonies from Europe must pass through England and pay customs duties. However, an elaborate system of rebates, or drawbacks, permitted colonists to buy goods about as cheaply through England as if bought directly.

The Navigation Act of 1673 was passed to prevent evasion by the colonists of earlier laws. This Act required shippers to pay the duties in the colonies or post a bond to guarantee that a given cargo would be taken only to England.

The Americans, especially in New England, evaded the Navigation Acts so that constant complaints were made by British appointed colonial customs officials to authorities in England. James II sought to reform the colonial government to secure enforcement of the Acts. The Dominion of New England and the Navigation Act of 1696 resulted from these reforms. This latter Act 1) required colonial governors to take an oath, under severe penalties, to enforce the trade regulations. 2) The laws were to be enforced by the Board of Trade and Plantations appointed by the king. 3) Customs officials could use writs of assistance that authorized them to search mercantile establishments without specific court approval.

The Molasses Act of 1733 sought to terminate a profitable trade between the American colonies and the non-English sugar islands of the West Indies and force the importation of sugar cane products from the British sugar islands. The act provided prohibitive duties on such foreign imports but it was not enforced.

British Regulation of Manufacturing and Currency—Since the English wished to prevent colonial competition in manufacturing, laws were passed against certain colonial industries. 1) The Woolens Act (1699) forbade the production of woolen cloth for export by the colonies. 2) The Hat Act (1732) forbade the manufacture of hats outside England except for sale in the colonies. 3) The Iron Act (1750) prohibited the manufacture of certain finished iron products in the colonies. These Acts actually had no serious effects upon the American colonies. The issuance of paper money by colonial legislatures was regulated by act of Parliament or by disallowance of such laws by their veto or suspension by the colonial governors.

⊙⊙ **Effects of the Navigation Acts**—English control of colonial trade, especially as the Acts were loosely enforced, brought mainly benefit to the colonies. Bounties were paid for crops such as indigo and silk, which would not have been grown otherwise, and for strategic goods such as naval stores and ship timbers. The colonists were also protected by the British navy. From 1721 to the start of the French and Indian War in 1754, the Acts were hardly enforced at all under Robert Walpole's policy of salutary neglect.

THE ECONOMIC LIFE OF THE COLONIES

The production of agricultural staples and of raw materials dominated the economy of the colonies. The natural resources of the American colonies determined their different ways of making a living and most colonial industries depended upon these resources for raw materials.

⊙⊙ **Agriculture in the South**—The climate, fertile soil, and a wide coastal plain penetrated by numerous streams that accommodated ocean-going vessels—these factors caused the Southern Colonies to turn to producing agricultural staples for export. Tobacco became the leading crop in most of the tidewater areas of Maryland, Virginia, and the Carolinas. Rice and indigo also were important crops in the Carolinas. These crops were exchanged with England and Europe for a wide variety of imports. Georgia produced some indigo and sea-island cotton for export. (Upland cotton was not an important crop until the 1790s.) These crops came to be produced by slave labor and by indentured servants as well as by the labor of small farmers.

Large plantations developed in the tidewater regions. The large planters came to dominate the political and social life of the South. As the planters enlarged their land holdings, the small farmers sold out and moved farther to the west where they usually produced tobacco or followed a subsistence type of farming.

⊙ **Agriculture in the Middle Colonies**—The Middle Colonies were designated as the "bread colonies," because they produced grain and other foodstuffs. Wheat was the leading crop but much corn was produced, as was true of all the colonies. The variety of food production included other grains, livestock, vegetables, and fruits. In the Middle Colonies, an annual fee, the quit-rent, was levied on all land. Although it was resented, it was levied and, especially in Pennsylvania and Maryland, frequently collected. As in Virginia, land was acquired at first as head-rights instead of by outright purchase which became the rule in the eighteenth century. Indentured servants or redemptioners served as the most important source of labor. Farms were usually small.

⊙ **The Agriculture of New England**—The infertile soil and stony land of New England and the lack of any export staple determined that New England farming would be self-sufficing. A large variety of good crops were grown. Land was held in fee simple. Unlike farmers in the other colonies, New Englanders settled new towns as a community undertaking. They lived together in the town and worked their fields in common. By 1700 most were living on their individual farms, the practice throughout the rest of the colonies.

Frontier Agriculture—The existence of cheap, fertile, unoccupied soil invited the landless to move out to the frontier to establish homes for themselves. Except in New England, this westward migration was undertaken by the individual pioneer. The pioneer settler learned how to build his log cabin in the vast forests that covered the eastern frontier. He opened a small clearing in the woods to plant his corn and vegetable patch by clearing underbrush and girdling the larger trees to kill them. The axe and the rifle were pioneer essentials. The pioneer supplemented his food crops by shooting wild game abounding in the woods. Life was simple and hard and the independent pioneer farmer developed into a rugged self-reliant individual. Frontier settlers often bought land on credit or borrowed money to make improvements. In debt, neglected and exploited by the eastern colonial aristocracy, the Westerners learned to think of their economic and political interests as being opposed to those of the East.

Industry—Shipbuilding, one of the largest colonial industries, centered in New England, but the Middle Colonies built a large tonnage also and some ships were built in the South. Naval stores were produced in all the colonies; North Carolina led in the production of pitch, tar, and turpentine. Saw mills in all the colonies produced lumber for export as well as for multiple local uses.

New England imported molasses from the West Indies and converted large quantities into rum for export and for local consumption. Iron ore was found throughout the colonies; after 1750 Pennsylvania, with abundant ore and wood for smelting it, became the leader in iron production. In New England and in the middle colonies much small hardware was produced by independent artisans. Flour milling was an important industry in New York and Pennsylvania; these two colonies exported large quantities of flour but all colonies produced flour for local consumption. Textile making was a home industry. Only a few looms made cloth for sale. Cloth was made of wool and flax, little cotton was used. Much cloth was imported from England. Home industries other than textiles included food preserving and the manufacture of furniture and farm tools. Various industries were stimulated in the Northern Colonies by the lack of specie or goods to exchange for imports from Britain.

Fur Trade and Fishing—All the colonies engaged in the profitable fur trade but it centered in Albany, New York, in the North, and in the South, Charleston exported large quantities of deerskins.

Fishing and whaling were thriving New England industries that kept several hundred vessels busy. Fish were caught in the Newfoundland Banks, relatively shallow waters of the North Atlantic, and exported for slave consumption in the West Indies plantations and exported to the Catholic nations of Europe.

✪✪✪ **Commerce**—The poor soil of New England caused her to turn to the sea not only for fishing but to engage in a thriving carrying trade for other regions. On their way to the West Indies, New England ships picked up cargoes of foodstuffs along the Atlantic coast. These cargoes were exchanged for molasses, sugar, ginger, and for bills of exchange used to pay for manufactured goods from England. After 1697 New England began to engage in the "triangular trade" involving slaves from Africa. The molasses from the West Indies was converted into rum in New England and in turn was exchanged for slaves on the African coast. The slaves were taken to the West Indies and the trading cycle would be repeated. The Middle Colonies also engaged in this trade.

The Southern Colonies shipped their staples of tobacco, rice, and indigo to England and exchanged them for manufactured goods for use in the South.

The Money Problem—The importation of manufactured goods from England constituted a severe drain on the supply of specie in the colonies and caused a shortage in their medium of exchange. Gold was earned in Africa and in the West Indies from the favorable balance of trade there. Spanish dollars, earned in the West Indian trade, supplied a large part of the colonial currency needs. The colonial legislatures issued paper money to relieve the shortage of currency. England forbade such issues after the paper money began to depreciate in value. In 1764 Parliament passed an unpopular law forbidding the issuance of paper money by the colonies.

✪✪ **Labor in the Colonies**—The development of the new lands of America and the exploitation of its resources required a large supply of labor. Immigrants themselves became landowners as soon as they had saved enough money to buy cheap, vacant land on the frontier. Free labor, skilled or not, was always scarce and in heavy demand in colonial times.

The largest source of labor in the colonies came from immigrants who contracted to serve from three to seven years in payment for their ship passage to America. In America these contracts were auctioned to the highest bidder—these were the indentured servants. They usually came as penniless individuals and many came after having been convicted or after having served prison terms for various crimes. Generally such indentured servants did not make the most desirable contributions to the American population.

Another class of bound servants, the redemptioners, should be distinguished from the indentured servants. These "free willers" came voluntarily and with families, usually had some savings, and made a more respectable contribution to American society. A great many redemptioners settled in Pennsylvania. Both kinds of bound, or bonded, servants were released at the end of their contract and usually given fifty acres of land and clothing and tools. Together they made up a majority of the immigrants in several of the colonies.

○ **Slavery**—Another large source of labor was slaves. New England used large numbers of Native Americans as slaves or traded them in the West Indies for African slaves. Native American slaves were used in the South too. However, Native Americans did not adjust to the conditions of slavery and slaves were imported from Africa beginning in 1619 when twenty were sold in Jamestown. At first, they were treated as bondservants, but by 1700, because of economic and social factors, chattel slavery evolved. After 1713 the importation of slaves increased rapidly, especially into the Southern Colonies where they could be employed in producing rice, indigo, and tobacco. Plantation owners preferred slave labor to bond-servants since they could exercise more control over slaves. At first the Northern Colonies accepted slavery as whole-heartedly as the South, but the economic factors prevalent in the North reduced the usefulness and need of slavery there.

CHAPTER BOOK LIST

Bailyn, Bernard, *The Origins of American Politics* (Capricorn).

Bidwell, P.W., and Falconer, J.I., *History of Agriculture in the Northern United States* (1925).

Bonomi Patricia, *A Factious People: Politics and Society in Colonial New York* (1971).

Bradford, William, *Of Plymouth* (Capricorn). Readings.

Bridenbaugh, Carl, *Colonial Craftsmen* (Phoenix). Best work on economic life of common people.

Gipson, L.H., *The British Empire Before the American Revolution* (15 vols., rev., 1958–1965).

Klein, Milton, and Cooke, Jacob E., eds., *A History of the American Colonies* (13 vols.) (1975). One on each colony, written by a specialist.

Labaree, L.W., *Royal Government in America* (1930).

Lemon, James T., *Best Poor Man's Country* (1972). Early Pennsylvania

Lovejoy, David S., *The Glorious Revolution in America* (1972). Good examination of a pivotal event in colonial America.

McCusker, John J., and Menard, Russell R., *The Economy of Colonial America* (1985). Most complete recent treatment.

Morgan, Edmund S., *American Slavery, American Freedom: The Ordeal of Colonial Virginia* (1975). The origins of slavery.

Morison, Samuel E., *Builders of the Bay Colony* (Houghton Mifflin).

Morison, Samuel E., *Maritime History of Massachusetts, 1783–1860* (Sentry). Gives colonial background.

Nash, Gary B., *Quakers and Politics* (1968).

Osgood, Herbert L., *The American Colonies in the Eighteenth Century* (four vols., 1957).

Perkins, Edwin J., *The Economy of Colonial America* (1980).

Rossiter, Clinton, *The First American Revolution* (Harvest). Causes of the Revolution.

Smith, Abbot Emerson, *Colonies in Bondage: White Servitude and Convict Labor in America, 1607–1776* (1947).

Sydnor, Charles S., *American Revolutionaries in the Making* (Free Press).

Walton, G.M., and Shepherd, J.F., *The Economic Rise of Early America* (1979).

Wertenbaker, T.J., *The First Americans* (1927). Emphasis on social and economic development.

REVIEW QUESTIONS

MULTIPLE CHOICE

1. In regard to the separation of powers between the executive, legislative, and judicial branches under the three types of colonial governments (1) there was no sharp distinction between the branches under any type (2) a sharp distinction existed in the corporate colonies only (3) a sharp distinction existed in all the colonies (4) a distinction existed in the royal colonies.

2. The General Court in the New England colonies (1) was primarily judicial in purpose (2) exercised legislative, judicial, and executive functions (3) exercised only advisory and judicial powers (4) was simply legislative in actual function.

3. Which distinct departure from English government developed in the colonies? (1) The legislatures refused to vote appropriations for unpopular executives (2) the exercise of the right of petition (3) representatives in the assemblies were required to be residents of the district from which they were elected (4) writs of assistance were protested.

4. In regard to the requirements for the voting privilege the colonies in comparison with England (1) were more restrictive (2) permitted about the same proportion of persons to vote (3) no clear generalization may be drawn (4) were definitely more liberal.

5. Which statement is *not* true regarding the predominant type of local government in these groups of colonies? (1) Town meetings characterized local government in New England (2) town meetings predominated in local government in the Middle Colonies (3) a combination of town and county government prevailed in the Middle Colonies (4) county government prevailed in the Southern Colonies.

6. Mercantilist controls of the economic life of the colonies began with restrictions on (1) shipping (2) manufacturing (3) European markets (4) the fur trade.

7. The Dominion of New England was created primarily to (1) enforce religious uniformity (2) make royal control more effective (3) provide defense against Native Americans (4) unite New England as a single colony.

8. Which list includes the most colonies noted for political and religious liberalism? (1) Georgia, North Carolina, Maryland, New York (2) Rhode Island, Pennsylvania, South Carolina, Maryland (3) Rhode Island, Pennsylvania, Maryland, North Carolina (4) Rhode Island, Pennsylvania, Maryland, Massachusetts.

9. Which crop was *least* important economically in the colonial South? (1) corn (2) tobacco (3) cotton (4) indigo (5) rice.

10. Which of the following was *not* a typical transaction in the triangular trade of the New England shippers? (1) The exchange of rum for slaves in Africa (2) the exchange of slaves for molasses in the West Indies (3) the acceptance of African bills of exchange (4) the sale of colonial foodstuffs in the West Indies.

11. Which of these is inconsistent with the principles of mercantilism? (1) Government subsidies to encourage new or lagging industries (2) freedom of individuals to conduct foreign trade without regulation by government (3) regulation to secure a favorable balance of trade (4) economic self-sufficiency of nations.

12. Which source of labor was *least* used in the colonies? (1) "Free-willers" (2) African slaves (3) indentured servants (4) Native American slaves.

TRUE-FALSE

13. Royal charters were often used as instruments for initiating new colonies.

14. The office of the colonial governor originated as the leading official of the joint stock corporation.

15. The greatest source of conflict in colonial government was between the governor and assembly.

16. England's long experience in ruling overseas colonies found her well prepared to govern the American colonies successfully.

17. The law-abiding trait of Englishmen made the enforcement of England's trade regulations easy in the colonies.

18. The effects of British trade regulations were uniformly stifling to the economy of the colonies.

19. The production of silk and cotton never ranked very large in the economy of the colonies.

20. The Middle Colonies were proprietary and their ruling families collected quit-rents from the landholders.

21. Exports of the colonies were mainly of finished, luxury goods.

22. Fishing and whaling never bulked large in the economy of New England.

23. The main source of earnings of gold and silver in colonial foreign trade was in England.

24. The large immigration of indentured servants provided an excess labor supply during much of the colonial period.

25. In the South, African slaves were imported only as a last resort since indentured servants were a more satisfactory source of labor.

COMPLETION

26. Other than religion the most common qualification for voting was the _____ qualification

27. The English _____ law was the basic law in the colonies.

28. The _____ was the basic unit of local government in the South.

29. Other than the justices of peace the leading local official in the South was the _____ .

30. A leading objective in a mercantilistic economy was the achievement of a favorable _____ .

31. The early laws for regulating the trade of the colonies were known as the _____ acts.

32. Goods which could be sold only within the empire were known as the _____ articles.

33. General search warrants known as _____ were used to enable customs officials to search for smuggled goods.

34. Other than silk, a prominent crop in the South which was encouraged by bounties was _____ .

35. Cotton grown in colonial times in Georgia was mostly of the _____ type.

36. The amount of land, usually fifty acres, given for paying the passage of an immigrant to Virginia was known by the term _____ .

37. Pitch, tar, and such materials used in shipbuilding were known collectively by the term _____ .

38. Other than flax, clothing in the colonies was made mainly from _____ .

39. The typical patterns of foreign trade developed by the Northern Colonies was known as the _____ trade.

40. Free-will indentured servants were also known as _____ .

CHRONOLOGY / CHAPTER 4

1517 Luther began Protestant Revolt in Germany.

1534 English Church separated from Roman Catholic Church.

1636 Harvard University founded.

1639 Baptists first organized in Rhode Island.

1647 Public elementary school law passed in New England.

1649 Toleration Act passed in Maryland.

1690 John Locke's theory of "natural rights" expounded.

1692 Salem witchcraft trials.

1693 William and Mary College founded.

1701 Yale University founded.

1704 *Boston News-Letter,* first regular newspaper, began publication.

1710 Beginning of large migration of German Protestants to English colonies; soon followed by Scotch-Irish Presbyterians.

1732 *Poor Richard's Almanac* began publication; continued to 1757.

1734 The Great Awakening, evangelical religious movement, began and continued until 1756.

1735 Zenger Trial won freedom of the press.

1747 Franklin began experiments with electricity.

1776 Adam Smith published *The Wealth of Nations.*

Chapter

4

SOCIAL AND INTELLECTUAL LIFE IN THE COLONIES, 1607–1763

Basically, American society and culture was English. However, 1) the special conditions of the frontier and the opportunities for the common man in a rapidly expanding economy developed self-confident individualists, and 2) the mingling of many different nationalities developed a new kind of people, or nationality, in America.

THE PEOPLE OF THE COLONIES

Population growth was rapid in America. 1) Immigration brought a steady flow of people into a land that offered opportunity and freedom. 2) A high birth rate was experienced because of a high rate of infant survival, probably owing to the improved nutrition of the mother, economic factors, and social approval of large families.

❂❂ **Immigration of Non-English Colonists**—The three main people to come to America in colonial times were 1) Palatine Germans, 2) Scotch-Irish, and 3) African slaves.

The Germans began emigrating in large numbers after 1710, when Parliament permitted the naturalization of foreign Protestants. They were ready to leave Germany because many of them were not members of the established Lutheran Church, and therefore they had no comfortable home there; the frequent wars and poverty also helped to drive them out. William Penn systematically advertised his colony and made land available on easy terms in order to coax them to settle there, tactics that were very successful. They became known as the Pennsylvania Dutch.

The Scotch-Irish had orignally been settled in northern Ireland in an effort to drive out the native Catholic population. Changes in the Navigation Acts as they applied to Ireland created very hard times there and the Scotch-Irish, largely Presbyterian, began to leave about 1700. They settled, often squatting, further west than the Germans because they lacked means to buy land, even on Penn's easy terms. Many of them followed the valleys of the Allegheny Mountains into western Virginia and the Carolinas.

Other non-English European immigrants included the Huguenots (French Protestants) who settled in the Carolinas. The Irish came in steadily throughout the colonial period and many lost their special identity as they were readily absorbed in colonial life. Scots and Scot Highlanders settled in the Carolinas and Georgia. The Dutch in New York, a few Swiss and Swedish settlers in the Delaware Valley also composed a part of the American colonial population.

✪ **Social Classes**—Social stratification, though very definite in America, was less pronounced and less rigid than in Europe. The aristocracy did not originate from any consequential immigration of nobility but was made up of the higher officeholders, clergymen, and other professional people and also included wealthy merchants and shipowners, landowners and planters of English origin. Economic achievement early gave rise to higher social status in America. A distinction developed between the office-holding aristocracy with English background and the native aristocracy among whom economic achievement counted heavily. Rapid development also made it difficult to retain wealth and position; there was always someone new pushing up from below.

The middle class was composed of farmers, tradespeople, and artisans. The middle class made up the larger part of the population. The third social class was that of unskilled, free laborers. A fourth distinct group included the indentured servants and African Americans.

RELIGION IN THE COLONIES

Religion and the religious outlook strongly affected the attitude of people toward all aspects of life in colonial times much more so than today. Since the more radical Protestants were the subjects of persecution in Europe, they came to America for refuge. Thus, America developed what Edmund Burke called "the dissidence of dissent, and the Protestantism of the Protestant religion." The large number and variety of religious denominations and sects that came to America for freedom eventually forced the growth of religious toleration.

✪✪✪ **The Puritans of New England**—Puritan characteristics have exerted a stronger influence over America than those of any other religious group. The outstanding religious tenet of these followers of John Calvin was that of predestination, the belief that God had predetermined those to be saved. Puritans engaged in much soul-searching to learn whether they were among the "elect." Puritan individuals concerned themselves with their own improvement and that of others. They upheld high moral standards. "Blue laws" were enacted under Puritan influence to require observance of the Sabbath by church attendance and to prohibit certain activities considered as ungodly. Although Puritans came to America to enjoy religious freedom for themselves, they persecuted Baptists, Quakers, Jews, Catholics, and others. However, this intolerance was characteristic of most religions of the sixteenth century. In church organization the New England Puritans were Congregational, that is, they believed each church should be independent of the outside control of a supervisory hierarchy. The largest denomination in Rhode Island was the Baptist; they thrived there under the liberal toleration that began with Roger Williams.

✪ **Religion in the Middle Colonies**—The most notable feature of the religious life of the Middle Colonies was its variety. The Quakers were the most numerous denomination in Pennsylvania and New Jersey. The Scotch-Irish brought a large Presbyterian group and the Germans introduced many Lutherans and various Pietist sects, such as the Mennonites and Moravians. In New York were the Dutch Reformed and German Reformed churches. Many New England Puritans settled in northern and central New Jersey. There was no particular religious denomination associated with the settlement of New York.

✪ **Religion in the Southern Colonies**—In the tidewater region of the South the Anglican Church was dominant and was the established church which all were required to support by the payment of tithes. Catholics survived only as a tiny minority in Maryland, in spite of the religion of the proprietor. The easygoing Anglicans in the South contrasted sharply with strait-laced Puritans of New England. In the back country of the South, Presbyterians, Baptists, and Quakers were prominent.

The Witchcraft Trials—In Europe and in America in the seventeenth century belief in witchcraft was universal. A mass hysteria developed in Salem in 1692 when some young girls, who had been listening to the voodoo lore of two West Indian slaves, spitefully accused some older women of casting spells over them. Hundreds were accused and nineteen hanged before the trials were finally stopped after prominent persons became the victims of the accusers. Puritan leaders were discredited by the trials.

✪✪ **Religious Toleration**—The notion that religious freedom grew naturally in the colonies is false. Most of the Protestant churches took their particular beliefs very seriously and objected to other Protestant churches almost as much as they did to the universally detested Catholic Church. Movements such as the Great Awakening (see following page) led to doctrinal disputes and divisions into two or more denominations where there had been only one church. This was in spite of efforts to restrict the franchise or even residence to members of the founding church of the colony, efforts that were especially severe in Massachusetts.

Although religious toleration was attempted in Maryland, Pennsylvania was the first colony to successfully maintain a policy of toleration; its example proved the practicality of toleration. The rationalism of the Enlightenment further weakened the severity of religious laws, but probably the most effective force working for religious toleration was simple necessity, for as time went on, every colony had a number of religions practiced within its boundaries—too many to allow rigorous persecution of dissenters.

❂ **The Great Awakening**—The growth of secular mindedness and disinterest in religion in the early eighteenth century brought a reaction in favor of religion. This movement, the Great Awakening, an evangelical religious crusade active around 1750, originated from the influence of Jonathan Edwards, an able Congregationalist theologian in Massachusetts. From New England the religious enthusiasm spread all over the American colonies and exerted a particularly strong influence in the frontier regions. The movement was characterized by zealous, emotional preaching that brought the conversion of large numbers.

The Great Awakening had these consequences: 1) It increased the membership of the small, dissenting evangelical churches. 2) It injected emotionalism into religion everywhere. 3) As a democratic movement, it appealed to the poorer folk and weakened the Anglican Church and British authority. 4) It aroused a greater concern for mankind, improved manners and morals, and led to the establishment of several religious colleges.

CULTURE IN THE COLONIES

English language, literature, law, customs, religion, and thought dominated the cultural life of the colonies.

Education—New England's Puritan emphasis upon the value of schooling brought educational leadership to this section. In 1647 Massachusetts required every town of more than fifty families to maintain a public elementary shcool, although many communities did not obey the law. By 1689 all of New England except Rhode Island had followed this example, with varying results. In the Middle Colonies education was limited by the fact that it was regarded as a church rather than a public function. In the South private tutors were hired by one or more families jointly where they could afford to do so and public schools were not provided.

The Latin grammar schools of New England were about the only secondary schools in all the colonies. Of the nine colleges founded in the colonies before the Revolution, all were connected with religious groups. Harvard (1636) was founded first. Next William and Mary (1693) was founded and Yale in 1701. Colleges were provided for the training of ministers primarily and, therefore, taught classical languages and theology.

Periodical Journalism—The first colonial printing press was set up in 1639. The first newspaper published one issue in 1690 after which it was suppressed. The first regularly published newspaper, the *Boston News-Letter*, was published in 1704. By 1765, 43 newspapers were being issued; these small weeklies printed local news, advertisements, and selected items from other papers. A precedent in establishing freedom of the press in America was achieved in 1735 when John Peter Zenger was acquitted of libeling Governor William Cosby in his *New York Weekly Journal*; the acquittal was based on a finding that the disputed statements were true. The first magazine was published in 1741. The first almanac was published in 1739 in New England. The almanacs, published annually, contained a variety of practical information, jokes, poems, bits of wisdom, and served as calendars and astrological guides. Benjamin Franklin's *Poor Richard's Almanac* (1732–1757), one of the better ones, is best known.

Literature in the Colonies—Early writings dealt with the founding of several of the colonies. New England literary output was the most extensive in the seventeenth century; it dealt with religious subjects and the history of the colonies. Without an educated public there was little interest in literature as such. Philadelphia by the 1740s developed literary consciousness and became the literary center of the colonies. American writing was provincial and derivative until Philip Freneau's early poems appeared in the 1770s.

✪ **Effects of the Enlightenment**—The medieval mind accepted unquestioningly religious dogmas as explanations of the nature of the universe. The Enlightenment, or Age of Reason, came when Nicolas Copernicus, the Polish astronomer, and others like him, contradicted the long-accepted science of the middle ages. Copernicus proved that the sun and not the earth was the center of the universe. These teachings brought further doubts of the old dogmas and led to more observation, experiment, and new rational, empirical explanations of nature. When rationalism soon came to be applied to understanding the nature of man and society, the unquestioned dependence upon religious authority rapidly weakened.

In America, as in Europe, rationalism caused man to turn his attention to applying the laws of science and the understanding of nature to the improvement of his lot on earth instead of merely accepting his present miseries in hope of eternal salvation. Cotton Mather and other leading Puritan divines reconciled religion with the findings of science. By 1700 America was embracing more humanitarian, secular, and liberal ideas. The colonists came to accept the ideas of progress and of the right to freedom of opportunity for man. Philosophers sought natural laws to explain man's social behavior. The doctrine of natural rights of man was applied to justify revolution against political tyranny.

Benjamin Franklin was the most outstanding scientist in the American colonies. Franklin was interested in science for its utility in helping people live better. He invented a practical iron stove and made other studies of heating, introduced useful plants to America, studied electricity, and made innumerable experiments and many discoveries. John Bartram, a Pennsylvania botanist, made observations of plant life throughout the colonies, planted the first botanical garden in America, and corresponded with Linnaeus.

⊙⊙ **The Influence of European Thinkers**—Certain British political philosophers strongly influenced American thought. John Locke *(Two Treatises of Government, 1690)* justified the Glorious Revolution of 1688 and its deposition of James II on the grounds that James had violated a social contract with his people. The contract legitimized government, but only under certain conditions; when the conditions were broken, the people were justified in revolting. The influence of European thinkers such as Jean Jacques Rousseau *(Social Contract, 1762)* was comparatively slight. English republican writers of the seventeenth and eighteenth centuries had a much more profound effect on the colonists, instilling in them a distrust of executive authority and a belief in the fragility of republican government, depending as it did on the constant efforts of an enlightened and virtuous citizenry.

Deism—A small but influential number of educated men in the colonies accepted the Deism of the European free thinkers. Deism, a religion based on reason and science, repudiated the supernatural teachings of religion and attacked sectarianism. The Deists held that a benevolent God operated in the universe through natural laws and did not intervene constantly in the life of man. In America Benjamin Franklin, Thomas Jefferson, and Thomas Paine were prominent Deists.

FORCES FAVORING AND OPPOSING COOPERATION BETWEEN THE COLONISTS

The British Atlantic seaboard colonies that eventually fought together in the cause of independence were united by certain common factors that did not attract other British colonies to them. At the same time powerful disjunctive forces worked even among the seaboard colonies to frustrate efforts to unify them. Among the forces that later operated to draw them together, the common opposition to royal tyranny was the culminating one.

⊙⊙ **Unifying Forces Among the Colonists**—1) As the population of the colonies increased and transportation by roads and by ocean grew, the geographic obstacles were partially surmounted by increased trade and travel. A postal service established by the British promoted communications. Benjamin Franklin as Postmaster General improved this service. 2) The fact that all Americans were immigrants who had left their old countries to endure the hardships of pioneering gave them a common psychological bond and unity against mother country domination. 3) The need to unite for protection against the Native Americans had driven the colonies into cooperation. 4) The dominant English language, laws, literature, and customs united them. 5) Certain political institutions that developed in America gave the colonies something in common against the mother country. These were the use of written charters, the opposition everywhere to the power of the governors, the methods of voting by written ballot, and the high regard for representative government.

OO Divisive Forces Among the Colonists—1) The geographic factors of wide rivers, vacant spaces, and the great distance from Massachusetts to Georgia kept the colonists apart. 2) Differences in climate and topography caused the colonies to develop different economic interests but there was little to draw them together in any mutual exchange of goods. 3) Class differences remained fairly distinct and continued to divide the people within each colony. British policy, however, often supplied grievances that overcame these differences. Small farmers and large planters, seaboard moneyed classes and poor Western farmers, debtors and creditors found themselves facing the common antagonist. 4) Differences in national origin and religion kept colonists apart. The growth of toleration, intermarriage, and the common hardships of frontier life helped overcome these differences. 5) Disputes broke out between the colonies over boundaries, tariff duties, and issues of paper money.

CHAPTER BOOK LIST

Bonomi, Patricia U., *Under the Cope of Heaven* (1986). A more general treatment of the Great Awakening.

Boorstin, D.J., *The Americans: The Colonial Experience* (1958). Interpretive and controversial.

Boyer, Paul A., and Nissenbaum, Stephen, *Salem Possessed* (1974). Study of the witchcraft trials.

Buel, Joy and Richard, *The Way of Duty* (1984). Charming study of a Connecticut woman's life in the mid to late 18th century.

Cremin, Lawrence A., *American Education: The Colonial Experience, 1607–1783* (1970). Most complete treatment.

Crevecouer, J.H. St. John, *Letters From an American Farmer* (Dolphin, Everyman, and others). A classic on American ways.

Cronon, William, *Changes in the Land* (1983). Ecological changes brought about by colonization in North America.

Demos, John, *A Little Commonwealth* (1971).

Demos, John, *Entertaining Satan: Witchcraft and the Culture of Early New England* (1982). Witchcraft in a more general context.

Gaustad, Edwin S., *The Great Awakening in New England* (1957).

Greene, Jack P., *Pursuits of Happiness: The Social Development of the Early Modern British Colonies and the Formation of American Culture* (1988). Different and interesting interpretation.

Greven, Philip, *Four Generations* (1969).

Jordan, Winthrop D., *White Over Black* (Penguin).

Lockridge, Kenneth A., *A New England Town: The First One Hundred Years, 2nd ed.* (1985). A study of Dedham, Massachusetts.

May, Henry F., *The Enlightenment in America* (1974).

Morgan, E.S., *The Puritan Family* (1944).

Morison, S.E., *Intellectual Life of Colonial New England* (Cornell). Brief survey of cultural development.

Powell, Sumner C., *Puritan Village* (Wesleyan).

Schneider, H.W., *Puritan Mind* (Ann Arbor). An interpretation of the Puritan heritage.

Simpson, Alan, *Puritanism in Old and New England* (Phoenix). Brief, favorable interpretation.

Starkey, Marion, *Devil In Massachusetts* (Dolphin). Study of witch trials.

Winslow, Elizabeth, *Jonathan Edwards: 1703–1758* (Collier). Pulitzer Prize biography of an influential intellectual.

Wright, Louis B., *The Cultural Life of the American Colonies* (1957). Excellent survey.

REVIEW QUESTIONS

MULTIPLE CHOICE

1. Which of the following people settled farthest west in the largest numbers in the English colonies? (1) The French (2) the Germans (3) the Scotch-Irish (4) the Irish.

2. The aristocracy of the colonies was made up mainly of (1) noblemen from England (2) officeholders with English backgrounds and well-to-do American merchants and landowners (3) rich men and officeholders of English birth (4) only of descendants of noblemen regardless of national origin.

3. The Anglican Church was more strongly entrenched in which group of colonies? (1) The Southern (2) the New England (3) the Middle.

4. Radical Protestants within the Anglican Church who wished to eradicate all traces of Catholicism were the (1) Congregationalists (2) Pilgrims (3) Puritans (4) Presbyterians.

5. Which pair of colonies was most noted for religious toleration? (1) Maryland and New York (2) Pennsylvania and Rhode Island (3) Pennsylvania and Georgia (4) North Carolina and Rhode Island.

6. The Great Awakening (1) was limited almost exclusively to the region west of the Appalachians (2) affected the religious life of all the colonies but flourished most in the West (3) was a revival of religion among the older denominations mainly (4) was a leading cause of the American Revolution.

7. During the colonial period education at all levels progressed most in which section? (1) South (2) West (3) Middle Colonies (4) New England.

8. Which statement about literature in the colonies is *not* true? (1) By 1765 many newspapers were being issued (2) almanacs were a popular annual publication (3) colonial literature showed remarkable creativity and originality (4) many early writings dealt with religion and the history of the colonies.

9. The Enlightenment of Europe (1) had no appreciable effect upon colonial thought (2) decidedly influenced colonials, including New England divines (3) influenced only freethinkers like Benjamin Franklin (4) brought greater emphasis upon spiritual values.

10. The Deists (1) rejected the supernatural and opposed sectarians (2) clung to the belief in God's intervention in the lives of individuals (3) found few prominent Americans among their followers (4) promoted a resurgence of religion by 1775.

11. Which is the exception to the following unifying forces operating among the people of the thirteen colonies? (1) Increased trade and travel (2) the common experience of immigration from Europe (3) political institutions originating in the colonies (4) economic influence of climate and topography.

TRUE-FALSE

12. Two basic forces in the development of American national character have been opportunity under frontier conditions and the mingling of heterogeneous peoples.

13. The early German immigrants settled largely in the Southern Colonies.

14. There was more uniformity in religion in the Middle Colonies than in the colonies to either the north or the south.

15. From the earliest times in America social stratification tended to be less rigid than in Europe.

16. Economic achievement early became a greater determinant of an individual's social standing in America than elsewhere.

17. The strongest religious influence in America has been that of the Puritans.

18. The religious beliefs of the Puritans came to be institutionalized in the Episcopalian Church.

19. The more radical Protestant and evangelical religious denomina tions flourished in the frontier regions.

20. The term "witch-hunting," in reference to ill-founded mass fears, originated from the hysteria attending the witchcraft trials in Massachusetts.

21. The Great Awakening is the name given to the American phase of the same movement known as the Age of Reason in Europe.

22. River transportation and good roads served as a unifying force among the colonies.

23. The influence of the frontier in colonial times exerted a unifying force among Westerners.

COMPLETION

24. The usual religious denomination of the Scotch-Irish immigrants was _____ .

25. The French Protestants who settled in the Carolinas are also known by the name _____ .

26. Laws regulating personal behavior in matters of morals and the observance of the Sabbath are known as _____ .

27. The New England witchcraft trials centered at the town of _____ .

28. The first college founded in America was _____ .

29. After Boston what other colonial city became a center of literary activity? _____ .

30. The Enlightenment in Europe began at about the time of _____ who proved the earth was not the center of the universe.

31. The most outstanding scientist in the colonies was _____ .

32. A religious philosophy known as _____ was based on science and reason.

MATCHING

33. John Calvin	a. Reconciled religion with science in New England
34. Jonathan Edwards	b. *Social Contract*
35. John Peter Zenger	c. Solar theory
36. Benjamin Franklin	d. The Great Awakening
37. Philip Freneau	e. Early national poet
38. Cotton Mather	f. Freedom of the press
39. John Locke	g. *Poor Richard's Almanac*
40. Adam Smith	h. Predestination
41. Jean Jacques Rousseau	i. "Natural rights"
	j. Advocated laissez-faire economics

THE AMERICAN REVOLUTION
1763–1789

CHRONOLOGY / CHAPTER 5

1637 Pequot War.

1675 King Philip's War.

1689 King William's War began; ended by Treaty of Ryswick, 1697.

1702 Queen Anne's War began; ended by Peace of Utrecht, 1713.

1744 King George's War began; concluded by Treaty of Aix-la-Chapelle.

1754 Albany Congress met.
French and Indian War began; ended with Treaty of Paris, 1763.

1763 Pontiac's (Indian) War.
Proclamation of 1763.
Paxton Boys uprising.

1764 Sugar Act passed and enforced. Currency Act forbade colonial paper money.

1765 Stamp Act. Stamp Act Congress. Quartering Act.

1766 Declaratory Act.

1767 Townshend Acts.

1768 Regulator Movement began; ended in 1771.

1770 Boston Massacre. Repeal of Townshend duties except tea tax. Period of calm began, ended 1773.

1773 Tea Act gave monopoly to British East India Company. Boston Tea Party.

1774 Intolerable Acts and Quebec Act passed by Parliament. First Continental Congress met.

1775 Lexington and Concord engagements with British troops. Second Continental Congress met.

1776 Declaration of Independence adopted July 4.

Chapter

5
COLONIAL RESISTANCE TO BRITISH RULE, 1763–1776

> Until the French and Indian War, the colonies generally felt weak and hemmed in on the north, west, and south by foreign powers such as France and Spain. British protection, even if it involved regulation of their foreign trade and, to an extent, their domestic economies, was welcome. After 1763 the character of British rule changed and it no longer appeared beneficial.
>
> The resistance to England may be systematized under five phases: 1) the first protests up to 1764; 2) the Grenville program, 1764–1766; 3) the Townshend acts, 1767–1770; 4) the period of calm, 1770–1773; and 5) the Tea Act and its consequences, 1773–1776.

WAR IN THE COLONIES

Early threats to the security of the colonists came from the Native Americans. Later, when the colonies became involved in Britain's struggles for empire with European rivals, the colonists were unavoidably drawn into these conflicts.

The Indian Wars—Early conflicts with Native Americans were localized, but when the British became engaged in war with her rivals for colonial empire, mainly with France, various tribes were drawn into these wars by alliances with one side or the other. Wherever the Europeans arrived, the Native Americans at first were usually friendly and helpful. As the white settlements expanded into their hunting grounds and mutual outrages occurred, conflicts broke out.

In New England the Puritans despised the Native Americans and, when wars occurred, they killed the men and sold women and children into slavery. The Pequot War (1637) broke out when the Pequots sought revenge for the mistreatment they were accorded. In the brief war hundreds of Pequots were killed and sold into slavery. After the war relative peace reigned in New England for nearly forty years.

In 1675 King Philip's War broke out as the New Englanders seized Native American lands and sought to rigidly regulate Native American conduct. Murder and looting raged in the frontier settlements. The costly war took a heavy toll in lives, many frontier settlements were burned, and the whole of New England was threatened. Again hundreds of Native Americans were killed and sold into slavery. The war finally ended after three years. Henceforth, Native American warfare in New England occurred repeatedly in connection with the imperial wars between France and England.

In the Middle Colonies the Dutch and then the English in New York fought local tribes to win Manhattan but later developed trade and maintained friendly relations with the powerful Iroquois confederacy in upper New York. In Pennsylvania the Quaker policy of friendship and fair dealing prevented warfare.

In Virginia a large scale war broke out in 1622 when Opechancanough led the tribes in a determined war against white settlements. The war lasted three years, 357 Virginians were killed, but the Native Americans were defeated by systematic destruction of their corn fields. In 1644 Opechancanough, now old and blind, promoted the massacre of 500 whites. As usual after the defeats of the Native Americans, they were forced to cede more lands to the settlers. Peace was again broken in 1676 when Native Americans began attacks that precipitated Bacon's Rebellion. The Carolinas too had their share of Native American warfare, the worst being the bloody Tuscarora War in 1711.

⚙ **Britain's Imperial Wars**—The Spanish were eliminated as a serious rival before Britain began efforts at colonizing North America. Her first rival there, the Netherlands, was eliminated in three short wars in the 1650s and 1660s, thus securing the Middle Colonies of New York, New Jersey, and Pennsylvania for Britain. She then engaged in a series of European and imperial wars with France, all of which involved the colonies, took up much of the period between 1689 and 1815, and are sometimes referred to as the Second Hundred Years War.

The Second Hundred Years War began when William of Orange became King of England in 1689. King William's War (1689–1697) brought the colonies into their first world war. New England captured Port Royal, Nova Scotia, but the English failed to take Canada. Deadly raids by Native Americans spread over the New England frontier. The Treaty of Ryswick (1697) restored peace without any territorial gains by either side.

Queen Anne's War (1702–1713) paralleled the War of Spanish Succession in Europe. Native American attacks again raged on the New England frontier. Port Royal was again captured (1710). In 1790 the New England and Middle Colonies organized forces to aid the British in an attack on Montreal, but the expedition ended after the loss of eight transports and a thousand men in a sea disaster at the treacherous entrance to the St. Lawrence River. The Peace of Utrecht ended the war in 1713 in a decided victory for Britain over France and her ally, Spain. The British won 1) Nova Scotia, Newfoundland, and the Hudson's Bay region in America, 2) Gibraltar in Spain, and 3) the Asiento that gave Britain a 30-year monopoly of the African slave trade with South America.

King George's War (1740–1748) began in Europe where it was known as the War of Austrian Succession. Because New England suffered from French-inspired Native American attacks and French competition in the fisheries and fur trade, the New Englanders organized an expedition to take Louisbourg on Cape Breton Island. They succeeded in 1745. The indecisive peace came with the Treaty of Aix-la-Chapelle in 1748 and Louisbourg was restored to France.

THE FRENCH AND INDIAN WAR (1756–1763)

The French and Indian War (called Seven Years War in Europe) began in America as a struggle over the Ohio Valley. It brought an end to the French empire on the mainland of North America.

○○ **Background of the War in America**—By 1750 the French, numbering about 100,000 in the vast holdings of New France, took genuine alarm at the westward advance of the English colonists who numbered about 2,000,000. Both France and Britain claimed the territory east of the Mississippi River. King George II in 1749 granted 200,000 acres beyond the Allegheny Mountains to the Ohio Company, a group of Virginia land speculators. From Pennsylvania, fur traders invaded this region, threatening to win control of the Native American trade. The French constructed a string of forts in the Ohio country to check these incursions of the British. In 1754 the governor of Virginia sent a twenty-one year old provincial officer, George Washington, with a body of colonial soldiers, to push the French away from the forks of the Ohio. A short engagement at Fort Necessity in present-day western Pennsylvania, resulted in Washington's surrender and the start of the war. The French went on to complete Fort Duquesne at the forks.

○○○ **The Albany Congress**—When the British encouraged the colonists to cooperate with them against the Native Americans, representatives from seven colonies met at Albany. Benjamin Franklin, representing Pennsylvania, proposed a plan of union, creating a colonial council to supervise defense, western expansion, and Native American affairs. It could levy taxes to finance military efforts. Neither the British government nor the various colonial assemblies were ready for this, however, and the plan failed on both sides of the Atlantic, although it did prefigure later, more successful efforts.

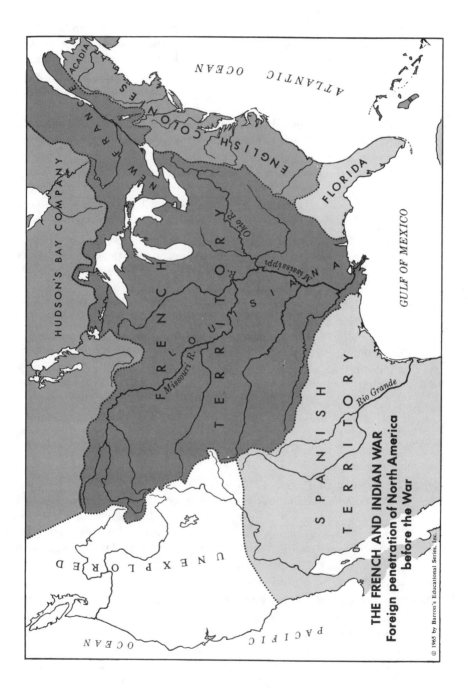

THE FRENCH AND INDIAN WAR
Foreign penetration of North America
before the War

○ **Advantages of the Combatants**—In the French and Indian War the British enjoyed 1) the advantage of the world's strongest navy. 2) In Europe Frederick the Great with the strongest army in Europe fought as Britain's ally. 3) The English colonists in America outnumbered the French colonists about 15 to 1. 4) Under the forceful leadership of William Pitt a new spirit was aroused among the British forces and unity of command was achieved. 5) The French had too much territory to defend while the English colonists, concentrated and self-sufficient, were supported by a varied agriculture and industry.

The French possessed the advantages of 1) numerous and powerful Native American allies while the usually cooperative English Native American allies, the Iroquois, remained neutral. 2) The French colonists were better disciplined and more loyal to their government. The British colonies acted like independent states and cooperated only when exposed to immediate danger. 3) The French had better overall command in the war while the British at first lacked unified control.

○ **Military Events of the War**—The commander of the British forces in America, General Edward Braddock, cut a road through the wilderness from Fort Cumberland, Maryland, northwestward to take Ft. Duquesne. Braddock's army was ambushed and he suffered his notorious defeat within about seven miles of Ft. Duquesne (1755). In 1756 the European phase of the war broke out and the war became a global contest. The British forces, divided into four armies in America, suffered disheartening defeats in the first two years.

William Pitt's assumption of power in 1758 brought about a remarkable shift in the war. Britain captured Louisbourg, Fort Frontenac (on Lake Ontario), and Fort Duquesne that year. Quebec, the center of French power in Canada, fell the next year and, in 1760 Montreal was taken and France was virtually eliminated from the war in North America. British victories in Europe and India forced the French to negotiate a peace in 1763.

○○○ **The Treaty of Paris, 1763**—By the terms of the treaty: 1) France ceded Canada and all territory east of the Mississippi River to Britain; 2) the French and Spanish islands in the West Indies were returned to their original owners; 3) Spain ceded Florida to Britain for the return of Cuba; 4) France transferred the Louisiana territory west of the Mississippi to Spain as compensation for Spain's loss of Florida; and 5) Britain retained lands she had won from France in India.

○○○ **Consequences of the French and Indian War**—With the virtual expulsion of the French from North America (they retained only two small islands in the Gulf of St. Lawrence), the French and their Native American allies were eliminated as a threat to the colonists. Also, their considerable efforts during the war had demonstrated the increasing strength of the colonies and several campaigns, involving troops from various colonies, had familiarized them with other areas. The colonies thus gained an increased sense of their own importance in the British Empire.

Conversely, the British believed the colonists should have contributed much more than they did and resolved to govern them more closely in the future. Also, the increased costs of imperial administration brought about by the newly acquired territories convinced the crown of the necessity of securing a revenue from the colonies, as well as a revamped administrative structure for colonial relations. Neither of these problems would be dealt with in a manner considerate of colonial interests and feelings.

REACTION TO THE NEW COLONIAL POLICY

Parliament previously had dealt hardly at all with colonial administration, mostly from a fear of increasing the power of the crown. George III overcame this fear, partly by patronage and bribes, partly because of the clear necessity of the case, and "King in Parliament" proceeded to try and reorganize colonial administration. In seeking to bring the colonies under a "due subordination" to the mother country, the crown tried to bring the colonies under a strict system of administration in place of the old, slipshod ways. In addition, the effort to secure a tax revenue antagonized colonial merchants who saw the British monopoly of colonial trade as a substantial, however indirect, contribution to the empire.

THE GRENVILLE PROGRAM, 1763–1766

More immediately responsible for the new colonial policy than George III was George Grenville who became prime minister in 1763.

The First Protests—Before the French and Indian War was over, attempts made to enforce the revenue laws brought friction. In 1761 the Boston merchants employed a brilliant young lawyer, James Otis, to protest the legality of the writs of assistance. (Writs of assistance permitted customs officials to search commercial establishments without specific authorization by a court.) The courts upheld the writs and applied them in all the colonies. Public opinion crystallized in favor of Otis's arguments that the writs were a tyrannical invasion of the ancient rights of Englishmen.

Another case, the Parsons' Cause, also alarmed England as the colonists denounced the British government and defended rights of the colonists as British subjects. In the Parsons' Cause, Anglican ministers appealed to the Privy Council to disallow a Virginia law that, in effect, reduced their salaries. When the Privy Council disallowed the act, the ministers sued to recover back pay. The jury, swayed by the protests of Patrick Henry against the right of the Privy Council to disallow colonial laws, defiantly awarded the ministers only one penny damages.

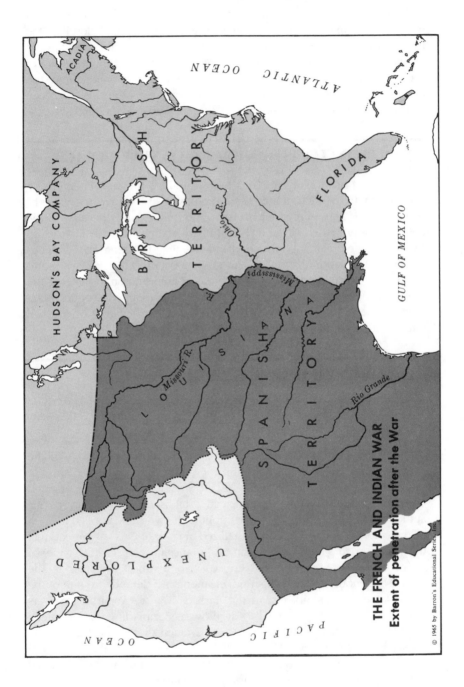

THE FRENCH AND INDIAN WAR
Extent of penetration after the War

© 1965 by Barron's Educational Series, Inc.

✪✪✪ **The Proclamation of 1763**—As an immediate consequence of the war, the British government was forced to settle the problem of Native American policy in the territories west of the Allegheny divide. The westward migration of white settlers aroused the Native Americans who struck back in Pontiac's Rebellion in 1763. British officials were responsible for pacifying the Native Americans, regulating the fur trade, and establishing government in the former French territories.

The Proclamation Act of 1763 1) created a Native American reserve west of the Allegheny divide, forbade settlement west of the proclamation line, and required removal of settlers already there. 2) The Act required the licensing of Native American traders, and 3) forbade private purchase of land from the Native Americans.

The Act offended settlers, traders, and land speculators and aroused a storm of protest in the colonies. Powerful groups of land speculators and migrating settlers caused the breakdown of the Proclamation. The line was moved westward bit by bit to accommodate land speculators. Settlers ignored the law and carried American settlement to the west of the mountains in three areas: 1) the Pittsburgh area, 2) the Watauga valley in eastern Tennessee, and 3) the fertile Blue Grass region of central Kentucky, where they were led by Daniel Boone. In response to the frontier settlers, the Native Americans attacked in Lord Dunmore's War in Kentucky in 1774.

✪✪✪ **The Grenville Tax Program**—George Grenville's program to raise greatly increased revenue from the colonies was needed to finance military garrisons for defense against the Native Americans and to relieve British landlords and merchants of part of their heavy tax burden. The taxes fell during the hard times after the French and Indian War and had to be paid in scarce colonial specie. To collect the revenues 1) measures were begun to prevent smuggling. The British resorted to the use of ship patrols, writs of assistance, strengthening of the customs service, and provisions for trial of accused smugglers without the benefit of juries. 2) The Sugar Act of 1764 replaced that of 1733. Although duties were cut by one-half on molasses from non-British sources, this levy was to be collected. The earlier one had been meant to prohibit the traffic by making it unprofitable; this new Act was to produce a revenue. 3) The Currency Act (1764) prohibited further colonial issues of paper money. 4) The Stamp Act (1765) levied an internal revenue tax in the form of stamps to be purchased and affixed to specified documents and publications such as newspapers. 5) The Quartering Act (1765) required the colonial legislatures to supply barracks and part of the cost of maintaining 10,000 British troops in the colonies.

✪✪✪ **Opposition to the Revenue Measures**—All of these acts were resisted, but the most attention was centered on the Stamp Act because it affected the most people, especially those previously untouched by

Britain's mercantile regulations, in many acts of ordinary life, and it was to be collected in coin, always scarce in the colonies.

Public opinion against the tax was aroused by the Virginia House of Burgesses when Patrick Henry won the passage of the Virginia Resolves condemning the Stamp Tax as a violation of their rights to be taxed only with the consent of colonial legislatures. Other legislatures took similar action. Massachusetts called the Stamp Act Congress (1765). This Congress, the first one called only by the colonists, met in New York City and was attended by representatives of nine colonies. It phrased its resolutions in a respectful tone, but it nevertheless firmly denied that Parliament could tax anyone not represented in it, and asserted that the colonists were not represented there.

Mobs broke out in riot in various places. The Sons of Liberty organized, and by threats, by tarring and feathering, and by burning the stamps forced the collectors to resign. Non-importation agreements were similarly enforced against British goods. But the most effective weapon of protest was almost universal defiance of the Act; by the end of 1765, it had been set aside. Parliament, confronted with the choice of sending an army to enforce the act or repealing it, chose the latter. First, however they resolved in the Declaratory Act (1766) that they had the power to legislate for the colonies in all cases whatsoever. They clearly intended by this Act to assert their right to tax the colonies, an assertion denied with equal force by the colonists.

THE TOWNSHEND PROGRAM

When the Rockingham ministry, which had presided over the repeal of the Stamp Act, fell, it was replaced by one headed by Charles Townshend. He sought favor with the influential land owners by cutting the land tax, replacing the lost revenue with new taxes on American trade. When he died in 1770, he was replaced by Lord North.

❂❂ **The Townshend Acts (1767)**—1) Townshend suspended the New York assembly for failure to vote supplies for British troops. Townshend singled out New York for punishment to avoid arousing all the colonies. 2) Duties were levied on colonial imports of glass, lead, paint, paper, and tea. These external taxes were presumably acceptable to the colonials. 3) Another measure created a board of customs commissioners and gave them authority to issue the writs of assistance to prevent smuggling.

❂ **Colonial Opposition**—The Boston merchants organized another boycott against British imports in protest and other colonies joined them. In Boston, Samuel Adams made himself leader of the protest. Adams stirred the Massachusetts legislature into issuing the *Circular Letter* denying the right of Parliament to levy external taxes. In Pennsylvania John

Dickinson wrote his influential *Letters from a Farmer* attacking external taxes. The colonists had admitted Parliament's power to levy regulatory duties, but denied its right to raise a revenue from them. Samuel Adams also aroused the "liberty boys" who mobbed and tarred and feathered the customs collectors. Adams spread stories in the newspapers of imaginary atrocities by the British troops that had been stationed in Boston to protect the customs agents. When the "redcoats" were badgered and attacked by a mob of "liberty boys" they fired into the crowd and killed several persons. To keep alive resentment against the British, Adams publicized this incident as the "Boston Massacre" (1770).

The ministry of Lord North recommended and Parliament repealed all the Townshend duties except the tax on tea. The colonists felt they had won a second major victory.

The Period of Calm, 1770–1773—After the repeal of the Townshend duties a period of relative quiet and prosperity ensued until the colonies were aroused by the Tea Act. This period of quiet disturbed some colonial leaders, such as Sam Adams, who may already have resolved on independence, but knew how few people were in agreement at that time. He and others managed to keep Britain's offenses in the public eye. In 1772 they organized the Committees of Correspondence throughout the colonies to spread propaganda against the royal government, to exaggerate British mistakes, and to defend the rights of the colonists.

In 1772 Rhode Island smugglers burned the British revenue cutter *Gaspee* when it ran aground in Narragansett Bay. The Regulator Movement (1768–1771), a small scale civil war in western North Carolina against Governor Tryon, broke out among frontiersmen in protest against extortionate taxes, corrupt courts, and underrepresentation—all attributable mainly to the upper class domination. An earlier uprising in Pennsylvania, the Paxton Boys (1763), also took place because of a recurring Western grievance against lack of protection against Native American disturbances. The Western movements were symptomatic of deeply felt grievances of poor frontiersmen against discrimination and unfairness of government of the upper classes in the East.

CONSEQUENCES OF THE TEA ACT OF 1773

This measure was passed by Lord North to save the British East India Company from bankruptcy.

✪✪✪ **The Tea Act**—The Act 1) relieved the East India Company of all taxes on tea save the one levied by the Townshend Acts, and 2) permitted it to sell its tea directly to American retailers. The Company could not compete with smuggled tea and immediately antagonized the merchants, most of whom dealt in tea, smuggled or legal, and were now frozen out of the trade.

The merchants then joined those who had continued to resist the British. Everywhere, except in Boston, the dutied tea was turned back to Britain without undue disturbances. But in Boston, because of the obstinacy of Governor Thomas Hutchinson, the tea had to be destroyed, leading to the Boston Tea Party in 1773.

✪✪✪ **The Coercive Acts (Intolerable Acts) (1774)**—Lord North and George III decided upon a policy of coercion against Massachusetts. The policy was to be carried out by four Acts passed by Parliament: 1) The port of Boston was closed pending payment of damages for the destroyed tea. 2) The Massachusetts Government Act revoked the provincial charter and subjected the colony to severely restricted self-government there. 3) A third Act provided that accused royal officials might be tried outside Massachusetts. 4) A quartering Act required the Massachusetts legislature to provide lodging and food for British troops.

✪✪ **The Quebec Act (1774)**—The Quebec Act brought out the strong anti-Catholic prejudice of the colonists and led to charges that it was a preliminary step to establishing the Anglican Church—or even the Catholic Church—throughout the colonies. This law 1) extended the boundaries of Quebec to include the territory north of the Ohio and east of the Mississippi River; 2) recognized the legality of the Roman Catholic Church in all of Quebec; and 3) gave political rights to Catholics.

The Quebec Act antagonized the American Protestants who feared it might be, according to rumors, an initial step to enforce the authority of the Anglican Church (which seemed to be little different from the Catholic Church) over the Protestants. The Act recognized both freedom of religion for Catholics and the French law in civil cases, law which did not provide trial by jury. The ever powerful interests of land speculators feared the law would hinder their sales of land in the West, and fur traders did not welcome control over their activities by royal officials at Montreal.

✪ **The First Continental Congress**—The colonists, aroused by the Coercive Acts and the Quebec Act, headed a call of a rump session of the dissolved assembly of Virginia and chose delegates to meet in the First Continental Congress in Philadelphia in September, 1774. Instead of isolating Massachusetts as intended, the Coercive Acts aroused all the colonies. Members were chosen by the assemblies or by local Committees of Safety.

The Continental Congress, with representatives from every colony except Georgia, turned out to be more radical than most colonial leaders expected. It passed 1) the Suffolk Resolves, which declared the Coercive Acts null and void and encouraged forcible resistance; 2) the Declaration of Rights and Grievances, which stated the American position of freedom from parliamentary taxation, while accepting trade regulation; 3) the Continental Association, a non-importation, non-exportation agreement, which also created a network of local committees to enforce its provisions, in effect, a coercive law passed by a body with no authority whatsoever. The delegates then resolved to meet again the following May, if their grievances had not been resolved.

THE DECLARATION OF INDEPENDENCE

Majority opinion in the colonies did not embrace the idea of independence until compelled to do so by George III's resort to force of arms to subdue them.

❂❂ **Lexington and Concord**—The Continental Congress approved preparations for defense, and the people of Massachusetts collected munitions and trained "Minutemen" to meet British aggression. General Thomas Gage dispatched 1,000 troops on the night of April 18, 1775, to march out from Boston to Concord to seize a store of gunpowder collected by the rebels. Paul Revere rode to give the alarm and the Minutemen appeared the next day to meet the British force at Lexington. Shots were exchanged (it is not known who fired first) and eight militiamen were killed. The redcoats marched on to Concord and found that most of the powder had been removed. On their return to Boston the British lost 273 men as they were fired upon continually by farmers in ambush. Word of the bloodshed spread throughout the colonies and colonial armed resistance began.

❂ **The Second Continental Congress**—Congress met, as previously planned, on May 10, 1775. The moderates, led by John Dickinson of Pennsylvania, delayed a declaration of independence. Congress, however, made plans to raise an army and made George Washington its Commander-in-Chief. Congress offered conciliation with Britain in the Olive Branch Petition which George III curtly rejected. Congress responded next with a Declaration of the Causes and Necessity of Taking up Arms. The colonies were not seeking independence but a redress of grievances and a return to relations with the mother country as existed before 1763.

❂❂ **Immediate Causes of a Declaration of Independence**—Military engagements occurred for more than a year before the colonists abandoned reconciliation and took the final step of declaring independence. They decided upon the complete break because 1) British military activity indicated the intention of dealing with the colonies only after they had surrendered to force. Early victories made the Americans optimistic. 2) The British use of the Hessian mercenaries, Native Americans, and African Americans alarmed the colonists. 3) The Prohibitory Act of Parliament closing all colonial ports until the colonists abandoned resistance seemed to leave no alternative but a declaration of independence which would enable them to seek foreign assistance. 4) Thomas Paine's publication of *Common Sense* crystallized public opinion. *Common Sense* condemned the British government and George III and pleaded the advantages of independence. 5) Radicals among the common people gained increasing influence in the colonial assemblies and replaced conservative delegates in the Continental Congress.

✪✪✪ **The Declaration of Independence**—Congress appointed a committee headed by Thomas Jefferson to draft a formal declaration of independence. A resolution of independence was adopted on July 2 and the Declaration of Independence itself, giving reasons for the break, was approved on July 4, 1776. Thomas Jefferson wrote the Declaration, but Congress made certain changes in it. The preamble stated the compact theory of John Locke as the philosophical basis of the revolution. The second part enumerated the grievances against the King. The final statement declared the existence of independence.

The Declaration strengthened the radicals. The patriots now had the definite goal of independence to fight for. People became divided as they were forced to choose either the Patriot or Loyalist cause. With independence as the Patriot war aim, the French government gladly gave secret aid in the breakup of the British empire.

✪✪✪ FUNDAMENTAL CAUSES OF THE AMERICAN REVOLUTION

The causes of the Revolution were complex. The following factors help to explain the decision for independence.

1) The American colonists had long become accustomed to a large degree of independence and self-determination during the century and a half of neglect and of separation from England. Many had come to America in the first place to enjoy more freedom. When Tory England sought to regulate, tax, and govern them with a strong hand, she introduced a change the colonials did not wish to accept and one which sympathetic Whigs in the homeland often protested.

2) The multiple unwise British policies threatened or hurt the vital interests of important groups—merchants, fur traders, settlers, manufacturers, debtors, workers, taxpayers, land speculators, and Protestants. British policies drove the divided colonials together.

3) The timing of the reorganization of the colonial system might have been designed to provoke resistance. Rigid regulation began in 1763 when the colonies felt more self-confident and independent. The tax burden was increased during a postwar depression made worse by restrictions on the supply of currency.

4) The constitutional disagreement over the status of the colonies caused much of the friction with Britain, as the colonists refused to accept a subordinate position in the empire or the idea of "virtual representation," used to justify the mother country's unrepresentative Parliament and extended to America by Grenville in 1764.

5) The religious factor strongly influenced a large proportion of the Americans. Many had come to America as radical Protestants and had left England and Europe under unpleasant circumstances. They disliked the Anglicans whom they considered as next to Catholics and they feared the possible appointment of an Anglican bishop in America.

6) There were psychological reasons for colonial resentment of British rule. Americans resented privileges enjoyed by Englishmen as opposed to Americans. Americans resented being held in contempt as colonials and disliked the sharp class distinctions drawn by the English.

7) The settlers in America had evolved into a different society and nationality from that of Britain. A third of the population were of non-English origin and the English settlers themselves had come to be Americanized. The simple fact of geographical separation is a basic factor in all independence movements among colonial peoples.

8) Intellectually, John Locke's philosophy of the natural rights of man and of social contract was adapted to rationalize the struggle for independence.

9) The feasibility of independence appealed to a numerous people spread over a large, rich land. They saw no reason to submit to rule by the small island far across the Atlantic waters. The prospects of foreign aid were encouraging. The revolt came not so much from desperation as from the bright prospects of the future.

Independence in time was inevitable; it would have been impossible to prevent, but it might have evolved more gradually as it did with the Commonwealth countries now nominally loyal to the British Crown.

CHAPTER BOOK LIST

Andrews, C.M., *Colonial Background of the American Revolution* (Yale). Basic causes of the separation.

Bowen, Catherine D., *John Adams and the American Revolution* (Universal). Careful biography by an admirer.

Brown, R.S., *Middle-Class Democracy and the Revolution in Massachusetts, 1691–1780* (1955). Denies thesis that the Revolution was a class conflict.

Brown, Wallace, *The King's Friends: The Composition and Motives of the Loyalist Claimants* (1965). One of the better books on the Loyalists.

Bushman, Richard, *From Puritan to Yankee* (1967).

Foner, Eric, *Tom Paine and Revolutionary America* (1976). Political ideology behind Paine's writing.

Gipson, L.H., *The Coming of the American Revolution, 1763–1775* (1954). Critical of the colonists.

Gross, Robert A., *The Minutemen and Their World* (1976). Excellent study of the town of Concord, 1760–1802.

Higginbotham, Don, *The War of Independence: Military Attitudes, Policies, and Practices, 1763–1789* (1983). Best military history of the War for Independence.

Kerber, Linda, *Women of the Republic* (1980).

Labaree, Benjamin W., *The Boston Tea Party* (1964). Valuable study.

Middlekauf, Robert, *The Glorious Cause: The American Revolution, 1763–1789* (1982). Complete treatment.

Miller, J.C., *The Origins of the American Revolution* (1943). Begins with 1760.

Morgan, E.S., *Birth of the Republic: 1763–1789* (University of Chicago). An excellent brief survey.

Parkman, Francis, *Montcalm and Wolfe* (Collier). By a great American historian of the French and English struggle to control America.

Peckham, Howard, *Pontiac and the Indian Uprising* (Phoenix). Biography of America's most formidable Native American chief.

Quarles, Benjamin, *The Negro in the American Revolution* (1961).

Rossiter, Clinton, *Seedtime of the Republic* (1953). Discusses background of the Revolution.

REVIEW QUESTIONS

MULTIPLE CHOICE

1. Which of the following colonies suffered least from conflicts with the Native Americans? (1) Pennsylvania (2) Massachusetts (3) Virginia (4) South Carolina.

2. Which was the greatest of the imperial wars preceding the French and Indian War? (1) Queen Anne's War (2) King William's War (3) King George's War (4) King Philip's War.

3. In the colonial wars between France and Britain before 1756 (1) the British were generally successful but gained little territory from France (2) the British usually experienced severe defeats (3) the British gained large cessions of French territory (4) no changes in territorial ownership were made.

4. The French and Indian War began (1) with hostilities in Europe (2) in a conflict over the Ohio Valley (3) in a dispute over the succession to the throne of Austria (4) because the British encouraged Native American raids against Quebec.

5. The Treaty of Paris of 1763 included all of these provisions *except* (1) France ceded Canada and the eastern Mississippi Valley to Britain (2) Spain ceded Florida to Britain (3) France was permitted to keep Nova Scotia (4) France transferred the western Louisiana territory to Spain.

6. Which was *not* a British problem of government arising out of the French and Indian War? (1) Promoting the settlement of the Ohio Valley (2) the prevention of conflict between Native Americans and whites west of the Appalachians (3) the financing of military defenses in America (4) devising stricter controls over colonial foreign trade.

7. In the fifteen years preceding the Revolution the first protests of the colonists against British measures were against (1) the Stamp Act (2) the writs of assistance (3) the Townshend duties (4) the Proclamation Line.

8. The Proclamation of 1763 included provisions upon all the following points *except* (1) the settlement of whites west of the Proclamation Line (2) providing revenues for policing the Native American reserve (3) the licensing of fur traders (4) private purchase of Native American lands.

9. The colonists protested most strongly against the Stamp Act because (1) it taxed newspapers and political pamphlets (2) they believed the revenue was not needed (3) it required a host of British officials for enforcement (4) they were not represented in Parliament.

10. The Declaratory Act was passed to (1) regain the good will of the Americans (2) assert the right of Parliament to tax the colonies in all cases (3) assert Parliament's right to levy only external taxes (4) uphold primarily the theory of virtual representation.

11. The Townshend Acts provided for all *except* (1) the suspension of the New York assembly (2) duties on certain colonial imports (3) the theory of representation in Parliament (4) the issuance of writs of assistance.

12. In the Boston Massacre the number of people killed was (1) almost fifty (2) over twenty (3) sixteen (4) about five.

13. Which was *not* a grievance of the Western frontiersmen against the ruling aristocracy in the various colonies? (1) Lack of adequate representation in the assemblies (2) lack of support in fighting Native Americans (3) extortionate taxation (4) measures to prevent smuggling.

14. Which of the following events occurred last? (1) The Townshend Act (2) the Stamp Act (3) the Tea Act (4) the Declaratory Act.

15. The Quebec Act (1) was passed to punish the assertive New Englanders (2) provided for an Anglican bishop to govern the New England churches (3) provided for the government of Quebec (4) forbade the colonists to enter the Ohio country.

16. Which of these named events occurred first? (1) The First Continental Congress (2) the Boston Tea Party (3) the Townshend Acts (4) the Committees of Correspondence.

17. The battles of Lexington and Concord were fought when the British commander sought to (1) station troops in the interior of Massachusetts (2) seize supplies of gunpowder held by the rebels (3) demonstrate British readiness to deal with resistance (4) arrest Samuel Adams.

18. With regard to the desire for independence, a majority of Americans up to 1775 probably (1) were determined to gain complete independence (2) did not wish to restore the relationship existing before 1763 (3) simply wished to restore amicable relations with Britain (4) only wanted a larger degree of self-government.

19. Which was *not* one of the immediate causes for adopting the Declaration of Independence (1) The British use of Hessian mercenary troops and African Americans against the colonists (2) an act of Parliament closing all colonial ports until the Americans ceased resistance (3) the fighting at Lexington and Concord (4) the influence of Thomas Paine.

20. The principal author of the Declaration of Independence was (1) John Locke (2) Patrick Henry (3) James Madison (4) Jefferson.

21. The Declaration of Independence listed among other tyrannical acts of the King all of the following *except* (1) the appointment of a multitude of officials to harass the colonists (2) maintaining standing armies without the consent of colonial legislatures (3) the threat to appoint an Anglican bishop to America (4) encouraging Native American attacks against frontier inhabitants.

22. The Declaration of Independence did all of the following with which exception? (1) Stated the compact theory of government as a basis for revolution (2) provided a statement of the war aims of the Revolution (3) asserted the existence of independence (4) stated the wrongdoings of the King.

TRUE-FALSE

23. The first serious Native American uprising in New England was the Pequot War.

24. Whenever the British and Americans became involved in wars with France the Native Americans usually joined the enemy and ravaged one frontier or another.

25. In the War of Spanish Succession the British won all of Canada from the French.

26. The French and Indian War began in America in a struggle over the Ohio valley.

27. The Albany Plan failed to be adopted because the colonies were afraid to give up local power to a central government.

28. The American colonies showed a strong willingness to cooperate with Britain in the French and Indian War.

29. In the French and Indian War the American colonists gained confidence in themselves and contempt for British military ability.

30. Although the Americans argued that the writs of assistance were illegal they were upheld by the British courts.

31. The Proclamation of 1763 proved ineffective since the British were forced to move the line westward bit by bit and the frontiersmen ignored it.

32. The Stamp Tax was levied during a time of depression following the French and Indian War.

33. The colonists admitted the right of Parliament to collect indirect taxes.

34. The Regulator Movement in North Carolina was a frontier protest mainly against failure of the ruling classes to provide defense forces against marauding Native American bands.

35. The Tea Act attempted to secure colonial acceptance of both an indirect tax and a British monopoly.

36. From the beginning the main goal of the majority of Americans was complete independence from Britain.

37. The large proportion of colonists of non-English origin largely explains their readiness to revolt.

COMPLETION

38. The worst Native American war in New England was _____ War.

39. The Second Hundred Years War began when _____ became King of England.

40. In Europe Queen Anne's War ended with the Peace of _____ .

41. When Washington was defeated by the French at Great Meadows he was forced to surrender his fort called _____ .

42. The Albany Plan of Union was proposed by which colonial leader? _____ .

43. In the French and Indian War the victorious English general at Quebec was General _____ .

44. In the Treaty of Paris, 1763, Spain ceded _____ to Britain.

45. Coming to the English throne in 1760 was _____ .

46. In a case of early defiance of England, a Virginia jury awarded Anglican clergymen only token damages. The case is known as the _____ .

47. A Native American uprising known as _____ Rebellion pre ceded the Proclamation of 1763.

48. A fertile region in Kentucky settled early by followers of Daniel Boone was the _____ region.

49. Organized opponents of the Stamp Act who resorted to violence were known as the _____ .

50. While the Americans defended the theory of actual representation, the British upheld what they called _____ representation.

51. The mobs in Boston who badgered the "redcoats" were called the _____ .

52. During the period of calm in relations with the British, Adams and the revolutionists spread propaganda and information through the _____ .

53. The _____ was a name given to an uprising in western Pennsylvania against the Native Americans.

54. Boston was punished for the Tea Party by British laws known in America as the _____ .

55. The First Continental Congress met in the year _____ .

56. The moderates favored the _____ Plan proposing a colonial union with an American parliament.

57. The first battle of the Revolution was fought as _____ .

58. The Second Continental Congress in 1775 made a final offer of reconciliation with Britain known as the _____ Petition.

59. Thomas Paine wrote the pamphlet by the name of _____ which convinced the public of the desirability of independence.

60. The political party in power in England during the Revolution was the _____ Party.

MATCHING

61. George Grenville	a. *Letters from a Farmer*
62. James Otis	b. Leading Revolutionary agitator in Boston
63. William Pitt	c. Led British to victory in French and Indian War
64. John Dickinson	d. Wrote the Declaration of Independence
65. Edward Braddock	e. Passed first revenue measures against the colonists
66. Samuel Adams	f. Led protest against writs of assistance
67. Thomas Jefferson	g. Leader in the First Continental Congress
68. Patrick Henry	h. Defeated in march on Fort Duquesne
	i. Caused passage of Virginia Resolves

CHRONOLOGY / CHAPTER 6

1775 Second Continental Congress met.
First military action of the Revolution at Lexington and
    Concord.
Battle of Bunker Hill.

1776 Thomas Paine wrote *Common Sense.*
Declaration of Independence adopted.
Washington retreated from Long Island and Washington
    Heights.

1777 Battle of Saratoga fought, the turning point of the Revolution.
Eleven states adopted new constitutions.
Articles of Confederation submitted to the states by Congress.
Washington at Valley Forge in winter of 1777–1778.

1778 Franklin signed treaty of alliance with France.
British began campaigns in the South with capture of
    Savannah.
George Rogers Clark began campaign in Illinois, finished
    in 1779.

1781 Admiral de Grasse sent by France to America.
Capture of Cornwallis at Yorktown.
Articles of Confederation ratified.

1783 Treaty of Paris recognized American independence.

Chapter

6

THE WAR FOR AMERICAN INDEPENDENCE, 1776–1783

> The war beginning in America gave France an opportunity to avenge her defeat in the Seven Years War and thus became another in the succession of worldwide colonial wars. In America the Revolution was primarily a hard struggle for independence but to a limited extent was a political and social revolution.

❂❂ RESOURCES OF THE OPPOSING FORCES

Estimates of the relative proportion of those supporting independence (the *patriots*) to those who stayed loyal to Britain (*loyalists* or Tories) are extremely difficult to make. Many Americans were never forced to choose sides as they lived in areas far from the fighting or governmental authority. Those who did choose the crown, however, did not overwhelmingly come from any one class or ethnic group. One can generalize that royal officials, Anglican clergy, and settlers recently arrived in the colonies, especially if they were non-English, tended to be more loyal than patriot. Settlers in the Carolina back country, with grievances against their colonies' leaders, also tended to choose the crown. Several states confiscated the property of loyalists. Those who left, possibly as many as 100,000, rather than live in a republic, went to Canada, the West Indies, or Britain.

❂❂ **Comparison of Military Strength**—1) In numbers the British had a much larger population to draw upon for troops but depended upon volunteers and, to a large extent, upon hired troops, mercenaries from her allies in Germany. After the war spread to other parts of the world, Britain had to divide her forces. The patriot army under Washington never numbered much more than 18,000 at any given time. 2) In discipline, training, and experience the British forces were definitely superior but this advantage could not be exploited in the wilderness conditions in America. The American forces were of two types, the Continental Army and the state militia. At first, the Continental Army was hampered by short enlistments and poor training, but it improved steadily throughout the war until some of its regiments equalled the British in effectiveness. The militia often would not serve outside their own state but usually arose bravely to any local emergency. 3) Long distances worked against the British. Troops had to be shipped across the Atlantic and shifted along exterior lines in the colonies. The patriots, fighting on home grounds, shifted on interior lines, and the militia assembled quickly and fought well in localities where the British troops appeared. Distance from England aggravated the British supply problems. 4) The British received support from Native American allies in the frontier regions and offered freedom to slaves in the South to encourage their enlistment. The Americans enjoyed the aid of French troops and of the French navy at the decisive battle of Yorktown. American privateers did great damage to British shipping.

○○ Comparison of Financial and Other Advantages—1) Great Britain, a mature and wealthy nation, enjoyed greater credit and economic resources for conducting war. The patriots faced a difficult problem of financing and raising supplies. The Continental Congress and the separate states raised funds by selling bonds; both issued paper money in the form of bills of credit so liberally that the bills came to be almost worthless. Loans were obtained from France, Holland, Spain, and from American patriots. Requisitions of money were levied against the states but often went unpaid. Patriot troops suffered severely for lack of supplies. Robert Morris became the financial leader of the Revolution. 2) Americans convinced of the justice of their cause fought better and had the moral advantage of defending their homes. 3) The war in England was not popular enough to secure enlistments or raise funds readily. 4) The Americans fought on familiar terrain; the British were not acclimated to the weather and living conditions in America. 5) Great Britain found herself alone in the war except for Prussia and smaller German allies. France and Spain actively took the American side and in 1780 the Netherlands was at war with England. Other nations of Europe in 1780 formed the League of Armed Neutrality against England because of English abuses of the commercial rights of neutral nations. 6) The loosely united states lacked a center of political and economic power, i.e., a real capital. Even the British occupation of Philadelphia, 1777–1778, did not hinder the American effort.

MILITARY CAMPAIGNS OF THE WAR

Equally important to Washington's military ability in leading the Continental forces was the example of his character and courage.

○ From Bunker Hill to Princeton—After Lexington and Concord the British withdrew to Boston. The Americans suffered heavy initial losses at Bunker Hill in Boston (June, 1775) but the next year Washington forced the British to abandon Boston (April, 1776). The British forces next established headquarters at New York under Sir William Howe. Washington lost the battles of Long Island and Washington Heights (1776) and retreated to New Jersey. He continued to retreat across New Jersey into Pennsylvania. In December Washington attacked and defeated the Hessians at Trenton and defeated British troops at Princeton.

✪✪ **British Plan of 1777**—General John Burgoyne proposed to lead a British army south from Canada into New York via Lake Champlain where he would be joined by Colonel Barry St. Leger marching east from Lake Ontario along the Mohawk Valley. These two forces were to join Howe at Albany and sever the colonies. St. Leger's forces, including Iroquois allies, were checked by General Nicholas Herkimer. Burgoyne's forces were surrounded and captured by General Gates at the Battle of Saratoga (1777). For reasons not fully understood Howe failed to cooperate in the campaign and moved his troops south instead. Saratoga proved to be the turning point of the war because it brought the crucial support of France. Washington's troops, defeated by Howe at Brandywine, suffered through the winter (1777–1778) at Valley Forge.

✪✪ **The French Alliance**—The American victory at Saratoga caused the French to sign a formal treaty of alliance and enter the war openly and

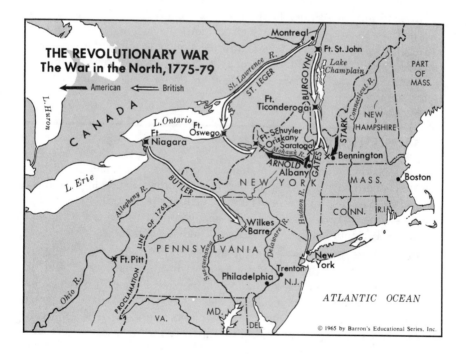

THE REVOLUTIONARY WAR
The War in the North, 1775-79

← American　⇐ British

© 1965 by Barron's Educational Series, Inc.

vigorously on the side of the Americans. The French government had secretly sent many supplies earlier, through a fictitious trading company, to the patriots and had equipped American privateers in her ports.

Benjamin Franklin, sent to France to negotiate a treaty of alliance, urged the French minister Vergennes to enter the war. The victory at Saratoga convinced Vergennes that the Americans could win victories. In 1778 France signed a treaty of military alliance under which the war would be continued until both nations were ready for peace. A second treaty providing for mutual trade was also signed. Spain entered the war as an ally of France, indirectly as an American ally. The generous French supplies and military aid were indispensable to American victory.

○○ **The Last Years of the War, 1778–1781**—In 1778 the British decided to invade the South to take advantage of the greater loyalist sentiment there. They captured Savannah in 1778 and Charleston in 1780. The Americans were next defeated at Camden, South Carolina, but at King's Mountain frontiersmen destroyed a large British force. Cornwallis was able to occupy the coastal cities in the Carolinas, but American guerrilla leaders regained control of the interior. In the Illinois country George Rogers Clark campaigned successfully in 1778 and 1779 for his state of Virginia and gained this territory north of the Ohio from the British.

In 1780 Benedict Arnold's unsuccessful attempt to deliver West Point to the British and the threat of Cornwallis's army greatly distressed Washington. This situation was relieved by the decision of the French to send an army under Rochambeau to America. In 1781 Admiral de Grasse was sent to America with a French naval force and additional troops. Upon hearing of Lord Cornwallis's move to the Yorktown peninsula, Washington combined forces with the French to surround the British and force their surrender. The victory proved complete and the fighting ceased.

THE TREATY OF PARIS

Occasional attempts during the war to restore peace met no success. After Yorktown, British opinion opposed further expenditure for war and strongly favored peace. The wartime ministry of Lord North fell and his successor Lord Shelburne sent his agent to Paris to negotiate with American commissioners on a basis of independence.

○ **Peace Negotiations**—Franklin, already in Paris when peace negotiations began, was later joined by John Adams and John Jay. The treaty of alliance between France and Spain required France to continue the war until Spain should regain Gibraltar. After France delayed negotiations unduly and the American negotiators learned that she planned to compensate Spain at American expense, the American negotiators

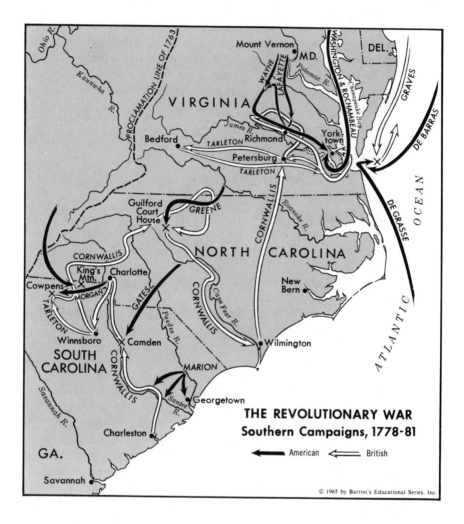

THE REVOLUTIONARY WAR
Southern Campaigns, 1778-81

◄——— American   ⇐═══ British

© 1965 by Barron's Educational Series, Inc

decided to make a separate peace with Britain, contrary to the terms of the French alliance.

By a preliminary separate treaty signed in 1782 Britain conceded such favorable boundaries as compared with those sought by France and Spain that French objections were ignored and the final treaty was signed in September, 1783.

✪✪✪**Terms of the Treaty**—By the terms of the Treaty of Paris (1783) 1) Britain recognized American independence; 2) the northern boundary was fixed on the Canadian border and along the Great Lakes. The Mississippi River became the western boundary. In the South, American territory extended to Florida. (In a separate treaty England returned Florida to Spain). 3) American fishing privileges off

Newfoundland were recognized. 4) The United States agreed to make "no lawful impediment" to prevent British creditors from collecting debts owed by Americans. 5) Freedom of navigation of the Mississippi by both Americans and British nationals was provided. 6) Congress was to recommend to the states the restoration of confiscated loyalist property.

THE INTERNAL REVOLUTION

In addition to independence the Revolution produced far-reaching internal changes in American society.

○ **Political Changes in the States**—Upon separation from the mother country it was necessary for the thirteen states to establish new machinery of government. Early in 1777 eleven states had adopted new constitutions; Rhode Island and Connecticut retained their colonial charters with a few changes. The rest of the states adopted new constitutions, which differed as their experiences under their charters differed. The major influence on these constitutions, other than their commonly shared heritage of British constitutionalism, was the history of the particular colony.

More significant changes in government made by the new state constitutions may be noted. 1) Some guarantees of popular rights were included in every constitution, with trial by jury in serious cases, prohibition of unreasonable bail or punishment and unjustifiable searches, and guarantees of religious toleration and freedom of the press common. 2) The privilege of voting was based on property requirements and in some cases religious tests, mild for that day, such as belief in God and the Trinity and acceptance of Protestantism. 3) Annual or frequent election of legislative bodies was designed to keep them responsive to the popular will. 4) The governor's office was much reduced in power as a result of the colonists' experiences with royal governors in the recent past. Later revisions frequently strengthened the governor's authority. 5) The principle of separation of powers and checks and balances was paid lip service, but the weakness of the governors and state courts generally made the legislatures supreme.

○○ **Provisions of the Articles of Confederation**—The framework of a new central government to provide a more permanent union of the states was drawn up by a committee appointed by the Continental Congress soon after independence was declared. John Dickinson, from Pennsylvania and one of the most influential leaders in the Revolution, was the chief writer of the Articles of Confederation. Provisions of the Articles reflected the impulses of the Revolution. The states feared a strong central government and planned to keep it weak to preserve the sovereignty of the separate states and the freedom of individuals.

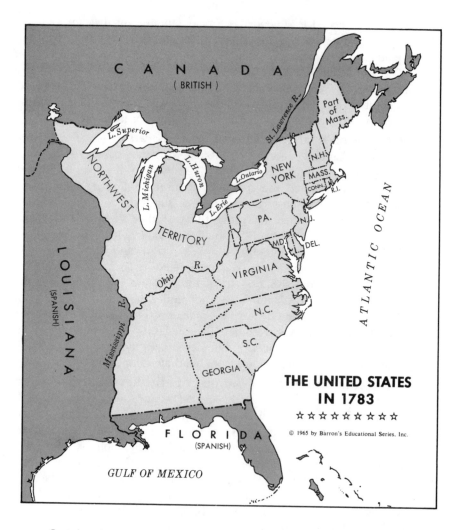

C A N A D A
(BRITISH)

L. Superior

NORTHWEST

L. Michigan   *L. Huron*

L. Erie   *L. Ontario*

St. Lawrence R.

Part
of
Mass.

N.H.

NEW
YORK

MASS.

CONN.   R.I.

TERRITORY

PA.   N.J.

Ohio R.   MD.   DEL.

VIRGINIA

L O U I S I A N A
(SPANISH)

Mississippi R.

N.C.

S.C.

GEORGIA

ATLANTIC OCEAN

**THE UNITED STATES
IN 1783**

☆ ☆ ☆ ☆ ☆ ☆ ☆ ☆ ☆

© 1965 by Barron's Educational Series, Inc.

F L O R I D A
(SPANISH)

GULF OF MEXICO

Certain necessary powers were given to the central government. It could build a navy and raise an army, declare war, make treaties and manage foreign relations. It could regulate the value of coins and borrow, spend, and issue money. It could not levy taxes, but it could make requisitions upon the states. It could not draft troops or regulate trade. Powers not given to the central government were reserved to the states. Generally, it can be said that the Confederation Congress possessed many powers, but no means to execute those powers.

✪✪✪ **Weaknesses of the Articles**—Serious weaknesses of the confederation government showed up soon after its adoption. Specific weaknesses of the Articles may be enumerated: 1) It required the affirmative vote of nine of the thirteen states to pass any important legislation. 2) A unanimous vote was needed to amend the Articles; this meant that any one state could exercise a veto against amendment and that the Articles could not be adapted to changing conditions. 3) There was no single elective executive, only committees in Congress. 4) No ordinary system of courts was provided. 5) No export or import duties could be collected for revenues. Without this authority the Confederation was deprived of an effective lever to use in bargaining with foreign powers for trade privileges.

⊙⊙ Ratification of the Articles of Confederation—Late in 1777 the Articles of Confederation were submitted to the states for ratification; they were to go into effect when ratified by all of the state legislatures. Most states accepted the Articles within the following year, except Maryland. She refused to do so until the states gave up their claims to the Western territories; Maryland felt that the Western lands would enable some states to dwarf the smaller states. In 1781 New York broke the bottleneck by surrendering her weak claims and next Virginia gave up her lands and ratification was completed in 1781. Land speculators helped bring about this cession of the Western territories since they believed they could obtain these lands under more suitable terms from the central government. It was also maintained by those who wished to strengthen the central government that the lands would provide revenue and the distribution of such public domain would give the weak government a function that would command attention.

⊙ Economic and Social Changes of the Revolution—1) Some effects of the war were only temporary. The war caused a scarcity of finished goods; home industries sprang up to meet the needs. Wages rose but not nearly so much as prices. The large issues of paper currency caused severe inflation. Speculation and profiteering on account of wartime shortages by many groups, not just farmers and businessmen, was widespread but ended with the return of peace. 2) Manufacturing increased as it was freed of British restrictions, but American commerce was excluded from trade with the British West Indies. 3) Some of the confiscated loyalist lands was sold in smaller tracts to individual farmers, but much of it was restored to the original owners or their heirs. Restrictions on the inheritance of land, such as primogeniture and entail, were removed, but these had been of very slight significance. Quit-rents and tithes were abolished. 4) Restrictions were removed against the settlement of the Western lands. 5) The inconsistency of holding slaves caused all of the states north of Maryland to abolish slavery before 1805, and most of the Southern states stopped the importation of slaves. 6) As for religion, several of the churches were reorganized as national churches. The Episcopal and Presbyterian churches were reorganized independently of the British mother churches. The Methodists under the leadership of Francis Asbury established in 1784 the Methodist Episcopal Church as independent of the British Anglican Church. The

Roman Catholics made John Carroll Bishop of Baltimore, the first Catholic bishop in America.

CHAPTER BOOK LIST

Adams, Randolph G., *Political Ideas of the American Revolution* (Barnes and Noble).

Alden, J.R., *The American Revolution* (1954). A general brief history of the war.

Bailyn, Bernard, *The Ideological Origins of the American Revolution* (Harvard).

Brinton, Crane, *Anatomy of Revolution* (Vintage). Study of the pattern of great revolutions.

Burnett, S.C., *The Continental Congress* (1941). Colonial politics in the war.

Cress, Lawrence D., *Citizens in Arms* (1982). Various social aspects of the military experience.

Dull, Jonathan R., *A Diplomatic History of the American Revolution* (1985). Standard and complete.

Flexner, J.T., *Benedict Arnold Case* (Collier). Abridged interpretation.

Jameson, J.F., *The American Revolution Considered as a Social Movement* (Beacon). Brief but significant.

Mackesy, Piers, *The War for America* (1964).

Morgan, E.S., *The Birth of the Republic, 1763–1789* (1956). Brief survey.

Paine, Thomas, *Common Sense and Other Political Writings* (Bobbs-Merrill). Readings.

Royster, Charles, *A Revolutionary People at War* (1979). See also Cress and Shy for military coverage.

Shy, John W., *A People Numerous and Armed* (1976). See also Cress and Royster for same topic.

Van Every, Dale, *Company of Heroes: The First American Frontier, 1775–1783* (Mentor). Stimulating and accurate.

REVIEW QUESTIONS

MULTIPLE CHOICE

1. In the support of the patriot cause which group showed the greatest division as between the Northern and the Southern Colonies? (1) Large landholders (2) frontiersmen (3) workers (4) debtors.

2. In which way did the French contribute the most to the American victory? (1) The example set for other nations of Europe (2) the timely assistance of French naval forces (3) by grants of liberal loans (4) the assistance of Native American allies.

3. The Battle of Saratoga was a decisive engagement because it showed (1) that a combination of British and Native Americans would be beaten (2) that British commanders would not coordinate their efforts (3) the French that the Americans had the ability and will to fight for victory (4) the French that America would not need any substantial assistance.

4. In the overall development of the war, the military campaigns of the American Revolution (1) began in the Middle Colonies, spread to the South, and ended in New England (2) began in New England and ended in Pennsylvania (3) began in New England and ended in the South (4) began simultaneously in the Middle and Southern Colonies but ended in New England.

5. The French entered the alliance with the Americans in 1778 primarily to (1) help establish democracy in America (2) aid Spain in regaining Gibraltar (3) recover lost prestige and avenge her earlier defeat by Britain (4) regain Louisiana.

6. In the American Revolution military activity was (1) limited to American and Canadian soil (2) limited to land fighting in America and naval engagements in the Atlantic (3) of significance only in America (4) almost worldwide.

7. Which are the correct dates for both the Battle of Yorktown and the Treaty of Paris? (1) 1783, 1784 (2) 1777, 1783 (3) 1781, 1783 (4) 1782, 1783.

8. In the negotiations preceding the Treaty of Paris (1) the Americans delayed agreement, hoping to win Canada (2) the French prolonged bargaining to regain the West Indies (3) the Spanish haggled long for the return of Cuba (4) the delay was caused by Spanish desire to regain Gibraltar.

9. New constitutions of the states after independence was declared (1) weakened the power of the executive (2) generally failed to provide bills of rights (3) provided no methods of raising revenues for state governments (4) abolished the upper house of the assemblies.

10. Of the three branches of government under the Confederation, the least provision was made for (1) the judiciary (2) the legislative (3) the executive.

11. Which was the critical issue in the states' adoption of the Articles of Confederation? (1) The regulation of the importation of slaves (2) the claims to the Western lands (3) the regulation of foreign trade (4) the inclusion of a bill of rights.

12. Which are the correct dates for the period the Confederation was in effect? (1) 1781 to 1790 (2) 1777 to 1790 (3) 1781 to 1789 (4) 1783 to 1789.

13. In the democratic changes following the Revolution all of the following were abolished *except* (1) quit-rents (2) titles of nobility (3) laws of primogeniture and entail (4) property qualifications for voting.

TRUE-FALSE

14. Small farmers and Southern planters both were more likely to join the patriot cause.

15. Conscription of troops and unity of public opinion gave the British great advantages against the Americans.

16. Great Britain suffered the disadvantage of fighting almost without allies during the American Revolution.

17. The British took the war into the South in 1778 in the belief that the worst centers of resistance should be destroyed first.

18. In the Treaty of Paris the British agreed to terms that may be considered fairly generous.

19. By the Treaty of Paris the Americans promised to guarantee the return of loyalist property.

20. The constitutions of the new states increased the powers of the governors.

21. A unanimous vote was required to amend the Articles of Confederation.

22. Extensive powers to levy tariffs and regulate trade were given to the Confederation.

23. The Revolution brought an increased desire to maintain slavery.

COMPLETION

24. During the Revolution small sea powers in Europe combined in a defensive alliance known as the League of _____ .

25. An ally of France's but not of the United States in the Revolution was _____ .

26. German mercenary troops defeated at Trenton were known as the _____ .

27. In 1777 cooperating with Burgoyne, _____ led Native American allies against the Americans in western New York.

28. The turning point of the Revolutionary War was the Battle of _____ .

29. The alliance between America and France was agreed upon in two treaties, one was a treaty of military alliance, the other a _____ treaty.

30. The notorious American traitor of the Revolution was _____ .

31. France delayed negotiating the peace treaty because she had promised to help Spain regain _____ .

32. Connecticut and _____ kept their colonial charters with only a few changes.

33. It was _____ that insisted that the other states give up claims to the disputed lands in the Northwest.

34. Taxes known as _____ for the support of established churches were abolished during the Revolution.

MATCHING

35. Benjamin Franklin	a. Captured Northwest posts
36. John Burgoyne	b. Negotiated with Franklin
37. Cornwallis	c. Wrote Articles of Confederation
38. William Howe	d. Guided Revolutionary finances
39. George Rogers Clark	e. Organized the Methodists
40. Vergennes	f. Defeated at Saratoga
41. Robert Morris	g. Bishop of Baltimore
42. John Dickinson	h. Tory commander in New York
43. Francis Asbury	i. Negotiated alliance with France
44. John Carroll	j. Captured at Yorktown
	k. Leader of Native American troops

CHRONOLOGY / CHAPTER 7

1781 Confederation Period began with ratification of the Articles of Confederation and ended with organization of the new government in 1789.

1784 Ordinance for organizing the Northwest Territory passed but replaced by the Northwest Ordinance of 1787.

1785 Land Ordinance passed by Confederation Congress.
Creek War in Georgia.
Jay-Gardoqui Treaty negotiated with Spain but not ratified by Congress.

1786 Shays' Rebellion in Massachusetts.
Annapolis Convention, a step toward the Constitutional Convention at Philadelphia.

1787 Northwest Ordinance passed.
Constitutional Convention met at Philadelphia in May.
Delaware became first state to ratify Constitution.

1788 Spain reopened Mississippi River to Western commerce.
Ratification of Constitution completed by nine states.
Federal government began to function.

1789 Washington inaugurated as first President under the Constitution.

Chapter

7

THE CONFEDERATION PERIOD AND THE CONSTITUTION, 1781–1789

The Articles of Confederation, ratified in 1781, provided for a central government of the United States to take the place of the Continental Congress. The Articles provided for a weak central government since the states feared a strong central authority after their recent experience with British domination. When the Confederation proved to be too weak for the best interests of the American people, the present Constitution was adopted and a federal union created.

DEVELOPMENTS IN THE WEST

The Ordinance of 1785 provided for the distribution of lands in the West; the Ordinance of 1787 provided for government and the formation of the states in the Old Northwest.

Early Provisions for Government in the West—The cession of the lands and the surrender of authority by the states in the Northwest was neither complete nor final in 1781 when they supposedly acceded to the demands of Maryland. At the same time that the states retained claims to certain blocks of land in the territories they had ceded, they also persisted in extending their authority of government over pioneers who had settled there. Confusion was caused also by the attempts made at self-government by the settlers. Virginia considered Kentucky as one of her counties and North Carolina asserted the same claim over Tennessee.

In 1784 Congress made important decisions regarding the Western territory. First, it was decided the territory would be organized ultimately as states equal to any of the original thirteen. Next, the Ordinance of 1784, sponsored by Jefferson, provided for the creation of ten self-governing districts which would eventually be admitted as ten new states. Lobbyists of the land companies succeeded in replacing the Ordinance of 1784 before it could be put in effect and the Ordinance of 1787 took its place.

©©© The Ordinance of 1787—This Act of Congress, sometimes called the Northwest Ordinance, provided: 1) that the area north and west of the Ohio River would be divided into at least three, but not more than five, territories. 2) Territories would go through three successive stages of government as the population increased. In the first stage the unorganized territory, completely subject to Congress, would be governed by appointed officials. In the second stage the inhabitants could, after reaching 5,000 persons, organize the territory, elect a two-house territorial legislature, and send a delegate to Congress. In the third stage, after attaining a population of 60,000, the territory could draft a constitution and apply to Congress for admission as a state. Slavery was prohibited in the area. This ordinance set a precedent for the organization of territorial government and the admission of states over the whole West as other territories were acquired.

©©© The Land Ordinance of 1785—The Ordinance of 1785 provided for: 1) the survey of the public domain into townships six miles square which, in turn, would be subdivided into sections one mile square (of 640 acres). 2) The sections were to be sold at auction at the minimum price of $1.00 an acre. The minimum sale of 640 acres favored land speculators since only they had such a large sum of cash—the Act did not provide for sales on credit. The Act set the pattern for subsequent surveying of public lands.

Land Policy in the Southwest—Large numbers of settlers poured into the region of Kentucky and Tennessee during and following the war and occupied much of this region. State claims to these lands of the Southwest were not disputed as in the Northwest and were therefore either granted to individuals or land companies by the states or were not ceded until after 1790. This explains the absence of any federal regional ordinances for the government of the Southwest. These lands of the Southwest were already occupied over large areas before the surveys took place in the Northwest. The states of the Southwest sold their Western lands at low prices, rewarded veterans with land grants, and gave land away to encourage settlement. Lands were located by individuals and bounds designated by natural or geographical lines. Counties and individual land holdings assumed irregular shapes, and much litigation took place before conflicting claims were settled.

©© The Northwest Posts—The Treaty of Paris required the British to surrender their posts in the Northwest territory to the Americans, something they refused to do. Formally, the British were holding the posts until the United States executed other provisions of the Treaty; actually, they wished to retain control of the fur trade and the Native Americans in the area. In spite of repeated demands and the efforts of John Adams as minister in London, the British retained the posts until 1796, as the United States lacked any means to coerce the British into executing the treaty.

○ **Trouble with Spain in the Southwest**—Although Spain had aided the United States in the war with Britain, she feared the aggressiveness of the United States and the influence of America's liberal political ideas upon her colonial subjects. 1) The most serious dispute with Spain was the American right to navigate the lower Mississippi River. Spain possessed both banks of the lower part of the river. The use of the Mississippi was vital to American pioneers in the upper Ohio valley for the transportation of bulky produce. 2) Another dispute between the two countries arose over the boundary between Spanish Florida and the United States. The area in dispute, paralleling the northern boundary of Florida, was known as the Yazoo Strip. 3) Spanish friendship and alliance with the Native American tribes of the Southwest was another sore point. The Spanish and the Native Americans had a common interest in blocking American frontier expansion in Georgia and Tennessee. In 1785 war broke out between the Creeks and the state of Georgia. 4) The United States also wished to gain trading privileges in the Spanish West Indies.

John Jay and the Spanish diplomat Gardoqui negotiated a treaty in 1785 to settle these sources of friction, but the Senate failed to ratify it because it sacrificed Southern interests in the navigation of the Mississippi for Northeastern trading privileges in the West Indies.

James Wilkinson, commander of American forces in the Southwest, took advantage of the settlers' discontent to conspire with Spanish authorities to separate Kentucky from the Union. The plot failed when Madrid opened the Mississippi to American traffic in 1788, but it demonstrated how weak the area's attachment to the Union was. Wilkinson's treachery was undetected.

COMMERCIAL AND FINANCIAL DIFFICULTIES UNDER THE CONFEDERATION

Failure to solve satisfactorily the commercial and financial problems revealed grave weaknesses in the Articles of Confederation.

○ **Commercial Problems**—Interruption of American foreign trade by independence brought depression, but the Confederation government, without control over customs duties, lacked bargaining power to win trading privileges from England and Spain. England enforced severe restrictions upon American trade with the West Indies, and the trade negotiations with Spain failed to open trade with Spanish West Indian colonies. American shipping and foreign commerce declined, while imports of foreign goods drained the country of specie.

Differing tariff and trade policies of the states made it difficult to conduct domestic trade, and foreign trade was restricted by the refusal of some states to comply with trade treaties negotiated by the Congress. The lack of a uniform currency also hindered domestic trade.

✪✪ **Financial Problems**—Having no power of taxation, Congress requisitioned contributions from the states, but they often failed to meet their payments. The national government could not pay interest on the heavy war debt nor could it meet current expenses. Insufficient funds were provided by the sale of public lands. Attempts, only slightly successful, were made to borrow money to meet current expenses. States refused to amend the Constitution to permit Congress to levy tariffs for revenue.

The depression of the 1780s brought a fall in prices, increase in the value of scarce specie, and severe distress to private debtors who could not meet their obligations. Demands for paper money arose. In seven states debtors controlled the legislatures and inflated the currency with paper money. In the other six states the creditor class refused the demands for paper money. Distressed farmers rioted in parts of New England in response to foreclosures for taxes and debts.

During the winter of 1786–1787, Daniel Shays, a Massachusetts veteran, led a popular effort to prevent the courts from collecting debts. Exaggerated reports of the event's severity induced a fear that anarchy was about to overcome Massachusetts and possibly other states. These fears helped persuade Congress to approve the call for the Philadelphia convention in February 1787.

✪✪✪ **The Movement for More Effective Government**—Events such as Shays' Rebellion, along with other signs of weak government in the states and the generally weak posture of the United States in foreign affairs combined to convince many that a stronger central government was needed. A successful (1785) meeting at Mount Vernon between delegates from Maryland and Virginia to resolve trade problems in the Chesapeake Bay area led to a 1786 meeting at Annapolis to discuss commercial problems throughout the Union. Although the meeting was unrepresentative, it sent a resolution to the Congress urging a general convention of the states to amend the Articles of Confederation and make them "adequate to the exigencies of the Union."

THE CONSTITUTIONAL CONVENTION

The Confederation Congress approved the call for a convention, fixing May 14, 1787 in Philadelphia for the meeting. All the state legislatures except Rhode Island chose delegates. When the delegates met, they decided to deliberate in secret and to draw up a completely new frame of union, not just propose amendments.

○ **Leadership**—Although Alexander Hamilton of New York had originally been very involved in organizing the meeting, he played only a minor role in it. James Madison of Virginia presented a plan that gave the larger states the predominant share of power, but most of it was rejected and the final product had very little to do with his original plan. His careful notes, published after his death, are the principal record of debates. The presence of George Washington and Benjamin Franklin, with the popular favor they carried with them, helped to legitimize the meeting; Washington as president of the meeting was especially significant. Patrick Henry and a number of other state leaders stayed away as they distrusted strong government. John Adams and Thomas Jefferson were both abroad (London and Paris respectively), representing the United States as diplomats.

○ **The Delegates**—The delegates were young, but already experienced in government and generally well educated. Although they tended to be wealthy, they kept in mind that the product of their labors would have to be approved by more representative bodies, and resolved to produce a government both practicable and workable.

COMPROMISES OF THE CONVENTION

The more important provisions of the Constitution were arrived at by compromise.

○○○ **Representation in Congress**—When the small states compelled Madison to abandon his plan for strictly proportional voting, the "Great Compromise" was effected where the states would be represented proportionally in the House of Representatives, which would also initiate all tax bills. The Senate would consist of two persons from each state and would have significant powers in appointments and foreign affairs.

Since the North and the South disagreed on how slaves should be counted to determine representation and direct taxes, it was resolved that every five slaves would count for three free persons in determining both. Suffrage requirements were left up to the states.

○○ **Commerce and Other Powers**—The North and South disagreed also over the powers of Congress over commerce. The Southern states agreed to federal control over foreign and interstate commerce. The question of slave importation was compromised by allowing it to continue for 20 years more (until 1808). The debate over tariffs was settled by permitting the federal government to collect import duties but not export duties.

It was decided early that the national government would be one of "enumerated powers," that is, all powers not granted the central government were reserved to the states or to the people. Among the powers listed were those of borrowing money, declaring war, maintaining military forces, establishing postal services, and making laws necessary to carry out these delegated powers.

✪ The Executive—There was much disagreement over the executive branch. It was finally decided there would be a single executive called the president who would be chosen for a term of four years but might be reelected. Distrust influenced the decision that the president should not be elected by Congress nor directly by the people. The result was an electoral college to be made up of electors from each state, equal in number to a state's senators and representatives. Each elector was to vote for two candidates for the presidency, the candidate winning the most votes to become president and the next candidate to become vice president. If no candidate won a majority, the House of Representatives, each state having one vote, would elect the president.

The Confederation government had shown the need for a strong executive; the president was given large powers. He 1) was to execute laws passed by Congress; 2) could call Congress into session and might veto acts of Congress subject to having such veto overridden by a two-thirds vote of both houses; 3) could make treaties with the "advice and consent" of two-thirds of the Senators present; 4) was made commander-in-chief of the army and navy; 5) and was given extensive power of appointing officials.

The Judiciary—There was little debate on the judiciary. Congress was to establish a Supreme Court and lower courts and appoint judges for life tenure. The jurisdiction of the federal courts was defined. The doctrine of judicial review, i.e., the power to pass upon the constitutionality of acts of Congress, was not stated or denied and it was probably expected that the Supreme Court would assume this power as indeed it did.

✪✪ Special Features—Provisions were made for amending the Constitution. Amendments may be proposed by a two-thirds vote of both houses of Congress or by vote of two thirds of the state legislatures. Ratification of amendments is done by three fourths of the states either in their legislatures or by special conventions.

The question of national supremacy was not settled. Sovereignty was not explicitly invested in the central government; this conflict was avoided by substituting the word "federal" for "national." It was stated that sovereignty rests in the people but as between the states and the federal government, this point was left to be settled later—by the Civil War.

Ratification of the Constitution—It was provided that the Constitution would go into effect as soon as nine state conventions, used to avoid the special interest of state assemblies, approved it. The conventions were thought to be the next best thing to a popular vote, which was deemed impractical. There was a good bit of opposition to the Constitution and those favoring it had to work vigorously to get it approved.

❍ **The Anti-Federalists**—Arguments against ratification were that the 1) Constitution had been written secretly by representatives of the well-to-do; 2) the delegates had exceeded their powers in writing an entirely new instrument; 3) there was no "bill of rights" to protect citizens against tyranny; 4) the powers of the states had been too sharply curtailed; and 5) that it would permit tariffs to be passed by the Northeastern states for their special benefit.

The Anti-Federalists included back country farmers, debtors, sectionalists, and those like Samuel Adams and Patrick Henry who feared centralized control. Many of the poor feared the powers of taxation of the federal government and disliked the prohibition of paper money issues by the states.

❍❍ **The Federalists**—Some, who were convinced that the United States needed a stronger frame of union to survive both the vagaries of the states as well as the challenges of foreign governments not basically friendly to a republic, favored the Constitution. Merchants trading abroad, farmers interested in the export market, city artisans, and those with an interest in foreign trade were the major economic interest to vote yes. Federalist spokesmen put the Constitution forward as a reasonable and safe answer to the problems of the Confederation, an answer that could be amended to correct defects that soon became apparent, such as the lack of a bill of rights.

By July 1788, nine states had ratified the Constitution, but neither New York nor Virginia had yet approved. For the critical New York state contest Hamilton, Jay, and Madison wrote articles in support of adoption. Later these articles were published as *The Federalist,* the greatest classic in the literature of American political theory. When Virginia ratified, New York soon followed her. North Carolina waited for the addition of the Bill of Rights. Last of all (1790), Rhode Island ratified after being threatened with an economic boycott by the United States Congress. With Rhode Island's ratification, all of the original 13 states had indicated acceptance.

CHAPTER BOOK LIST

Brant, Irving, *James Madison, The Nationalist* (1948). Detailed study of a leading framer of the Constitution.

Collier, Christopher and James L., *Decision in Philadelphia* (1987). The Constitutional Convention, a complete, clear treatment.

Corwin, E.S., *The Constitution and What It Means Today* (Atheneum). Twelfth edition of a systematic, standard work.

Farrand, Max, *Framing of the Constitution of the United States* (Yale). A classic in constitutional history.

Jensen, Merrill, *Articles of Confederation* (University of Wisconsin). An interpretation of conflicting interests in the American Revolution.

Jensen, Merrill, *The New Nation, 1781–1789* (1950). Interesting standard treatment.

Kenyon, Celia, *The Antifederalists* (Bobbs-Merrill).

Main, Jackson Turner, *The Anti-Federalists: Critics of the Constitution* (1961). Scholarly.

Main, Jackson Turner, *The Sovereign States, 1775–1783*. The states during the War for Independence.

McLaughlin, A.C., *Foundations of American Constitutionalism* (Premier). Brief.

Robinson, David L., *Slavery in the Structure of American Politics, 1765–1820*. The role of slavery at the Constitutional Convention.

Rossiter, Clinton, *The Grand Convention* (Macmillan).

Williamson, Chilton, *American Suffrage from Property to Democracy, 1760–1860* (1960). How voting requirements were lessened.

Wood, Gordon S., *The Radicalism of the American Revolution* (1992). An analysis of the transforming effect of the Revolution on American society and government.

Zilversmit, Arthur, *The First Emancipation* (1961). The end of slavery in the Northern states.

REVIEW QUESTIONS

MULTIPLE CHOICE

1. The greatest significance of the Northwest Ordinance is that it (1) provided for trial by jury (2) provided a precedent for the transition of territories to statehood (3) it set public land aside for schools (4) it provided for five new states in the Old Northwest.

2. Which was *not* a provision of the Ordinance of 1785? (1) The survey of the public domain to create townships of 36 sections (2) prohibition of slavery in the Northwest (3) only cash sales of land (4) the minimum sale of 640 acres.

3. Which was not a point of dispute between Spain and the United States during the 1780s? (1) The navigation of the Mississippi River (2) Spanish alliance with Native American tribes of the Southwest (3) the boundary between Florida and the United States (4) American trading privileges in Florida.

4. The Jay-Gardoqui Treaty negotiated with a foreign power failed to win Senate approval because it (1) made no reference to the Northwest posts (2) contained no provision in reference to the Native Americans (3) failed to concede territory to the United States (4) sacrificed rights of navigating the Mississippi for trading privileges in the West Indies.

5. Which important advantage did the Americans lose in separating themselves from the British Empire? (1) Trade with the British West Indies (2) marketing agricultural surpluses in Britain (3) the carrying trade of the British Empire (4) loans from England.

6. The meeting between Maryland and Virginia delegates leading to the Constitutional Convention was called to discuss (1) foreign relations (2) public policy (3) paper currency (4) trade problems in the Chesapeake Bay area.

7. Which statement about Shays' Rebellion is true? (1) It was caused by debt foreclosures (2) the rebellion succeeded in its goal (3) in its effect it made the creditor classes everywhere feel more secure (4) it arose over a problem peculiar to Massachusetts.

8. Which leader was *not* present at the Constitutional Convention? (1) Jefferson (2) Madison (3) Franklin (4) Hamilton.

9. The Great Compromise of the Constitutional Convention decided the conflict over the (1) slavery issue (2) election of the president (3) tariff (4) representation of the states in Congress.

10. The Electoral College system for choosing the president was designed (1) because of the lack of rapid transportation (2) to preserve states' rights (3) as an economy measure (4) because of a distrust of the masses or powerful individuals.

11. Amendments to the Constitution may be made by the following *except* which one? (1) Proposal of two thirds of the state legislatures and ratification by three-fourths vote of both Houses of Congress (2) proposal by two thirds of the state legislatures and ratification by three fourths of the legislatures (3) proposal by two-thirds vote of Congress and ratification by three fourths of the state legislatures (4) proposal by two thirds of the state legislatures and ratification by three fourths of the states in special conventions.

12. Which of these provisions of the Constitution relating to slavery are correct? (1) Sixty percent of the slaves would be counted for purposes of representation (2) slave importation was permitted for twenty years (3) slavery was forbidden north of the Mason-Dixon line (4) 1 and 2 above are correct (5) 2 and 3 above are correct.

13. The Anti-Federalists included a large proportion of all of the following groups *except* (1) debtors (2) sectionalists (3) large planters (4) those afraid of federal power to tax.

14. Which state was last to ratify the Constitution? (1) New York (2) Rhode Island (3) North Carolina (4) South Carolina.

TRUE-FALSE

15. The Ordinance of 1784 never went into effect; it was replaced by the Ordinance of 1787.

16. The Ordinance of 1787 had little influence upon the organization of territories and the admission of states later.

17. The Land Ordinance of 1785 appears to have been designed for the benefit of small farmers.

18. The British encouraged Native American tribes in the Northwest to make trouble for the United States, but Spain was innocent of such trouble making in the Southwest.

19. Under the Confederation, Congress had no power of taxation nor could she collect requisitions from the states.

20. The delegates to the Constitutional Convention had instructions to amend the Articles, not to write a new Constitution.

21. It was decided that slaves should not be counted for purposes of determining representation.

22. Presidential electors from each state are equal in number to the members of the House of Representatives from a state.

23. The Constitution explicitly provides that the Supreme Court may pass upon the constitutionality of acts of Congress.

24. The campaign in the states for ratification were hard fought and often won only by small majorities.

25. The Federalists were strongest among the lower economic groups.

COMPLETION

26. Kentucky at first was considered as a county belonging to _____ and Tennessee was claimed by _____ .

27. During the Confederation Period the United States disputed the northern boundary of Florida and claimed territory known as the _____ .

28. According to the Ordinance of 1787 a territory needed a population of _____ to apply for statehood.

29. Plotting with Spain in the Southwest was a high-ranking army officer by the name of _____ .

30. Leader of the distressed farmers in western Massachusetts was _____ .

31. The first meeting leading to the Constitutional Convention met at _____ , the second at _____ .

32. The Articles of Confederation were ratified in the year _____ , the Constitutional Convention met in the year _____ , and the Constitution was ratified by the original 13 states in _____ .

33. The prestige of _____ and _____ helped to legitimize the Constitutional Convention.

34. Distrusting strong government _____ did not attend the Convention.

35. Jefferson did not attend the Constitutional Convention because he was in _____ at that time.

36. Senate ratification of a treaty requires a vote of what proportion to its members? _____

37. The power of the Supreme Court to pass upon the constitutionality of acts of Congress is known as the power of _____ .

38. Those favoring ratification of the Constitution were known as the _____ .

39. _____ was the last state to ratify the Constitution.

THE EARLY REPUBLIC
1789–1861

CHRONOLOGY / CHAPTER 8

1789 Congress met in early April and declared Washington
elected President.
Washington inaugurated as President.
Congress passed the Bill of Rights, Judiciary Act, and Tariff
Act.
French Revolution began.

1790 Capital moved to Philadelphia.
Hamilton's financial measures enacted and completed in
1791.

1791 Bill of Rights ratified by states.
Bank of the United States chartered by Congress.
Whiskey Tax passed.
Vermont admitted to the Union as the fourteenth state.

1792 Kentucky admitted.

1793 Neutrality proclaimed in war in Europe.
Louis XVI executed in France; Citizen Genet's behavior leads
to his recall and discredits the pro-French group.

1794 Jay Treaty negotiated.
Whisky Rebellion in western Pennsylvania.
"Mad Anthony" Wayne won Battle of Fallen Timbers.
Congress defines rights of neutrals at sea.

1795 Pinckney Treaty negotiated.

1796 Tennessee admitted.

1797 XYZ Affair leads to war with France.
John Adams inaugurated as President.

1798 Undeclared naval war with France began, lasted until 1799.
Alien and Sedition acts followed by Kentucky and Virginia
Resolutions.

1800 Jefferson elected President in House of Representatives.
Treaty with France restored peace and abrogated alliance
of 1778.

8
THE FEDERALIST PERIOD, 1789–1801

Upon ratification of the Constitution in 1788 the Confederation Congress ordered elections held in the states for choosing the officers of the new government. The government began functioning when the newly elected Congress convened in April 1789. The supporters of the Constitution gradually coalesced into the Federalist Party, which guided the government until 1801, but not without significant defections as the strains of both foreign and domestic policy disputes divided them.

✪✪ INAUGURATION OF THE NEW GOVERNMENT

In early April 1789, Congress met in the old City Hall in New York City, counted ballots of the presidential electors, and declared George Washington unanimously elected President and John Adams Vice President. Trade had already revived and the new administration began auspiciously under the halo of prosperity. Although the nation had a great potential, its government, experimental and revolutionary, was challenged by strong enemies and difficult problems.

President Washington assumed office April 30, 1789, in New York City, the first capital under the Constitution. (In 1790 the capital was moved to Philadelphia and in 1800 to Washington.) Both houses of Congress were controlled by supporters of the Constitution. The new administration busied itself setting precedents, establishing ceremonial procedures for the future, and creating the machinery to make the government operative.

James Madison pushed Congress to redeem the implicit promise made to the Anti-Federalists to amend the Constitution with a bill of rights. Twelve amendments were submitted to the states; ten were ratified by 1791, guaranteeing freedom of the press, religious liberty, trial by jury, and other popular freedoms.

To meet urgent needs for revenue, Congress passed a tariff act levying only light duties. A light tonnage duty was levied on goods imported in American ships but a heavy duty levied on goods coming in foreign ships.

The Judiciary Act of 1789 created a Supreme Court with a Chief Justice and five associate justices and a system of lower federal courts. John Jay was appointed the Chief Justice of the Supreme Court.

Congress created three executive departments in 1789—State, War, and Treasury—and the offices of attorney-general and postmaster-general. Thomas Jefferson was made Secretary of State, Alexander Hamilton, Secretary of the Treasury, and Henry Knox, Secretary of War. It would be some time before the secretaries would be referred to as the cabinet; it did not receive statutory recognition until the twentieth century.

HAMILTON'S FINANCIAL PROGRAM

Hamilton soon emerged as the most influential member of Washington's cabinet. He prepared a series of reports for Congress on fiscal matters; these recommendations were substantially enacted into law. Hamilton's purposes in his financial policies were to establish the credit reputation of the government, to bind the capitalist classes to the government, and to enlarge the powers of the federal government.

○○ **The Program for Managing the Debt**—Congress dealt with three kinds of government debt arising from the Revolution: 1) federal debt owed foreigners, 2) federal domestic debt owed Americans, and 3) state debts.

Congress readily agreed to refunding the foreign debts at par. The domestic debt, made up of many kinds of securities, had depreciated to about 25 cents on the dollar. When Hamilton proposed refunding the domestic debt at par, those who had bought the depreciated certificates profited immensely, but few were surprised at the move. Anti-Federalists in Congress opposed the measure since it would enrich speculators instead of the original holders, but the securities were refunded at face value.

Hamilton proposed the assumption of state debts by the federal government, but suffered successive defeats in Congress, mainly because of Southern opposition. Hamilton won Jefferson's support by agreeing to locate the capital in the South (Washington, DC).

Hamilton had no fear of a heavy federal debt. Instead he argued that investment by the moneyed interests in federal securities would bind these important classes to the federal government.

○○ **The Bank of the United States and the National Currency**—Hamilton also proposed the establishment of a national bank; it was created in 1791. It was needed 1) to provide a sound, uniform paper currency for the business needs of the country by issuing paper money and 2) to provide fiscal services to the government of short-term lending, of acting as a depository of government funds, and helping individuals pay taxes by making loans to them.

The agricultural South opposed the bank but the Act passed Congress. Before signing it Washington asked Jefferson and Hamilton for advice. Jefferson agreed with Madison, supported a strict construction of the Constitution, and stated that Congress was not explicitly authorized by the Constitution to create a bank. Hamilton, wishing to set a precedent for loose construction, argued that the power to charter the bank was implied (doctrine of implied powers) since it was needed to issue currency, an explicit power. Without stating his reasons, Washington signed the bill, perhaps out of respect for Congress and because he was himself uncertain.

The Mint Act of 1792 provided for a government mint to coin both gold and silver.

✪ **Excise Taxes and the Tariff**—In 1791, when Hamilton asked for an excise tax on various commodities, he broke a promise to Congress that no new taxes would be needed to finance his program. The excise was a convenient tax, but one much resented in British and American political culture. The tax on distilled liquors was especially unpopular in the West where much of the whiskey was not sold but rather exchanged for labor and goods. Throughout the West, farmer-distillers resisted the tax, most strongly in western Pennsylvania where the Whiskey Rebellion occurred in 1794. Hamilton accompanied militia sent west to enforce federal law. The rebellion was suppressed and showed the ability of the government to enforce its laws.

Hamilton wanted the United States to remain a commercial-agricultural nation with strong ties to Great Britain. The tariffs he recommended were essentially tariffs for revenue, not the protection of manufactures.

ORIGINS OF THE POLITICAL PARTIES

Hamilton's policies and his influence with President Washington inspired opposition in Congress organized and led by James Madison. The supporters and opponents of the administration would eventually form the Federalist and Republican parties.

✪✪✪ **Federalists**—The Federalists, headed by Hamilton, favored a commercial nation led by the well-to-do. The party represented wealthy merchants, planters, commercial farmers, and, initially, the artisans of the cities. In the South, commercial men and tidewater planters supported it. They expected the federal government to advance business interests and favored a broad interpretation of the Constitution to aid it in its work. When the wars of the French Revolution affected American interests, the Federalists favored their largest trading partner, the British.

✪✪✪ **The Republicans**—The Republicans, organized by Madison but eventually led by Jefferson, represented Southern farmers, frontiersmen, and others who wished to see the central government exercising only restricted powers. City artisans and merchants who wished to break the stranglehold Britain had on American trade later joined the party, as did those repelled by the excessive pro-commercial and pro-British policies of the Federalists. Others who supported France as the champion of democracy and human rights became Republicans. The party originated in the Congress as opposition to administration measures mounted in the 1790s.

Both sides considered the development of political parties deplorable and saw themselves as advocating the correct national policies. Not until the 1830s would the coordinating role of parties in the federal government be recognized and appreciated.

NATIVE AMERICAN RELATIONS IN THE WEST

The outbreak of the Revolution unleashed hordes of pioneers impatient to settle the West. Vermont, seeking recognition since 1777 as a separate state from New York, won the recognition of Congress in 1791 when she was admitted as the first new state. Kentucky, organized at first as a county of Virginia, was admitted in 1792. Tennessee, which North Carolina had sought to control, gained statehood in 1796. The intrusions of whites in Native American lands provoked atrocities by the Native Americans and created an annoying problem for the administration.

Pacification of Native Americans in the Northwest—British agents at the Northwest posts encouraged the Native Americans to resist white encroachments and to believe they would receive British aid in case of war with the whites. Early campaigns in the regions of Ohio and Indiana were poorly prepared and led to Native American successes which only made the Native Americans bolder. Washington appointed the competent "Mad Anthony" Wayne to punish the tribes. He prepared his force thoroughly and spent the winter in the Native American country in 1793–1794. At the Battle of Fallen Timbers (August 1794), he crushed the Native Americans within sight of the British post, Fort Miami. The Native Americans were demoralized by Wayne's demonstration that they could expect no active aid from the British. In the Treaty of Greenville (1795) Wayne restored peace and forced the defeated tribes to cede extensive lands in Ohio and Indiana.

Native American Relations in the Southwest—In the southwest the Spanish encouraged the Creek Indians under Chief Alexander McGillivray to attack frontier settlements. George Washington used his influence to make peace with McGillivray by treaty in 1790. In two years the Native American chief denounced the treaty because the Spanish had induced him to do so. Tennesseans by 1794 had defeated the Native Americans in several campaigns.

By the Indian Intercourse Act of 1796 the federal government undertook to regulate more effectively relations between the Native Americans and white traders and settlers in order to protect the natives and prevent friction with settlers.

PROBLEMS IN DIPLOMACY

When the French Revolution began in 1789, most Americans sympathized with the reformers, believing that they were following the earlier example of the American Revolution. With the execution of Louis XVI in January 1793, however, and the increasing radicalism of the Revolution, Americans began to take sides, with the Federalists generally favoring Britain who went to war with France in 1793, and the Republicans siding with the French.

✪✪ **American Neutrality and Citizen Genet**—When Washington learned in April 1793 of the outbreak of war between France and Britain, and that the new French republic had dispatched a minister to the United States to obtain American assistance as provided by the Treaty of Alliance of 1778, he consulted with the cabinet about appropriate policy. He decided to declare American neutrality in the conflict and to receive the minister, but with no great ceremony.

Citizen Edmund Genet landed in Charleston, South Carolina, and, without bothering to present his credentials at the capital, began immediately to try to use the United States as a base from which to launch attacks on Spanish and British colonies. Secretary of State Jefferson, who welcomed Genet in Philadelphia in May, was so angered by his tactless disregard of American interests, that he, along with the rest of the cabinet, voted for his recall in August. This discredited the pro-French group in America and seemed to confirm some of the charges made by the Federalists against the French Republicans.

✪ **British Interference with American Commerce**—American exporters and shippers soon began to enjoy a wartime boom after the British navy drove French ships off the seas. American shippers profited especially from the carrying trade between the French West Indies and France. Congress defined and asserted by law (1794) the rights of neutrals. The British navy, controlling the seas, sought to enforce rules favoring Britain in the struggle with France.

Since 1776 the United States had asserted a definition of neutral trading rights favorable to the neutral carrier. 1) "Free ships make free goods," that is, goods not contraband owned by a belligerent subject could not be taken from a neutral vessel. 2) Contraband was defined strictly as goods used only for warlike purposes; food stuffs especially were excluded. 3) Blockades could not be conducted on the high seas, but had to be mounted immediately outside the port in question. The British countered with the unilateral "Rule of 1756," a trade not permitted in peacetime could not be conducted in wartime and a liberal definition of contraband, including foodstuffs, which, however, would be purchased rather than seized. Blockades were usually enforced by stopping vessels on the high seas and seizing them if they appeared to be headed for an area under blockade. Finally, Britain insisted on removing her subjects from American vessels wherever found for forced service in the Royal Navy. This practice of "impressment," however necessary it might have been for manning the navy, diminished American independence and frequently ensnared native-born American citizens, a group even the British recognized as exempt from impressment. Britain, following a rule of inalienable allegiance, did not recognize the naturalization of British subjects. British interests and American policy directly conflicted on all these points.

✪✪✪ **The Jay Treaty (1794)**—A combination of events in early 1794 caused a crisis in Anglo-American relations that required a special mission. Washington sent Chief Justice John Jay to London 1) to secure compensation for recent seizures of American vessels; 2) to effect the evacuation of the Northwest posts; 3) to obtain a commercial treaty, if possible. Wayne's recent victory at Fallen Timbers and rumblings from the League of Armed Neutrality against Britain favored the American effort, but Hamilton's disclosure of American bargaining tactics to the British minister in Philadelphia cancelled the favorable circumstances. Jay could also have pushed harder for further concessions that the British were ready to make.

Jay's Treaty as finally approved provided for 1) commissions to fix damages payable to Americans for ships seized and to settle boundary disputes. 2) The British agreed to withdraw from the Northwest posts; and 3) an unsatisfactory commercial treaty that made few concessions to the United States was signed. Republicans and others severely criticized the treaty, which was approved by the Senate only after deleting an especially objectionable article. While it managed to soothe relations with Britain, the treaty seriously antagonized the Republicans and caused some Federalists to defect to their ranks. Because it gave Spain the impression that the United States and Britain had entered a secret alliance, it won generous concessions in the Pinckney Treaty.

✪✪ **The Pinckney Treaty (1795)**—The disputes with Spain over navigation of the Mississippi, the Yazoo Strip, and Native American intrigue were carried over from the Confederation period. The Spanish feared that British friendship with the United States might encourage the United States to attack Spanish Louisiana; Spain wished to mitigate American antagonism.

In Madrid Thomas Pinckney took advantage of this situation to negotiate the Treaty of San Lorenzo, popularly known as Pinckney's Treaty.

Under its provisions: 1) Spain agreed to accept the 31st parallel as the southern boundary of the United States, thus conceding the Yazoo Strip; 2) Spain conceded the right of navigation of the Mississippi along with 3) the right of deposit at New Orleans for three years, and 4) promised to stop the Native Americans in Florida from raiding into white territory.

Pinckney's Treaty was hailed in America as the great victory it was; the fears of the western frontiersmen were quieted; and rapid westward expansion was now resumed.

THE ADMINISTRATION OF JOHN ADAMS, 1797–1801

Jay's Treaty and other events of Washington's second term as President brought Thomas Jefferson out of the retirement he had enjoyed since leaving office in December 1793. He found the Republican Party, the work primarily of James Madison, an effective, albeit loosely organized political force.

The Election of 1796—In publishing his Farewell Address, Washington positively refused a third term in 1796. The Federalists refused to support their now unpopular leaders, Jay and Hamilton. They turned to the able and upright aristocrat John Adams for the Presidency and the popular Thomas Pinckney for the Vice Presidency. The Republicans chose Jefferson and Aaron Burr of New York for President and Vice President respectively. Adams barely won in the electoral college with 71 votes to 68 for Jefferson. Under the existing constitutional provision for choosing the president and vice president these two men from opposing political parties were elected to serve together. Adams soon had to face the worst problem of his administration, that of relations with France.

❂ **The XYZ Affair (1797)**—When the French learned the provisions of Jay's Treaty, they resented the favorable treatment given Britain and the unfavorable position in which they were placed. They also suspected a secret alliance. France retaliated by ordering her naval commanders to enforce restrictions like those of the British against American ships. The Federalist election victory in 1796 further alienated the French who continued their confiscation of American shipping. President Adams sent C. C. Pinckney, Elbridge Gerry, and John Marshall to Paris in 1797 to negotiate for damage payments for the ships seized and to restore good relations.

In a cynical reaction to the Revolution, the corrupt Directory had come into power in France. As a preliminary to negotiations, Foreign Minister Talleyrand demanded bribes from the American emissaries, who refused to pay them. The reports of their reception in Paris, in which the French agents were referred to as X, Y, and Z, were published in America, and caused a popular furor. War seemed imminent.

The Undeclared Naval War with France—Congress voted large sums for the army and navy (and created a separate Navy Department in 1798) and repealed all the treaties with France. The navy completed construction of 23 warships, armed merchantmen, and authorized hundreds of privateers to prey on French shipping. Hamilton, leader of the Federalist faction eager for war, was made head of the army. The undeclared naval war lasted two years and resulted in losses of over 80 vessels by both sides. President Adams refused to yield to the clamor of his party for war, believing the national interest called for avoidance of a full-scale conflict.

The French government, like Adams, did not want war and indicated willingness to restore peaceful relations. Adams appointed a commission that reached France in 1800. Napoleon Bonaparte had just gained control and found it advantageous to restore peace. The Convention of 1800 abrogated earlier treaties with France, provided for settlement of the damage claims arising from captured ships, and agreed to the principle that neutral ships make neutral goods.

✪✪✪ The Alien and Sedition Acts (1798)—Federalists jumped at the opportunity the war with France presented to strengthen their party and weaken the burgeoning Republicans. They passed a set of laws known as the Alien and Sedition Acts. The Alien Acts struck at recent French, Irish, and other liberal immigrants who had flocked to the Republican Party. 1) The period of residence required for naturalization was increased from five to fourteen years. 2) The president was empowered to order dangerous aliens out of the country.

The Sedition Act forbade not only conspiracies against the laws, but also criticism of the laws, and the actions and statements of president, cabinet, and Congress. While no aliens were actually deported (although some left voluntarily to avoid deportation), about 25 persons were indicted and 15 were convicted under the Sedition Act; they were punished for disagreeing with the Federalist administration. Ironically, these prosecutions sparked a substantial increase in Republican newspapers.

✪✪✪ The Kentucky and Virginia Resolutions (1798)—James Madison, retired at his Virginia estate, and Thomas Jefferson cooperated in writing resolutions criticizing the Alien and Sedition Acts, both to channel popular anger about them against the Federalists and to start the campaign of 1800. Madison's resolutions, passed by the Virginia assembly, declared the acts unconstitutional and claimed that the states could "interpose" themselves between the federal government and the citizen. Jefferson's, which flatly declared the Acts "void and of no force," were passed by the Kentucky assembly. Implicitly, the resolutions, especially Jefferson's, claimed for the states the right to define the Constitution and nullify acts deemed to violate it. Almost certainly, neither Jefferson nor Madison meant such an extreme interpretation, but the resolutions began the doctrine of nullification and were later used by pro-slavery Southerners to justify their actions.

○○ **The Election of 1800**—The Federalists chose John Adams and C. C. Pinckney of South Carolina. The Republican candidates were Jefferson and Aaron Burr. The main issue of the campaign was the Alien and Sedition Acts; in these laws the Federalists had gone too far in trying to perpetuate their stay in office and Jefferson took advantage of this. The war spirit against France had quieted down and could not be turned against Jefferson. Renewed English interference with American commerce was turning the public against the pro-British Federalists. The growth in the federal debt and the increase in military expenditures enabled the Republicans to accuse the Federalists of extravagance and militarism. The Federalists were further weakened by the quarrel between Hamilton and Adams. Adams himself, a person of high character, was lacking in political ability while Jefferson and Burr both were shrewd and popular. There was much mud-slinging in the campaign; the Federalists pictured Jefferson as an atheistic, immoral, and dangerous radical.

The election was deadlocked when two leading candidates, Jefferson and Burr, tied in the electoral college. The tie threw the election into the House of Representatives where the Federalists could block selection of a president, but not select one themselves. They contrived a stalemate in the hope of securing concessions from either Jefferson or Burr. Hamilton feared Burr's election. He was a rival of Burr in New York politics, believed that he had no principles, and considered Jefferson the lesser of two evils. Thus, he urged the Federalists to elect Jefferson, which they did on the thirty-sixth ballot.

Twelfth Amendment (1804)—The elections of 1796 and 1800 disclosed a serious flaw in the procedure provided by the Constitution for the choice of the president and vice president. Therefore, the Twelfth Amendment was ratified in 1804, before the election of that year. The amendment provided that candidates must stand for either one office or the other but not for both. A candidate could not be eligible for either office, as was the case in 1800, depending upon whether he received the most or the second most votes. This amendment also prevents the choice of a president and vice president from opposing parties, as happened in 1796.

CHAPTER BOOK LIST

Adams, Henry, *The United States In 1800* (Cornell). A classic.

Banning, Lance, *The Jeffersonian Persuasion: The Evolution of Party Ideology* (1978). Ideology of the Republican Party.

Bartlett, Richard A., *The New Country: A Social History of the American Frontier 1776–1890* (1972).

Chambers, William N., *Political Parties in a New Nation: The American Experience, 1776–1809* (1963).

Charles, Joseph, *Origins of the American Party System* (Torchbooks). Brief monograph.

Clark, Thomas D., *Frontier America* (1969).

Combs, Gerald A., *The Jay Treaty: Political Battleground of the Founding Fathers* (1970). An excellent study of the interaction between foreign policy and domestic politics.

Cooke, Jacob E., *Alexander Hamilton* (1982).

Cunliffe, Marcus, *George Washington* (New American Library). Short, accurate interpretation.

De Conde, Alexander, *The Quasi-War* (1966).

Ferling, John, *The First of Men: A Life of George Washington* (1988).

Jones, Robert F., *George Washington: A Biography* (1986, rev. ed.). For the student and general reader.

Kurtz, S.G., *Presidency of John Adams* (Perpetua). Deals with the Federalists' fall from power and important events of the Adams administration.

Livermore, Shaw, Jr., *The Twilight of Federalism* (1962).

Miller, J.C., *Alexander Hamilton: Portrait in Paradox* (1959). Best biography of Hamilton.

Miller, J.C., *Crisis in Freedom* (1951). About the Alien and Sedition Acts.

Miller, J.C., *The Federalist Era, 1789–1801.* (1963). Best survey of the period.

Peterson, Merrill D., *Thomas Jefferson and the New Nation: A Biography* (1970). Good, relatively brief biography.

Smith, James Morton, *Freedom's Fetters: The Alien and Sedition Laws and American Civil Liberties* (1956). Definitive.

Varg, Paul A., *Foreign Policies of the Founding Fathers* (Penguin).

REVIEW QUESTIONS

MULTIPLE CHOICE

1. Which was *not* a part of Hamilton's financial program? (1) Refunding the foreign debt at par (2) levying an excise tax (3) refunding depreciated state issues of paper money at par (4) levying substantial tariff duties.

2. The charter of the first Bank of the United States gave it all of the following functions except (1) minting money (2) acting as a depository of government funds (3) issuing paper currency (4) handling the sale of government bonds.

3. The first state to enter the Union after independence was (1) Kentucky (2) Vermont (3) Tennessee (4) Maine.

4. Which was *not* a Hamiltonian policy? (1) Giving the creditor class a strong stake in the success of the government (2) friendship with Britain (3) broadening the powers of the federal government (4) rapid repayment of the federal debt.

5. In the Northwest Territory, the British (1) accepted to relinquish control of the fur trade in exchange for monetary compensation (2) signed a treaty with Adams to undertake a joint pacification of Native Americans (3) promised to aid the Native Americans if they went to war with the white settlers (4) sent aid to Native Americans at the Battle of Fallen Timber.

6. Citizen Genet came to the United States officially to (1) establish a base for regaining New France (2) negotiate an alliance with the United States (3) make use of favorable provisions of an existing alliance with the United States (4) secure an American declaration of war against Great Britain.

7. Which statement regarding the Jay Treaty is *not* true? (1) The treaty drove Spain into an alliance with the United States (2) threats of the League of Armed Neutrality against Britain favored the American negotiations (3) Hamilton's assurances to Britain weakened Jay's bargaining position (4) Jay failed to exert his best efforts on behalf of the United States.

8. The least satisfactory provision incorporated in the Jay Treaty related to (1) impressment (2) commerce (3) boundaries (4) the Northwest posts.

9. In the Pinckney Treaty Spain made valuable concessions to the United States because (1) Spain was in danger of attack from France (2) the United States had mobilized troops on the Florida border (3) Spain feared the United States had made an alliance with England (4) Spain had lost the good will of the Native Americans of the Southwest.

10. Who was *not* a candidate for the presidency in 1796? (1) Jefferson (2) Washington (3) Burr (4) John Adams.

11. Which did *not* have the effect of turning France and the United States against each other before the XYZ Affair came up? (1) The Alien and Sedition Acts (2) the Jay Treaty (3) French confiscations of American ships (4) the Federalist election victory of 1796.

12. Which is *not* true of the Alien and Sedition Acts? (1) An important purpose was to strengthen the Federalists politically (2) naturalization requirements were increased (3) under the Alien Act many were deported by legal processes (4) under the Sedition Act some were imprisoned.

13. Which statement about the Kentucky and Virginia Resolutions is *not* true? (1) The Kentucky resolution was written by Jefferson (2) the Virginia resolution was written by Madison (3) they constituted the first assertion of the doctrine of nullification (4) they helped the Federalists win election in 1800.

14. Which of these is *not* an explanation of the Federalist defeat in 1800? (1) Accumulated grievances against the Federalists going back to the Whiskey Rebellion (2) the Federalist tariff policy since 1789 (3) the Alien and Sedition Acts (4) the Kentucky and Virginia Resolutions.

TRUE-FALSE

15. The first tariff act passed in 1789 levied high duties and therefore may be designated as a protective tariff.

16. Jefferson quickly became the most influential member of Washington's cabinet.

17. Although foreign debts were refunded at par by the Federalists, domestic debts were paid off at a considerable discount.

18. Hamilton believed a large debt would strengthen the federal government by binding the moneyed classes to it.

19. The Federalists represented the interests of the business classes and the Anti-Federalists the interests of the farmers.

20. Political parties at first were looked upon as undesirable.

21. Jefferson supported Citizen Genet at all times since Jefferson thought he would strengthen the Anti-Federalists politically.

22. By declaring that "free ships make free goods" the United States in the 1790s upheld its right as a neutral to trade with either belligerent.

23. It is not true that John Jay was pro-British.

24. The party of Jefferson is the ancestor of the present day Republicans.

25. John Adams staunchly refused to follow Hamilton's partisan advice, advice that would have gotten the United States into war with France.

26. No persons were penalized by the Federalists under the Sedition Act.

27. Under the Kentucky and Virginia Resolutions the states as well as the Supreme Court would have the right to declare acts of Congress unconstitutional.

COMPLETION

28. When Congress first met under the Constitution it was at _____ .

29. The first ten amendments, known as the _____ were soon added to the Constitution.

30. The first Secretary of the Treasury, appointed by Washington, was _____ .

31. Hamilton favored assumption of the Revolutionary War debt of the states but _____ was opposed.

32. Congress chartered the Bank of the United States in the year _____ .

33. Hamilton favored loose construction of the Constitution, but _____ advocated _____ construction.

34. Hamilton argued that Congress might constitutionally charter the Bank of the United States under the doctrine of _____ .

35. The Whiskey Tax, an internal revenue tax, was a kind of tax also known as an _____ .

36. In the struggle between Britain and France the Federalists took the side of _____ .

37. The first new state admitted to the Union was _____ ; soon afterwards _____ and _____ were admitted.

38. The French Revolution began in the year _____ .

39. In the war between Britain and France a French agent called _____ commissioned privateers to sail from American ports to operate against British shipping.

40. The principle of international law enforced by the British and which stated that trade not open to a nation in time of peace could not be conducted in time of war was known as the _____ .

41. Materials for waging war which may be legally seized on the high seas by belligerents are known as _____ of war.

42. A blockade not enforced by ships on actual patrol along the enemy coast is referred to as a _____ blockade.

43. John Jay in negotiating his unpopular treaty made it possible for another diplomat by the name of _____ to negotiate a more successful treaty.

44. In 1796 _____ was elected President.

45. In the undeclared naval war against France in 1798 hundreds of _____ were authorized to prey on French shipping.

46. The _____ Act, 1798, provided heavy penalties for false or malicious statements against government officials.

47. The Kentucky Resolution was written by _____ .

48. The constitutional procedure for electing the president and vice president was changed by the _____ Amendment.

MATCHING

49. John Jay

a. Creek chief

50. Thomas Jefferson

b. First Chief Justice of the Supreme Court

51. Alexander Hamilton

c. Treaty of San Lorenzo

52. Anthony Wayne

d. Candidate for President in 1800

53. Thomas Pinckney

e. Secretary of State under Washington

54. Talleyrand

f. Battle of Fallen Timbers

55. Alexander McGillivray

g. Author of the Whisky Tax

56. Aaron Burr

h. Corrupt foreign minister

i. Secretary of War under Washington

CHRONOLOGY / CHAPTER 9

1798   Eleventh Amendment ratified to limit suits against states in federal courts.

1800   Harrison Land Law passed.

1801   Jefferson inaugurated as President, served until 1809.

1803   Louisiana Purchase Treaty.

        Marbury v. Madison established power of judicial review by Supreme Court.

1804   Hamilton shot in duel with Burr.

        Twelfth Amendment ratified to change method of electing president.

        Lewis and Clark began expedition to the Pacific, returned in 1807.

1805   Essex decision made against American West Indies shipping.

1806   Pike began exploration of the southwest, returned in 1807.

        Burr expedition down the Mississippi River.

        Berlin-Milan decrees and British Orders-in-Council issued, 1806–07.

1807   Burr acquitted of treason charges.

        British *Leopard* attacked American Chesapeake.

        Embargo Act stops American exports to foreign countries.

1809   Nonintercourse Act.

1810   Macon's Bill No. 2.

1811   Bank of the United States allowed to expire.

1812   Congress declared war against Great Britain.

1814   British invaders burned Washington, DC.

        Hartford Convention voiced opposition to War of 1812.

        Yazoo claimants finally received payment.

        Treaty of Ghent restored peace with Great Britain.

1815   Battle of New Orleans.

JEFFERSON, MADISON, AND THE WAR OF 1812, 1801–1815

The Presidential inauguration of Jefferson in 1801 marked the end of Federalist control of American politics. The Federalists continued as an opposition party until they were discredited for their anti-war position in 1812 and their activities during the war itself. Agricultural, democratic, and Western influences replaced commercial, autocratic, and Eastern domination of the young republic. This period was marked also by the serious distractions of and involvement in the Napoleonic Wars in Europe.

EARLY YEARS OF THE JEFFERSON ADMINISTRATION

Jefferson later described his election in 1800 as a revolution in the spirit of the government. Although they may not have constituted a revolution, significant changes did take place. First and most important was the peaceful transfer of power that took place on March 4, 1801, when Jefferson was inaugurated. Few countries have managed this peaceful transfer at all, and the United States did it after only 12 years under the Constitution. Also, the Jeffersonians devoted themselves to paying off the national debt ($32 million was retired under Jefferson) and doing away with all internal taxes, the anthesis of Hamiltonian finance. Finally, Jefferson attempted to achieve foreign policy goals by commercial coercion, not force, actual or implied.

Jefferson, the Man—Although Jefferson belonged to one of the leading families in Virginia he was not a part of the tidewater aristocracy but a well-to-do back country planter. Nevertheless, as a large land and slave holder, he did belong to the landed aristocracy. He was well educated and had many cultural and scientific interests. He drew the architectural plans for his home at Monticello and introduced plants for the improvement of American agriculture. He was Deist in religion.

OOO Political Ideals of Jefferson—Jefferson's political philosophy was influenced by both his reading of the French liberal philosophers and his experience living in the Virginia piedmont. He showed his liberalism early in the Revolution. In the Virginia legislature he worked to abolish the relics of feudalism and for the separation of church and state. He had great faith in public education and the free press; he worked for a more humane penal code and advocated the emancipation of slaves. He believed that government should be kept weak. As a states' right advocate he favored a relatively weak federal government and a strict construction of the Federal Constitution. To him the ideal government was one run by well-informed, self-respecting farmers. In office he kept foremost in mind the interests of both farmers and Westerners.

O Jefferson's Initial Acts as President—Some Federalists expected Jefferson to strike a wildly radical keynote in the inaugural address. Instead, he sought to conciliate his defeated rivals and soothe their fears. He spoke of the similarities between the Federalists and Republicans. Not being an effective speaker, he began the practice of sending written messages to Congress, to be read by a clerk. Hereafter, until President Woodrow Wilson (1913–1921), only the inaugural addresses would be delivered orally. In his cabinet he made James Madison Secretary of State and Albert Gallatin of Pennsylvania Secretary of the Treasury. His appointees represented the well-to-do planter class and other agriculturists. Jefferson found a near-monopoly of Federalists in appointive office when he was inaugurated; he removed Federalists until a slim majority of government employees were Republicans. The Alien Act and the Sedition Act had expired before Jefferson's term began; the Naturalization Act was liberalized in 1802.

The Army and Navy—Republican fiscal policies differed sharply from those of the Federalists. As noted, Jefferson and Gallatin reduced the national debt and repealed all internal taxes, especially the detested whiskey excise responsible for the 1794 disturbances in Pennsylvania. Government expenses were pared drastically to match the loss in revenue. The army and navy suffered much to drastic reductions. Many worn out naval vessels needed to be retired, and Jefferson replaced them with about 200 small gunboats equipped with a single gun. This policy was ridiculed when, after a tropical storm, one boat of this "mosquito fleet" was washed eight miles inland and stranded in a corn field. This naval policy left the country unprepared for the War of 1812. Tariff duties produced abundant revenues due to brisk trade with the French West Indies.

The War with Tripoli—The European nations had long paid tribute to the piratical seafaring Barbary states on the north coast of Africa. The Federalists had followed the custom of paying tribute even after several frigates had been added to the navy. In 1801 Tripoli, dissatisfied with the amount of her tribute, declared war on the United States. For four years American ships fought these pirates. In 1805 peace was restored, but the American navy continued intermittent fighting to defend the nation's shipping against the pirate states until 1815 when Commodore Decatur dictated a lasting peace that ended the demands for tribute and ransom.

The Judiciary—The Judiciary Act of 1801, passed in the last months of the Adams administration, was a worthwhile reform and expansion of the federal judiciary. Unfortunately, President Adams immediately filled all the new positions it created and the Senate confirmed his nominees. The Republicans, especially Jefferson, criticized these "midnight appointments," a term that actually covered all appointments made after December 10, 1800, when Adams learned of his electoral defeat.

OOO*Marbury v. Madison* (1803)—Jefferson ordered Secretrary of State Madison to hold all appointments not yet delivered pending repeal of the 1801 Act. One of these appointees, William Marbury, named as federal justice of the peace for the District of Columbia, sued for delivery of his certificate under Section 13 of the Judiciary Act of 1789, which made such matters original jurisdiction for the Supreme Court. Chief Justice John Marshall found that Secretary Madison illegally withheld the certificate, but that the Court was powerless to remedy the greivance, as Section 13 was unconstitutional. Thus, Marshall had it both ways; he reproved his cousin, President Jefferson, for violating the law, but avoided any formal confrontation with the executive.

The Court's assertion of judicial review was not especially controversial. If Marshall had claimed judicial supremacy for the Court, there would have been objections, but he did not. Most of the popular objections to the decision centered on the implied rebuke of the President, not the finding as to Section 13. By the time the decision was given (February 1803), the 1801 Act had been repealed and, essentially, the original federal court system restored by the Judiciary Act of 1802. Thus, as Jefferson said, he did not remove the judges from the bench, but the bench from the judges.

The Impeachment of Justice Chase (1805)—The Republicans began to seek a defense against the Federalist justices of the Supreme Court. The right of impeachment offered a possible defense. The Republicans now attempted to remove Justice Samuel Chase by impeachment in Congress. He was rightfully charged with partisanship for an anti-Republican tirade he had made in court but irrelevant charges brought against him caused the Senate to fail to convict. The case did cause the Federalist justices to be more judicious in their criticisms.

⊙ **Land Legislation**—Two opposing positions determined the terms of federal land laws. One position held that the lands should be disposed of to produce maximum revenue, the other that land should be sold on terms advantageous to small farmers. As time passed, the pioneer's view that land should be disposed of to promote rapid settlement gradually made headway.

The first federal act providing for the distribution of land was the Ordinance of 1785; it provided that the minimum purchase would be 640 acres and the minimum price $1 an acre. There was no provision for credit to accommodate the small farmer. This law was framed to produce revenue and to favor the land speculator. The next act (1796) increased the minimum to $2 an acre but permitted credit for one year for half the purchase price, but little land was distributed under this law.

The Harrison Land Law of 1800, sponsored by William Henry Harrison, delegate from the Northwest Territory, allowed a minimum purchase of 320 acres. Credit terms permitted a down payment of only a fourth of the purchase price and extended credit for four years. This Act represented a strong concession to the Western settlers. The Act of 1804 liberalized the law further by reducing the minimum purchase to 160 acres. The Act of 1820 reduced the minimum size of a purchase to only 80 acres and the minimum price to $1.25 an acre, but the credit system was abolished because of mass defaulting in payments by Western settlers. Under these laws the land was first put up for sale at auction where much of it sold above the minimum price. It was under these more liberal laws that the eastern basin of the Mississippi was settled before 1840.

The rapid settlement of Ohio, partly stimulated by the liberal Land Act of 1800, gave it enough population for Congress to admit it as a state in 1803.

⊙ **The Yazoo Claimants**—The complex problem of the Yazoo land companies is of multiple significance. The problem began in the early 1790s with the sale by a bribed Georgia legislature of western lands to four land companies owned by stockholder-land speculators in the East. A subsequent legislature (1795) annulled the corrupt sale. The land companies sued Georgia in the federal courts. Georgia agreed to surrender her land claims to the United States government (which disputed Georgia's claims to the lands anyway) if Congress would compensate the Yazoo land claimants. Jefferson approved the settlement but the extreme states' rightists in his party, the "Quids," led by John Randolph of Virginia, stubbornly refused to vote the necessary appropriation. The sniping from Jefferson's own party arose from those who disliked his policy of conciliating the Federalists. The payment was not voted until 1814 after Randolph left Congress.

The Yazoo problem was significant in these respects: 1) it resulted in the 11th Amendment (1798) which denies the right of citizens of another state or a foreign nation to sue one of the states in a federal court. 2) The dispute delayed the settlement of those parts of western Georgia which became the states of Alabama and Mississippi. 3) It was one of the main issues giving rise to the Quids. 4) In the case of *Fletcher v. Peck* the Supreme Court upheld the sanctity of business contracts by denying Georgia the right to unilaterally annul the contract of sale. 5) It calls attention to the ever present background influence of land speculation in America.

THE LOUISIANA PURCHASE, 1803

The settlement of Kentucky, Tennessee, and the upper Ohio valley by American pioneer farmers in the eastern half of the Mississippi basin made the control of the lower Mississippi at New Orleans of extreme economic importance to the United States. Large quantities of produce were floated down river to New Orleans. Previously, interference with this movement of goods had caused great hardship to American shippers.

✪✪✪ **Revival and Abandonment of French Ambitions in Louisiana**—The French transferred Louisiana to Spain in the Treaty of Paris of 1763, but retained an interest in it. This was especially true after 1783, when French policy aimed, quietly and inconspicuously, to keep their ally, the United States, confined close to the Atlantic and relatively weak. After Napoleon Bonaparte came to power in 1799, he decided to revive France's North American empire. He forced Spain to give Louisiana back in the Treaty of San Ildefonso (1800), and dispatched General Jacques Leclerc to Santo Domingo to reconquer that island from former slaves led by Toussaint L'Ouverture. Leclerc was successful and L'Ouverture was sent to France to die in prison, but the island's second line of defense, yellow fever, then decimated the French forces, taking even General Leclerc. Since the island was seen as an essential base for the development of Louisiana, Napoleon, 1) having failed in Santo Domingo, 2) realizing that Britain or the United States could take the territory, and 3) needing money to resume his European wars, decided to sell Louisiana.

✪✪✪ **The Louisiana Purchase Treaty**—Jefferson was already alarmed about the prospect of the French reacquiring Louisiana—the territory had not yet been transferred—when news of the closure of the Mississippi to American traffic by the Spanish arrived early in 1803. Fearing violent action by Westerners, action that could lead to war, he sent James Monroe to Paris to assist the resident minister, Robert R. Livingston, in acquiring New Orleans and Florida. Monroe found

Livingston settling details on a treaty purchasing all of Louisiana (including New Orleans but not Florida) for $15 million. No boundaries were stated in the treaty. Jefferson was temporarily dumbfounded by the news, and by the fact that he could see no constitutional provision permitting the federal government to acquire land. But the opportunity was too good to ignore and he allowed himself to be talked into executing the treaty and letting the voters decide. In October 1803, the treaty was approved, appropriations made, and a temporary government for Louisiana drawn up. The actual transfer into American hands occurred in December. Only the Federalists criticized the treaty as unconstitutional.

○○ **Early Exploration of Louisiana**—Jefferson immediately secured an appropriation from Congress for the exploration of the region beyond the Mississippi. In 1804–1806 Meriwether Lewis and William Clark, chosen by Jefferson, led their famous expedition up the Missouri River, across the continental divide in the Rockies, and down the Columbia River to the Pacific. Zebulon M. Pike led an expedition to explore the region of the upper Mississippi in 1805 and in 1806 led a more famous exploration across the Great Plains to the southern Rockies and thence into New Mexico.

THE ROLE OF AARON BURR

The ambitious Aaron Burr, an unprincipled, self-seeking politician from New York, earned his disrepute in three significant scandals; he caused serious embarrassment for Jefferson.

The Federalist Secession Plot—The ratification of the Louisiana Purchase Treaty and the reelection of the popular Jefferson in 1804 determined certain Federalists to plot the secession and possible union with Canada of New York and New England. They turned to Aaron Burr who had been thrown aside by Jefferson as his Vice Presidential running mate in 1804. (Jefferson was alienated from Burr by his equivocal conduct during the House Presidential voting in 1801.) The plot called for the election of Burr as governor of New York. Hamilton exposed the plot and secured Burr's defeat. New England secession was not revived again until the War of 1812.

The Hamilton-Burr Duel—This most famous of duels in American history resulted from Burr's repeated political defeats at the hands of Hamilton. Burr chose to avenge himself and challenged Hamilton to a duel in 1804. Burr aimed to kill; Hamilton's death forced Burr into exile from the East. The custom and ceremony of dueling characterized the rougher elements of American society until public opinion and legal sanctions outlawed it after the Civil War.

The Burr Expedition (1806)—Burr decided, like some other Americans whose careers in the East had been blocked, to go West to seek a new career. (Besides, dueling was more accepted in the West and Hamilton less popular there.) Burr sought to exploit remnants of Western discontent and plotted to separate Western states from the Union to establish a new government. He approached the ministers of England and Spain for aid. He floated an expedition down the Ohio and Mississippi and drew the treasonable General James Wilkinson, head of the American army in the West, into his schemes. When Wilkinson recognized that the plans would fail, he gave the plot away. Burr was arrested and taken to Richmond for trial.

At Burr's trial (1807) for treason politics played an undue part under the presiding judge, Chief Justice John Marshall. Marshall, who disliked Jefferson, favored Burr who was Jefferson's enemy now. The court ruled that to be guilty of treason the accused had to be present at the time Burr's armed expedition began its journey down the Ohio—an unreasonable bit of hair-splitting. Burr was found not guilty.

DEFENSE OF THE RIGHTS OF AMERICAN NEUTRALITY

Napoleon's renewal of war in 1803 against England and her allies revived the earlier American difficulties of upholding her shipping rights at sea against Britain and France. By 1805 Napoleon had control of the continent of Europe, and Britain had control of the seas. Each opponent in the deadly struggle needed to choke off the ocean commerce of the other. The United States enjoyed a profitable trade in supplying both belligerents.

○○ British Maritime Policies—Britain sought to stop the American carrying trade between the French West Indies and France. 1) In the Essex decision (1805) Britain applied the rule of 1756 to stop even the indirect shipment of French West Indian produce by way of United States ports. Such a broken voyage, the British court ruled, was the same as a direct voyage, and the British navy began seizing such ships. 2) Desperate Britain, short of sailors to man her vessels, actively practiced impressment of seamen from American ships. She was careless in impressing not only deserters from British ships but took naturalized Americans and some native-born American sailors. In the most outrageous case of impressment (1807), the British warship *Leopard* bombarded the unwary American warship *Chesapeake* just outside American waters. One deserter and three sailors were removed after the American ship had suffered 21 casualties. Jefferson could have led the aroused nation to war over the incident. 3) Britain also issued the Orders-in-Council which forbade neutral trade with France and her allies and declared a blockade of European ports in nations occupied by France. Only by violating these British regulations could America conduct trade with Europe.

French Policies—Napoleon in retaliation against Britain issued decrees to starve England into submission. 1) The Berlin Decree (1806) declared a blockade of the British Isles. 2) The Milan Decree announced that any neutral ship obeying the British Orders-in-Council would be confiscated, even when they came to trade in French ports. Under these decrees the French also confiscated large numbers of American ships.

✪✪✪ **Jefferson's Policies**—Jefferson and Madison resolved to secure British and French recognition of American neutral rights by using commercial coercion, the denial of the American market to Britain, and American goods to everyone. In 1806 Congress passed the Nonintercourse Act that forbade the importation of certain British goods; the act took effect in December 1807. After negotiations following the *Chesapeake* affair failed to secure satisfaction from the British, Jefferson proposed and Congress approved an embargo on all American exports and foreign voyages by American vessels. This took effect with the Nonintercourse Act.

The British made good the loss of the American market by exploiting a newly opened South American market. Despite severe efforts by the administration, American compliance with the Acts was not high and they were much criticized, especially in New England, which returned to Federalism in the election of 1808. As the last act of his administration, Jefferson signed the repeal of the Embargo and bequeathed the problem to his successor, James Madison.

The Nonintercourse Act (1809) forbidding trade with Britain or France, but allowing it with all other countries, was an attempt to maintain at least the appearance of commercial coercion. The Act offered to repeal the embargo against either country if anti-American regulations were repealed. Without authority, British minister David Erskine negotiated an agreement lifting British regulations in return for the end of the American embargo. When London repudiated the agreement, Americans accused her of negotiating in bad faith.

✪ **Macon's Bill No. 2 (1810)**—The Nonintercourse Act, being unsuccessful, was replaced by President Madison with Macon's Bill No. 2. This Act permitted reopening of trade with both England and France and offered to stop trade with the enemy of the nation that first repealed its laws against American trade. Napoleon took advantage of this offer to issue a confusing statement that apparently revoked France's regulations, provided Britain revoked hers. Despite its ambiguity and probable insincerity, Madison took it at face value in order to concentrate American efforts on Britain whose offenses were greater and who could be attacked in Canada.

Great Britain in June 1812, revoked her Orders-in-Council because of pressure from her own merchants and the growing threat of war with the United States. The attempt at conciliation came too late and Congress declared war against Britain before the news of the British concessions could arrive across the Atlantic.

THE WAR OF 1812

The measures of peaceful coercion against Britain and France employed by Jefferson were continued by Madison. Madison also tried negotiation without success. In 1810 a group of young Republican Congressmen from the West known as the "War Hawks" were elected. Their impatience to break the stalemate by war helped push Madison into a struggle for which the country was not prepared and which ended without victory.

✪✪✪ **Causes of the War**—1) British enforcement of her rules of international law since 1805 was deeply resented by many Americans. These violations of American rights included a) the seizure of American ships and other interference with American trade, and b) the impressment of American seamen. The interference with American commerce aroused the ire of Westerners since it interfered with the marketing of their produce and brought depression to the Ohio valley. 2) The insolent attitude of British diplomats and British contempt for the American people kept Americans antagonistic to Britain.

Other causes for the war also arose from Western antagonisms to the British. 3) Native American attacks in the West were attributed to British encouragement and to British arms that found their way into the hands of the Native Americans. The notable Native American chief Tecumseh and his brother, the Prophet, inspired Native American tribes in the Northwest to unite and take a stand against further land cessions and demoralization by whites. William Henry Harrison fought an initial battle at Tippecanoe and the Native Americans rose all over the frontier. The War Hawks believed that war against the British in Canada would stop this source of Native American incitement and provide the occasion for thorough destruction and pacification of the Native Americans.

4) Some Americans hoped to annex Canada and Spanish Florida. These attacks were intended to pacify the Native Americans as much as to annex land. The War Hawks loudly proclaimed that Canada could be taken by merely marching into it.

While there was certainly no unanimity in the demand for war, when it did come, it was with a national majority in Congress favoring it. The younger members from the West and South provided much of the leadership for the war, but those sections could not pass the declaration themselves. Support was forthcoming from every section of the country, even New England, which provided 12 yeas (and 18 nays) in the House. Madison's reelection over DeWitt Clinton of New York by an electoral vote of 128 to 89 in 1812 was probably a good indication of the relative popularity of the war.

○ **American Lack of Preparedness**—In spite of all the clamor for war, Congress found it impossible to obtain more than a small proportion of the number of soldiers authorized. Americans disliked national military service and preferred to enlist in the poorly disciplined militia. The militiamen were incompetently led by men too old, too young, or chosen by political influence; but the men themselves refused to leave their own states. The navy consisted of about a dozen warships to oppose Britain's 800.

Financially, the nation was unprepared. Revenue, produced chiefly by tariffs on imports, had been insufficient for some time because of the trade stoppages. Jefferson's hated internal revenue taxes had to be used to help finance the war. Furthermore, New England opposition left the country badly divided. When the rechartering of the national bank came up in 1811, it would have passed if President Madison had publicly asked for it. But Madison regarded such activity as improper and the measure failed in the Senate by Vice President George Clinton's tie-breaking vote. State banks were left free of necessary discipline over issues of bank notes. Such a flood of paper was issued that specie payment had to be suspended before the end of the war.

○ **American Campaigns Against Canada**—Military action began in 1812 with three separate invasions of Canada; none succeeded. The overcautious old General Hull panicked and surrendered his force at Detroit. Court-martialled and sentenced to be shot, he was pardoned by Madison because of his record in the Revolution. The invasion across the Niagara River failed because the militia refused to follow the regular army across the border. General Dearborn's planned invasion at Lake Champlain failed to cross the border when his militiamen refused to set foot on Canadian soil.

In 1813 the Americans achieved decided success. General William Henry Harrison succeeded Hull in the Northwest. Subsidiary to Harrison's preparation for the capture of Fort Malden was the construction of a fleet on Lake Erie. This naval force under Oliver H. Perry cleared the lake of British vessels and eliminated this threat to American communications in Canada. Next, Harrison won a decisive victory in the Battle of the Thames. Tecumseh, leader of the Native Americans who had allied with the British, was killed and the Native American power broken. To the east of Lake Erie the planned invasions all failed or soon turned back.

✪ The War in 1814—The British entered American soil at five points in 1814. An effort against the American post at Niagara was turned back in July and a similar attempt, using Lake Champlain as a corridor, was stopped in September at Plattsburgh when American lake vessels sunk the British ships supplying their troops. However, a raid led by British General Ross directed against Washington in August succeeded in capturing the city and destroying its public buildings. A similar attempt at Baltimore immediately afterwards failed. About 100 miles of the Maine coast was temporarily occupied. The final British effort was directed against New Orleans.

✪✪ Jackson and New Orleans—In the Southwest the war began in 1813 when the Creeks, stirred up by Tecumseh, massacred a large number of whites who had taken refuge at Fort Mims, Alabama. General Andrew Jackson led Tennessee troops in a resounding victory against the Creeks at Horseshoe Bend in Alabama. After this Jackson was appointed to the command of all American forces in the Southwest and ordered to New Orleans to counter the British invasion under General Pakenham. A force of 10,000 veterans of the Napoleonic campaigns marched across an open field against Jackson's frontier sharpshooters. American losses were negligible; the British lost 2,000 men. The battle was more decisive in promoting Jackson's political career than in ending the war—the victory came two weeks after the peace had been signed.

✪✪ The War at Sea—The overwhelmingly outnumbered American navy fighting alone was doomed to defeat. No fleet engagement occurred at sea, but numerous ship-to-ship encounters ended in victories for the American vessels which carried more guns and sail than did British warships. British commerce suffered frightful losses from both American warships and numerous privateers.

The British blockade beginning in 1813 confined most American ships to port by that summer, except for the *Constitution* and intermittent offensives by five other warships. American commerce was effectively blockaded at all ports except in New England where ports were exempted because of their willingness to trade with the enemy and their outspoken sympathy with Britain. The heroic naval victories on the lakes were subsidiary to land movements but crucial to American victories in the vicinity of Lake Erie and Lake Champlain.

✪✪ New England and the War—The agricultural dynasty that came to power in 1801, with Jefferson and his Republican successors, followed policies offensive to the commercial interests of Federalist New England. The trade stoppages applied against the European belligerents brought depression to seaports everywhere; for this New England blamed the American government more than Britain. New England financiers refused to buy war bonds, merchants and farmers sold provisions to the

British forces in Canada, and the states withheld their militia from the campaigns in Canada. Enlistments were discouraged and open sympathy with England prevailed.

The Hartford Convention (1814) marked the culmination of New England opposition. It was actually an effort by moderate Federalists to soften the extreme feelings against the war in some parts of the section, especially western Massachusetts. That state, along with Connecticut and Rhode Island, sent delegations while New Hampshire and Vermont were partially represented. The convention declared the war intolerable and called for several constitutional amendments, including a two-thirds vote for declarations of war, embargoes, and the admission of new states, no counting of slaves for representation, and no successive presidents from the same state. These resolutions were presented shortly after the news of the victory at New Orleans and the Treaty of Ghent had arrived in Washington and thus came as an anticlimax to what now appeared as a successful war. The Federalists were not planning to secede, simply protest, but they managed only to appear ridiculous.

✪✪✪ **The Treaty of Ghent**—Armistice negotiations began soon after the declaration of war but deadlocked on the issue of impressment. In 1813 Russia offered mediation. Madison appointed American Minister to Russia, John Quincy Adams, as head of the delegation, and Federalist Senator James A. Bayard and Republican Albert Gallatin as its members. Later two more Republicans were added, one being Henry Clay. The able delegation of Americans eventually met the second rate diplomats that Britain sent to Ghent.

Negotiations began with extravagant and unacceptable demands on both sides. The Americans became more conciliatory when news of defeats, especially the raid on Washington, arrived. Napoleon's surrender in May 1814 turned the war into one for the benefit of Canada, which, combined with the poor state of the British effort there, and the obviously greater importance of European affairs for Britain, brought about a similar change of heart by Britain.

The Treaty of Ghent as finally signed in December 1814, provided for no territorial changes or other concessions. The rights for which the United States fought the war were abandoned. Concrete provisions for the settlement of differences called for the appointment of commissioners to meet later and settle questions of boundaries, fisheries, a trade agreement, and rights on the Great Lakes.

✪✪✪ **Consequences of the War**—1) The war won British respect for the fighting ability of American seamen and the ability of American diplomats. 2) American dislike of Britain was renewed and extended after the war, but the maritime issues ceased to cause trouble with the restoration of peace. 3) Defeat of the Native American tribes opened the whole area east of the Mississippi to settlement. 4) The return of peace in Europe, leaving America free of the distraction of war, permitted American concentration upon her own territorial expansion and other matters. 5) The war increased the American spirit of nationalism and overcame disruptive forces of sectionalism. 6) Trade interruptions before and during the war forced a significant growth of American manufacturing.

CHAPTER BOOK LIST

Buel, Richard, Jr., *Securing The Republic: Ideology in American Politics 1789–1815* (1972).

Coles, Harry L., *The War of 1812* (University of Chicago).

Corwin, E.S., *John Marshall and the Constitution* (1919). By a specialist in constitutional history.

Cresson, William P., *James Monroe* (1946).

Cunningham, Noble E., *The Jeffersonian Republicans in Power* (University of North Carolina).

De Conde, Alexander, *This Affair of Louisiana* (1976). The Louisiana Purchase.

Egan, Clifford, *Neither Peace Nor War* (1983). Franco-American relations.

Ellis, Richard E., *The Jeffersonian Crisis: Courts and Politics in the Young Republic* (1971). What the Anti-Federalists might have done.

Ketcham, Ralph, *James Madison: A Biography* (1971). Good one-volume treatment.

Koch, Adrienne, *Jefferson and Madison: The Great Collaboration* (1950). A survey of this period and the Federalist period.

Malone, Dumas, *Jefferson and The Rights of Man* (1951). On Jefferson's liberalism.

Perkins, B., *Causes of The War of 1812* (Holt). Presents different interpretation.

Rutland, Robert A., *Madison's Alternatives: The Jeffersonian Republicans and the Coming of the War, 1805–1812* (1975).

Sheehan, Bernard W., *Seeds of Extinction: Jeffersonian Philanthropy and the American Indian* (1973). Brilliant study of Jefferson's rationale for his policy towards Native Americans.

Smelser, Marshall, *The Democratic Republic 1801–1815* (Harper & Row).

Spivak, Burton, *Jefferson's English Crisis: Commerce, the Embargo, and the Republican Revolution* (1979). Anglo-American relations.

Tucker, Richard W., and Henderson, David C., *Empire of Liberty: The Statecraft of Thomas Jefferson* (1990). Modern study of Jefferson's foreign policy ideas and practice.

Van Deusen, Glyndon, *Life of Henry Clay* (1937). The most complete biography of the Great Compromiser; deals with his role as a "War Hawk" in 1812.

White, Leonard, *The Jefffersonians* (Macmillan).
Wiltse, Charles M., *The New Nation 1800–1845* (Hill & Wang).
Young, James Sterling, *The Washington Community: 1800–1828* (1966).
Social and political study of the Jefferson administration and its physical setting.

REVIEW QUESTIONS

MULTIPLE-CHOICE

1. After election as President, Jefferson (1) sought to root out Federalist policies (2) followed a conciliatory policy towards Federalists, although many were removed from office (3) renewed the Alien and Sedition Acts (4) raised tariff duties.

2. Jefferson's administration did all *except* which one of the following? (1) Repealed the Whisky Tax (2) abolished the Bank of the United States (3) rapidly reduced the national debt (4) reduced the size of the navy and army.

3. Which of the following classes would you expect to benefit most from the policies of Jefferson? (1) Shipowners (2) bankers (3) merchants (4) small farmers.

4. Jefferson received the most notable opposition to his desire to settle the Yazoo land controversy from (1) the land companies (2) the "Quids" and Randolph (3) the Federalists (4) the state of Georgia.

5. The Land Law of 1800 revised earlier legislation by (1) making it easier for settlers to acquire land (2) benefiting land speculators (3) increasing federal revenues (4) sharing land revenues with the states.

6. The aim of the initial negotiations relating to the purchase of Louisiana was to (1) acquire control of the mouth of the Mississippi (2) expand the fur trade in the West (3) eliminate Spanish claims there (4) acquire a vast increase in territory.

7. In which of these acts did Jefferson's administration do the most to violate his previously held political philosophy? (1) The Embargo Act (2) the Barbary Wars (3) the purchase of Louisiana (4) the refusal of Marbury's commission.

8. Aaron Burr was not punished for treason because (1) there was no evidence of a treasonable plot (2) Chief Justice Marshall favored Burr in his conduct of the trial (3) Burr escaped into exile (4) it was proved he intended to attack Spanish territory.

9. In the Essex decision (1) Britain forbade neutral trade with France (2) the court held that free ships do not make free goods (3) Britain ruled that the indirect carrying of French West Indian produce by American ships was illegal (4) the right of impressment was upheld.

10. The *Chesapeake-Leopard* Affair aroused Americans against England for all reasons *except* which one? (1) The *Chesapeake* was an unarmed vessel (2) the attack occurred barely outside American waters (3) the *Chesapeake* was a naval vessel (4) the tricky manner in which the British stopped the Chesapeake was resented.

11. The Embargo Act (1) was endorsed by New England shippers (2) brought respect for American maritime rights (3) was repealed when no longer needed (4) failed almost completely to win its objectives.

12. Which of these events occurred last? (1) Ratification of the Twelfth Amendment (2) the decision of *Marbury v. Madison* (3) the Embargo Act (4) the *Chesapeake-Leopard* Affair.

13. All are causes of the War of 1812 *except* which one? (1) The desire of Western farmers for access to European markets (2) impatience of Westerners with Native American attacks (3) New England's impatience with British seizure of her ships (4) land hunger of Western frontiersmen.

14. Spain, in the War of 1812, was (1) completely neutral (2) an ally of the United States (3) an ally of Britain (4) an ally of France.

15. In the War of 1812 the most disastrous defeat of the British occurred at (1) New Orleans (2) Baltimore (3) the Battle of the Thames (4) Lake Erie.

16. The most extreme action taken by the Hartford Convention was to (1) recommend several amendments to the Constitution (2) recommend secession by New England (3) withdraw the militia from active service (4) nullify the embargo.

17. In the negotiation of the Treaty of Ghent the two outstanding American diplomats were (1) C. C. Pinckney and W. H. Harrison (2) Henry Clay and John Quincy Adams (3) Henry Clay and W. H. Harrison (4) John Adams and James Monroe.

18. Which was *not* a consequence of the War of 1812? (1) British respect for fighting ability of the American navy (2) destruction of Native American power east of the Mississippi River (3) British recognition of American maritime rights (4) decrease in sectional strife.

TRUE-FALSE

19. Jefferson's election represented a victory of the small farmers and plain people over a commercial aristocracy.

20. Jefferson took full advantage of his victory over the Federalists by wholesale removals of old officeholders and radical changes in government.

21. Jefferson practiced economy in government and worked to reduce the national debt.

22. The executive and judicial branches of the national government worked together in amicable relationship under Jefferson.

23. The direction of land legislation under Jefferson was inconsistent with the Jeffersonian political philosophy.

24. Georgia finally surrendered her land claims to the federal government on condition that Congress compensate the Yazoo claimants.

25. The Louisiana Purchase Treaty stated that West Florida and Texas were parts of the Louisiana Territory.

26. In one of his plots Aaron Burr planned to take part in a secession movement of New York and New England.

27. In the Essex Decision Britain ruled that the United States might engage in the shipment of goods from the French West Indies to France if such goods were first landed in the United States.

28. Even though both Britain and France captured American ships the profits were so great during the Napoleonic Wars that American shippers continued the trade.

29. The Nonintercourse Act permitted imports from the rest of the world but not from all parts.

30. Great Britain revoked her Orders-in-Council just before the United States declared war on her.

31. One of the most influential reasons the West favored war in 1812 was the opportunity it would give to break the power of the Native Americans in the West.

32. New England voted for Madison in 1812.

33. Failure to recharter the national bank left American finances in a sorry state during the War of 1812.

34. General Pakenham was responsible for capturing Washington.

35. After a great victory over the Creeks at Horseshoe Bend, Jackson went on to defeat the British forces attempting to take New Orleans.

36. Had the War of 1812 continued the American navy would undoubtedly have won the war at sea.

37. In the Treaty of Ghent the British made important concessions to the United States.

COMPLETION

38. Jefferson drew the architectural plans for his home at _____ .

39. As evidence of his friendship towards the Western farmers Jefferson won early repeal of the hated _____ Tax.

40. Jefferson's small gunboats built for the navy were derisively referred to by his enemies as the _____ fleet.

41. Peace with the Barbary States was finally dictated in 1815 by Commodore _____ .

42. The judges appointed by the outgoing President Adams on his last day in office came to be called the _____ judges.

43. In the case of _____ the Supreme Court asserted the right of judicial review.

44. In a move against the growing power of the Federal justices on the Supreme Court, the Republicans attempted to remove the intemperate Justice _____ .

45. The Land Law of 1800 reduced the minimum land purchase from 640 acres to _____ acres; in 1804 the minimum sale was further reduced to _____ acres.

46. The Yazoo land controversy resulted in the passage of the _____ Amendment to the Constitution.

47. Napoleon in the Treaty of _____ forced Spain to transfer Louisiana back to France.

48. Jefferson sent _____ to explore the Louisiana Territory in 1804.

49. In his treasonable plot in the West _____ tried to gain the help of another traitorous schemer named _____ but this general revealed the plot.

50. British seizure of sailors from American ships was known by the term _____ .

51. In his wars against England Napoleon tried to starve England by the effects of his _____ and _____ decrees; the British retaliated with their _____ .

52. Jefferson's first important measure to gain respect for American commercial rights was known as the _____ Act; it was succeeded by the _____ Act.

53. The War of 1812 was least popular in the _____ states.

54. The great leader of the Northwest Native Americans in the War of 1812 was _____ .

55. The militant Western Congressmen who favored the declaration of the War of 1812 were called the _____ .

56. General _____ won an important victory against the Native Americans and British at the Battle of the Thames.

57. General Andrew Jackson won a great victory over the British in the Battle of _____ .

58. The high point of sectional opposition to the War of 1812 came at the meeting known as the _____ .

59. The War of 1812 caused a great increase in the American spirit of _____ .

MATCHING

60. William Henry Harrison   a. Secretary of State under Jefferson

61 Toussaint L'Ouverture   b. Secretary of the Treasury under Jefferson

62. James Madison   c. Made an agreement with the United States that was soon revoked

63. John Randolph

64. Zebulon M. Pike   d. Began negotiations for the Louisiana Purchase

65. David Erskine   e. British general in the War of 1812

66. Oliver H. Perry   f. Sponsored more liberal land law in 1800

67. Albert Gallatin   g. Defeated General Le Clerc

68. Robert Livingston   h. Leader of the Quids

69. J. Q. Adams   i. Naval hero of the War of 1812

j. Helped negotiate the Treaty of Ghent

k. Led exploration of the Southern Rockies

CHRONOLOGY / CHAPTER 10

1803 Ohio admitted.

1806 Foreign trade stoppages foster American industry until 1816.

1807 Fulton's steamboat, *Clermont,* steamed up the Hudson.

1811 National Road begun.

1812 Louisiana admitted.
War of 1812 began, ended in 1814.

1816 Bank of the United States chartered again, protective tariff
passed, and other nationalistic measures.
Indiana admitted.

1817 Monroe inaugurated as President.
Bonus Bill for federal aid to roads vetoed; construction of
Erie Canal begun.
Mississippi admitted.
Jackson invaded Florida.
Rush-Bagot Agreement with Britain.

1818 Bank of the United States began to force state banks to
redeem paper money in specie.
Illinois admitted.
Convention of 1818 settled disputes with Great Britain.

1819 Panic caused by policies of the Bank of the United States.
Alabama admitted.
Adams-Onis Treaty.
McCulloch v. Maryland upheld constitutionality of the Bank.

1820 Land Act of 1820 lowered price of land.
Missouri Compromise. Maine admitted.

1821 Missouri admitted.

1823 Monroe Doctrine announced.

1824 John Quincy Adams elected President in House of
Representatives.

1825 Adams inaugurated President. Erie Canal completed.

1826 Anti-Mason movement began.

Chapter

10

A PERIOD OF STRONG NATIONALISM, 1815-1828

The American and French Revolutions inspired democratic nationalistic movements, and the Napoleonic Wars aroused national self-consciousness in Europe and America. Just as the nations of Europe arose against the foreign aggression of Napoleon so did the War of 1812 arouse a belated pride in America in its military victories over the British. In America people everywhere, convinced of the superiority of democracy over the European systems of monarchy and aristocracy, took a boastful pride in the new society they were creating.

NATIONALISTIC LEGISLATION FOR ECONOMIC DEVELOPMENTS

In 1815 President Madison, in the midst of a war scare with Great Britain, requested several measures with the twin purposes of improving the nation's defensive ability as well as serving some national goals. Subsequently, 1) the Second Bank of the United States was chartered to restore the national banking network that had been so badly missed during the War of 1812; 2) the Tariff of 1816 temporarily implemented the principle of protection; 3) appropriations were made to continue the Cumberland (National) Road from the capital to the Ohio River; 4) the army and navy were increased.

❂❂ **The Second Bank of the United States**—After the Jeffersonians allowed the charter of the Bank of the United States to expire in 1811, the state banks were left to themselves to supply the nation's currency needs. Bank notes in circulation doubled by 1816. Shortage of gold and silver in the West and South forced state banks to suspend specie payment and left the nation with a multiplicity of bank note issues of uncertain value. To halt the expansion of unsound currency, to stop paper money inflation, and to provide a federal depository, John C. Calhoun and Henry Clay moved to revive the national bank.

In 1816 Congress chartered for twenty years the Second Bank of the United States modeled after the earlier bank in organization and created for the same functions. The Second Bank of the United States differed 1) in having a much larger capitalization and 2) in provisions for branch banks.

The Panic of 1819—The Second Bank of the United States did not immediately check the excesses of the state banks but loaned its own bank notes lavishly. Land speculators borrowed bank notes in large amounts to buy government land, and land sales boomed. In 1818 the national bank suddenly began forcing the state banks to redeem their paper in specie. Banks had to demand payment of loans when due. A money panic ensued and all prices collapsed as debtors sold property to raise cash. Many debtors were forced into bankruptcy. The drastic action of the bank made it many enemies, particularly in the West. As consequences of the depression, many states passed more liberal bankruptcy laws and abolished imprisonment for debt. Congress in the Land Act of 1820 lowered the price of land to $1.25 an acre but abolished sales on credit.

○ **The Tariff of 1816**—The growth of nationalism, the increase in factories, and deliberate English dumping of textiles to crush the infant industry in America brought support for the first protective tariff in the United States. Tariff rates were increased to levels intended to favor American manufactures as well as to produce revenues for the treasury. Daniel Webster, representing still predominantly commercial Massachusetts, opposed the tariff; Henry Clay, responding to the interests of Kentucky's wool and hemp producers, favored it along with John C. Calhoun, temporarily out of step with his fellow South Carolinians. In time, Webster and Calhoun would both reverse their positions on the tariff.

Federal Aid to Internal Improvements—The rapid settlement of the western hinterlands created a dire need for roads and canals, but financing them imposed a heavy burden on the West. Nationalistic sentiment favored road and canal construction by the federal government as did the need to facilitate trade between the East and the West. In his 1815 message, Madison had warned that the Constitution had to be amended before federal money could be spent on interstate roads and canals. Accordingly, in 1817 he vetoed the Bonus Bill applying the $3 million bonus that the Second Bank of the United States had paid to the government for its charter to internal improvements although he approved of the purpose. Neither Madison nor Monroe prevented the use of revenues from land sales for the extension of the Cumberland Road, clearly a national road, but in 1822 Monroe vetoed appropriations for its repair. The major burden of financing internal improvements was regarded as a state function and generally was left to the states.

THE WESTWARD MOVEMENT

The westward movement gained momentum rapidly after the Revolution. The frontier advance, slowed by the War of 1812 and accompanying Native American uprisings, was quickly resumed after 1815. The movement may be likened to a procession. At the head were hunters, traders and explorers; after them came subsistence pioneer farmers. When progressive farmers had taken over and population density reached about six persons per square mile, the frontier vanished or moved farther out. The largest westward surge up to this time, that after the War of 1812, is called the Great Migration.

Causes of the Great Migration—1) The pacification and removal of Native American tribes during and after the War of 1812 opened all lands east of the Mississippi to settlement. 2) The exhaustion of old cultivated soils in New England and on the eastern seaboard in the South along with the magnet of rich, virgin soils in the West spurred the migration of farmers. 3) Generous terms for purchase of land, beginning with the Harrison Land Act of 1800, invited settlers into the public domain. 4) Transportation facilities provided by such improvements as the National Road and the Erie Canal opened the way. 5) And there was the opportunity to escape political, social, and economic discrimination in the static communities of the East and of Europe.

The Routes of Migration—Up until 1830 pioneers took road, canal, and steamboat routes as follows. Beginning in the North, 1) after 1825 the Erie Canal offered a through route by barge for migrants from New England and New York into Lake Erie; before the canal was completed these migrants took the Genesee Road from Albany to Buffalo. These settlers moved into the plains south of the Great Lakes. 2) In Pennsyl-vania they took the Lancaster Turnpike at Philadelphia to Lancaster, crossed the mountains at Bedford, then to Pittsburgh and the Ohio. Picturesque flatboats with family and livestock could be seen in large numbers floating down the Ohio during heavy migration.

To the South, 3) the Cumberland (National) Road from Maryland, following the route of Braddock's march, also gave access to the Ohio valley, for migrants from the South. On this route there were years when an almost steady stream of migrants were seen walking, pushing wheelbarrows, driving livestock loaded with their few possessions, or riding in carts and wagons. Pittsburgh, the focus of the routes from the East, became the early gateway to the West, not only for pioneer families but for trading and exploring expeditions. 4) Much further south, pioneers from Virginia and the Carolinas took the Wilderness Road across the Cumberland Gap into Kentucky and Tennessee. 5) After the early 1820s settlers rode steamboats from New Orleans up the Mississippi and its tributaries.

Migration was not organized by large groups. Most migrants were separate families of pioneer farmers.

○ Influence of the Frontier on American Character—As early as the late colonial period, commentators suggested that the colonists had evolved from being simply transplanted Europeans into a new nationality, Americans. The success of the War for Independence and the reaffirmation of American independence by its "victory" in the War of 1812 furthered this idea. In 1893, Frederic Jackson Turner believed that the "existence of an area of free land, its continuous recession, and the advance of American settlement westward, explains American development." It instilled character traits such as independence, self-confidence, individualism, inventiveness, and adaptability. But later writers have charged that Turner overlooked frequent conservatism and imitativeness on the frontier, the fact that many emigrants moved in ethnic groups and maintained European ways in their communities as long as possible. He also neglected the influence of Native Americans and did not take notice of the presence of African Americans in the West. Whatever effect the frontier might have had on the American character, it is certain that it was not the only influence producing the somewhat vulgar, bumptious nationalists of the early nineteenth century.

The West in National Politics—In 1803 Ohio was admitted to the Union and Louisiana in 1812. States resulting from the Great Migration were admitted in rapid succession—Indiana in 1816, Mississippi in 1817, Illinois in 1818, and Alabama in 1819. Population in the West continued to grow even more rapidly after statehood. When Western states after 1820 constituted an important bloc, lively competition ensued between the North and South to win the political alliance of these Western senators and congressmen. Westerners wanted cheap land, internal improvements, and were inclined to favor high tariffs and cheap money. The early political influence of New England diminished as the West grew in population.

GROWTH OF INDUSTRY AND TRANSPORTATION

American business life until the War of 1812 was centered in such commercial activities as shipping and trade. America exchanged raw materials for English and other European manufactures instead of developing any extensive domestic industry. English manufactures were superior, and she enjoyed certain advantages over America in producing them. After independence, American transportation facilities were greatly improved.

○ Causes of the Rise of Factories—The stoppages of trade by embargo after 1806 and by the War of 1812 sharply curtailed the importation of manufactures. The American market for manufactures now belonged to American producers. This proved a great stimulus to industry. Investment capital that had been absorbed by commerce now flowed into manufacturing. Liberal bounties were offered by state and local governments, and manufacturing was encouraged as patriotic enterprise. The textile industry, always at the forefront of industrialization, grew rapidly along with the manufacture of iron goods, leather goods, woodenware, and paper.

❍ Location of the Factories—New England became the leading center of industry, especially in textiles, because 1) manufacturing came to replace the New England mercantile activities; 2) New England had abundant water power and labor, and 3) her shippers and merchants were prepared to distribute finished goods to American markets to the south.

In the Middle Colonies iron and iron goods manufacturing developed because of the abundance of iron ore and nearby coal deposits. The South gave much thought to developing industry but soon concentrated on growing cotton and other agricultural raw materials which proved more profitable for the employment of slave labor.

Significance of Advances in Technology—The opportunities for profit in ever-widening domestic and world trade and the relatively high cost of labor motivated enterprising American businessmen and inventors to devise machines and other means of increasing production. Technological advance has been an outstanding determinant in the expansion of the Western World. More than anything, technological improvements in transportation, industry, and agriculture made possible the unexpectedly rapid conquest of the wilderness and the settlement of the frontier regions.

❍❍ Advances in Technology—John Fitch invented the steamboat in 1790, but Robert Fulton navigated the first practical vessel in 1807 when the *Clermont* steamed upstream on the Hudson. Steamboats were ideally suited for the rivers of the Midwest as they could move on very shallow water and their need for fuel could easily be met from the abundant forests; by 1830 there were more than 200 steamboats on the Mississippi. New Orleans was to become the center of the steamboat traffic that served the rivers of the West and the seaports of the East and of Europe.

Eli Whitney invented the cotton gin in 1793 and removed the bottleneck to the expansion of cotton plantations in the South. Cotton cultivation spread so rapidly that it was an influence in the Senate's eliminating an article of Jay's Treaty in 1795 that prohibited its export. Even more important in the long run was Whitney's application of the principle of interchangeable parts, basic to assembly line, mass production industries.

❍❍ Roads and Canals—Turnpikes offered all-weather overland transportation for the first time in America. The first of these, the Lancaster

Turnpike from Philadelphia to Lancaster, was built in 1794. Turnpikes were toll roads, often employing macadamized engineering of the roadbed. The success of the Lancaster road set off a wave of private financing, construction, and operation of turnpikes. Many were aided by state and local governments but could not operate profitably and eventually all had to be taken into the public roads system.

Water transportation offered the best hope for conquering space, before railroads were proved feasible, after 1830. The Erie Canal, remarkable for its day, was begun in 1817 through the persuasion of DeWitt Clinton, Governor of New York. Completed by 1825, the canal carried barges from New York City to Buffalo on Lake Erie. After this, New York City increased her lead in population and commerce over Boston and Philadelphia. The example it set for cheap, speedy transportation started a canal building boom in America. By 1824 the Pennsylvania Canal System, including the engineering marvel of a portage railroad system across the mountains, connected Philadelphia and Pittsburgh. Eventually several canals were built to connect the Great Lakes with tributaries of the Ohio and the Mississippi. Canals were financed mainly by the states; some were privately financed.

AGREEMENTS WITH BRITAIN AND SPAIN

Several minor controversies with Great Britain were settled by commissions as provided by the Treaty of Ghent. With Spain, the problems relating to Florida were settled by its acquisition.

Negotiations with Britain—Several agreements after the War of 1812 can almost be viewed as part of that treaty. In 1815 a commercial treaty substantially expanded commerce with Britain. An 1817 agreement, the Rush-Bagot Agreement, provided for naval disarmament on the Great Lakes, paving the way for the eventual abandonment of fortifications on the Canadian border. The Convention of 1818 fixed the boundary with Canada at the 49th parallel from the Lake of the Woods to the Rocky Mountains, with the area beyond the mountains to be occupied jointly. American fishermen were also allowed to use the waters off Newfoundland.

Florida Before 1819—Following the Treaty of Paris, 1783, Spain regained Florida from Britain. West Florida, the panhandle extending from the Perdido River westward along the Gulf coast to the Mississippi, was the first part to fall to the Americans. Americans wanted Florida because of the proximity of Florida to New Orleans, the desire to navigate the rivers flowing through Spanish Florida into the Gulf, the fertile soil, and the failure of Spain to suppress border outlaws and Native Americans there.

The United States acquired Florida in four separate annexations: 1) The disputed Yazoo Strip along the northern border was conceded in the Pinckney Treaty. 2) West Florida was taken in 1810. American settlers, encouraged by American officials, revolted against Spanish authority and President Madison proclaimed it American territory. 3) The occupation of West Florida was completed in 1813 when General Wilkinson took Mobile as ordered to do. 4) In 1817 during the Seminole War with the United States General Andrew Jackson invaded the main part of the province, known as East Florida, and took Pensacola. The invasion convinced the Spanish they ought to sell Florida to the United States.

✪✪ **The Adams-Onis Treaty (1819)**—The so-called Florida Treaty is more appropriately known as the Adams-Onis Treaty since it settled more than the Florida question. Jackson's invasion raised doubts that the Spanish could hold Florida and John Quincy Adams convinced Onis that Spain ought to sell it. The treaty provided: 1) for the cession of Florida to the United States in return for American settlement of claims of her citizens against Spain. 2) Equally important, the other main provision defined the boundary between the Louisiana Purchase and Spanish possessions to the southwest. Roughly, the boundary was drawn along the present boundaries of Texas on the east and north, thence along the Arkansas River to the Rockies and along the 42nd parallel to the Pacific. Spain thus surrendered her claims above the 42nd parallel to the United States in return for the surrender of American claims to Texas. The ratification of the treaty was delayed until 1821 because of a dispute over land titles in Florida.

JOHN MARSHALL AND THE SUPREME COURT

John Marshall, a Federalist, was appointed by President Adams as Chief Justice of the Supreme Court in 1801. Marshall served on the Court as Chief Justice for 34 years, longer than any other justice has served in that position. During this long tenure he stamped his strong influence upon the Court and its decisions.

✪✪✪ **Marshall's Influence**—John Marshall, another Virginian, fought in the American Revolution. He attended William and Mary College and soon made himself recognized as a leading lawyer and politician in his home state. He served as one of the commissioners sent to France in what came to be known as the XYZ Affair. After his appointment to the Court, his kindly personality and convincing logic won over other members, including Republican appointees, so that the Court came to reflect his leadership. As the Republicans turned more nationalistic they came to approve many of his decisions. Time after time the Court established and exercised its power to declare acts of Congress and the states unconstitutional. Marshall's decisions enhanced the power of the federal government and helped to create a more secure climate for business by reinforcing respect for business contracts.

❍ **Two Early Decisions**—In the case of *Marbury v. Madison* (1803), discussed earlier, the Court asserted the prerogative of judicial review.

In *Fletcher v. Peck* (1810) the Court declared unconstitutional the act of the legislature of Georgia annulling the contracts providing for the sale of land to the Yazoo companies. The decision is significant for two reasons: 1) it upheld the sanctity of business contracts by declaring that contracts could not be canceled except by mutual agreement of contracting parties, and 2) the decision asserted the Court's power to declare unconstitutional acts of state legislatures. Several other cases established the power of the Supreme Court to overrule state legislatures and state courts in legislation or in decisions in conflict with the Federal constitution.

❍ **Dartmouth College Case (1819)**—The Republican legislature of New Hampshire annulled the charter of Dartmouth College because it was a center of Federalist influence. The Supreme Court declared the annulment to be null and void. The decision helped protect private schools from political interference and made it more difficult to regulate business corporations. The charter as an obligation of contract could not be impaired by a state government. States now began to add clauses permitting unilateral revocation or amendment to all new charters.

❍❍❍*McCulloch v. Maryland* **(1819)**—A conflict between state and federal governments arose when Maryland levied a tax on bank notes issued by a branch of the Bank of the United States in Maryland. In this famous decision 1) Marshall gave legal recognition to the doctrine of implied powers and recognized the constitutionality of the national bank. 2) The right of a state to tax an instrumentality of the federal government was denied because "the power to tax is the power to destroy."

Gibbons v. Ogden **(1824)**—The state of New York granted a monopoly of steam navigation in the state. In this case Marshall extended the meaning of the commerce clause in the Constitution to include transportation. The decision held that Congress was supreme in all aspects of interstate commerce and could not be limited by the states in this area. This interpretation of the commerce clause was essential to developing the economic unity of the United States. The decision helped establish the large federal powers over interstate commerce.

THE STRUGGLE OVER MISSOURI

Dispute over the slavery question suddenly interrupted the era of good feelings between the sections when Missouri applied for statehood in 1819.

○○ **The Tallmadge Amendment**—Representative James Tallmadge of New York introduced an amendment to the Missouri statehood bill that would have 1) prohibited the further introduction of slaves into Missouri and 2) would have freed at the age of 25 all children of slaves born in Missouri after its admission to statehood. Sharp, angry debate over the right of Congress to legislate on the slavery issue ensued. The decision as to whether Missouri would become a slave or free state was critical since it threatened to upset the hitherto fortuitous balance of free and slave states in the Senate. The free states already had more votes in the House. The South feared that the prohibition of slavery by Congress would set a precedent leading ultimately to the prohibition of slavery.

○○○ **The Missouri Compromise**—The Tallmadge Amendment failed to pass the Senate. The first break towards the solution of the issue began in 1820 when the admission of Maine (a part of Massachusetts at the time) was proposed. The essential provisions of the Missouri Compromise provided: 1) that Missouri be admitted as a slave state and Maine to be admitted as a free state and 2) that the territory north of the line of 36' 30° be "forever free." This permitted new states admitted south of the line to become slave states. This appeared to have settled the issue until Missouri adopted a constitution prohibiting free African Americans from entering the state. Antislavery members now refused to recognize Missouri. Finally at Clay's suggestion a resolution passed Congress requiring that Missouri never enact laws denying citizens of other states their rights under the Constitution. In 1821 Missouri was admitted.

The angry debate over the admission of Missouri was significant for several reasons: 1) The North had expressed its moral objections to slavery and the South now felt forced to defend its "peculiar institution." 2) The South began denying the right of Congress to exclude slaves from the territories. 3) This was the first assertion of the only politically feasible antislavery position in American politics: opposition to the extension of slavery.

THE MONROE DOCTRINE

This statement of foreign policy indicated the determination of the United States to prevent Europe from interfering in affairs of the Americas.

○○ **Background of Monroe's Statement**—During Spain's involvement in the Napoleonic Wars, her colonies in Latin America seized the opportunity to declare their independence. By 1882 most of Latin America had successfully established its independence but Spain refused to recognize the new governments. The United States welcomed the independence of these nations that had, like herself, thrown off the yoke of the European powers. Americans, who had been excluded from Latin American trade by the Spanish monopoly, were eager to establish commercial relations. The United States recognized their independence in 1822.

Russia in 1812 extended her interests southwards from Alaska along the Pacific Coast by establishing Fort Ross just north of San Francisco. In 1821 the Russian Czar proclaimed a monopoly of trading rights as far south as the 51st parallel and warned ships of other countries not to enter waters within 100 miles off the coast. Monroe and his Secretary of State John Quincy Adams were alarmed by this expansionism of Russia.

✪✪✪ **Europe's Attitude Towards Latin America**—The conservative reaction in Europe following the defeat of Napoleon did not approve of the revolutionary events in Latin America. Beginning with the Holy Alliance of Austria, Russia, and Prussia, the European monarchies determined to suppress democratic uprisings and preserve peace against revolutionary movements in Europe. The enlarged association of the European powers, called the European Concert, soon included France, where the monarchy had been restored, and Spain. The members of the Concert agreed to the selection of various members to apply military intervention to suppress republican revolutions and actually did so in Italy and Spain.

It was well known that the King of Spain would welcome aid in reestablishing control in her American colonies. England opposed intervention in the affairs of other nations of Europe and was especially alarmed at the threat of restoration of the colonies to Spain. She had begun exploiting South American markets and wished to continue selling there; she also feared that France might assist Spain in the reconquest of South America, receiving colonies in return and recovering her international position.

✪✪ **The British Proposal**—The British Whigs shared a common interest with the United States in preventing Russian, French, or Spanish expansion or intervention in America. George Canning, the Foreign Secretary, wrote Richard Rush, American minister to England, and proposed a joint declaration in which Britain and the United States would 1) disclaim any intention of acquiring Spanish-American territory and 2) warn other nations not to interfere in America. The proposal was referred to President Monroe.

Monroe called upon former Presidents Jefferson and Madison for advice about taking such an important stand that might involve the United States in war as an ally of England. The former Presidents favored the joint declaration. The more astute John Quincy Adams urged that the United States take an independent position and not tag along behind Britain in the statement of policy. Besides, the self-denying clause in reference to Spanish America might embarrass the United States if it should undertake expansion to the south.

✪✪✪ **Statement of the Doctrine**—The wisdom of Adams's view came to be accepted. Monroe, therefore, stated the famous doctrine in a written message to Congress. Briefly, it stated that 1) America was no longer open to colonization by European powers and 2) that the United States would not interfere in the local affairs of European nations and 3) warned Europe not to interfere with the republic form of government in America.

The pronouncement had no great immediate importance. European powers thought it unnecessary and presumptuous and Latin Americans realized that Britain, not the United States, protected them from reconquest. Later the Monroe Doctrine was employed to prevent intervention of European powers in Latin America. It was used later to justify America's traditional policy of isolationism. Theodore Roosevelt used it to justify intervention in Latin-American affairs by the United States to preclude European intervention there.

THE ELECTION OF 1824

The presidential campaign of 1824 marked the end of the Era of Good Feeling and the revival of strong sectionalism; this is indicated by the sectional origins of the candidates.

✪✪ **Political Background of the Election**—In 1820 James Monroe was supported by all sections of the country and the Federalists failed to nominate an opponent to him. The Federalist Party had completely dissolved; therefore, neither party saw fit to hold a congressional caucus to nominate candidates as was done before 1820.

In 1824 the democratic spirit of the country refused to permit a small group of congressmen and senators to choose the candidate for the Republican Party. Less than a third of the Republicans in Congress attended a caucus that nominated William H. Crawford. The other candidates received nominations chiefly from the state legislatures or at mass meetings. The candidates were chosen for their personal popularity and their identification with the sections of their origin. The rivalry was thus personal and sectional and not between national parties.

✪ **Crawford, Candidate of the Southern Planters**—The candidate named by the small Republican caucus and intended to maintain the succession of the Virginia dynasty was William H. Crawford of Georgia. Formerly a strong nationalist, Crawford had now swung back to emphasizing states' rights. A representative of the planter aristocracy, he was an able and independent-minded leader. Crawford was the politicians' favorite in the race until a physician's treatment incapacitated him late in 1823. He was still a semi-invalid during the presidential contest in 1824.

○ **Adams, Candidate of the Industrial Northeast**—Another very able candidate, John Quincy Adams, son of John Adams and the choice of New England, enjoyed great advantages in the race. His long experience as a diplomat, his education and high-mindedness, his service as Senator from Massachusetts and as Secretary of State under Monroe qualified him for the office. Unfortunately he was plainly ambitious, cold, unpopular, and somewhat inept in politics. In his political views he served as a spokesman for the new industrialism of New England. As a nationalist, he favored high tariffs, the national bank and internal improvements.

○ **Clay, Candidate of the Upper Class West**—Henry Clay of Kentucky, practical-minded, popular, and shrewd, began his career as a lawyer. As a member of the United States House of Representatives he was chosen repeatedly as its Speaker. He served on the peace commission in making the Treaty of Ghent. He saw that a politician should represent various interests and earned his reputation as the "Great Compromiser." Clay favored what he called the "American System" that summed up the Whig policies after 1830. The American System called for tariffs to build up national industries for the benefit of the whole country. Tariff revenues were to be used for internal improvements to help not only the West but the whole national economy.

Jackson, Candidate of the New Democracy—Andrew Jackson, who grew up in the Carolina and Tennessee back country, served in the War for Independence while only a boy. He held several high political offices but won national popularity as a soldier-hero fighting Native Americans, Spanish, and British. Jackson personified the desirable and undesirable qualities of Westerners. Politicians recognized the value of his popular appeal. In the campaign he took no strong stand on controversial issues. He opposed the caucus system as being undemocratic, argued the need for new blood in office, and stood for the right of the common people to a greater voice in government. He had the support of workers in the East and, in fact, had more national support than any other candidate. John C. Calhoun of South Carolina as Jackson's running mate strengthened Jackson's cause over the South.

○○ **Election Results**—Jackson led with 99 electoral votes representing all sections except New England. Adams ranked second with all electoral votes of New England and New York state. Crawford, third, won the votes of Virginia and Georgia. Clay, winning in Ohio, Kentucky, and Missouri, got almost as many votes as Crawford.

Since Jackson did not receive a majority, the election had to be decided in the House of Representatives. Clay as Speaker of the House exercised powerful influence there. He favored Adams who approved his American System which the other candidates did not endorse. Clay could not be expected to vote for his hated rival Jackson, or for Crawford who was incapacitated. Clay's influence elected Adams.

OO Political Consequences—Upon taking office President Adams chose Clay as his Secretary of State. This office was the traditional route to the presidency; it seemed that Adams and Clay had bargained to make each other President! In the first place the Jacksonians argued that their candidate, with the plurality, was the popular choice and should have been supported by Clay. Now they cried "corrupt bargain" and said Clay had cheated the people out of their choice. Clay never lived down the untrue and malicious charge.

The next election campaign began immediately as politicians began gathering around Jackson. The Jacksonians soon came to be known as the Democratic-Republican Party or Democratic Party; the Adams and Clay forces called themselves the National Republicans until 1832. After 1832 they called themselves "Whigs."

THE ADMINISTRATION OF JOHN QUINCY ADAMS

The Adams administration accomplished little. Jackson's followers vilified Adams and Clay throughout the term. After the congressional elections of 1826 Adams' opposition gained control of the House. Constructive measures supported by Adams were ridiculed by his opponents.

O The Adams Program—Adams met an unfortunate response to the nationalistic program he requested in his first message to Congress. He went on record in favor of a tougher bankruptcy law, the Bank of the United States, internal improvements financed by revenues from protective tariffs, a department of the interior, a national university, and the advancement of scientific knowledge. The Democrats, as the opposition soon came to be known, criticized centralization of power and ridiculed the novel proposals to aid education and science.

Aid for internal improvements was voted more generously than ever before but not enough to meet the President's requests. Adams tried to secure just treatment for the Creek Native Americans in Georgia and lost what support he had there to Jackson, the Native American fighter.

The Panama Congress (1826)—Clay enthusiastically favored the meeting, initiated by Simon Bolivar, of the American nations at the Panama Congress. The meeting was planned in order to promote democratic institutions and trade. The Democrats sought to make political hay out of the naming of the delegates to the meeting and for a long time delayed the necessary appropriation. The Panama Congress adjourned before an American delegate could get started.

❍❍ The Tariff Issue—The growth of manufacturing in the northeast increased the support there for higher tariffs. Rates were increased in the Tariff of 1824, but wool growers and manufacturers met to draft a bill for still higher rates. Clay and Adams supported the higher schedules. In 1828 the Jackson forces with Southern connivance devised a complicated measure incorporating rates so high that it would be defeated—so they thought. The bill passed when a slight change was made to please New England. New England's principal interest was now manufacturing and its representatives supported protective tariffs.

The Tariff of 1828 raised rates so high that the South called it the "Tariff of Abominations." Calhoun of South Carolina led his state to issue its *Exposition and Protest* against the use of the tariff power to provide protection instead of revenue, as intended by the Constitution according to Calhoun. The paper asserted the right of "interposition" of a state against unconstitutional action of Congress. The arguments of the Kentucky and Virginia Resolutions were revived now as a call to action.

❍ The Anti-Mason Movement—A movement against the Masonic Lodge that began in 1826 was exploited by New York politicians to turn public sentiment against Jackson, who was a Mason. It began with the publication of a pamphlet by a former Mason, in which he claimed to reveal the secrets of Masonry. The former Mason was kidnapped, taken to Niagara Falls, and nothing more was heard of him. The Lodge was already disliked in the West because of its exclusiveness. The anti-Mason movement developed into a political party as new issues were added to attract popular support. The anti-Masons are of significance because 1) it was the first third party in American politics. 2) Men who rose with the anti-Masons later joined the Whigs and still later many became prominent Republicans. 3) The party held the first national nominating convention to select a presidential candidate (1831).

❍❍ The Election of 1828—The tariff issue and the American System were the leading constructive issues in the campaign, but the emphasis was upon personal vilification. "Dirty" politics were actively employed by both sides as appeals were made to the newly enfranchised masses. The worst kind of slander and the old cry of "corrupt bargain" were repeated against Adams and Clay. Jackson too was victimized by the National Republicans who created a scandal of adultery against him and turned his crude frontier fights against him. Jackson and Calhoun won by 183 electoral votes to 83 for Adams.

CHAPTER BOOK LIST

Ammon, Harry, *James Monroe* (1971). One-volume biography.
Baker, Leonard, *John Marshall* (1974). The standard biography.

Bemis, S.F., *John Quincy Adams and The Foundations of American Foreign Policy* (1949). A diplomatic history of the period 1795–1829.

Billington, Ray A., *Westward Expansion* (1974).

Boorstin, David, *The Americans: The National Experience* (Random).

Corwin, John, *John Marshall and The Constitution* (1919). Brief book by a student of constitutional history.

Dangerfield, George, *Awakening of American Nationalism 1815–1828* (Harper & Row).

Dangerfield, George, *The Era of Good Feelings* (1952). Well-written synthesis.

Eaton, Clement, *Henry Clay and The Art of American Politics* (Little, Brown).

Gates, Paul W., *The Farmer's Age: Agriculture: 1815–1860* (1960).

North, Douglas C., *The Economic Growth of the United States: 1790–1860* (1961).

Perkins, Dexter, *The Monroe Doctrine, 1823–1826* (1927). The standard study.

Prucha, Francis P., *American Indian Policy in the Formative Years* (1962).

Remini, Robert V., *The Election of Andrew Jackson* (1963). Brief and lively.

Taylor, George R., *The Transportation Revolution, 1815–1860* (1951).

REVIEW QUESTIONS

MULTIPLE CHOICE

1. In the results of the war at sea in the War of 1812 the British (1) suffered serious losses only on the Great Lakes (2) suffered no serious losses due to American action (3) nearly always won in ship-to-ship duels with American warships (4) suffered frightful losses of commercial shipping due to American action.

2. In 1816 the Republicans were prepared to charter a new Bank of the United States because (1) they had absorbed most of the Federalists (2) experience in the War of 1812 showed the need for the Bank (3) their desire to prevent the revival of the Federalist Party (4) the need to hold Western loyalty to the party.

3. The Tariff of 1816 was passed (1) mainly to increase federal revenues (2) to win political support for the Republicans (3) to prevent British manufacturers from crushing new American industries (4) without any support from the South.

4. Which of the following statements about the pattern of westward migration is *not* true? (1) Streams of migration often followed available land or water transportation routes (2) migration very often followed the same lines of latitude (3) prosperity rather than depression was accompanied by the heavier migration (4) migrants were more likely to originate in the East rather than from the area nearest to that being occupied.

5. Which roadway to the West was the same as the Cumberland Road? (1) The National Road (2) the Wilderness Road (3) the Cumberland Gap (4) the Genesee Road.

6. The frontier developed several traits of character in Americans. Which is the exception? (1) Energetic, hard-working (2) world-mindedness and doubts about democracy (3) boastfulness and optimistic attitudes (4) initiative and self-reliance.

7. Which was the most important immediate cause of the rise of manufacturing in the United States (1) Growth of the textile industry (2) New England water power (3) stoppages of trade by the embargoes and the War of 1812 (4) patriotic appeals and the growth of nationalism.

8. Which is *not* a correct explanation of the delayed rise of manufacturing in the United States? (1) English manufactures were of better quality than American (2) investment capital was employed more profitably in shipping and trade (3) interruption of trade by wars (4) the abundance of raw materials.

9. The National Road (1) was financed by the states (2) was eventually extended to St. Louis (3) was not an all-weather road (4) had its repairs financed by tolls collected by the states.

10. By the Rush-Bagot Agreement the United States and Britain (1) demilitarized the Great Lakes (2) agreed to divide Oregon along the 49th parallel (3) settled the Maine boundary line (4) agreed not to build forts on the 49th parallel.

11. By the Adams-Onis Treaty (1) the United States acquired the Yazoo Strip (2) Adams gave up the American claim to Cuba (3) the United States acquired Florida (4) Spain gave up her claim to Texas.

12. Which of these decisions made it more difficult for the state governments to regulate business corporations? (1) Dartmouth College case (2) *Marbury v. Madison* (3) *Cohen v. Virginia* (4) *Gibbons v. Ogden*.

13. In *Fletcher v. Peck* the Supreme Court held that (1) a state could not enact a law impairing the validity of a contract (2) the federal government controls interstate traffic on rivers serving as a boundary between states (3) Georgia could not deprive Native Americans of their reservation lands (4) "The power to tax is the power to destroy."

14. In *McCulloch v. Maryland* the Supreme Court did all of the following *except* (1) declare that the obligation of contract could not be revoked by a state legislature (2) declare that the "power to tax is the power to destroy" (3) uphold the doctrine of implied powers (4) deny the right of a state to tax an instrumentality of the federal government.

15. The Tallmadge Amendment was hotly debated because it (1) was designed to make Missouri a free state (2) sought to legislate upon slavery in the territories (3) threatened to introduce slavery into Missouri (4) called for the immediate emancipation of slaves in Missouri.

16. The debate over the admission of Missouri to statehood is significant for all *except:* (1) it caused the South to rationalize the institution of slavery (2) it led to Southern denial of the right of Congress to exclude slavery from the territories (3) it delayed the admission of Maine (4) threats of secession were voiced by both North and South.

17. The country not belonging to the Holy Alliance was (1) Russia (2) Great Britain (3) Austria (4) Prussia.

18. The Monroe Doctrine in effect stated that (1) Europe and America were separate and neither should interfere in the internal affairs of the other (2) the Holy Alliance would not be permitted to reconquer Spanish America (3) America was subject only to colonization by the United States (4) the United States would defend democratic governments everywhere.

19. All were provisions of Clay's American System except which one? (1) High tariffs to protect infant industries (2) federal financing of internal improvements (3) low tariffs and state support of internal improvements (4) a national bank with branches in the states.

20. Which statement is *not* true regarding the candidates in the election of 1824? (1) They represented different sections (2) most were nominated by state legislatures or mass meetings (3) all were well known (4) each represented opposing political parties.

21. The correct ranking of the candidates in the election of 1824 in order of electoral votes received is (1) Jackson, Adams, Crawford, and Clay (2) Adams, Jackson, Clay, Crawford (3) Jackson, Clay, Adams, Crawford (4) Adams, Clay, Jackson, Crawford.

22. As President, John Quincy Adams favored all *except* (1) higher tariffs—(2) reduced federal spending (3) the Bank of the United States (4) internal improvements federally financed.

23. The presidential election of 1828 (1) resulted in a victory for Jacksonian Democracy (2) vindicated the policies of Adams (3) was a clean campaign (4) represented a victory of business interests.

TRUE-FALSE

24. In the early nineteenth century, the South had hoped that industry would be established in their section of the nation.

25. By 1820 Republican political attitudes had changed so much that they voted liberal appropriations and assumed the major burden of road building.

26. By 1820 the depleted fertility of soils in the older states drove farmers westward in search of new, fertile soils.

27. Pittsburgh did not serve as a gateway to the West for either pioneers or exploring parties.

28. Several new states were admitted to the Union from 1812 to 1820.

29. The principle of interchangeable parts was first applied by Eli Whitney.

30. The large eastern seaport cities waited for the development of the railroads for drawing in the Western commerce instead of building canals.

31. The American invasion of Florida in 1817 convinced the Spanish they could not hold it if the Americans should decide to take it.

32. In addition to losing Florida, Spain lost nearly all of her American colonies after 1815.

33. Marshall's influence as Chief Justice was almost as great as that of any justice since his time although he served only briefly.

34. As the Republicans elected one president after another they became more and more like the Federalists.

35. Marshall's decisions strongly upheld the sanctity of business contracts.

36. Marshall's most significant decision was his declaration that a corporation is a person having the rights of any citizen.

37. The Missouri Compromise provided that territories north of the 32nd parallel would be free and those south of it would be slave.

38. The reactionary monarchies of Europe after 1815 sought to suppress republican revolutionary movements.

39. England's interest in Latin-American independence grew chiefly out of her idealistic desire to promote democracies everywhere.

40. The notion of warning the Continental powers to stay out of Latin America originated with the British Foreign Secretary.

41. The Monroe Doctrine assumed enormous significance in international law immediately.

42. The Monroe Doctrine came to be used to uphold American isolationism.

43. Of the presidential candidates in 1824 Clay and Adams held the most dissimilar political beliefs.

44. Jackson's well-defined political program accounts for his great popular appeal in 1824.

45. John Quincy Adams' constructive program of nationalistic legislation was defeated by demagogues who misrepresented it.

46. The election of Jackson in 1828 brought a "revolution" in American politics comparable to the "Revolution of 1800."

COMPLETION

47. The Second Bank of the United States was chartered in the year _____ for a period of _____ years.

48. When the Bank of the United States began forcing state banks to redeem paper in specie it precipitated the _____ .

49. The first protective tariff was enacted in the year _____ .

50. After 1825 the _____ offered the greatest route for westward migration north of Pennsylvania.

51. Migrants from the South who wished to float down the Ohio River, first traveled over the _____ or _____ Road to reach the Ohio valley; migrants taking the route through Kentucky first went through the Gap to gain access to the _____ Road.

52. The cotton gin was invented in the year _____ .

53. The _____ Turnpike was the first important American turnpike built.

54. The first great canal built in America was the _____ Canal.

55. Britain and the United States agreed to demilitarize the Great Lakes in the _____ Agreement, but the boundary was extended along the 49th parallel by the _____ . In the latter settlement Britain and the United States agreed that Oregon would be subject to _____ .

56. The United States acquired the remainder of Florida in the _____ Treaty in the year _____ .

57. In the case of _____ the Supreme Court said Georgia could not cancel the Yahoo contracts.

58. The Bank of the United States was declared constitutional in the case of _____ .

59. The federal power over interstate commerce was greatly enlarged in the case of _____ .

60. The debate over the admission of Missouri began with the _____ Amendment; at the same time Missouri was admitted _____ was also admitted.

61. Russia extended her claims southward from Alaska and in 1812 built in California a settlement named _____ .

62. The first alliance in Europe formed to uphold the principle of monarchy was known as the _____ and included the three powers of _____ .

63. The statesman who influenced most the final decision shaping the Monroe Doctrine as stated in the year _____ was _____ .

64. New England's candidate in 1824 was _____ . When Adams named his Secretary of State his opponents immediately charged there had been an agreement known as a _____ .

65. An attempt under Adams to provide closer relations in Latin America was made at the _____ .

66. In 1828 in his _____ Calhoun condemned the Tariff of 1828 as unconstitutional.

67. The first third party in the United States was the _____ Party.

MATCHING

68. James Madison   a. Built the Erie Canal

69. Robert Fulton   b. Upheld federal power by court decisions

70. Eli Whitney   c. Vetoed the Bonus Bill in 1817

71. DeWitt Clinton   d. Secretary of State under John Quincy Adams

72. Andrew Jackson   e. Made proposal leading to the Monroe Doctrine

73. John Marshall   f. Caused great expansion of cotton plantations

74. George Canning   g. Originally suggested the Monroe Doctrine

75. William H. Crawford   h. Presidential candidate of the Southern aristocracy in 1824

76. John C. Calhoun

77. Henry Clay   i. Developed the first successful steamboat

     j. Close political ally of Jackson's until 1830

     k. Invaded Florida

CHRONOLOGY / CHAPTER 11

1821 Stephen F. Austin began American settlement in Texas.
1828 Jackson (Dem.) elected President.
Tariff of Abominations passed.
1829 Jackson inaugurated as President.
1830 Webster-Hayne debates over nullification theory.
Jackson-Calhoun confrontation at Jefferson Day banquet.
Jackson vetoed Maysville Road Bill.
1832 Jackson reelected after veto of Bank Bill.
Tariff of 1832 failed to reduce rates.
Nullification Ordinance passed by South Carolina.
Jackson issued Nullification Proclamation.
1833 "Force Bill" passed. Compromise Tariff passed.
1836 Texans won independence at the Battle of San Jacinto.
Distribution Bill signed.
Specie Circular issued.
1837 Van Buren (Dem.) inaugurated as President.
Panic of 1837.
1838 Aroostook war.
1840 Harrison, first Whig President elected. Liberty Party entered race.
1841 Harrison died after one month as President; succeeded by Tyler.
Preemption Act passed.
Independent Treasury repealed.
Tyler vetoed bills to charter a national bank.
1842 Webster-Ashburton Treaty settled difficulties with Great Britain.
Tariff of 1842 enacted, a Whig protectionist measure.

Chapter

11

THE ADMINISTRATIONS OF JACKSON, VAN BUREN, AND TYLER, 1829–1845

> For twelve years Jackson and his chosen heir held the Presidency after the victory in 1828. The new democracy coming to power with Jackson's election represented the rise of the plain people—small farmers and workers—to an influence in government. Jacksonian Democracy also stood for the influence of the new West across the Appalachians. While Jeffersonian philosophy espoused government for the people by capable, educated leaders, Jacksonian philosophy believed the people could best govern themselves.

BEGINNINGS OF JACKSONIAN DEMOCRACY

Distinct changes in laws, practices, and popular attitudes gave rise to Jacksonian Democracy and were in turn accelerated by the new equalitarian spirit. These innovations taken together brought a distinct break with the earlier generation, a "revolution" comparable to that of the election of Jefferson in 1800. Revolutions in Europe after 1830 manifested this same spirit of reform.

●●● **Political Changes**—1) Political democracy had been considerably extended by 1828 by the abolition in the states of all property qualifications and of the remaining religious qualifications for voting and office-holding. 2) Presidential electors, at first chosen by state legislatures, came to be chosen by popular vote. 3) New state constitutions made an increased number of offices elective instead of appointive, and terms of office were shortened. 4) The choice of presidential nominees by caucus and by state legislatures gave way to nominating conventions where the people were more adequately represented. 5) Political parties as we know them today took form. Political machines organized voters and, to win elections, conducted vigorous and rough campaigns among the plain people. Most of these changes had occurred or had begun to occur before Jackson arrived on the scene; what made them significant now was the return of competition to presidential politics with the rise of the second party system.

6) The "spoils system" of rewarding loyal party workers with government jobs came to be more actively practiced. The frontier influence on Jacksonian Democracy deprecated the value of education and experience; any ordinary person of good intentions was considered capable of discharging the duties of public office. New blood in office was advocated by the adage "a new broom sweeps clean." Rotation in office was preferred to permanent office-holders who might come to regard themselves as a privileged aristocracy.

7) Jackson took a new view of the presidency. As the chosen servant of the people, Jackson believed the president should assume wide prerogatives and exercise vigorously the powers of his office. He defied Congress and the Supreme Court when he felt they did not adequately represent the interests of the people. Jackson exercised the veto power freely; he vetoed more bills than all his predecessors combined.

○ **Social and Economic Changes**—1) The westward expansion offered new opportunity for the lower classes and enabled them to escape the restraints of the conservative communities in the East. A ferment of new religious and social thinking defied the old affirmations. 2) Humanitarian movements, many of European origin, reflected a deep concern for the improvement of the lot of underprivileged and unfortunate persons. Movements were promoted to secure women's rights, to abolish slavery, to humanize treatment of the insane, to prohibit the use of intoxicating beverages, and to experiment with economic organization through communal societies. 3) Increasing opportunities for education and political understanding were opened by the growth of free public schools and of the press. 4) Eastern workers in urban industry organized to improve their opportunities. The Jacksonians, with their belief in minimum government, had little to do with these reforms and social movements.

○○ **The New Administration**—Jackson's Presidential inauguration in 1829 symbolized the "revolution" that had taken place. The people crowded into Washington to celebrate the overthrow of the aristocrats. At the White House reception the mob trampled in muddy boots on fine carpets and broke delicate furniture.

In his first cabinet Jackson appointed his eager supporter, Martin Van Buren, as Secretary of State. Other cabinet members were not outstanding and served merely as administrators. For executive and political advice Jackson consulted a "kitchen cabinet" of close friends led by his ghost writer Amos Kendall and by William B. Lewis, his adviser on petty politics. About ten percent of the officeholders were removed in the application of the rule "To the victor belong the spoils," stated by a Jackson supporter. Adams' men were replaced with Jackson supporters.

Jackson had never announced any program. He merely intended to meet problems as they came up.

THE JACKSON-CALHOUN SPLIT

John C. Calhoun had been Jackson's Vice Presidential running mate in 1824 and was elected with him in 1828. Calhoun expected to become the leading influence next to Jackson in the new administration and after four years to succeed the aged Jackson to the Presidency. Van Buren soon arose as a rival to Calhoun's aspirations.

The Eaton Affair—A quarrel over the social acceptability of Secretary of War Eaton's wife worked against Calhoun's hitherto cordial relationship with Jackson. Eaton had married Peggy O'Neill shortly before the inauguration; she was the daughter of the hotel keeper where Eaton had boarded. Gossip against her reputation and her humble origin made her unacceptable to the other cabinet wives who ostracized her. Calhoun and his wife refused to accept her, but Jackson, whose wife also had been the victim of malicious gossip, tried to force the cabinet wives to accept her. Martin Van Buren, like Jackson, a widower, joined the President in showing courtesies to Mrs. Eaton.

The Jefferson Day Banquet—Calhoun and South Carolina Democrats attempted to use the occasion of the Jefferson Day banquet, early in 1830, to maneuver Jackson into going on record in favor of Calhoun's states' rights views. Jackson, with advance warning, offered the toast: "Our Federal Union—it must be preserved!" Calhoun managed to toast states rights in reply but became resentful of the public rebuff he had received.

Calhoun's Censure of Jackson—Van Buren's friends worked to widen the breach. Crawford wrote a letter in which he revealed that Calhoun in 1818 had recommended Jackson's censure for hanging two British subjects during the invasion of Florida. Jackson now branded Calhoun his enemy, and their political alliance ended in 1830. Consequently, Van Buren became Jackson's choice for the succession. Soon afterwards Jackson reorganized his cabinet, named Eaton as Governor of the Florida Territory and thereby ended the social feud over Mrs. Eaton at Washington. Van Buren became Ambassador to England.

WESTERN PROBLEMS

Jackson fell heir to the Native American problems of the Adams administration. He now clarified his stand on the issues of internal improvements and land distribution.

○ **Conflicts with Native Americans**—Jackson took the viewpoint of the frontier settlers toward the "Indian problems" and worked to facilitate removal of the Native Americans. The policy of removal had already been established.

The Cherokees in Georgia hoped to avoid removal. They farmed their land, conducted schools, and had otherwise adopted the white man's ways. Georgia claimed their lands and opened them to settlement. In the case of *Worcester v. Georgia* (1832) the Supreme Court ruled that Georgia had no jurisdiction over the Cherokees and that they came under the protection of the federal government. Georgia refused to obey the decision, and Jackson refused to enforce the Supreme Court decision by sending troops to Georgia.

Other Native American removals caused Black Hawk's War (1832) against the Fox and Sauk in Illinois and the Seminole War (1837–1842) in Florida. By 1835 nearly all Native Americans had been removed.

○○ **Internal Improvements**—Jackson's view on federal aid for internal improvements was not known until he vetoed the bill for construction of a road from Maysville to Lexington, Kentucky (May 1830). He reasoned, in this famous veto, that the road lay entirely within Kentucky. To vote federal aid, state roads would require an amendment to the Constitution. Jackson now lost supporters who before had hoped he would approve such appropriations. The Whig Party began to take shape as the malcontents deserted Jackson.

○ **The Land Question**—Westerners were unsatisfied by the Land Act of 1820. They agitated for land on more favorable terms. Senator Thomas Hart Benton of Missouri served as their leading spokesman. 1) "Squatters" who had illegally settled on the public domain asked for preemption laws that would give them the first right to buy the land after it was surveyed and put up for sale. 2) As a means of making lands available at a lower price, Benton and many of the Democrats proposed the principle of graduation, that is, unsold land would be gradually reduced in price according to a schedule fixed by law or, finally, would be given away.

Easterners opposed easy terms of land sale since the Western lands drained away population and tended to raise wages in industry. Daniel Webster of Massachusetts and Clay favored distribution of the revenues from public land sales among the states. The West did not want land sold to raise revenue under any conditions. The South opposed distribution since it would both drain the treasury surplus and support demands for higher tariffs. The debate over land policy remained a fundamental difference between the Democrats and Whigs.

THE TARIFF AND NULLIFICATION

Calhoun continued active as the spokesman for the anti-tariff South. The South wanted revision of the high rates of the Tariff of 1828.

✪✪ **Why the South Opposed the Tariff**—The agricultural states of the South exported cotton, tobacco, and rice, taking in return manufactured goods from the North, Britain, and Europe. Since the tariff created a protected market for Northern manufacturers, protection that raised the prices all consumers paid, as well as providing 90 percent of the revenue of the federal government, the South felt it was supporting both Northern manufacturers and the government more than the other sections. Also, by making it more difficult for British cloth to be sold in the United States, the tariff reduced that market's demand for cotton. Southeastern planters, whose worn-out soil gave lower yields than their Southwestern competitors' virgin soil, illogically but vehemently blamed their financial problems on the tariff. Working with a combination of accurate and mistaken perceptions, the South made the tariff the explanation for all their problems.

✪✪✪ **The Webster-Hayne Debates**—In the course of the debates over land policy, Senator Samuel A. Foote introduced a resolution to stop land sales. The South proposed an alliance with the West against the manufacturing East. The discussion in time turned to the tariff question. The discussion of the tariff raised the question of its constitutionality. Senator Hayne of South Carolina in the debates became the mouthpiece of Calhoun who, as Vice President, presided over the Senate. Hayne stated the grievances of the angry South and again put forward Calhoun's nullification theory. In January, 1830, Daniel Webster replied to Hayne's contentions; he argued that the ultimate sovereignty rested in the people and not in the state governments. A state could not by itself declare an act of Congress unconstitutional and nullify it. Many Westerners agreed with the South on the tariff but refused to accept the nullification theory. Jackson made his opposition clear at the Jefferson Day dinner.

✪✪ **The Tariff of 1832**—With election year approaching, Jackson in December 1831, recommended that Congress revise tariff rates downward. The national debt was almost paid off and excessive revenues were pouring into the treasury. The revised tariff passed Congress in July 1832. It kept protective rates firmly in place and lacked only certain features that the protectionists had disliked.

✪✪✪ **Nullification by South Carolina**—The nullifiers in South Carolina immediately elected delegates to a convention that in turn proceeded to pass the Nullification Ordinance (November 1832) declaring the tariffs of 1828 and 1832 null and void. The convention prohibited tariff collections in the state and promised secession if the federal government should use coercion to enforce the collection of duties.

Jackson answered with his famous Nullification Proclamation (December 1832) denying the right of a state to nullify a law of the United States. As tension increased, the Senate passed the "Force Bill" (February 1833) authorizing the President to use military force against South Carolina. At the same time Clay secured the passage of the Compromise Tariff which provided for steady, gradual reduction until 1842 when no duties would exceed 20 percent. South Carolina accepted the compromise and called another convention that repealed the Nullification Ordinance and nullified the Force Act. Jackson ignored this last act of defiance from South Carolina. Southern defensiveness, henceforth, centered around the slavery question.

THE WAR OVER THE BANK, 1832–1836

The charter of the Second Bank of the United States, issued in 1816, expired in 1836. Henry Clay, who expected to receive the presidential nomination of the National Republicans (predecessor to the Whigs), submitted a re-charter bill in 1832. He believed Jackson would not dare veto the bill in an election year, thus giving Clay's people the victory of a re-charter; if Jackson did veto the bill, Clay believed he would be defeated in the election.

✪✪✪ **Dislike of the Bank**—1) Various elements in the nation disliked the tight money policy of the Bank. Debtors favored easy money and low interest rates; land speculators liked a plentiful money supply since it facilitated land sales financed with loans of paper money from the state banks.

2) Bankers owning state-chartered private banks (some run responsibly, others deserving the tag "wildcat banks") disliked its competitive and disciplinary power. The Bank often tested the specie reserve behind the bank notes of private banks by collecting them and presenting them for redemption in specie. This forced the little banks to keep adequate reserves of specie which they would have preferred to lend at interest.

3) Others opposed the privilege all banks enjoyed of creating and lending paper money, which tended to exaggerate the fluctuations of the business cycle. 4) The ruthlessness of banks in foreclosing mortgages in the past had made enemies of many debtors. 5) Nicholas Biddle, the president of the Bank, used its vast power to corrupt Congressmen and pay for favorable newspaper publicity.

Jackson disliked all banks but especially resented Biddle's use of the Bank's lending power to influence politics. Congress passed the bill to recharter but Jackson vetoed it, and in his veto message issued a ringing denunciation of it as a privileged monopoly used to enrich a "few at the expense of the many." Actually, as we shall see, the expiration of the Bank was a great loss to the country. Biddle and Jackson both share the blame for its demise.

✪✪✪ **The Election of 1832**—The Democrats renominated Jackson and chose Van Buren as his running mate. At this convention the Democrats adopted their traditional "two-thirds rule" to assure Van Buren's nomination. Conservatives and opponents of Jackson nominated Clay as the candidate of the National Republican Party in a convention in December 1831. This convention also adopted the first party platform. Earlier, the anti-Masons had nominated (1831) William Wirt as their candidate. The Bank and the charges against Jackson as a tyrant were the main issues. Jackson who had identified himself with the Masons and the fight against the privileged moneyed classes won a resounding victory.

Biddle began to tighten credit, after the election, in an effort to demonstrate that threats against the Bank were frightening to the business community. The brief credit stringency backfired against Biddle, and Jackson now decided to destroy the Bank instead of waiting for it to expire in 1836. Jackson ordered government deposits removed. They were placed in selected state banks ("pet banks") by his loyal Secretary of the Treasury, Roger B. Taney.

✪ **Inflation and Panic**—Without the curbs of the National Bank to prevent liberal issues of banknotes, many newly founded state banks, chartered under existing lax state banking laws, made liberal loans. A great increase in loans and money in circulation stimulated a business and speculative boom. State banks increased their loans when deposits of federal funds were made with them. Land speculators borrowed money freely to purchase government land. Land sales quintupled from 1834 to 1836. Western states indulged in a frenzy of subsidizing road and canal building by selling bonds to Eastern banks and British bankers. In 1836 Jackson signed an act, the Distribution Bill, to "deposit" the surplus treasury funds with the states, actually a gift, made in proportion to their population. The new deposits stimulated an inflation already gone too far.

Private bank notes of little or no value were flooding into public land offices, causing serious loss of revenue. Jackson dealt with it by issuing the Specie Circular, requiring only coin in payment for public land. The deflationary effect of retiring so much coin, along with recent downturns in Europe, plunged the United States into the Panic of 1837, a depression lasting several years.

PROBLEMS IN FOREIGN RELATIONS UNDER JACKSON

The blunt President's shirt-sleeve diplomacy enjoyed unusual success. The Texas Revolution and proposals for her annexation created resentment in Mexico.

○ Jackson's Success with the British and French—By relaxing discriminatory trade regulations against British vessels, Van Buren succeeded in getting Britain to open the West Indies trade to American shipping in 1830.

The Spoliation Claims against France arose from the French confiscations of American shipping during the French Revolution and Napoleonic Wars. France could not deny the validity of the claims but postponed settlement indefinitely. After Louis Philippe became King of France (1830) Jackson succeeded in signing a treaty by which France would pay most of the American claims. When the first installment came due the French treasury refused payment. After patiently waiting until 1834 Jackson asked Congress to authorize the seizure of French property if France did not appropriate the funds for payment. The French government took great affront, recalled its minister, and refused to pay until Jackson apologized. Jackson issued a statement denying any intention of insulting the French but not an outright apology. The French government began payments in 1836.

○ The Texas Revolution—In 1820 Moses Austin secured Spanish permission to colonize families in Texas. After his death, his son, Stephen F. Austin, took possession of the land grants in 1821 and secured confirmation of the colony's charter from the newly independent government of Mexico. In 1825 Mexico encouraged further immigration with an act introducing the empresario system under which large grants were offered colonizers who would settle several hundred families. Terms of land sales were far more generous than in the United States and settlers from the South flocked in to cultivate the rich soils.

Friction soon developed between Mexico and the settlers for several reasons. 1) Mexico failed to solve annoying problems and provide services of local government. 2) Texans did not take seriously their promises to accept Roman Catholicism, the established church of Mexico. 3) conflicts over the payment of Mexican customs duties, 4) Mexican determination to abolish slavery, 5) subordination of the province of Texas to Mexican-dominated Coahuila, and 6) the prohibition of further immigration into Texas—all these contributed to mutual dissatisfaction.

The independence movement began when the Texans failed to secure satisfaction of their grievances. The Mexican dictator General Santa Anna led an army into Texas to establish Mexican control. The Texans declared their independence in March 1836. The Mexican army killed all the Texan defenders of the Alamo, a mission in San Antonio which the Texans undertook to defend. General Sam Houston, an old friend of Jackson, retreated towards the Louisiana border with his force but, at the Battle of San Jacinto in April 1836, annihilated the larger Mexican army in a surprise attack. Santa Anna, as a prisoner of the Texans, recognized Texan independence, but Mexico later repudiated the agreement made by Santa Anna.

The Republic of Texas, with Sam Houston chosen president, was established and requested annexation to the United States. The United States Congress recognized Texas independence but President Jackson took no precipitate steps to annex the republic. He wished to avoid war with Mexico and feared the disruption of the Democratic Party if he antagonized the antislavery Northerners. The issue of annexation of Texas, which would become a slave state, prevented annexation until 1845.

VAN BUREN'S ADMINISTRATION

Van Buren firmly believed that the federal government should have as little as possible to do with the private economy, that it was up to individuals, not the government, to bring the nation out of the depression. Accordingly, he proposed nothing to remedy the nation's economic problems.

The Election of 1836—Two noteworthy aspects of the election were the entrance of the Whig Party and the fact of Jackson's choosing Van Buren for his successor. Between 1834 and 1836 the Whig Party took shape; it absorbed the National Republicans, the anti-Masons, anti-Jackson Democrats, and others who found a common cause in opposing Jackson. While strongest in the North, the Whigs were not a sectional party, gaining support from merchants, manufacturers, well-to-do farmers, and native-born workmen throughout the country. There was considerable difference of opinion within the party, and it was held together by its strong leaders, Webster, Clay, and Calhoun.

The Whigs were so disunited that they neither nominated a presidential candidate nor drafted a platform. Three sectional candidates were put forward; while this could have had the effect of throwing the election into the House of Representatives, it was not intended. Van Buren won a majority of electoral votes.

✪ Van Buren and the Panic of 1837—Causes of the panic other than 1) the Specie Circular were 2) a depression in England that caused investors there to sell American canal and bank stocks, 3) overexpansion of credit, 4) the speculative mania of the preceding years, and 5) crop failures.

Within a month after Van Buren's inauguration in 1837 all signs indicated that the country was in a serious depression. Hundreds of banks and other businesses failed. Land and commodity prices collapsed. Unemployment spread and wages fell. The depression lasted for several years. The Whigs, who blamed Jacksonian financial ideas and practices, began to make notable political gains. Van Buren adhered to his philosophy of negative government and did not advise any measures to combat a depression. He stopped further distribution of the treasury surplus and authorized an issue of $10,000,000 in treasury notes to meet the federal deficit.

❍ The Independent Treasury Question—The depression experience turned major attention to the search for a solution to the problem of creating sounder banks and limiting the issuance of bank notes. It was recognized that the large increase in bank notes had produced an inflationary bubble after 1833.

Van Buren and the Democrats came to believe that government should be divorced from banking by requiring government revenues to be held in government offices where received. These funds stored in vaults could not be used as a fractional reserve by bankers to expand bank note issues. The use of government offices as depositories was called the Independent Treasury or Sub-treasury system. Both state banks and a national banking system were opposed. Specie would replace paper as circulating currency except for limited issues of federal notes. This hard money policy of the Democrats was opposed by the Whigs who advocated a United States Bank. Whigs preferred depositing government funds in state banks to Van Buren's Independent Treasury and defeated the Independent Treasury Bill in 1837 and 1838.

A faction of extremists sprang up in the Democratic Party and opposed all banks, credit, and bank note currency; they favored specie only. This group, nicknamed the Locofocos, were strongest in western New York state but had considerable influence in adjoining states. Their influence finally secured the passage of Van Buren's Independent Treasury system in 1840. The government abandoned its responsibility for establishing a regulated national currency.

TYLER'S ADMINISTRATION, 1841–1845

The Whigs elected their first President in 1840 and gained control of Congress as well but lost their victory with Harrison's death. After this, disagreement between the legislative and executive branches prevented the realization of most of the Whig program.

❍❍ The Election of 1840—The Democrats renominated Van Buren. The Whigs chose William Henry Harrison, the old Native American fighting hero of the War of 1812; Harrison's demonstrated popularity in the election of 1836 and the powerful support of Whig leaders won him the preferment over Clay. Clay was without doubt the most able and prominent leader of the Whigs, but a combination of opponents defeated him for the nomination, and in Congress his well-known position on many issues had alienated certain groups. John Tyler of Virginia, an anti-Jackson Democrat who had joined the Whigs and was also a Clay supporter, was chosen as Vice President. The Whigs failed to draw up a platform because of their conflicting views on important issues. A new party, one opposed to slavery, nominated James G. Birney and became known as the Liberty Party. After this time, the slavery issue was injected into all national political campaigns.

In the campaign some attention was given to the political issues of the Independent Treasury and the Bank, but personalities received by far the greater emphasis. Whigs pictured Van Buren as an effete dandy and created the image of Harrison as a rugged man of the people. This "Log Cabin and Hard Cider" campaign associated these symbols of the pioneer Western farmer with Harrison who lived in a fine country home. The public blamed Van Buren and the Democrats for the depression; this did more than anything to defeat them.

The Whigs won the Presidency and control of both houses of Congress, but their joy was brief. After a month in office, Harrison died. For the first time, the Vice President had succeeded to the Presidency. Tyler made good his assertion that he was now President, not acting-President as some thought. A states-rights Virginian put on the ticket to appeal to Southerners driven out of the party by Jackson's anti-nullification stand, he vetoed most of the Whig program.

✪ Whig Legislative Program—Henry Clay assumed control of the Whigs in Congress but was never able to win the cooperation of the conscientious and stubborn President Tyler who disagreed with the whole Whig program.

The Independent Treasury Act was soon repealed, but Tyler vetoed the act of Congress to establish a third national bank. Tyler vetoed a modified bank bill that also failed to meet his objections. The expiration of the Tariff of 1832 forced Congress to legislate a new tariff act in 1842; this act restored duties to the levels of 1832. The act was defended as a revenue measure. Tyler's Whig cabinet resigned in 1841 in protest against his opposition to their program.

✪✪ Preemption Law—The Preemption Act (1841) was probably the most significant measure of the Tyler administration. Democrats in Congress forced the Whigs to fulfill their campaign promise of recognizing the right of preemption. Squatters who moved into unsurveyed federal lands had long agitated for the first right to buy the land they had taken once it was put up for sale. The settlers argued that as pioneers they had undergone the risks, labor, and hardships of conquering the wilderness, that the government owed them this special consideration. The Preemption Act provided that a settler could claim 160 acres and exercise the right to buy it at the low price of $1.25 an acre. Previous measures had recognized this right under certain circumstances, but the Act of 1841 gave the Westerners a victory by recognizing the principle of preemption.

○○ Anglo-American Controversies—Several controversies with Britain, occurring during Van Buren's administration, reached a critical state in 1840. Most of these were settled by the Webster-Ashburton Treaty after Tyler had become President. Webster was appointed as Secretary of State by Harrison.

1) The so-called Aroostook War (1838) referred to fighting between lumberjacks on the border of Maine and New Brunswick in Aroostook County. General Winfield Scott arranged a truce between the two sides but the threat of more serious fighting continued.

2) The *Caroline* Affair (1837) arose from a Canadian rebellion against Britain. The *Caroline,* an American ship, that had been furnishing supplies to the rebels, was burned by Canadian loyalists who had crossed the American border to do so.

3) In the McLeod case, New York state had arrested a Canadian loyalist soldier, McLeod, who boasted in a barroom that he had killed the American who lost his life in the *Caroline* Affair. England demanded McLeod's release, but New York tried and acquitted him. A law in 1842 provided that cases involving aliens under orders of a foreign government should be tried in federal courts.

4) In the *Creole* case an American vessel, the *Creole,* transporting slaves to the deep South, was forced by a slave mutiny to put in at Nassau in the Bahamas. There the British freed the American slaves as they had done before when ships were driven by storms into British ports. The South grew angry at such British interference.

5) Another source of friction was the British slave patrols off the African coast; American ships were searched to suppress the slave-smuggling there.

6) The conflict in claims to Oregon remained unsettled. 7) Britain had a new issue with Americans because the states during the depression had repudiated bonded indebtedness owed to British investors.

○○ THE WEBSTER-ASHBURTON TREATY (1842)

Webster and Ashburton both wished to make an amicable settlement of the several difficulties between their respective governments. 1) Settlement of the Maine-New Brunswick boundary dispute was facilitated by the discovery by each of maps favoring the opposing claims. The claims were compromised with the United States gaining slightly more than half of the disputed territory. 2) Ashburton expressed regret for the sinking of the *Caroline,* and 3) the Treaty promised to avoid "officious interference" in freeing slaves in such cases as the *Creole.* 4) Both countries agreed to patrol the African coast to suppress the slave trade. The dispute over Oregon remained to be settled later; the defaulted state debts were settled in private arrangements between individual creditors and states.

CHAPTER BOOK LIST

Belohlavek, John, *"Let the Eagle Soar!" The Foreign Policy of Andrew Jackson* (1985).

Benson, Lee, *The Concept of Jacksonian Democracy* (Princeton).

Boorstin, David, *The National Experience* (Random).

Coit, Margaret, *John C. Calhoun* (Sentry). Pulitzer Prize biography; full length, one volume.

Ellis, Richard B., *The Union at Risk: Jacksonian Democracy, States Rights, and the Nullification Crisis* (1987). Excellent treatment.

Freehling, William W., *Prelude to Civil War: The Nullification Controversy in South Carolina, 1816–1836* (1966).

Gunderson, Robert C., *The Log Cabin Campaign* (1957).

Hammond, Bray, *Banks and Politics In America* (1957). Hamiltonian view.

McCormick, Richard P., *The Second American Party System* (1966).

McNickle, D'Arcy, *The Indian Tribes of the United States* (Oxford). Survey of Indian policy.

Meyers, Marvin, *Jacksonian Persuasion, Politics and Belief* (Vintage). Interpretive.

Pessen, Edward, *Jacksonian America: Society, Personality, and Politics* (1979). Deflates the myth of the Jacksonians as great democrats.

Peterson, Merrill D., *The Great Triumvirate: Webster, Clay, and Calhoun* (1987). Favorable but fair treatment.

Satz, Ronald N., *American Indian Policy in the Jacksonian Era* (1975).

Schlesinger, Arthur M., Jr., *Age of Jackson* (New American Library). Stimulating account of the nature of Jacksonian democracy.

Sellers, C.G., *James K. Polk: Jacksonian, 1795–1843* (1957). Accurate.

Smith, Timothy L., *Revivalism and Social Reform* (Harper and Row).

Van Deusen, Glyndon G., *The Jacksonian Era 1828–1848* (Harper & Row).

Ward, J.W., *Andrew Jackson: Symbol of an Age* (Galaxy).

White, Leonard D., *The Jacksonians* (Free Press).

Wilents, Sean, *Chants Democratic: New York City and the Rise of the American Working Class, 1788–1850* (1984).

Wiltse, C.M., *John C. Calhoun, Nullifier* (1949). Sympathetic.

REVIEW QUESTIONS

MULTIPLE CHOICE

1. Which pair of factors gave the most support to Jackson? (1) The common people and the South (2) the upper classes and the South (3) the common people and the West (4) the common people and the Northwest.

2. Which is *not* one of the features of Jacksonian Democracy? (1) Nomination of presidential candidates by conventions (2) large-scale removal of officeholders of the defeated party (3) vigorous organized campaigning among the people (4) long tenure of office-holders.

3. Jackson's "Kitchen Cabinet" was made up mainly of (1) his old cronies (2) newspapermen and political advisers (3) leading Democratic politicians (4) close family friends and relatives.

4. The Eaton Affair's significance is that it (1) showed the feeling of Jackson for the common people (2) it caused Van Buren to be made minister to England (3) it caused Jackson to abandon extreme states rights views (4) led to the elimination of Calhoun as Jackson's successor.

5. Jackson vetoed the Maysville Road Bill because (1) the road lay entirely within a single state (2) he opposed all internal improvements (3) he wished to defy Henry Clay (4) he was seeking to create a campaign issue.

6. The principle of graduation in land sales meant that (1) land prices would be increased annually to discourage settlement (2) revenues would be distributed to the states according to population (3) prices of unsold land would be steadily reduced to encourage buyers (4) first settlers had an option to buy land they had cleared.

7. The greatest significance of the Webster-Hayne debates is that (1) they showed that the West would oppose restrictions of land sales (2) they showed the South was dependent upon agricultural exports (3) the South asserted the right of nullification of federal laws considered unconstitutional (4) revealed the split between Jackson and Calhoun.

8. After the Nullification Controversy ended in 1832 (1) the Whigs managed to increase tariff rates substantially (2) the Democrats lowered tariff rates after Texas was annexed in 1845 (3) tariff rates were stabilized immediately in a gesture of conciliation (4) tariffs were reduced over a ten-year period.

9. What action did Jackson take against the Second Bank of the United States after the election of 1832? (1) He closed branch banks competing with state-chartered banks (2) he ordered his Secretary of the Treasury to deposit no more funds with the bank and to withdraw deposits (3) he ordered the Bank closed (4) he removed Biddle from the presidency of the Bank.

10. Jackson won the election of 1832 in spite of his veto of the bank bill because (1) Jackson appealed to the prejudices of the masses (2) experts recognized the Bank's charter as mainly a piece of class legislation (3) the Bank was generally accepted as unconstitutional (4) most of the Bank's stock was owned by Englishmen.

11. The greatest numbers of people moved to the West (1) in immediate response to improved land laws (2) when bankruptcy and hard times occurred (3) when the nation's economy was booming (4) in response to patriotic appeals.

12. In his relations with foreign nations Jackson (1) exhibited rare tact and finesse (2) was successful even though blunt (3) had little success in dealing with France and England (4) opposed the annexation of Texas.

13. Which was *not* a cause of the Texan Revolution? (1) A dispute over the Rio Grande as the boundary between Texas and Coahuila (2) Mexican plans to abolish slavery (3) a decision to halt American immigration to Texas (4) political turmoil in Mexico and inefficient government for Texas.

14. The annexation of Texas was (1) delayed until Van Buren's administration (2) opposed by Jackson and New England (3) was favored by Jackson but failed in the Senate (4) desired by neither Mexico nor Texas before 1840.

15. Van Buren favored the deposit of federal funds in (1) government offices over the country (2) a national banking system (3) a rechartered Bank of the United States (4) state chartered banks.

16. Presidential candidates in 1840 included (1) Harrison, Van Buren, and Tyler (2) Birney, Harrison, and Van Buren (3) Birney, Tyler, and Van Buren (4) Harrison, Polk, and Clay.

17. All of these are trends up to 1862 in the successive land laws providing for distribution of the public domain *except* which one? (1) Provisions for the acquisition of smaller blocks of land (2) reduction in the cost (3) provisions favoring the actual settler (4) increasingly liberal credit terms.

18. The Preemption Law was designed to favor (1) settlers who bought surveyed land at auction (2) Eastern purchasers (3) Western land speculators (4) "squatters" who claimed unsurveyed lands.

19. The Webster-Ashburton Treaty settled all *except* (1) the question of slave patrols off the African coast (2) the Maine-New Brunswick boundary dispute (3) the *Caroline* dispute (4) the partition of Oregon.

TRUE-FALSE

20. Paralleling the democratic movement known as Jacksonian Democracy were the Revolutions of 1830 in Europe.

21. Jacksonian Democracy gave greater emphasis upon the value of experience and education for public officeholders.

22. Jackson vetoed fewer bills than all his predecessors combined.

23. Demands for social and humanitarian reforms accompanied the demand for political reforms under Jacksonian Democracy.

24. Martin Van Buren's wife was glad to accord social acceptance to Peggy Eaton.

25. The Maysville Road veto is significant because it clarified Jackson's stand on the important issue of internal improvements.

26. Webster, Clay, and other Whigs opposed the distribution to the states of proceeds from land sales.

27. Calhoun opposed protective tariffs because he felt they favored Southern industry over Southern agriculture.

28. Liberal loans of paper money caused inflationary booms which seemed to benefit the speculating classes.

29. Although Jackson disliked all banks he viewed the Bank of the United States as a privileged monopoly.

30. Mexico gave little encouragement to the Americans who insisted on settling in Texas.

31. In 1836 the new Whig Party chose no single candidate to oppose the Democratic candidate.

32. The Locofocos were extremists in the Democratic Party who opposed all bank note currency.

33. John Tyler, who became President upon Harrison's death, was a former Democrat from Virginia.

34. The Whigs tried to evade their campaign promise of preemption, but the Democrats forced them to act upon the bill.

35. The Webster-Ashburton Treaty was truly a compromise settlement of quarrels between the two nations.

COMPLETION

36. By 1832 the choice of presidential nominees by _____ had given way to choosing them at _____ .

37. Jackson was first inaugurated President in the year _____ and Van Buren in _____ .

38. The famous social quarrel in Jackson's first term came about when the Secretary of War named _____ married the woman _____ . Prominent in refusing to accept her was the wife of the Vice President, Mrs. _____ .

39. The famous battle of the toasts over states' rights occurred at the _____ Day banquet.

40. Jackson refused to enforce a Supreme Court decision handed down in the case of _____ .

41. Jackson vetoed a famous internal improvements bill in the _____ Road Bill.

42. The leading spokesman of Westerners who wanted more favorable terms for acquiring government land by small farmers was _____ .

43. Settlers who took up land before it was surveyed were called _____ .

44. South Carolina tried to void the Tariff of 1832 in the _____ , but Jackson replied with his _____ and had Congress pass the _____ which permitted him to use the military power against South Carolina. The dispute was compromised by the act of Congress known as the _____ .

45. Opposing Jackson for the Presidency in 1832 was _____ who ran on the _____ issue.

46. Loosely managed state-chartered banks were called _____ banks, but Jackson placed new deposits in banks nicknamed the _____ banks.

47. The Panic of 1837 was touched off by Jackson's instructions to the land offices known as the _____ .

48. Texas won its independence in the year _____ at the Battle of _____ .

49. In 1840 the victorious Presidential candidate was _____ of the _____ Party.

50. The land law of 1841 favoring the squatters is known as the _____ Act.

51. An American ship called the _____ was burned by Canadian loyalists in 1837; another ship taken to the Bahamas by mutinous slaves was called the _____ . These two controversies with Britain over the ships and other disputes were settled in the _____ Treaty in the year _____ .

MATCHING

52. Amos Kendall
53. James G. Birney
54. Martin Van Buren
55. John C. Calhoun
56. Samuel A. Foote
57. Daniel Webster
58. Nicholas Biddle
59. Roger B. Taney
60. Stephen F. Austin
61. Sam Houston

a. Recommended censure of Jackson
b. Upheld national sovereignty
c. Jackson's obliging Secretary of the Treasury
d. Jackson's leading adviser
e. Wanted to stop sales of western lands
f. Led Texans to victory
g. Chosen as Jackson's successor
h. Nominee of Liberty Party
i. Took first colonists to Texas
j. Ran for President in 1832
k. Head of the Bank of the United States

CHRONOLOGY / CHAPTER 12

1769 Spanish Franciscan mission established at San Diego.

1812 Astoria opened as trading post by John Jacob Astor.

1820s Many Americans settle in California during decade.

1821 William Becknell made trading trip to Santa Fe on Santa Fe trail.

1826 Jedediah Smith blazed first overland trail from the east to California.

1830s Decade of early missionary activities in Oregon.

1832 Bonneville fur trading expedition to Far West. Wyeth expedition to Oregon country.

1836 Texas won independence.

1841 First pioneer settlers migrate overland to California.

1842 Commodore Jones seized Monterey.

1843 Large migration of pioneers to Oregon.

1844 Polk (Dem.) elected President on issue of annexation of Texas.

1845 Polk inaugurated.
Texas annexed. Slidell Mission to Mexico.

1846 Bear Flag Republic proclaimed in California.
Mexican War began. Taylor campaigned in northern Mexico; Kearny to California.
Oregon Treaty with Great Britain divided Oregon country.
Sub-Treasury law and Walker Tariff (reduced rates) passed.
Wilmot Proviso introduced to exclude slavery from territory acquired from Mexico.

1847 Mexico City taken by General Scott.
Brigham Young began colonizing Mormons at Great Salt Lake.

1848 Treaty of Guadalupe Hidalgo ended Mexican War.
Whigs elect their second President, General Taylor.

1849 Taylor inaugurated as President.

1850 Taylor died: succeeded by Millard Fillmore.

12
THE OCCUPATION OF
THE FAR WEST, 1821–1848

From colonial times Americans had grown accustomed to moving
into the vacant lands of the West to engage in trade or agriculture.
They had come to think of the occupation and annexation of new
lands as a part of the natural order of events. In the 1840s the term
"Manifest Destiny" was used to describe what was thought to be
the obvious destiny of the United States to encompass all of North
America. In the 1840s the United States added Texas, Oregon,
and the great Southwest including New Mexico and California.
The Mexican War was fought in the process.

TEXAS

The annexation of Texas was delayed only by the touchy question of
slavery. The possibility of a British foothold in Texas and the election of
President Polk brought the immediate annexation of Texas.

❂ **The Texas Question**—Abolitionists asserted that the settlement, the
revolution, and the attempts to annex Texas were all parts of a plot of
slaveholders of the South. Northern Whigs opposed annexation since
several slave states could be organized in that vast area. While Southern
state legislatures adopted resolutions favoring annexation, those in the
North adopted resolutions opposing it. Failure of the United States to act
forced Texas to withdraw its offer of annexation in 1838 and to proceed
to seek commercial treaties and loans from European powers. While
some Texans never stopped hoping for annexations, others decided that
independence was, after all, the best course of action.

British Interest in Texas—The interests of Great Britain favored
close ties with Texas. An independent Texas could be used to counter-
balance the power of the United States. Since Britain and Texas both
favored a free trade policy, Britain could exchange her manufactures for
Texas cotton without the hindrance of tariff duties. Abolitionists in
Britain hoped that Texas would abolish slavery in return for a large loan.
Texas could become a base of operations against slavery in the United

States. In 1843 Britain and France negotiated a truce between Mexico and Texas to halt Mexican plans to reconquer Texas. The Texan minister informed Washington that Texas was no longer interested in discussing annexation. This only served to make the American government more eager.

Friction with Mexico—In 1843 President Santa Anna of Mexico notified the United States that Mexico would declare war if the United States annexed Texas. The American Secretary of State John C. Calhoun late in 1843 notified the Texas minister that the United States wished to reopen negotiations for annexation. President Sam Houston of Texas proceeded cautiously to avoid offending Britain but agreed to the proposals early in 1844 on condition the United States provide military and naval protection. A treaty was drawn up but rejected in the Senate when abolitionists fears were aroused. The danger of war with Mexico also brought votes against the treaty. President Tyler next tried to get Congress to pass a joint resolution of annexation but Congress adjourned. The annexation question then became a campaign issue in 1844.

⊙⊙ The Election of 1844—The Democrats refused to nominate Van Buren who had taken a stand against the annexation of Texas. Instead, James K. Polk, a Jacksonian Democrat from Tennessee and the first dark horse nominee in American political history, was nominated for the Presidency. Clay won the Whig presidential nomination as their most prominent candidate. Clay at first stated his opposition to the annexation of Texas but in a letter he later indicated he would accept annexation under certain conditions. Offended Northern Whigs now refused to support Clay and instead voted for the Liberty Party candidate, James G. Birney.

Polk and the Democratic platform strongly favored "the reoccupation of all of Oregon and the reannexation of all of Texas." Public opinion over the nation definitely favored expansion regardless of the slavery issue. The Liberty Party, calling for the non-extension of slavery, may have attracted enought votes to defeat Clay. Polk won a decisive victory and the Democrats also won control of Congress. It was clearly a mandate for territorial expansion.

⊙⊙ The Annexation of Texas—When Congress convened in December 1844, Tyler again recommended the annexation of Texas. In February 1845, the Senate and the House approved a joint resolution, which required only a simple majority vote, empowering the President to negotiate a new treaty with Texas for annexation. The resolution provided 1) Texas was to be admitted without a preliminary period of territorial status 2) and might be divided into as many as five states. 3) Texas would pay her own debt but 4) could retain her public lands. 5) The application of the Missouri Compromise line would permit slavery in Texas. The resolution passed Congress, and Tyler signed it three days before his term expired. Texas was admitted to the Union in December 1845, and formally installed her state government in February 1846. Oregon came next—also the result of the territorial ambition of James K. Polk.

OREGON

The first American pioneer settlers on the Pacific coast settled in Oregon when it was claimed by both the United States and Great Britain. Large numbers of migrants made it necessary to settle the question of ownership.

❂❂ **British and American Claims to Oregon**—The Oregon country extended westward from the crest of the Rockies and between the 42nd parallel and 54°40′ on the north. British claims to Oregon were based on 1) the voyages of Drake, Cook, and Vancouver and the land explorations of Mackenzie. 2) The extensive fur-trading activities of the North West Company and the Hudson's Bay Company and its domination of Oregon since 1812 further buttressed British claims.

American claims were based on 1) the discovery and exploration of the Columbia in 1792 by Captain Robert Gray; 2) exploration by the Lewis and Clark Expedition; 3) American fur-trading activities including John Jacob Astor's establishment of Astoria in 1811; and 4) the right of settlement.

Joint occupation agreements in 1818 and 1827 provided that citizens of both countries could trade and settle in Oregon.

❂ **American Traders in Oregon**—The first American fur-trading activities were conducted by New England merchants who traded for furs with the Native Americans along the coast. Furs were exchanged for tea and other goods in China. Astor organized the Pacific Fur Company in 1810, which established the trading post of Astoria on the Columbia. Within a few months his agents were forced to sell the post to the Canadian North West Company because of the War of 1812. After this the British dominated Oregon through the Hudson's Bay Company under the benevolent control of John McLoughlin. The Company founded outposts through Oregon, engaged in extensive farming and ranching, and gathered furs over a large part of the Pacific coast.

Before 1832 the only Americans in Oregon were on trading and trapping expeditions. In the 1820s Hall J. Kelley, a Boston schoolteacher, took a fanatical interest in the American occupation of Oregon. He aroused interest in Oregon and petitioned Congress to aid emigration there. Nathaniel Wyeth, also from Boston, led a fur-trading expedition into Oregon in 1832. He found he could not compete successfully with the well-entrenched Hudson's Bay Company.

☉ The Settlement of Missionaries and Pioneers—A published report of Native Americans asking that missionaries be sent to Oregon aroused the enthusiasm of several churches. The Methodists sent Reverend Jason Lee to start a mission in the Willamette Valley in 1834. The Presbyterians sent Reverend Marcus Whitman into eastern Oregon to found a mission. Father Pierre de Smet, famous Jesuit missionary and explorer, arrived to help in the founding of Catholic missions already begun months earlier. The missionaries sent enthusiastic reports of the Oregon country in letters published in the East.

Pioneer settlers beginning in 1841 established the long wagon caravan route of the Oregon Trail. This most famous of American pioneer trails began at Independence, Missouri, led northwestwards to the Platte River and ascended into Fort Laramie and then crossed South Pass, Wyoming, through the Rockies to Fort Hall on the Snake River. From Fort Hall the trail led down the Snake and then crossed the high plateau lands to the Columbia and on to the Willamette valley. Large scale migration in 1843 began with a covered wagon caravan of 1,000 persons. The pioneers in Oregon followed the American tradition of establishing their own provisional government and asked for annexation to the United States.

☉☉ The Oregon Treaty (1846)—In December 1845, Polk asked Congress for authority to take the necessary steps to fulfill his commitment to take Oregon. The impending war with Mexico indicated the need to make a friendly settlement with England. The actual occupation of Oregon by thousands of impatient American settlers gave the United States a stronger claim by right of possession. Fearing that Americans might raid her Fort Vancouver on the north bank of the Columbia, the Hudson's Bay Company withdrew to Vancouver Island. A compromise was now arranged by which the 49th parallel boundary was extended to the Pacific, with a notch in it to keep all of Vancouver Island Canadian. Now Polk could concentrate on the settlement of the differences with Mexico.

THE SOUTHWEST

American interest in the Southwest beyond the Great Plains was awakened by fur traders and trappers during the 1820s and 1830s. After Mexico gained independence in 1821, Americans began trading with Santa Fe. From New Mexico, fur trappers soon explored into California and learned of its attractions also. In the early 1840s settlers began taking up land in Mexican California. The acquisition of New Mexico and California became an important goal of the Polk administration.

☉ The Santa Fe Trade—Spain had forbidden American trade in New Mexico, but enough trading had occurred to reveal its profitability. In

1821 William Becknell, after an invitation from Mexican soldiers, made a trading trip to Santa Fe and realized a profit of several hundred percent. Beginning in 1823 wagon trains assembled in western Missouri at Independence and other points and began an active trade of Yankee manufactures and cloth for Mexican silver, furs, mules, and other items. The trail, following the Arkansas River much of the way, approximated a straight line pointing southwestward to Santa Fe. This trade was not of significant proportions economically but it aroused further American interest in the Southwest.

The Mountain Men—In the early 1820s fur-trading expeditions, organized by companies such as the Rocky Mountain Fur Company, became active in gathering furs by trading and trapping. Individuals or small parties of "mountain men" explored the whole area beyond the Great Plains in search of beaver and other valuable furs. Under the "rendezvous" system "free trappers" would meet company traders at a designated place to exchange their catch for trading goods or cash. Outstanding among the mountain men was the pious Jedediah S. Smith. At the head of parties of trappers, he blazed a new trail (1826) from the Great Salt Lake southwestward to southern California and then northward into Oregon. These fur traders and trappers opened routes through the mountains and across the deserts, discovered fertile lands, and served as guides for caravans of pioneer settlers.

California Under Spain and Mexico—California was settled first at San Diego in 1769, as part of the Spanish expansion from Mexico to the Northwest. The colonization was entrusted to the Franciscan fathers who founded numerous missions along the Pacific coast as far north as San Francisco. Presidios, or army posts, were established to protect and towns to grow provisions for the missions. The missions converted, civilized, and controlled a large population of unusually backward Native Americans.

After Mexico became independent, settlement was encouraged by liberal land grants to ranchers and farmers. Anti-clerical pressures in Mexico and California brought about the secularization of the missions in the 1830s; their land was granted to ranchers.

◊ American Intervention in California—The first Americans in California were New Englanders coming by ship to catch sea-otter along the coast and conduct a welcomed but illegal trade with the remote Spanish settlements. After 1820 whaling vessels conducted legal trading along the coast. A thriving hide and tallow trade sprang up during the 1820s to the mutual profit of Americans and Mexican missions and rancheros. American agents of the traders established themselves as Mexican citizens. Next came the mountain men. All made interesting reports of California resources.

Liberal Mexican land laws encouraged Americans to immigrate. The first overland settlers immigrated in 1841 and by 1844 several hundred

Americans had settled in the small valleys surrounding San Francisco Bay. They emigrated from the Missouri frontier along the Oregon Trail. At Fort Bridger they turned southwestward to follow the Humboldt River across Nevada. Through several passes they crossed the Sierra into the Sacramento Valley.

The farmer-settlers took little interest in becoming naturalized Mexican citizens and hoped that in some way California would soon be added to the United States. Thomas O. Larkin, an American merchant at the Mexican capital of Monterey, was appointed consul of the United States and also directed to see what he could do to stir up Mexican sentiment to join the United States. The Swiss-American John Sutter encouraged and gave much aid to American immigrants from his fort at Sacramento.

THE MEXICAN WAR, 1846–1848

Trouble between Mexico and the United States began after Texan independence. New Mexico and California were acquired as a result of the Mexican War.

✪✪✪ Causes of the Mexican War—1) Ineffective government in Mexico made it difficult for her to meet her financial obligations and protect the lives and property of Americans during her recurring revolutions. Polk was unable to secure payment of damage claims of American citizens against Mexico. 2) Mexico considered the annexation of Texas a hostile act and had warned it would lead to war. Attempts at annexation deeply offended Mexico. After annexation it was the disputed southern boundary of Texas and Mexico that led directly to war. (Mexico recognized the legality of the annexation of Texas, as a result of British negotiations, in May 1845, just before the war broke out.) 3) As to the boundary dispute, the United States claimed the Rio Grande as the southern boundary but Mexico considered the Nueces to be the boundary because it had been when Texas was a part of Mexico. 4) American intrusions in California alarmed Mexico. In 1842 Commodore Thomas Catesby Jones of the American navy, excited by rumors and thinking war had broken out with Mexico, seized Monterey. After Larkin convinced him he had acted mistakenly, he apologized and withdrew, but his action had revealed the desire to take California. In 1843 Mexico ordered the expulsion of American citizens from California and the exclusion of further immigration. Americans in California asked for American protection against arbitrary treatment.

✪✪ The Slidell Mission—Polk dispatched John Slidell to Mexico City in November 1845, to offer a settlement by which the United States would 1) assume claims of American citizens against Mexico in return for recognition of the Rio Grande boundary; 2) offer $5,000,000 for New

Mexico; and 3) offer $20,000,000 for California. Political turmoil in Mexico made Slidell's negotiations impossible. Mexican presidents did not dare to offend public opinion by receiving Slidell.

✪✪✪ **Outbreak of Hostilities**—The refusal of Mexico to negotiate convinced Polk that war was justified. He ordered General Zachary Taylor into the disputed territory just north of the Rio Grande. He expected hostilities that would more fully justify a declaration of war. Mexican troops crossed to the north bank of the Rio Grande and attacked American troops in April 1846. When Polk received the message he secured a declaration of war from Congress on May 12, 1846.

Many in the Northeast opposed the war, considering it an extension of slavery. The war was fought primarily by volunteers from the Mississippi valley and the Southwest.

CAMPAIGNS OF THE MEXICAN WAR

The war was fought in three main campaigns: 1) General Taylor's invasion of northern Mexico, 2) the conquest of New Mexico and California under the leadership of General Kearny, and 3) General Scott's march to Mexico City.

✪ **Taylor's Campaign**—General Zachary Taylor crossed the Rio Grande into Mexico at Matamoros in May 1846. Marching to the southwest, he captured Monterey in September and, in February 1847, won the Battle of Buena Vista against a force under General Santa Anna more than twice as large as his own force. These victories meant little as more than 300 miles of arid, mountainous terrain stood between Taylor and Mexico City. Political factors also intruded as Polk did not want to inflate the reputation of a potential Whig presidential candidate. Taylor stayed in northern Mexico.

✪ **Kearny in New Mexico and California**—In June 1846, Colonel Stephen W. Kearny, in command of an expedition to take California, marched over the Santa Fe Trail and along the Gila River to take charge in California. The war had begun there when the Bear Flag Republic was proclaimed by American settlers under the leadership of William B. Ide. Captain John C. Fremont's presence at the head of a surveying expedition apparently encouraged the revolt. Two weeks later when news of the war arrived, Fremont took over leadership of the Bear Flaggers and with his own men marched into southern California. Naval forces in the Pacific under Commodore Sloat and his successor Commodore Stockton, took the coastal towns of San Francisco, Monterey, and Los Angeles. When General Kearny arrived in San Diego he took command of all American forces and completed the conquest near Los Angeles.

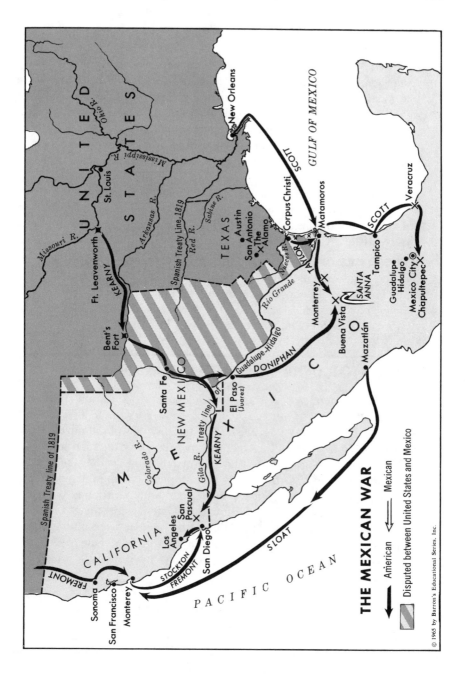

THE MEXICAN WAR

→ American

⇒ Mexican

◩ Disputed between United States and Mexico

© 1965 by Barron's Educational Series, Inc.

⊘ Scott's March to Mexico City—Late in 1846 General Winfield Scott was ordered to land his army at Vera Cruz to begin the conquest of Mexico City. The able leader won brilliant victories in hard fought engagements against the valiant Mexican defenders. Santa Anna's forces in Mexico City surrendered in September 1847. To draft a peace treaty Polk sent with Scott's forces Nicholas Trist, the chief clerk of the State Department who had learned his Spanish well in Cuba. Trist, after being recalled to Washington, undertook upon his own initiative to draft a treaty according to his original instructions. Meanwhile, enlarged American ambitions were ready to take much more, if not all, of Mexico. When Trist's treaty arrived in Washington, Polk reluctantly accepted the accomplished fact of a signed treaty. Protests of the abolitionists against adding new territory that might be opened to slavery suggested that the Treaty of Guadalupe Hidalgo should be accepted, which Polk reluctantly did.

⊘⊘⊘ The Treaty of Guadalupe Hidalgo (February 1848)—The terms of the treaty provided that 1) Mexico cede New Mexico and California and recognize the Rio Grande as the boundary of Texas; 2) the United States pay Mexico $15,000,000 for New Mexico and California and assume the claim of American citizens against Mexico.

⊘⊘ THE MORMON COLONIZATION OF UTAH

In the ferment of new social and religious ideas, Joseph Smith organized the Mormon Church at Palmyra, New York, in 1830. The tightly disciplined social order established by the disciples of the novel religion antagonized individualistic American frontier folk. Smith led his faithful to Kirtland, Ohio, in 1831, to Clay county, Missouri, in 1833, and in 1838 to Nauvoo, Illinois. As the tightly knit Mormon community gained converts, prosperity, and political power and openly sanctioned polygamy, the gentiles, or non-Mormons, turned violently against them. In the disorder that followed, Joseph Smith and his brother were murdered and the Mormons forced to leave Illinois. Early in 1846 Brigham Young, who had succeeded Smith, led the Mormons to Council Bluffs, Iowa. In 1847 Young began colonizing the Mormons in the vicinity of Salt Lake. Their numbers increased rapidly as converts were won in the East and in northern Europe. In 1850 Utah was organized as a territory with Brigham Young as its governor.

LEGISLATION UNDER POLK AND THE ELECTION OF 1848

With the acquisition of California, Polk had accomplished all the goals he had set for his administration: the acquisition of Oregon and

California, the lowering of the tariff, and the restablishment of the Independent Treasury.

The Tariff and the Sub-Treasury—With the support of the West and the South, Polk convinced Congress to lower the tariff and, hence, federal revenue, in the midst of a war; the Walker Tariff of 1846 was the first substantial cut since the compromise Tariff of 1833. He also secured the reestablishment of the Sub or Independent Treasury system begun by Van Buren and repealed under Tyler.

✪ **The Election of 1848**—Although the outbreak of the Mexican War aroused congressional debate over the slavery question, both major parties refused to inject this issue into the campaign. (Polk had declared he would serve only one term.) The Democrats nominated Lewis Cass of Michigan. The Whigs chose the popular hero of the Mexican War, General Zachary Taylor, a slaveowner from Louisiana. Millard Fillmore from New York became the Whig candidate for Vice President.

A third party entered the contest, the Free Soil Party. It promoted the non-expansion of slavery principle, recently revived as the Wilmot Proviso, adding to it free homesteads for settlers. It nominated Martin Van Buren. The party attracted former members of the Liberty Party, antislavery Whigs, and an antislavery faction of the Democrats called the Barnburners who refused to support Cass.

The Barnburners disagreed with the Hunkers and split the Democratic vote in New York state, causing Taylor and the Whigs to win the state and consequently the national election.

CHAPTER BOOK LIST

Acuña, Rudolfo, *Occupied America: A History of Chicanos* (1988). How Mexicans saw the war.

Anderson, Nels, *Desert Saints* (1942). On Mormon settlement of Utah.

Billington, Ray A., *The Far Western Frontier, 1830–1865* (1956). Good overview of expansion to the Pacific.

Coy, Owen, *The Great Trek* (1931). On the Gold Rush.

De Voto, Bernard, *Course of Empire* (Sentry). About the westward movement up to 1806.

Eisenhower, John S.D., *So Far from God: The U.S. War with Mexico* (1989). Good account for the general reader.

Farragher, John Mack, *Women and Men on the Overland Trail* (1979). Thoughts of the pioneers.

Foreman, Grant, *Five Civilized Tribes* (University of Oklahoma).

Foreman, Grant, *Indian Removal* (University of Oklahoma).

Graebner, Norman A., *Empire on the Pacific* (1955).

Gregg, Josiah, *Commerce of the Prairies* (Keystone). Classic account of the Sante Fe trade, published in 1844.

Hogan, William R., *The Texas Republic* (1969).

Horsman, Reginald, *The Frontier in The Formative Years 1783–1815* (Holt, Rinehart & Winston).

Jordan, Winthrop D., *The White Man's Burden: Historical Origins of Racism in the United States* (Oxford).

Limerick, Patricia, *The Legacy of Conquest* (1987). A very different view of the West.

Merk, Frederick, *The Monroe Doctrine and American Expansionism 1843–1849* (1966).

Pletcher, David M., *The Diplomacy of Annexation: Texas, Oregon, and the Mexican War* (1973). A complete study of the subject.

Sellers, Charles G., *James K. Polk: Continentalist, 1843–1846*. Describes Polk's election and his expansionist policies.

Singletary, Otis A., *The Mexican War* (Chicago). Brief account.

Turner, F.I., *Frontier and Section* (Prentice-Hall).

REVIEW QUESTIONS

MULTIPLE CHOICE

1. The campaign of 1844 was fought over (1) personalities (2) the question of territorial annexations (3) the slavery question (4) the national bank.

2. Texas was finally annexed to the Union for all these reasons except (1) the Texans finally relaxed their exorbitant demands (2) a real possibility existed that Texas might swing into a British orbit (3) annexation had been a campaign issue in 1844 (4) the spirit of Manifest Destiny.

3. The best American claim to Oregon was based on the immigration of which group? (1) Fur traders (2) missionaries (3) explorers (4) pioneer settlers.

4. Which name is not an American prominently associated with the settlement of Oregon? (1) John McLoughlin (2) Hall J. Kelley (3) Father De Smet (4) Marcus Whitman.

5. What is the best explanation of Polk's failure to take all of Oregon? (1) Southern opposition to adding more free states (2) the war threatening with Mexico (3) desire for the 49th parallel as the boundary (4) large British population in Vancouver.

6. The name most prominently associated with the opening of the Sante Fe trade is that of (1) Jedediah Smith (2) Zebulon Pike

(3) Manuel Lisa (4) William Becknell.

7. The Santa Fe Trail is most significant because (1) it led to the gold mines in California (2) Mexicans paid for goods with silver much needed as currency on the frontier (3) the trail came into immediate use for a large westward migration (4) it brought Americans into contact with the Southwest—New Mexico and California.

8. Which pair was least important in arousing American interest in California? (1) Traders and whalers (2) pioneer farmers and settlers (3) missionaries and miners (4) mountain men and explorers.

9. Which was the immediate cause of the Mexican War? (1) The clash of American and Mexican troops on the disputed boundary of Texas (2) the exclusion of Americans from California (3) the failure of the Slidell Mission (4) the annexation of Texas.

10. What are the correct dates for the beginning and end of the Mexican War? (1) 1845–1848 (2) 1846–1849 (3) 1846–1848 (4) 1845–1848.

11. Which leader did the most to bring the Mexican War to an end? (1) Scott (2) Taylor (3) Kearny (4) Fremont.

12. Who was not a presidential candidate in 1848? (1) Zachary Taylor (2) Lewis Cass (3) James K. Polk (4) Martin Van Buren.

13. Which pair of events did not occur at approximately the same time? (1) The Walker Tariff and the election of Taylor (2) the Compromise of 1850 and the death of President Taylor (3) Mormon migration to Utah and the Mexican War (4) the discovery of gold in California and the Treaty of Guadalupe Hidalgo.

TRUE-FALSE

14. The most powerful factor in preventing the annexation of Texas was fear of war with Mexico.

15. The primary British interest in Texas was commercial.

16. Several attempts were made in Congress to annex Texas before Tyler succeeded.

17. One of the earliest propagandists for the annexation of Oregon was Hall J. Kelley, a Boston schoolteacher.

18. Oregon was settled mainly through the efforts of antislavery societies that wished to make sure it would become a free state.

19. Polk agreed to the compromise over Oregon because he wished to concentrate military efforts on the war threatening with Mexico.

20. The Santa Fe was of less significance in stimulating interest in the Southwest than in the economic importance of the trade.

21. In California as in Texas the Mexicans welcomed American emi-

grants at first but later tried to prohibit further immigration.

22. American citizens going to California expected and hoped to become naturalized and permanent citizens of Mexico.

23. Even though Mexico rejected the Slidell Mission, Polk never gave up hope for peaceful settlement of the disagreements with Mexico.

24. Trist negotiated a treaty of peace with Mexico that gave the United States considerably less than Polk originally outlined in his instructions to Slidell.

25. A faction of Democrats in New York state called the Barnburners split the vote there and caused a Whig victory in 1848.

COMPLETION

26. The belief that the United States was due to expand and take over all of North America was summed up in the expression _____ .

27. In 1844 the Whig candidate _____ opposed the victorious Democrat _____ . The third party in this election was called the _____ Party.

28. Texas was annexed in the year _____ when Congress passed a _____ which provided Texas might divide herself into as many as _____ states.

29. The dominant British trading company in Oregon was the _____ Company; it was headed by the man _____ . The leading American fur-trading company in Oregon before 1812 was that of _____ .

30. Three missionary leaders prominent in calling attention to Oregon were the Methodist _____ , the Presbyterian _____ and the Catholic _____ .

31. The Oregon Trail began at _____ , Missouri, and crossed the Continental Divide at _____ , Wyoming.

32. Oregon was divided with Britain in the Oregon Treaty in _____ ; it continued the _____ as the boundary between Canada and the United States.

33. The Santa Fe Trail began at _____ , Missouri, and followed the _____ River for a great distance.

34. The fur men in the West were known as the _____ men; the greatest of them was _____ .

35. An American merchant at Monterey named _____ served as the American consul in California; at Sacramento _____ built his fort and aided American immigrants. In 1842 Commodore _____ of the American navy, thinking war had begun, seized Monterey.

36. In an attempt to settle the disputes with Mexico and acquire California and New Mexico President Polk sent _____ to Mexico late in 1845.

37. In the Mexican War the invasion of undisputed Mexican soil began when General _____ crossed the border at the _____ ; his greatest victory was at the Battle of _____ .The invasion of the Southwest was led by General _____ .

38. The founder of the Mormon Church was _____ and his successor who settled Utah was _____ .

CHRONOLOGY / CHAPTER 13

1790   Slater reconstructed English cotton spinning machinery in America.

1791   First Bank of the United States chartered.

1793   Whitney invented cotton gin.

1794   Lancaster Turnpike completed.

1807   Fulton invented first successful steamboat. Embargo Act stimulated growth of American factories.

1811   Construction of National Road begun. Charter of Bank expired.

1816   Second Bank of the United States chartered by Congress.

1817   Erie Canal construction begun.

1819   Cast-iron plow invented. Panic of 1819.

1820   Land Law of 1820 favored small farmers.

1830s   Time of rapid growth of labor unions.
Canal building boom. First railroads built early in decade.

1834   McCormick patented reaper.

1835   Colt patented revolver.

1837   Panic of 1837. Deere introduced steel plow in United States.

1839   Vulcanization of rubber discovered by Goodyear.

1840s   Heavy immigration of Irish and Germans brought plentiful labor supply for American industry for the first time.

1841   Preemption Act passed.

1842   American courts recognized right of collective bargaining by unions.

1844   Morse constructed first telegraph line.

1846   Howe invented sewing machine. Hoe rotary printing press invented.

1849   Gold Rush in California stimulated American prosperity.

1850   Illinois Central Railroad became the first to receive a federal land grant.

1851   Isaac Singer developed practical sewing machine.

Chapter

13

THE AMERICAN ECONOMY BEFORE THE CIVIL WAR, 1800–1860

The whole American economy expanded rapidly before the Civil War as the result of population growth, the development of export markets, and technological advances. The industrial revolution would soon lead to the domination of the nation by business interests, which would become well-entrenched by the Civil War.

Population in the United States grew from 4,000,000 in 1790 to 9,000,000 in 1815. By 1850 population was 23,000,000. Most of the increase was due to natural causes. From 1830 to 1850 about 2,000,000 foreign-born arrived, mostly from Ireland and Germany. The Irish took jobs in the cities of the Northeast and Midwest and afforded a large labor supply to industry for the first time. The Germans settled on farms, in the Midwest mainly.

AMERICAN AGRICULTURE

Agriculture dominated the politics and economy of the United States until the Civil War. Much progress was made in agricultural technology before 1860. The greatest change was the expansion of cotton growing. Climate caused large differences in Northern and Southern agriculture except in corn production which was common to both sections.

❂❂ **Southern Agriculture After 1800**—The outstanding change in American agriculture was the rapid expansion in cotton cultivation. When Eli Whitney invented the cotton gin (1793), he broke the bottleneck in the conversion of cotton to textiles and thereby opened up an ever growing demand for cotton fiber. The gin made economically feasible the cultivation of upland, short staple cotton. The gin could quickly cut the tightly clinging fibers from seeds of the upland cotton. Cotton cultivation was freed from its confinement to the coastal, sea-island climate where the loose-seeded, long staple variety grew.

By 1811 cotton production had increased forty times over the production of 1791. With the conclusion of the War of 1812 cotton production spread more rapidly than ever over new areas of the deep South as high prices for the staple encouraged the extensive use of slave labor. Small farmers also produced cotton in areas not so suitable for large plantation fields. "King Cotton" came to dominate the whole life and economy of the South. This cash crop brought great profits to producers and served to draw settlers into the virgin lands farther out on the frontier. Since cotton exhausted the fertility of the soil rapidly, fresh land was always in demand.

Sugar cane cultivation on large plantations in southern Louisiana increased and came to supply a large part of the country's need for sugar. Tobacco production continued in Virginia and Maryland as in colonial times and expanded into Kentucky and Tennessee. Rice production on plantations cultivated by slave labor prospered in South Carolina and Georgia until the Civil War. Southern farms, even slave plantations, tried to produce enough foodstuffs for self-sufficiency. Corn acreage was as large as any crop and more widespread geographically, but it was consumed on the farm and plantation.

○ **Northern Agriculture**—New England agriculture began to decline after 1800 because of the competition from new lands being opened in the Ohio valley. The centers of wheat and corn production shifted from the middle Atlantic states to the states of the Old Northwest. Livestock and grain production dominated the agriculture of the North. The characteristic unit was the small family farm. Centers of livestock production shifted to the West also. Cincinnati and Chicago successively became marketing and packing centers for hogs and cattle. The Midwest produced corn and hogs for export to the South. As the cities grew in population, surrounding farming lands turned to specialized vegetable, fruit, and dairy farming.

○ **Agricultural Inventions**—Markets in the cities of the East and in Europe provided an incentive to farmers to increase their output by the use of more efficient labor-saving equipment. The cast-iron plow (1819) only slowly replaced the wooden plow, because farmers believed the iron poisoned the soil. However, by 1830 iron plows had been accepted and were being mass-produced. Next, steel plows came into use, especially in prairie lands farther west where an efficient cutting edge was needed to break the heavy turf. John Deere took the lead in producing self-scouring efficient steel moldboard plows that could be drawn by horses. Horses in the North and mules in the South replaced the slower-paced oxen.

In harvesting, the long-bladed scythe was improved by the attachment of a cradle to catch the severed stalks. In the early 1830s in Virginia Cyrus McCormick developed a horse-drawn mechanical reaper.

After 1840 horse-powered machinery began to come into use. By 1860 over 100,000 reapers were being used by western farmers. After 1840 the mechanical thresher replaced the older methods of flailing by hand or treading by horses to separate the grain from stalks and husks. J.I. Case took the lead in manufacturing threshers. In the 1850s many experiments and actual application of steam power were being made in plowing and threshing. Grain production greatly increased and larger world markets were opened during the prosperous 1850s.

TRANSPORTATION

The immense growth of both domestic and foreign commerce after 1840 created a great need for transportation facilities. Steamboats and railroads developed to fill the need.

❂ The Shipping Industry—Although the colonies had developed a great shipping and shipbuilding industry, the typical American ship, the fast-sailing clipper, reached its perfection well before the Civil War. Americans developed the clipper ships because of the long distances traveled around South America into the Pacific Northwest and to the Far East. The long, narrow, tall-masted clippers gave America the lead in the world's carrying trade before the Civil War. After that England assumed the lead with fast steamships, and transcontinental railroad transportation began to replace the clippers that carried goods around Cape Horn into the Pacific.

Steamboating, on the Mississippi and elsewhere, reached its peak in the 1850s but continued to carry enormous tonnages on the rivers of America. It declined because of competition from canals, railroads, the danger of shipwrecks, and the deadly competition among the different transportation facilities.

❂ The Railroads—By far the most significant development in transportation was the building of railroads beginning in the 1830s. The advantages of rail transportation over other forms was in the greater speed and freedom from confinement of routes to waterways. The Eastern Seaboard cities built railroads to draw inland commerce to themselves or they built to make connections with sources of freight traffic such as canals and other waterways. Most were built with private financing, often subsidized by local and state aid. The first federal land grant to aid railroad financing was obtained in 1850 for the Illinois Central Railroad and by 1860 about 20,000,000 acres had been granted by various enactments to subsidize railroad construction. By 1860 an astonishing growth in railroads had taken place east of the Mississippi.

Numerous technological improvements were made. Wooden rails were replaced with iron and coal replaced wood as a fuel. As the necessary connections between lines were made, the Northwest became more closely linked to the East; the common economic interests thus created would draw them together during the Civil War.

BUSINESS AND INDUSTRY

Mercantile and shipping dominated American business life in the colonial and early national periods. Manufacturing, expanding rapidly since 1807, superseded commercial interests about the time of the Civil War.

⚙ **The Industrial Revolution**—The Industrial Revolution, or development of large scale manufacturing, was delayed in America because of 1) the superior quality of imported manufactures; 2) the lack of adequate, low-cost labor; 3) and the greater attraction of shipping, trade, and land speculation for investment capital.

The first large factories were built by textile manufacturers using water power in the Northeast. Samuel Slater introduced cotton spinning from England in 1791. Eli Whitney's development of the principle of interchangeable parts helped make mass production possible. The construction of the first telegraph line in 1844 by Samuel F. B. Morse brought rapid communication, an aid to business organization. In 1846 Elias Howe invented the sewing machine, but Isaac Singer developed a practical machine about 1851. The sewing machine made possible the ready-made clothing industry. Improved transportation enabled manufacturers to supply national markets from factories in the Northeast or the upper Midwest. The heavy immigration of the 1840s and 1850s furnished many of the workers for these larger factories. The powerful and prospering new industrialists grew impatient with Southern control of the nation's politics that prevented favorable legislation for business interests.

Corporations—The corporation as a form of business organization began to replace individual proprietorships and partnerships before the Civil War. A corporation is a legal entity, a person in the eyes of the law, created by charters granted by state governments usually, rarely by the federal government. The great advantage of the corporation is its ability to attract investment, risk capital for large scale enterprise. The legal provision of limited liability protected investors from risk of losing more than they had invested in the shares of an enterprise. By selling shares of stock, capital could be gathered from a multitude of investors. The best managerial talent could be commanded by corporations offering high salaries.

Corporations were used at first by banks and by transportation monopolies, both as a symbol of prestige and a means of raising capital. In manufacturing, the corporation device was first used in the textile industry. The corporation came to dominate American business after the Civil War.

♦ The Fur Trade—Important but sometimes overlooked in the early national economy was the fur business. This trade continued on a large scale after colonial times and expanded into the Far West. Furs were gathered by American trappers and hunters, as well as by traders who exchanged various manufactured goods with the Native American tribes. Furs were exported to Europe and China to be used for hats, clothing, and blankets.

After the purchase of Louisiana, St. Louis became the center of the fur business. Large companies organized as corporations; the business required much money for trading goods and yielded large profits but there were elements of large risk. John Jacob Astor, a poor immigrant boy from Germany, made himself the largest operator in the fur trade; the American Fur Company was his main firm. Astor became the first American millionaire and his was the first great business corporation. The fur trade was significant not only for its size but in speeding the opening of the West.

♦♦ Labor—The growth of industry was necessarily accompanied by the rise of a large wage-earning working class with its own distinct interests. In the early decades of the Industrial Revolution workers enjoyed little in the way of legislation or organization to protect their interests. Most mill workers in the textile industry worked 10 to 13 hours a day. A great many girls and children worked under conditions that varied from good to very bad. New England farm girls worked, until they married, for paternalistic employers under fairly favorable conditions. Exploitation occurred with the development of a permanent class of workers, a large part of whom were immigrants.

Labor organizations for bargaining purposes were not only not recognized by law but held by common law to be conspiracies against the public interest. However, they organized among the skilled workers in spite of opposition, even in colonial times. They usually organized in secret societies or as brotherhoods and on a local scale. Around 1830 unions experienced a rapid growth and by 1834 had 300,000 members. Beginning with the Jacksonian period they were a source of support in the Democratic Party in eastern cities. They conducted strikes for better wages and hours and worked for free public schools. They worked successfully also for the abolition of imprisonment for debt and for mechanics' lien laws. In 1842 the courts recognized the important right of organized labor to bargain collectively for higher wages.

CHAPTER BOOK LIST

Bidwell, P.W., and Falconer, J.I., *History of Agriculture in the Northern United States, 1820–1860* (1925). Detailed economic history.

Bodnar, John, *The Transplanted: A History of Immigrants in Urban America* (1985).

Bruchey, Stuart W., *Enterprise: The Dynamic Economy of a Free People* (1990). Economic development in the early nineteenth century.

Cochran, Thomas C., *Frontiers of Change: Early Industrialism in America* (1981). Overview of the subject by a veteran scholar.

Cohen, Henry, *Business and Politics in America from the Age of Jackson to the Civil War* (1971).

Fish, C.R., *The Rise of The Common Man* (1927). Much material on living conditions at this time.

Fogel, Robert W., *Railroads and American Economic Growth* (1964). Clear and complete survey.

Johnson, Paul, *A Shopkeepers Millenium: Society and Revivals in Rochester, New York, 1815–1837* (1979). Religion and the new industrial order.

Jones, Maddyn A., *American Immigration* (University of Chicago). Brief.

Knoebel, Dale T., *Paddy and the Republic: Ethnicity and Nationality in Antebellum America* (1985).

Martin, Albro, *Railroad's Triumphant: The Growth, Rejection, and Rebirth of a Vital American Force* (1991). The history of a basic American transportation facility.

Morison, S.E., *Maritime History of Massachusetts, 1783–1860* (Sentry). History of the era of clipper ships.

North, Douglass C., *The Economic Growth of the United States: 1790–1860* (Norton).

Sitterson, J.C., *Sugar Country* (1953). About Louisiana plantations.

Temin, Peter, *The Jacksonian Economy* (Norton).

Wallace, Anthony F.C., *Rockdale: The Growth of an American Village in the Early Industrial Revolution* (1980). How factories changed rural America.

REVIEW QUESTIONS

MULTIPLE CHOICE

1. The outstanding change in American agriculture from 1800 to 1850 was (1) production of tobacco in Kentucky (2) prosperity of the small farmer in the South (3) rice cultivation in South Carolina and Georgia (4) spread of cotton cultivation over the South.

2. The westward expansion of upland cotton farming in the South (1) resulted mainly from the invention of the cotton gin (2) resulted mainly from the surplus population of slaves (3) would have spread westward rapidly regardless of the cotton gin—because of favorable climate and soil (4) occurred mainly on lands cleared by slave labor.

3. Which name is most important in the development of harvesting machinery? (1) J.I. Case (2) Elias Howe (3) John Deere (4) Cyrus McCormick.

4. Which list shows the correct order of the beginning of each development in transportation? (1) Canals, railroads, clippers (2) railroads, clippers, steamships (3) clippers, steamships, railroads (4) steamships, railroads, canals.

5. Which probably did the most to reduce the importance of steamboats? (1) Canals (2) railroads (3) turnpikes (4) clipper ships.

6. The increase in business enterprises organized as corporations before 1860 is best explained by (1) the prestige given by a corporation charter (2) ability to hire best college graduates (3) corporate ability to raise risk capital for large enterprises (4) favorable federal legislation.

7. The Native American fur trade in the Louisiana Territory was opened by the (1) French (2) Spanish (3) British (4) Americans.

8. The fur trade with the Native Americans (1) yielded only small profits (2) in the United States came to be centered at St. Louis (3) was not suited to large-scale enterprise (4) was Kit Carson's main occupation.

9. Which statement about labor organizations before 1850 is incorrect? They (1) were usually organized as secret brotherhoods (2) were held to be conspiracies against the public interest until 1842 (3) organized active political parties (4) worked for free public schools.

10. Before the Civil War American inability to meet a great national need was most conspicuous (1) in the handling of the banking issue (2) in the provisions of federal land laws (3) in legislation providing for local and state government (4) in creating a body of national literature.

TRUE-FALSE

11. For the first time American industry had a sufficient labor supply when the heavy immigration came in about 1850.

12. Livestock and grain production dominated the agriculture of the Northwest.

13. Steam power was not introduced to the farm until after the Civil War.

14. English steamship competition and the transcontinental railroads did the most to end the era of the American clipper ships.

15. The construction of railroads flourished because they could transport heavier loads and bulkier produce than water transportation.

16. John Jacob Astor became the first American millionaire.

17. New England farm girls supplied a large part of the labor to operate the textile mills there and certainly most of them worked under the most unfavorable conditions.

COMPLETION

18. Before the Civil War the leading state in sugar production was _____ .

19. An early meat packing center before Chicago was _____ .

20. The leader in the improvement of the plow was _____ .

21. _____ is best known as a manufacturer of threshers.

22. The first railroad to receive a federal land grant was the _____ .

23. Cotton textile machinery was introduced from England by _____ .

24. The builder of the first telegraph line was _____ ; _____ is usually given credit for inventing the sewing machine but _____ developed the first practical machine.

CHRONOLOGY / CHAPTER 14

1817   Active antislavery movement resulted in organization of the American Colonization Society in 1817.

1825   Robert Owen founded New Harmony socialist colony in Indiana.

1826   Lyceum movement begun in Massachusetts.
American Temperance Society organized.

1830s   Dorothea Dix began crusade for humane treatment of insane.
Compulsory free public school movement active.

1830   Mormon Church organized.

1831   Garrison began publication of *The Liberator*.

1833   Oberlin College founded as the first coeducational college.

1836   "Gag rule" adopted in Congress to table antislavery petitions.
Mount Holyoke College for women founded.

1840   Liberty Party organized as first antislavery third party.

1841   Brook Farm, a Fourierist society, organized.

1846   Neal Dow secured passage of the first state prohibition law in Maine.

1848   First Women's Rights convention held.

1852   *Uncle Tom's Cabin* published.

1855   Amana Society of German Pietists settled in Iowa.

1860   By this date twenty Western states had founded universities.

Chapter

14
REFORM MOVEMENTS
BEFORE THE CIVIL WAR,
1815–1861

Americans after 1815 embraced many religious and social movements in pursuit of solutions for the problems, evils, and misfortunes of mankind. These movements were generally more active in the Northern states.

⊙ **Sources of Antebellum Reform**—1) A main assumption of the Enlightenment was that the world reflected the reasonable plan of God for humanity; all that had to be done was to uncover that plan and apply it to human institutions. Something of this survived into the nineteenth century. 2) As the United States became more of a political democracy, interest spread in educating and uplifting the common people, as they now had political power and must be taught to use it responsibly. 3) Evangelical Protestantism reinforced this tendency, adding to it the moral demands of religion. 4) Middle class Americans grew fearful that the working classes, without the social cement of the old hierarchical class system, would threaten the stability and order of society. Reform groups often aimed to make good citizens of these people.

⊙⊙⊙ **The Antislavery Movement**—The most active of the reform movements was that against slavery. Many antislavery societies promoted their cause before 1820. These early societies were most numerous in the border states of the South and were gradualistic in action. The outstanding national organization here was the American Colonization Society which began in 1817. It founded the African republic of Liberia on the west coast of Africa for colonizing African Americans. The societies worked to solve the race problem by transporting free African Americans to Africa. They soon discovered that they were transporting fewer African Americans than the number of African Americans being born in the country at the same time.

In 1831 William Lloyd Garrison, publisher of the radical abolitionist journal called *The Liberator,* condemned mild, gradual, and compensated emancipation and stridently worked for immediate emancipation without compensation. The radical abolitionist movement centered in New England. A second center of abolitionism, north of the Ohio River and led by James Birney and Theodore D. Weld, worked through religious appeals and favored gradual emancipation. Many prominent ministers and other crusaders were active in the abolitionist societies over the North. They flooded the country with antislavery literature. At first they sought to convince owners that slavery was a sin and attempted to secure voluntary emancipation. Later they turned to political action. (They organized the Liberty Party in 1840.) Abolitionists sent antislavery petitions of one kind or another to Congress where they were obligingly introduced by John Quincy Adams. Congress adopted the "gag rule" in 1836 and tabled such petitions without debate. Resorting to direct action, the abolitionists organized the so-called "Underground Railroad" to aid runaway slaves in making their way to freedom in Canada.

OO **Reaction to Abolitionism**—Northern reaction to the antislavery movement reflected the general racism of American society. Abolitionists were often attacked as radicals and troublemakers, with Garrison being mobbed in Boston and Elijah Lovejoy killed in Illinois.

In the South after 1830 abolitionists were completely squelched. In 1831 Nat Turner, an African American preacher, led a slave uprising in Virginia in which about 55 whites were killed. Garrison and the abolitionists were blamed. When Southern mobs attacked post offices to destroy abolitionist literature, postmasters stopped delivering such mail. The South was cognizant of ancient slave uprisings and of the uprising in Santo Domingo in the 1790s. Slave codes were tightened in Southern states and patrols established.

The South, placed on the defensive by abolitionist attacks, tried to justify their "peculiar institution" in every way they could. Professor Thomas R. Dew and others after him wrote intellectual defenses of slavery. They said that 1) the slave was better cared for and enjoyed more security than the Northern factory worker; 2) the African American slave was better off than in Africa; 3) slavery reflected the "natural order," in which the strong always dominated the weak; 4) slavery was accepted in Biblical times; and 5) national prosperity was based on the export trade and the slave-based economy of the South. Abolitionism added a highly emotional issue to the other quarrels between the sections. The South rallied more and more to the defense of slavery; in the North public opinion for one reason or another came to support the antislavery cause.

The Temperance Movement—The temperance movement agitated for the mitigation of the evils of alcohol even before abolitionists became active. Dr. Benjamin Rush during the American Revolution condemned alcoholic beverages as harmful to the health. Religious-minded reformers led the movement before 1820 and consolidated local temperance societies into the American Temperance Union. Those advocating the moderate use of alchohol frequently clashed with the "teetotalers," those who would prohibit alchohol totally. In the 1840s thirteen states moved to restrict the production or sale of alcohol in some way. In 1851, under the influence of Neal Dow, Maine passed a total prohibition law.

Treatment of the Insane—Dorothea L. Dix in the 1830s and 1840s led a crusade for more humane and rational treatment of the insane and feeble-minded. At that time people believed that the insane were morally responsible for their condition or viewed them with superstition. Little hope was held for the cure of these unfortunates. They were beaten, caged, and neglected. Dorothea Dix called public attention to the inhumane treatment accorded the insane and influenced state governments over the whole country to establish hospitals for them.

The Women's Rights Movement—From the earliest times women were kept politically and legally subordinate to men. They could not control property, make wills, vote, retain wages they had earned, or attend college. They might legally be given corporal punishment "with a reasonable instrument." As women became active in the various crusades and more articulate as writers, men began to recognize their achievements. Margaret Fuller (1810–1850) and Susan B. Anthony (1820–1906) led the crusade to give them the right to enter professions and to give them equality before the law. Their contemporaries Lucretia Mott and Elizabeth Cady Stanton called the first Women's Rights Convention in 1848. Gradually the movement gained favorable results through legislation in the states.

❍ **The Philosophic Communitarians**—Collective societies led by Utopian visionaries were a conspicuous part of the reforming zeal of the first half of the nineteenth century. Cooperative settlements were founded to demonstrate that shared property and work would promote a better life than the individualist life-style of most Americans. Others sought the same economic equality and segregated themselves also to realize religious and social ideals. Most of them failed after a few years except those held together by strong religious convictions. These various societies sought a solution to the economic and social evils arising from the inequalities and insecurity produced by the industrial revolution.

Robert Owen, a British mill owner and Utopian socialist, founded the colony of New Harmony in Indiana in 1825, in addition to other colonies in the United States and in Great Britain. Owen's unorthodox social ideas and his anti-religious views needlessly antagonized Americans. The colony, like some of the others, attracted too many visionaries and lazy and irresponsible persons. Hard working Americans preferred to enjoy the fruits of their labor rather than to share them.

The ideas of the French socialist, Charles Fourier, were tried in several colonies in America. Emerson and other intellectuals for a time tried the Fourierist ideas at Brook Farm. These New England transcendentalists were attracted by Fourier's emphasis upon the dignity of man; they disliked the fierce competitiveness of private enterprise. None of the 40-odd Fourierist societies succeeded; they proved impractical.

The Religious Communitarians—Religious colonies did succeed or at least survived for many years. The Amana Society, founded by German Pietists, who settled in Iowa in 1855, were notably successful in following a communitarian order until 1932.

Two early Protestant monastic societies were the Shakers and the Rappites. The Shakers organized communistic colonies in the Ohio valley and in New York. They carried on a flourishing agriculture but never attracted a large number of converts. The Rappites organized among German Pietists in Pennsylvania and lived at New Harmony, before they sold out to Robert Owen in 1824.

Reforms in Education—Free public schools financed by property taxes became an objective of reformers who argued that they were necessary for educating voters and citizens. Organized labor agitated for schools to provide more equality of opportunity for all and reduce the competition of children for jobs in industry. Horace Mann of Massachusetts in many ways promoted public education. He founded the first normal school, a two-year post-secondary institution to train teachers. He influenced all the Northern states to create tax-supported primary schools.

The lyceum movement began in Massachusetts in 1826. Well-known and popular educators and speakers were brought to towns during the winters to address adult audiences. Another development was the organization of subscription libraries all over the North by 1850. The first coeducational college, Oberlin, was founded in 1833, and Mount Holyoke College in 1836 was founded for women. Twenty Western states founded universities before 1860. As for secondary schools, private academies prevailed.

CHAPTER BOOK LIST

Bestor, Jr., A.E., *Backwoods Utopias* (1950). On communitarian socialists.
Boles, John B., *The Great Revival* (1972).
Commager, H.S., *Era of Reform, 1830–1860* (Anvil). Selected readings prefaced by helpful introductions; about reform movements.
Davis, David B., *The Problem of Slavery in the Age of Revolution 1770–1823* (1975).
Degler, Carl N., *At Odds: Women and the Family from the Revolution to the Present* (1980).
Ekirch, A.A., *The Idea of Progress in America, 1815–1860* (1944).

Flexner, Eleanor, *Century of Struggle: The Woman's Rights Movement in the United States* (Harvard).

McLoughlin, William G., *Modern Revivalism* (1959). Best general work on the Second Great Awakening.

Nye, Russel B., *The Cultural Life of the New Nation* (Harper & Row).

O'Neill, William L., *The Woman Movement* (Watts).

Richards, Leonard L., *"Gentlemen of Property and Standing": Anti-Abolition Mobs in Jacksonian America* (1970). Study of the frequent violence against abolitionists.

Rorabaugh, W.J., *The Alcoholic Republic: An American Tradition* (1979). Excellent survey of the temperance movement.

Ryan, Mary, *The Cradle of the Middle Class: The Family in Oneida County, New York, 1790–1865* (1981). On the cult of domesticity.

Smith, Timothy L., *Revivalism and Social Reform in Mid-Nineteenth Century America* (1957).

Stewart, James Brewer, *Holy Warriors: The Abolitionists and American Slavery* (1976).

Sweet, W.W., *Religion in the Development of American Culture, 1765–1840* (1952). Influence of churches.

Tyler, A.F., *Freedoms Ferment: Phases of American Social History to 1860* (1962). General survey.

Walters, Ronald G., *American Reformers, 1815–1860* (1978). A modern interpretation.

Walters, Ronald G., *The Antislavery Appeal: American Abolitonists After 1830* (1976).

REVIEW QUESTIONS

MULTIPLE CHOICE

1. The most radical abolitionist was (1) Benjamin Lundy (2) Ralph Waldo Emerson (3) William Lloyd Garrison (4) Elijah P. Lovejoy.

2. Which person was not an abolitionist? (1) William Lloyd Garrison (2) Thomas R. Dew (3) Elijah Lovejoy (4) Theodore Weld.

3. Communitarian societies and religious sects flourished in America because (1) there was a prevailing attitude of toleration (2) there existed vacant land where they might isolate themselves from disturbing influences (3) Americans were more religious than other peoples of European origin (4) the cooperative spirit usually predominated on the frontier.

4. The largest and most enduring communitarian societies were based primarily (1) on religious beliefs (2) on ideas of economic equalitarianism (3) on political and social ideals (4) on financial subsidies.

TRUE-FALSE

5. The earliest antislavery societies were the most radical.

6. The various reform movements flourished as much in the South as in the North.

7. Northern ministers almost universally shunned the abolitionist societies.

8. Abolitionists in the North received more ill-treatment in the southern Ohio valley than they did elsewhere in the North.

9. The South argued that slavery reflected the natural order of strong vs. weak found in nature.

10. The South reacted to antislavery propaganda by making numerous concessions to Northern opinions.

11. A leading problem the communitarians wished to solve was that of economic inequality.

COMPLETION

12. The American Colonization Society was responsible for the founding of the African republic of _____ .

13. Southerners in Congress prevented debate on antislavery petitions by adopting the _____ .

14. An organized system for aiding runaway slaves to escape to Canada was called the _____ .

15. An abolitionist killed by a mob in Illinois was _____ .

16. _____ was a Southern professor who wrote a book defending slavery.

17. Those who advocated complete abstinence from alcoholic beverages were called _____ .

18. The best known communitarian colony, located in Indiana, was known by the name _____ .

19. One of the most successful religious communitarian societies, located in Iowa, was that of the _____ Society.

20. An adult education movement made up of popular lecturers was known as the _____ movement.

21. The first coeducational college was founded at _____ , Ohio.

MATCHING

22. William Lloyd Garrison	a. Probably best known advocate of women's rights
23. Nat Turner	b. *The Liberator*
24. Benjamin Rush	c. Called for better treatment of the insane
25. Dorothea L. Dix	d. Founded first normal school
26. Neal Dow	e. British utopian socialist
27 Susan B. Anthony	f. Maine prohibitionist
28. Elizabeth Cady Stanton	g. His ideas tried at Brook Farm
29. Robert Owen	h. Slave leader
30. Charles Fourier	i. One of first to condemn alcoholic beverages
31. Horace Mann	j. Gradualistic abolitionist
	k. Called early women's rights conventions

THE CIVIL WAR PERIOD
1850–1865

CHRONOLOGY / CHAPTER 15

1846 Wilmot Proviso first introduced.

1848 Free-Soil Party, successor to Liberty Party, introduced slavery issue into a national election.

1850 Clayton-Bulwer Treaty provided that neither the United States nor Great Britain would construct an isthmian canal under exclusive control.

Compromise of 1850, among its various provisions admitted California as a free state, abolished slave trade in District of Columbia, and enacted a more stringent fugitive slave law.

1852 *Uncle Tom's Cabin* published by Harriet Beecher Stowe.

1853 Pierce inaugurated as President. Gadsden Purchase made from Mexico.

1854 Kansas-Nebraska Act provided for the organization of Kansas and Nebraska as territories. Republican Party organized.

Treaty with Japan opened two ports to the United States.

Ostend Manifesto failed to bring annexation of Cuba.

1856 Proslavery mob burned free-state capital at Lawrence in "Bloody Kansas"; John Brown retaliated with "Pottawatomie Massacre."

Republican Party nominated Fremont, its first presidential candidate. Buchanan (Dem.) elected President.

1857 Buchanan inaugurated as President.

Representative Preston Brooks assaulted Senator Sumner for "The Crime Against Kansas" speech.

Dred Scott case awarded the South a victory.

Panic of 1857 bolstered confidence of the South.

Hinton Helper published *The Impending Crisis* attacking rule of slave aristocrats in the South.

1858 Lincoln-Douglas debates made Lincoln better known.

1859 John Brown's Raid at Harper's Ferry.

1860 Election of Lincoln, made possible by split of Democratic Party, caused Southern states to secede.

1861 Civil War began. Kansas admitted as free state.

Chapter

15
SECTIONAL STRIFE, 1850–1861

> After the Mexican War the controversy over slavery affected almost every issue in American politics. One provocative event after another aggravated relations until secession of the South led to the outbreak of the Civil War in 1861.

THE COMPROMISE OF 1850

The acquisition of the Southwest in the Mexican War raised the question of the status of slavery in the territories.

The Wilmot Proviso—In August 1846, David Wilmot, an antislavery Democrat from Pennsylvania, moved to amend a military appropriations bill with a proviso that slavery would never be permitted in any territory acquired from Mexico. Although it never passed, it was frequently offered as an amendment and kept opposition to the extension of slavery before the nation.

⊙⊙⊙ **Slavery in the Territories**—There were three views on the legality of slave-holding in the territories.

1) Southern view as stated by Calhoun maintained that Congress had no right to exclude slavery from the territories. The territories belonged to the whole nation. To exclude slavery would amount to the exclusion of slave owners and would deny their rights to take their property, the slaves, into territories that belonged to the whole nation. The South hoped that additional slave states might be brought into the Union to offset the free states of Oregon and Minnesota which would soon follow California as free states.

2) The North held that Congress had the legal right to legislate such provisions as it saw fit for the government of the territories including the right to legislate upon the status of slavery.

3) The moderates, mostly Northern Democrats, favored "squatter sovereignty" as suggested first by Lewis Cass of Michigan and which held that the residents of a territory should decide the status of slavery. Some held this view as a means of compromise, others simply believed

in local determination of such questions as a matter of democracy. Later Stephen A. Douglas gave the name "popular sovereignty" to this view.

4) Another view favored dividing the territory by the extension of the Missouri Compromise line of 36°30´ to the Pacific.

✪ The California Gold Rush—The discovery of gold not far from Sacramento in 1848 brought a sudden large inrush of "forty-niners" to California the next year. The military government proved inadequate for the needs of a population of 100,000. California drafted a constitution in 1849 and applied for admission as a free state. Again, as with Missouri's application for statehood, the South was alarmed by the prospect of being outvoted in the Senate by free state senators. A year later New Mexico and Utah applied for admission as free states. Extremists in the South favored immediate secession.

Apart from the slavery controversy, the phenomenal mass migration from all over the world to California greatly accelerated the settlement of the whole of the Far West. The inflationary effect of the golden metal poured into the channels of commerce stimulated worldwide prosperity during the 1850s.

✪✪ Debate and Enactment of the Compromise Proposals—Henry Clay and several other old Whig stalwarts presented legislation to settle not only the future of the Mexican Cession, but several other sectional issues as well. This legislation was offered in a so-called Omnibus Bill to be accepted or rejected as a package. It included the following: 1) California was admitted as a free state; 2) New Mexico and Utah were to be organized as territories with no reference to slavery; 3) Texas's public debt was assumed in return for her acceptance of a more restricted boundary than she claimed; 4) the slave trade (but not slavery) was banned in the District of Columbia; 5) a more stringent fugitive slave law.

The moderates led by Clay appealed to Congress to settle the issues and stop the dangerous squabbling over slavery. Daniel Webster sacrificed his political career in the North to support Clay's compromise in his famous "Seventh of March" speech. Webster argued that nature had banned slavery from the arid West, and he condemned the abolitionists for creating strife. Farmers and businessmen over the country, enjoying a new prosperity, did not wish to disturb it with further dispute over slavery. President Taylor, not a good politician, refused to work with either side to achieve compromise, but Taylor died suddenly in July 1850. Vice President Millard Fillmore, who favored the compromise, now became President. Stephen A. Douglas, a Democratic Senator from Illinois, took over management of the bill from the ailing Clay and separated it into five separate bills, the passage of which he secured by September.

✪✪ Consequences of the Compromise—After the compromise measures were adopted by Congress the South stopped its threats of secession, and relative quiet over the whole nation followed. The compromise supporters insisted that the slavery question had been permanently settled. Most of the provisions represented victories for the antislavery cause, but the North refused to accept the Fugitive Slave Law which represented the only clear-cut victory for the South. The North wanted jury trials for runaway slaves. Mass meetings resolved not to obey the law. State legislatures passed "personal liberty laws" prohibiting the use of local jails for holding runaways and otherwise blocked enforcement. The South accused the North of violating their part of the bargain. A larger consequence was the postponement of Southern secession until the North had become strong enough to prevent the disintegration of the Union.

○ **The Clayton-Bulwer Treaty (1850)**—The large gold rush to California and the sustained migration to Oregon dictated the need for better communications to the American Pacific coast than those afforded by horse and wagon across the western plains and mountains. The United States during the Polk administration secured exclusive transit rights across Panama in a treaty (1846) with the government of New Granada. American promoters wanted to construct a canal. Britain chose to check the possible American choice of an alternate route through Nicaragua by seizing Greytown (San Juan, Nicaragua). In the crisis that followed, the two powers chose to negotiate a compromise, the Clayton-Bulwer Treaty. It agreed that neither nation should fortify or exercise exclusive control over an isthmian canal. The treaty checked British expansion in Central America at a time when the United States was weakened by the slavery quarrel.

○ **The Election of 1852**—Results of this election seemed to reflect a national feeling for moderation. The Democratic dark horse candidate Franklin Pierce of New Hampshire won an overwhelming victory over the Whig nominee. The Whigs again characteristically nominated an old war hero, General Winfield Scott. The Free Soil Party entered a candidate but made a poorer showing than in 1848. The Whigs lost badly because their party was disintegrating in the South, ominously foreshadowing the end of national parties with strong support from both sections.

EXPANSIONISM OF THE PIERCE ADMINISTRATION

Pro-Southern Democrats controlled the Pierce administration, the Democratic Party, and Congress. Pierce was a mediocre President who had no profound understanding of how critical were the quarrels between the sections. The administration tried to distract attention from slavery by foreign expansion.

Commercial Expansion—To satisfy the expanding commercial interests Pierce sent a naval expedition under Commodore Matthew C. Perry to Japan to obtain privileges for American ships and protection for shipwrecked American seamen. Perry conducted the negotiations in a forceful, dignified manner that secured a treaty (1854) that opened two ports to the United States.

An effort at this time to annex Hawaii failed. A Reciprocity Treaty (1854) negotiated with Canada permitted free trade in many commodities and settled a number of minor disagreements.

✪✪ **The Ostend Manifesto**—An overly aggressive bit of Southern diplomacy tried to acquire Cuba from Spain. Southerners took advantage of Cuban dissatisfaction with Spanish misrule. Narcisco Lopez led filibustering expeditions from American ports between 1849 and 1850 and others threatened to do so. In 1854 a crisis arose when the Spanish seized the *Black Warrior*, an American ship, for violation of customs regulations. Spain answered Pierce's ultimatum with an apology.

In 1854 Pierce decided to take advantage of both difficulties within Spain and of French and British involvement in the Crimean War to take action regarding Cuba. The American ministers to England, France, and Spain were directed to meet at Ostend, Belgium, to plan concerted action to aid the American Minister Pierre Soule in Madrid. They drew up the Ostend Manifesto pointing out the importance of Cuba to the United States. The statement declared that Spain ought to sell Cuba to the United States. If Spain refused, the United States would be justified in seizing it by force. The Manifesto was a trial balloon that disclosed so much opposition in the North and in Europe that Pierce disavowed it. It showed how far the South would go to strengthen the slave interests of the country by trying to annex one or more new states.

THE ANTEBELLUM SOUTH

The South had developed a unique society and special interests giving rise to a kind of Southern nationalism. These differences brought conflict with the North and led to secession in an attempt to create an independent nation.

✪✪ **The People of the South**—The South developed a class system in contrast with the social structure of the North. Southern society may be conveniently divided into four main classes: 1) the planter aristocracy owning over 20 slaves; 2) the middle classes made up of small slave-owners, yeoman farmers, mechanics, and storekeepers; 3) the "poor whites"; and 4) the slaves.

The large planters, or "cotton snobs," who owned 20 or more slaves were only a small minority, but their wealth afforded them the leisure and means for exercising political and social leadership and they dominated the South. Most smaller slave-owners had recently risen from the yeoman farmer class. The great majority of the Southern whites belonged to the middle class, the yeoman farmer being the most common type. Class distinctions among Southern whites were not sharp and individuals might readily improve their status. Yeoman farmers hoped to and many did become large slave-owners. The small storekeeper was the most typical businessman. Business activity did not bring prestige equal to that of the small farmers. In the lower brackets of the middle class were the artisans of various kinds, spoken of as "mechanics." All these were independent, self-respecting, plain people. At the bottom of the middle classes were the well-paid but little respected overseers of slaves on large plantations.

The term "poor whites" correctly designated only a small minority. They were an ignorant, unambitious, slovenly lot. Some worked for wages; others were shiftless because of hookworm or other disease; some were petty criminals. They could take pride only in their nominal superiority to the slaves. The slave, without much opportunity of freedom and completely subordinate to the master's wishes, made up the lowest class. The slaves made distinctions among themselves according to the type of work required of them. At the bottom were the field hands; household workers and some slaves trained at such skills as blacksmithing ranked higher. Free African Americans enjoyed little more than personal freedom and were in danger of being kidnapped and forced into slavery.

Southern population, except for the African-American, was more homogeneous than that of the North. Most Southerners were of British origin and were Protestant. This homogeneous population was largely isolated in a predominantly rural society that produced a provincial outlook in most Southerners.

○ **Attitudes of Different Classes Toward Slavery**—Nearly all Southern whites, except those living in mountain areas where no slave plantations could exist, supported slavery. Most Southerners agreed it was the most desirable solution to the race problem, especially in areas where the whites were outnumbered as they were in some areas of rich soil and level fields where large plantations developed, as in the "black belt" in Mississippi and Alabama. Yeoman farmers hoped to grow rich and in time become large planters. Businessmen depended upon the patronage of slave owners. The artisans and laborers did not wish to see slaves free to compete with them in the labor market. The poor whites, conscious of their inferior status, wished to preserve more distinction than color alone provided. All Southerners appreciated the social control over the slaves that the system provided.

Treatment Accorded Slaves—Some slaves lived in more comfort and security than Northern factory workers or frontier dwellers, but most lived in rather crude cabins with little more than subsistence fare. They developed certain stratagems to avoid being worked too hard by their owners, which in turn brought responses from the owners, one of which was the threat or use of physical violence. Much depended on the character and ability of the individual owner.

Life was not as idyllic as Southerners of the magnolia and mockingbird school pictured it nor was it as brutal as abolitionist agitators described it. The well-being of the slave as valuable property physically able to work for the master's profit still permitted brutal treatment far short of incapacitation. Whatever the conditions might have been, the fact of slavery should have been enough to arouse the moral qualms and humanitarian sympathies of the white population.

✪ Detrimental Economic Effects of Slavery upon the South— Aside from moral and humanitarian considerations, 1) probably the worst effect of slavery was that it perpetuated a class system in the South. It not only kept the slave down as a caste, but it enabled large planters to control the South for the interests of their particular class. They dominated the courts, the legislatures, and the whole machinery of government. Tax laws and the apportionment of representation favored the planters. 2) Legislation and attitudes that favored plantation agriculture offered no encouragement to business and industry. Planters disliked the assertiveness of free industrial labor. This failure to encourage business activity proved to be a fatal weakness in the war with the North. Overspecialization made the South dependent upon the North for a long list of important manufactured goods. 3) Industrious, intelligent immigrants, such as the Germans, avoided the South. They were opposed to slavery in principle and did not wish to farm or work in competition with unfree labor. 4) Since hard manual labor was performed by slaves, the system produced contempt for manual labor.

THE KANSAS-NEBRASKA ACT

Mutual animosity between the sections survived the Compromise of 1850 in spite of prosperity and the insistence of moderates that the slavery issue had been settled. The personal liberty laws and abolition propaganda antagonized the South. Harriet Beecher Stowe's *Uncle Tom's Cabin* (1852) appealed to the emotions of the masses in the North and ended indifference by arousing them against slavery as a moral evil. The North organized its resentment after the passage of the Kansas-Nebraska Act.

✪✪✪ The Kansas-Nebraska Act—This Act: 1) established two new territories, Kansas and Nebraska; 2) it specifically repealed the Missouri Compromise which prohibited slavery north of 36°30′; and 3) provided that the inhabitants of the territories should decide the status of slavery themselves (the principle of popular sovereignty). Such an act was obviously favorable to the South.

The motives behind its passage were: 1) the desire on the part of Stephen A. Douglas, who introduced the bill, to open the way for the construction of a transcontinental railroad through the central route. Douglas, from Illinois, represented the interests of a group of railroad builders and land speculators in Chicago who, along with the state of Illinois would benefit from a railroad routed to Chicago. By organizing territorial government, the Native Americans could be removed and the land opened to settlement; otherwise, the Southern route might be chosen for the railroad. 2) The inception of the bill began with Senator Atchison of Missouri who sought an issue to help him win reelection by making an appeal to land-hungry Missourians. 3) Douglas himself, ambitious to win the Democratic Presidential nomination, saw an opportunity to win Southern support—it was expected that Kansas would become a slave state. 4) Douglas had already gone on record in favor of popular sovereignty as a matter of principle. He was more interested in other goals than in the outcome of the slavery issue about which he had no moral convictions. Douglas was surprised at the stormy reaction in the North after the bill was passed.

○○ Effect on the Political Parties—With the assistance of the powerful Democratic bloc, the Kansas-Nebraska Act easily passed and was signed by President Pierce. There was an immediate and strong grass roots reaction against it in the North, especially in the Northwest, a reaction that effectively wiped out the second party system of Whigs and Democrats. Northern Whigs went into either the new Republican Party or the anti-immigrant Know-Nothings, the Southerners went into the Democrats, and the Whig Party itself vanished. The Know-Nothings had a temporary burst of strength that did not last beyound 1856. Anti-Nebraska Northern Democrats also joined the Republican Party, which added opposition to slavery extension to other Northern issues in a sectional appeal for supporters.

○ The Struggle to Win Kansas—The Kansas-Nebraska Act caused civil war in Kansas. Northerners organized to win Kansas as a free state, but Missourians organized also to make Kansas slave. New England founded the New England Emigrant Aid Society to populate Kansas with antislavery voters to offset the normal tendency for Kansas to be settled by pro-slave migrants from the bordering state of Missouri. From the nearby Northern states antislavery immigrants came to take up lands for farming, not to win any cause. Antislave settlers easily outnumbered proslavery settlers. However, Missourians organized secret societies to send fraudulent voters into Kansas to win elections to make Kansas a slave state. In this way they elected a pro-slave territorial delegate to

Congress and in 1855 chose a pro-slave legislature. Governor Andrew Reeder protested but President Pierce removed him from office.

Next, the antislavery forces met at Topeka in October 1855, and drafted a constitution for the state prohibiting slavery. Pro-slave men refused to vote and the free state government was installed at Lawrence. In May 1856, a proslavery mob of "border ruffians" from Missouri burned Lawrence. John Brown, the fanatical abolitionist, retaliated by murdering five proslavery men in the "Pottawatomie Massacre." Subsequently about 200 persons were killed in guerrilla warfare in "Bleeding Kansas."

When Buchanan became President in 1857 he supported the proslavery cause and the Lecompton Constitution they had drawn up the same year. The voters overwhelmingly refused it. Buchanan favored the bill (1858) in Congress to admit Kansas under the Lecompton Constitution but it failed to pass the House. Kansas was asked to vote for a modified Lecompton Constitution but it was rejected in 1858. In 1861 Congress admitted Kansas as a free state after the Southern members had withdrawn from Congress.

The Assault Against Senator Sumner—During the debates over the events in Kansas, Senator Charles Sumner, a sharp-tongued abolitionist orator from Massachusetts, denounced Senator Butler of South Carolina in polished but insulting language in a long speech on "The Crime Against Kansas." Butler's neighbor, Representative Preston Brooks, also of South Carolina, avenged the remarks by beating Sumner over the head and shoulders with a cane. Southerners endorsed this act of gross violence by presenting a number of canes to Brooks and reelecting him after he resigned in the face of Northern protests. The North took up the quarrel and endorsed their protagonist by buying tens of thousands of copies of Sumner's provocative speech. The incident worsened relations between the North and South.

OO The Know-Nothings—The Know-Nothing Party originated from secret political orders organized to oppose the political influence of Irish and German immigrants and of the political machines that sought the immigrant's votes. It got its name from the instructions to members, who, when questioned about plans of the Anti-foreign party, were told to answer that they "know nothing." As a nationalist, anti-foreign movement it organized later under the name American Party. It was hoped it would become a national Party. In 1854 opponents of the Kansas-Nebraska Act joined the Party in large numbers. The Party quickly disintegrated after the election of 1856.

OOO The Republican Party—In response to the Kansas-Nebraska Act, Republicans arose in 1854 almost spontaneously to resist the extension of slavery into the territories. It grew rapidly as Free Soil men, antislavery Whigs, and anti-Nebraska Democrats joined it. Know-Nothings soon abandoned their Party to become Republicans. It attracted abolitionists, temperance advocates, and other reform groups. German immigrants in the Northwest joined it because they strongly opposed slavery. The Party also supported a higher tariff and federal money for the transportation improvements the North, especially the upper Midwest, felt were needed to continue economic expansion. These measures, as well as a homestead law, had been blocked by the Southern-dominated Democrats. The Republicans were a sectional party with a sectional program.

✪ The Election of 1856—The Democrats nominated James Buchanan of Pennsylvania for the Presidency. He favored popular sovereignty. He already had forty years experience in politics and in diplomacy but was too weak to serve in the crises that followed. He won an easy victory over his divided opponents. The Republicans nominated the popular, well-publicized army explorer and son-in-law of Senator Benton, young John C. Fremont of California. Many moderates refused to vote for Fremont who took a firm stand against slavery in the territories. The Know-Nothings nominated Millard Fillmore as the candidate of the American Party.

EVENTS LEADING TO SECESSION

Several events during the Buchanan administration convinced the South they could no longer, as a minority section, protect their interests against an aggressive majority in the North. Secession seemed to be the solution.

✪✪✪ The Dred Scott Case, 1857—This decision, legalizing slavery in the territories, was a great Southern victory but was uncertain since the North seemed determined to reverse it.

Dred Scott, a slave, sued for his freedom on the ground that his residence in the free territory north of the Missouri Compromise line and in the free state of Illinois had made him free. Scott was abetted by abolitionists who managed to get his case into the United States Supreme Court as a test case. The Court, headed by Chief Justice Taney from Maryland, dismissed the case for want of jurisdiction, because Dred Scott was not a citizen but still a slave without the right to sue. This was as far as the Court would have gone ordinarily in writing its opinion, but it now decided to hand down an *obiter dictum*, or gratuitous opinion, to settle the disputed question of slavery in the territories. The Court declared that as a slave Dred Scott was property, that the Fifth Amendment prohibited Congress from depriving any person of property without the process of law, and that property could be taken into the territories. It ruled that the Missouri Compromise had always been unconstitutional.

The South was delighted by this victory. The Republicans denounced it as partisan since seven justices in the Court were Democrats.

Republicans denounced the *obiter dictum* as having no legal justification. Republicans declared they would reverse the decision, once they gained control of the national government, by "packing" the Court. Their unwillingness to accept a decision of the highest court in the land alarmed the South.

The Panic of 1857—A sharp depression struck the country in 1857. It was caused by 1) the preceding years of overexpansion and overspeculation. 2) The Crimean War checked the flow of European capital into American investments and the return of peace in 1857 caused a fall in farm prices. However, recovery set in quickly when large quantities of grain and cotton were exported in 1858. The North blamed the Walker Tariff for the depression. The South suffered much less than the industrial North, gained confidence, and asserted that this proved the superiority of their economy to that of the North. In the election of 1858 the North voted strongly Republican and gave that Party the lead in the House of Representatives.

○○ **The Lincoln-Douglas Debates (1858)**—Stephen Douglas, the Democratic Senator from Illinois, ran against a young Springfield lawyer, Abraham Lincoln, for reelection. It was one of the first opportunities to test the strength of the new Republican Party. Lincoln challenged "the Little Giant" to a series of debates that centered on the slavery question. At Freeport, Lincoln sought to embarrass Douglas by asking if the people of a territory could, after the Dred Scott decision, lawfully exclude slavery from a territory. Douglas, in the "Freeport Doctrine," replied that the people of a territory could keep slavery out by not passing local police regulations necessary for its existence. Douglas won the election. His answer did not satisfy the South and helped to widen the growing split between Northern and Southern Democrats. Since the debates popularized Lincoln all over the North, they helped him win the Republican presidential nomination in 1860.

○ **Helper's *The Impending Crisis***—Hinton R. Helper, a North Carolinian, in 1857 published a "dangerous" book under the title *The Impending Crisis of the South*. He presented statistics and arguments to show that slavery was economically harmful to the South. He argued that slavery enriched the planters at the expense of the yeoman farmers. He asked non-slaveholders to abolish slavery on economic grounds. The book alarmed Southern leaders so much that it became dangerous to be found in possession of a copy of it; it threatened to turn the common people of the South against the planter ruling class.

○○ **John Brown's Raid (1859)**—The fanatic responsible for the Pottawatomie Massacre secured financial contributions from Northerners to carry out a plan to free the slaves by inciting a slave insurrection. Brown, in order to secure a supply of arms, captured the federal arsenal at Harpers

Ferry. As the alarm spread, forces gathered to take Brown and his men. The insurrectionists took refuge in a railroad roundhouse but were forced to surrender after ten of them were killed. A Virginia court tried Brown for treason; he was hanged with six of his followers. The South was horrified by the threat of a slave revolt and blamed the "Black Republicans" for it. After the executions the North made a martyr of Brown.

❂❂❂ **The Election of 1860**—The Democrats met at Charleston, South Carolina. There the Southern extremists demanded that the Party adopt a platform plank asking Congress to guarantee slave property in the territories. The Northerners under Douglas defeated the demand and adopted instead the Douglas policy of popular sovereignty. Southerners bolted the convention. The Northerners adjourned and met again at Baltimore to choose Douglas. Southern Democrats reassembled and chose John C. Breckinridge of Kentucky and endorsed the Dred Scott decision.

The Republicans met in Chicago. Lincoln, the more moderate candidate, was chosen in preference to Seward, an older politician but an extremist. They adopted a platform to appeal to various voter groups. They promised to 1) exclude slavery from the territories, 2) adopt a protective tariff, 3) enact a free homestead law, and 4) support railroad building with federal aid.

The Constitutional Union Party, emphasizing the preservation of the Union by compromise, named John Bell of Tennessee.

Lincoln won every state in the North except New Jersey. He gained only a minority of the popular vote. Breckinridge won the states of the lower South. Both sections voted for the extremist candidates. The South had declared that Lincoln's election would be the signal for secession and now proceeded to secede.

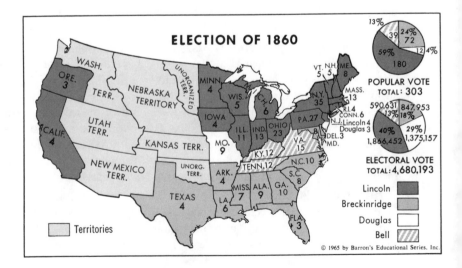

ELECTION OF 1860

POPULAR VOTE TOTAL: 303

ELECTORAL VOTE TOTAL: 4,680,193

Lincoln
Breckinridge
Douglas
Bell

Territories

© 1965 by Barron's Educational Series, Inc.

CHAPTER BOOK LIST

Beales, Carleton, *Brass Knuckle Crusade: The Great Know-Nothing Conspiracy* (1960). The American Party and its supporters.

Berlin, Ira, *Slaves Without Masters: The Free Negro in the Antebellum South* (1974).

Craven, A.O., *The Coming of the Civil War* (1942). Readable study of circumstances leading to the war.

Dumond, D.L., *Antislavery Origins of the Civil War in the United States* (Ann Arbor). History of the antislavery movement.

Filler, Louis, *The Crusade Against Slavery* (1960).

Foner, Eric, *Free Soil, Free Labor, Free Men: The Ideology of the Republic Party before the Civil War* (1970). Why the Republicans appealed to Northern voters.

Genovese, Eugene D., *The Political Economy of Slavery: Studies in the Economy and Society of the Slave South* (1965). A more general work than the title indicates.

Gienapp, William E., *The Origins of the Republican Party, 1852–1856* (1988). Best study of the organization.

Hamilton, Holman, *Prologue to Conflict: The Crisis and the Compromise of 1850* (1964). Excellent treatment.

Holt, Michael F., *The Political Crisis of the 1850s* (1978). The decline and fall of the Whig Party.

Jaffa, Harry V., *Crisis of the House Divided: An Interpretation of the Lincoln-Douglas Debates* (1959). Fine, concise analysis.

Levine, Lawrence W., *Black Culture and Consciousness: Afro-American Folk Thought from Slavery to Freedom* (1977). Good introduction to slave culture.

McPherson, James, *Battle Cry of Freedom: The Civil War Era* (1989). Narrative history on a grand scale.

Nichols, Roy F., *Disruption of American Democracy* (Collier). Pulitzer Prize winner about the background of the Civil War.

Oakes, James, *The Ruling Race: A History of American Slaveholders* (1982). History from the top down.

Potter, David, *The Impending Crisis, 1848–1861 (1976)*.

Stampp, Kenneth M., *The Peculiar Institution: Slavery in the Ante-Bellum South* (1956). Stresses the coercive features.

Sydnor, Charles S., *The Development of Southern Sectionalism 1809–1848* (1968).

REVIEW QUESTIONS

MULTIPLE CHOICE

1. The Wilmont Proviso stipulated that slavery be forbidden in (1) any new states north of 36°30′ (2) Kansas and Nebraska (3) unorganized territories (4) any territory acquired in the Mexican War.

2. With regard to slavery in the territories (1) the South held that Congress had full power to legislate (2) the North denied the right of Congress to interfere (3) the South held that Congress had no right to exclude slaves (4) Northern Democrats denied the right of squatter sovereignty.

3. For thirty years before the Civil War sectional conflicts centered chiefly around which pair of issues? (1) The sale of public land and westward expansion (2) tariffs and the slavery question (3) internal improvements and immigration (4) national expansion and railroad routes.

4. Which provision of the Compromise of 1850 is stated incorrectly? (1) California was admitted as a free state (2) popular sovereignty was adopted for New Mexico (3) slavery was abolished in the District of Columbia (4) a stringent fugitive slave law was passed.

5. The immediate response to the Compromise of 1850 was one of (1) acceptance by the North (2) Northern rejection of the Fugitive Slave Law (3) acceptance by the whole country (4) angry criticism by the South.

6. The Clayton-Bulwer Treaty provided that any canal across the Isthmus of Panama be (1) built by Britain and France (2) fortified by neither Britain nor the United States exclusively (3) built by the United States (4) built by New Granada under joint British-American supervision.

7. The Ostend Manifesto (1) threatened the United States with war if Texas was annexed (2) led to the debate followed by the Compromise of 1850 (3) threatened secession by South Carolina (4) declared that Cuba rightfully belonged to the United States.

8. In the South before 1860 the largest social class was the (1) small slaveholders (2) "poor whites" (3) yeomen farmers (4) wage-earning whites.

9. Before 1860 the population of the South as compared with that of the North was (1) more homogeneous in origin (2) more international minded (3) more heterogeneous in origin (4) less provincial in outlook.

10. In attitude toward slavery in the South the (1) whites held strongly conflicting views (2) "poor whites" hated slavery (3) non-slaveholders were indifferent (4) small farmers endorsed slavery.

11. In the South slaves were accorded treatment by their masters that may be described as (1) varying with different masters (2) almost universally inhumane (3) generally exhibiting generous humanitarianism (4) less humane in the older sections.

12. All of the following were effects of slavery in the South *except*: (1) perpetuated a class system (2) engendered contempt for manual labor (3) discouraged progressive immigrants (4) encouraged business enterprise.

13. The Kansas-Nebraska Act put in effect a method of settling the slavery controversy that had been used earlier in (1) the Missouri Compromise (2) the Compromise of 1850 (3) California (4) Texas.

14. In his attitude towards slavery Douglas (1) showed much humanitarian concern (2) favored the right of Congress to decide its status in the territories (3) was more interested in other matters (4) wished to extend slavery.

15. The Kansas-Nebraska Act had which effect upon the slavery controversy? (1) Revived intense sectional feeling over the issue of slavery (2) had little observable effect (3) had a moderately quieting effect (4) exerted little concern in a time of general prosperity.

16. Which factor operating alone would have made Kansas a free state before 1860? (1) The wishes of Buchanan (2) a majority vote of Kansas settlers (3) the wishes of Pierce (4) measures of Congress.

17. What was the official name of the Know-Nothing Party? (1) Union (2) Nationalist (3) Nativist (4) American.

18. The occasion for the rise of the Republican Party was the (1) Kansas-Nebraska Act (2) demise of the Know-Nothings (3) Compromise of 1850 (4) Dred Scott decision.

19. Which group did not go into the composition of the Republican Party? (1) The Know-Nothings (2) the Northern Whigs (3) proponents of squatter sovereignty (4) those favoring high tariffs.

20. Which was not a reaction to the Dred Scott Case? (1) A Northern demand to reform the Supreme Court (2) an increase in sectional anger (3) the reelection of Preston Brooks to the House (4) virtual refusal of the North to accept the decision of the Court.

21. The Lincoln-Douglas debates are significant especially because they (1) indicated Lincoln was a radical abolitionist (2) won the Democratic presidential nomination for Douglas (3) caused the defeat of Douglas (4) made Lincoln's name well known in the North.

22. Which brought the sharpest increase in abolition sentiment in the North? (1) The publication of *Uncle Tom's Cabin* (2) the publication of *The Impending Crisis* (3) the Dred Scott decision (4) Douglas's Freeport Doctrine speech.

23. John Brown's motive in his "raid" was to (1) start a slave revolt (2) arouse Northern sympathy for the slaves (3) protest Southern control in Washington (4) dramatize Northern unpreparedness for defense.

TRUE-FALSE

24. The production of gold in California helped bring on worldwide prosperity in the 1850s.

25. Daniel Webster sacrificed his political future in the North to support the Compromise of 1850.

26. The election of 1852 indicated the desire of the majority to accept the Compromise of 1850.

27. Pierce was really an able President who has not been fully appreciated for his strong qualities.

28. The Pierce administration desired to purchase Cuba to protect American commercial interests in the Caribbean area.

29. The slaves among themselves recognized class distinctions according to the type of labor performed.

30. The largest single group in the South out of sympathy with slavery were the whites living in mountain areas away from plantations.

31. Laborers in the South generally opposed slavery since they believed in free labor.

32. The Kansas-Nebraska Act specifically repealed the Missouri Compromise.

33. Douglas favored making Kansas a slave state and his main interest was in preserving the balance in the Senate between North and South.

34. The Kansas-Nebraska Act destroyed the Whig and Know-Nothing parties and gave rise to the Republican Party.

35. Chiefly it was the efforts of the New England Emigration Aid Society that made Kansas a free state.

36. The Republican Party originated as a sectional party and soon attracted various reform groups.

37. It was a Southern-manned Supreme Court that handed down the Dred Scott Decision.

38. The Panic of 1857 buoyed the confidence of the South in its economic system.

39. Lincoln really won the debates with Douglas but lost the election in 1858.

40. In choosing Lincoln in 1860 the Republicans chose one of their most radical abolitionists for the presidential nomination.

COMPLETION

41. The _____ started the controversy between the North and South that led to the Compromise of 1850.

42. After California two other free states were admitted; they were _____ and _____ .

43. The California gold rush started after gold was discovered in the year _____ .

44. _____ was President shortly before but not at the time the Compromise of 1850 was reached.

45. The _____ laws were passed in the North to prevent enforcement of the Fugitive Slave Act.

46. _____ was elected President in 1852; he belonged to the _____ Party.

47. It was the _____ that secured a treaty from Japan to open two ports to the United States.

48. The _____ along the Gila River was the last territory added to the mainland United States.

49. The small farmer class in the South was known as the _____ farmer.

50. The leading party that arose to oppose the Kansas-Nebraska Act was the _____ Party.

51. The author of *Uncle Tom's Cabin* was _____ .

52. Two towns in Kansas were populated by the free state forces; they were _____ .

53. John Brown killed five proslave men in what was called the _____ .

54. President _____ tried more than once to bring Kansas in as a slave state.

55. The Republican Party was organized in the year _____ .

56. The Chief Justice who handed down the Dred Scott Decision was named _____ .

57. An important conflict involving European nations during the mid-1850s was the _____ War.

58. John Brown's Raid occurred at _____ in Virginia.

59. In 1860 the Southern Democrats nominated _____ for the Presidency.

MATCHING

60. Lewis Cass
61. Daniel Webster

62. Millard Fillmore
63. Winfield Scott
64. James Buchanan
65. Stephen A. Douglas
66. Preston Brooks
67. John C. Fremont
68. Hinton R. Helper
69. John Bell

a. "Popular sovereignty"
b. President who supported Lecompton Constitution

c. "Seventh of March" speech
d. First Republican presidential nominee
e. "Squatter sovereignty"
f. Whig nominee in 1852
g. *The Impending Crisis*
h. Successor to Taylor
i. Candidate of Southern extremists in 1860
j. Constitutional Union candidate
k. Resented slurs on South Carolina

CHRONOLOGY / CHAPTER 16

1860 Election of Lincoln. Secession of Southern states began.

1861 Confederate States of America organized. States of the upper South join the Confederacy.

April, Fort Sumter fired upon by Confederates. Opening of the Civil War.

July, First Battle of Bull Run.

Morrill Tariff raised rates to protectionist levels.

Trent Affair brought threat of war with Great Britain.

Napoleon III sent French troops into Mexico.

Serfs freed in Russia.

1862 Peninsula Campaign, a Union defeat. Battle of Antietam Creek in September, a Union victory and turning point of the war, followed by Emancipation Proclamation.

Homestead Act, Morrill Land Grant College Act passed.

Railroad to Pacific subsidized by federal government.

1863 Battle of Gettysburg defeats Confederate invasion army under Lee.

Capture of Vicksburg gave Union control of Mississippi River.

National Banking Act passed.

1864 Grant defeated in Wilderness Campaign. Atlanta captured in Sherman's March through Georgia.

Lincoln reelected under National Union Party ticket.

Wade-Davis Bill, embodying harsh reconstruction policy, vetoed by Lincoln.

1865 Lee surrendered at Appomattox Courthouse.

Lincoln assassinated.

Civil War ended.

Thirteenth Amendment abolished slavery.

✪✪✪ GREAT SIGNIFICANCE
✪✪ IMPORTANT TOPICS
✪ SECONDARY IMPORTANCE

16
THE CIVIL WAR, 1861–1865

Neither North nor South foresaw that secession would bring almost total war. The struggle that followed employed for the first time such technology of recent warfare as the submarine, the iron-clad ships, the machine gun, the repeating rifle, observation balloons, trench fighting, telegraphy, and railroads. It was the world's greatest war between the Napoleonic Wars and World War I. It was also the most consequential event since the achievement of American independence, for it moved agriculture out and put business in power in Washington, now the capital of a country ruled by a single, supreme government. It is the most compelling, the most dramatic event in the nation's history.

THE SECESSION PROBLEM

Despite the specific guarantee of slavery where it now existed in the Republican platform, the slave states felt they had to exercise the right of secession that some had claimed. Since the Southern-dominated Democratic Party had lost the presidency, the South felt it could no longer control the federal government's policies and had to secede to safeguard its "peculiar institution," slavery.

✪✪ **The Secession Movement**—South Carolina adopted, in December 1860, its "Ordinance of Secession" in a convention elected by the people. By late February 1861, six other states of the lower South followed her lead. They now chose delegates to meet at Montgomery, Alabama, to organize the Confederate States of America. Jefferson Davis of Mississippi was made President and Alexander H. Stephens of Georgia, Vice President. They adopted a constitution like that of the United States but with these differences: 1) the right to own slaves and move them from one state to another was guaranteed; 2) state sovereignty was recognized but nothing said about the right of secession; 3) protective tariffs were prohibited; and 4) the term of the president was limited to six years.

✪✪✪ **Causes of Secession and War**—The South justified secession because of various alleged infringements upon their constitutional rights by the North. Their complaints were based upon the events of the previous decade: the abolitionist propaganda against the South's key institution of slavery, the activities of the underground railroad, the enactment of the personal liberty laws by Northern legislatures, John Brown's raid, and the election of Lincoln by a purely sectional party and one hostile to slavery. The admission during the fifties of the new states of California, Minnesota, and Oregon gave the free states a majority in the Senate.

All Southern grievances related to slavery. No mention at the time was made of states' rights or of the tariff. The causes of the Civil War depended upon economic and moral considerations relating to slavery; it is most unlikely that it would have occurred if slavery had not existed. Other factors aggravated this issue or allowed it to lead to secession and war. The more immediate cause was the quarrel over the extension of slavery in the territories. The occasion of secession was Lincoln's election. Secession created a separate *de facto* government that was bound to result in a military struggle over many issues that could not be settled peacefully. Once the fighting began, the preservation of the Union and of Southern independence became the war aims of the opposing forces.

○ **Supposed Economic Advantages of Secession**—Secessionists argued that the South would prosper if independent, because 1) direct trade could be established with Europe which would keep Northern middlemen's profits in the South; 2) free trade would increase the market for agricultural exports and reduce the cost of imports; 3) the cost of labor (i.e., price of slaves) which had been increasing might be reduced by reviving the African slave trade; 4) it was expected that the South would develop its own manufacturing, banking, and transportation, and retain profits that had been going to the North; and 5) secession was expected to be peaceful.

○ **Northern Response to Secession**—A large minority of Northern opinion was willing to let the South depart in peace and was opposed to the use of force to preserve the Union. Many believed the quarrel might be patched up and the South brought back. President Buchanan sympathized with the South and did nothing either to safeguard federal installations there or to make the seceders' task more difficult.

The "Crittenden Compromise" was one of numerous plans considered in hopes of satisfying the South and restoring the Union. This compromise, proposed by Senator J.J. Crittenden of Kentucky, resembled the other plans and advocated "permanent amendments" to the Constitution. These would have provided: 1) for the protection of slavery in the states where it was legal; 2) approval of the domestic slave trade; 3) that the United States government guarantee payment for slaves escaping the South; 4) that Congress not abolish slavery in the

District of Columbia without the consent of Virginia and Maryland; 5) for reviving the Missouri Compromise line. Lincoln had little to say during the transition of the Presidency, but he opposed any agreement permitting the extension of slavery in the territories. The unwillingness of both sides to make concessions doomed favorable action in Congress on all proposals for compromise.

❍❍❍ **The Problem of Fort Sumter**—Federal military property in the South was immediately taken over by the Southern states. Attention concentrated on Fort Sumter located on a defensible island in the harbor of Charleston, South Carolina. The South could not permit the Federals to retain this fort within such an important seaport. Lincoln expressed a conciliatory tone in his inaugural address. Lincoln faced a delicate decision in handling the Fort Sumter problem. He decided to maintain the fort by sending provisions only but to avoid any offensive measure. Lincoln could not alienate the border states by any action making the North appear as the aggressor. Southern "fire eaters" in Charleston fired the first shots (April 12, 1861) at the fort. The fort surrendered on the 14th. On the 15th Lincoln called for volunteers and declared a blockade of Southern ports. Both sides prepared for war.

In May and June, the states of Virginia, Arkansas, North Carolina, and Tennessee seceded after lively debate. The northwest counties of Virginia organized as West Virginia and were admitted to the Union in 1863. Border states of the South that did not secede were Missouri, Kentucky, Maryland, and Delaware.

❍❍ **Advantages of the North**—A Northern victory was favored by several factors. 1) The North had a population almost three times that of the South (which was also over one-third slaves) and large numbers of immigrants came in not only to work but to enroll in the military forces. 2) The industrial resources of the North were both great and diversified. The South had almost no industries to produce the necessities of war or of its civilian economy. The wealth of the North during the war actually grew faster than it was dissipated by the destruction of war. 3) In addition, the agriculture of the North was more diversified and food crops bulked large in production. The South suffered starvation toward the end of the war. Large wheat crops were exchanged in England for war materiel. 4) The weakness of the Confederate government was advantageous to the North. The North avoided constitutional scruples and Lincoln exercised unusual powers in prosecuting the war. The Confederate government sacrificed the national interest to preserving states' rights and individual liberties at a time when discipline and sacrifice were called for. 5) Control of the navy gave the North a great advantage by enabling it to maintain a blockade of Southern ports.

❍❍ **Advantages of the South**—1) British and French cotton mills depended upon Southern cotton. The South believed that cotton was so important that Britain and France would break a Northern blockade to secure raw cotton. They believed the North could not do without Southern cotton. Both Britain and France did give help and encouragement to the Confederacy. 2) The superior training of Southern men in the military arts and their outdoor life proved of great value. 3) Southern military leaders were more able than Northern, as shown in the defense of Richmond and the heavier casualties among Northern troops. 4) The defensive character of the war favored the South. Confederates fought on familiar ground. 5) Opposition of the Copperheads, or "Peace Democrats," Southern sympathizers in the North, weakened the Union cause.

MILITARY EVENTS OF THE WAR

The Union defeat at the first Battle of Bull Run (June 1861) showed that the war would not be a short one. With the South on the defensive, the North followed what came to be called the Anaconda strategy. It was devised by General Winfield Scott, who then retired and left the field to younger men. It called for a three-pronged attack, one from the north upon the Confederate capital, Richmond, the second a naval blockade of the southern coast to deny the South foreign goods and weapons, and the third, a drive down the Mississippi, then the Tennessee and Cumberland Rivers, thus surrounding the South and crushing its ability and will to resist, as the Anaconda snake crushes its prey.

❂ **The Eastern Campaigns**—The first battle of the war occurred in the Eastern theater. The war continued until Lee abandoned Richmond (where the Confederate capital had been relocated after Virginia joined the Confederacy). Lee headed Richmond's defense throughout the war. Lincoln, however, had to make several changes before he found a satisfactory commander for the army of the Potomac. At the opening of the war 1) the aged General Winfield Scott headed the Union army. (He drew up the overall strategy of the war, the Anaconda Plan for choking off supplies to the South from all sides.) Under Scott, General Irwin McDowell headed the attacking forces at Bull Run. 2) McClellan succeeded Scott as commander in chief of Union forces and of the forces against Richmond. 3) Pope followed next, then 4) McClellan again, 5) followed by Burnside, 6) Hooker, 7) Meade, and finally 8) General Ulysses S. Grant led the Union forces to victory.

❂ **The First Battle of Bull Run**—The first important engagement of the war brought Union defeat at the Battle of Bull Run (July 1861) in Virginia just southwest of Washington, DC. The battle showed both sides how unprepared and inexperienced they were in war. The North learned the need for greater effort; the South felt reassured.

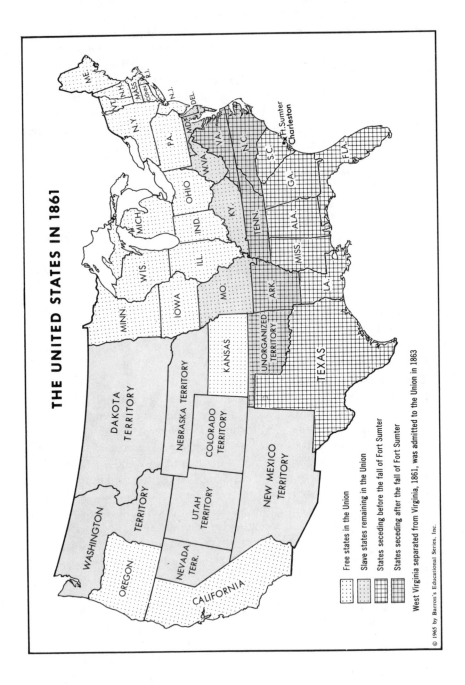

THE UNITED STATES IN 1861

Free states in the Union

Slave states remaining in the Union

States seceding before the fall of Fort Sumter

States seceding after the fall of Fort Sumter

West Virginia separated from Virginia, 1861, was admitted to the Union in 1863

❂ The Peninsula Campaign—In 1862 plans called for General George C. McClellan to land forces by sea on the peninsula between the James and York rivers and march toward Richmond. General McDowell led another large army at the same time from Washington toward Richmond. General Robert E. Lee brilliantly countered this strategy by dispatching a force under General Thomas "Stonewall" Jackson toward Washington, DC. Lincoln recalled McDowell's army. McClellan was driven back from Richmond in the Seven Days Battle and ordered back to Washington. Pope who had replaced McClellan suffered defeat in a march toward Richmond the same year in the Second Battle of Bull Run.

❂ The Battle of Antietam—In September 1862, Lee crossed the Potomac in an offensive into Maryland and toward Washington. McClellan, recalled to command to check Lee's invasion, met the Confederates at Antietam Creek in Maryland and won a crucial victory in a bloody engagement. Lee succeeded in escaping, however. This victory gave the North a great diplomatic advantage because it enabled Lincoln to issue the Emancipation Proclamation (from a position of strength) and thereby ensure that England would not actively take the side of the Confederacy. McClellan, who failed to follow his victory at Antietam, was replaced by General Burnside.

❂ The Eastern Theater, 1863–1865—In December 1862, at the Battle of Fredericksburg, Lee halted General Ambrose E. Burnside's advance to Richmond. At Chancellorsville (where "Stonewall" Jackson was killed) Lee defeated General Thomas Hooker, who had replaced Burnside in command in the East.

Lee carried the war into enemy territory in July 1863, at Gettysburg with a force of 80,000 men. But General George C. Meade defeated Lee's army and it now retreated back to Virginia. This had been the high point of Confederate hopes in the war. After Gettysburg Northern victory was only a matter of time. England and France now withheld cruisers intended for the Confederacy.

In 1864 in the Wilderness Campaigns, Lee defeated Grant, now in overall command of the Union armies. Grant lost 55,000 men in the campaign. He could not take Richmond but kept it under siege.

In April 1865, Lee tried to break out of Richmond since he was running out of supplies and in danger of being forced to surrender. When Lee's attempted breakthrough to escape Richmond failed, he surrendered to Grant at the famous meeting at Appomattox Courthouse. This virtually ended the Civil War.

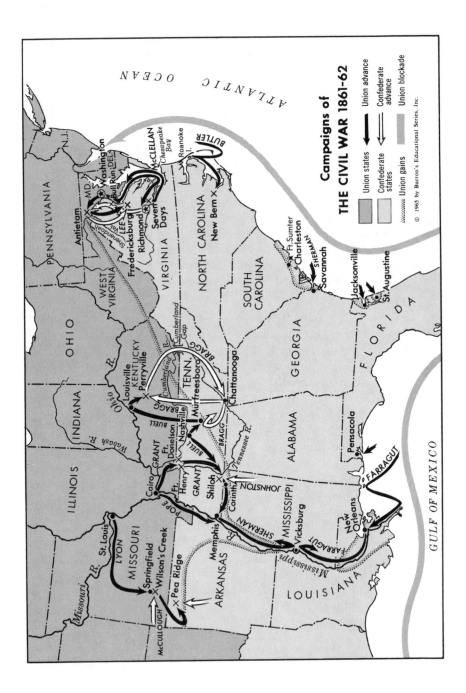

Campaigns of
THE CIVIL WAR 1861-62

Union states
Confederate states
Union gains
Union advance
Confederate advance
Union blockade

© 1965 by Barron's Educational Series, Inc.

THE WAR IN THE WEST
AND SHERMAN'S MARCH

Grant's successes in the West brought him rapid promotion until he was placed in charge of the campaign to take control of the Mississippi. The North needed to take the Mississippi to cut the Confederate armies off from supplies from the West.

Grant in February 1862, captured Fort Henry on the Tennessee River and Ft. Donelson on the Cumberland River. These victories opened the way for the invasion of the South. Grant advanced into Tennessee to capture the important railroad center of Corinth in April 1862. In the advance Grant fought the bloody Battle of Shiloh where the Confederate General Albert Sidney Johnston was killed. The Confederates evacuated Corinth, and General Henry W. Halleck took command of the Western army. In 1862 New Orleans was captured by Admiral David Farragut who then ascended the Mississippi and captured Natchez. Vicksburg, commanding the river, remained in Confederate control during a stubborn siege of several months.

In July 1863, Grant finally took Vicksburg. Now Union gunboats, controlling the entire Mississippi, severed the Confederacy. In September, Grant took the important railroad junction of Chattanooga in the victories at Chickamauga and Lookout Mountain. At this point General William T. Sherman took charge of the army in the West and began his "march to the sea."

✪✪ **Sherman's March**—Sherman's aim was to divide the South by marching southeast to Savannah on the Atlantic. In September 1864, with 100,000 men he took Atlanta, Georgia. In the march to Savannah he carried out a scorched earth policy of destroying everything in sight. His troops lived off the countryside. He wanted to destroy the productive resources and end the war more quickly. From Savannah, Sherman marched northward into South Carolina and North Carolina destroying cities and resources. In late April he forced the surrender of Joseph E. Johnston in North Carolina.

✪✪ THE WAR AT SEA

Northern control of the federal navy yielded great advantages from the beginning. Northern strategy of blockading Southern ports went into effect immediately. Its purposes were both to prevent the export of cotton (by which the South could earn foreign exchange) and prevent the importation of essential war goods. At first the South itself forbade the export of cotton, hoping to force Britain and France to break the Northern blockade. The blockade at first lacked enough vessels to be fully effective but ships were rapidly added to the patrols. Southern blockade runners at first managed to bring in some goods from the British Bahamas and West Indies.

The South made a clever effort to break the blockade by covering a wooden vessel with iron plates to withstand cannon balls. The Union intelligence learned of the preparations of the *Merrimac* and rushed to prepare its own ironclad, the *Monitor*. The ships met in a battle of several hours in Hampton Roads. The duel was indecisive but the *Merrimac* withdrew and never again challenged the *Monitor* or the wooden blockading ships. The ironclads foretold the coming of iron and steel navies. The blockade succeeded in starving the South not only of war supplies but civilian necessities and greatly aided the North in winning the war.

The Confederacy sank about 250 Northern merchant vessels with cruisers built in England. This British aid to the South constituted a serious violation of neutrality and gave rise to the Alabama Claims by which the United States demanded indemnification for damage done by the Confederate commerce raiders.

FOREIGN RELATIONS

The South hoped for English intervention; the North at best could hope only for strict English neutrality.

✪ **English Sympathy with the South**—When the war began, it was assumed that Great Britain would aid the South. 1) The landed aristocracy in Britain saw the Southern planters as a class with similar characteristics being oppressed by Northern factory owners. 2) Southern victory would weaken the United States, whose fast growing power was feared. 3) Both Britain and the South were free trade proponents. 4) British textile manufacturers needed Southern cotton, but, as the war began, there was already a large quantity of cotton in British warehouses, thus weakening the effect of this factor.

✪ **English Sympathy with the North**—Certain other factors in Britain operated to favor the Union cause. 1) Strongest of all was the antislavery sentiment in Britain. After the Emancipation Proclamation was declared in September 1862, England could not very well turn against the North that was fighting to free the slaves. 2) British liberals favored the Northern democracy. 3) English laboring classes, even though suffering from unemployment in the cotton mills, favored the North. Their evangelical Protestantism led them to favor emancipation. 4) A policy of neutrality would permit Britain to conduct profitable trade with the United States, but war would seriously damage British shipping. 5) Short wheat crops in Britain necessitated imports from the United States where large crops were harvested during the war. 6) To help the rebellious South would set a bad precedent that might lead to American aid to the Irish who were now agitating for Home Rule.

England recognized the Confederate rights as a belligerent but never recognized her independence.

⊙⊙ **The Trent Affair**—Late in 1861 the Trent Affair brought a serious crisis with Britain. The British packet *Trent* was stopped by a Union warship and two Confederate diplomats, James Mason and John Slidell, were removed. The North was jubilant at this reversal of similar events during the War of 1812. Britain sent an ultimatum demanding release of Mason and Slidell and an apology claiming a violation of England's rights and of international law. The men were released, partly because the American action mirrored earlier British actions when they had impressed seamen off American vessels.

As for the Union blockade of the South, Britain acquiesced in American policies. The doctrine of continuous voyage was enforced by Union warships to seize British goods ultimately destined for the South.

⊙ **Relations with France**—Napoleon III, Emperor of France, wished for a Southern victory even more than the British. The French built cruisers for the Confederacy and floated a large loan for the South. Napoleon's intervention in Mexico (1862) was made possible by the American Civil War. Seward protested the presence of French troops in Mexico in support of the puppet regime of Maximilian but could not at that time back up his demands with force.

Relations with Russia—Russia and other countries of Northern Europe favored the Union cause. Russia, like the United States, at odds with England from time to time, regarded the United States as a friend. Russia too had emancipated her serfs (1861) who were on the same level of servitude as the American slaves. In 1863 Russia sent her fleets to New York and San Francisco. This was regarded as a sign of friendly intentions and as a warning to Britain and France not to interfere on the side of the South. A result of American gratitude was the purchase of Alaska in 1867.

WARTIME GOVERNMENT IN THE NORTH AND SOUTH

Government and legislation in the North were determined by the necessity of winning the war and the promises made in the Republican platform of 1860.

⊙ **The Lincoln Cabinet**—Lincoln's choice of cabinet members was determined by the necessity of giving representation to the diverse political elements in the origin of the party. Seward of New York became Secretary of State and expected himself to assume the role of prime minister in relation to Lincoln as the nominal head of state. Some others took a disrespectful attitude towards Lincoln. Lincoln kept command of his subordinates by unusual tact, patience, humor, and understanding of the ambitious and scheming cabinet members.

○ Northern War Finance—The war was financed by 1) increasing excise taxes and raising tariff rates. Congress enacted the Morrill Tariff Act in 1861. The principle of protectionism was accepted and rates were raised to an average of 40 percent before the war was over. 2) An income tax with low rates was levied. 3) Greenbacks, irredeemable legal tender paper money, were issued. 4) Long- and short-term bonds were sold; here Jay Cooke was the financial genius who floated these issues for the North. 5) The National Banking Act (1863) required banks chartered under the Act to invest a third of their capital in federal bonds. The banks were permitted to issue national bank notes up to 90 percent of the value of bonds held as security for them. The Act was important in itself; it created a uniform paper currency and provided a more adequate banking structure for the business needs of the nation. Private bank note issues were driven out of circulation by a 10 percent tax in 1866.

○○○ Emancipation of the Slaves—In spite of his antislavery convictions Lincoln did not make emancipation of the slaves a war aim until late September 1862, and then only in unoccupied Confederate soil. Wherever slave territory came under Northern occupation the disposition of slaves was left to the military commanders, who followed divergent policies.

The Emancipation Proclamation was issued in September 1862, following the Union victory at Antietam. Lincoln had begun the war to restore the Union, not necessarily to free the slaves. The war aims were now expanded, partly to gain favorable public opinion in America and Europe, especially Britain, partly to deny a resource to the South. The Proclamation declared all those slaves in areas still in rebellion on January 1, 1863, to be free.

○○ Other Wartime Measures of the Lincoln Administration—The Homestead Act (1862) promoted the settlement of the West. The westward movement proceeded without interfering with the war effort. The Morrill Land Grant Act (1862) provided land grants to states for financing agricultural and mechanical colleges in all the states. The transcontinental railroads were chartered across the central route.

A Conscription Act in 1863 required counties to supply quotas of men for army service. It resulted in the Draft Riots in New York City in which hundreds were killed. Individuals could avoid the draft by hiring a substitute or by paying $300. Lincoln exercised unconstitutional powers in defiance of Congress to arrest political seditionists. Nevertheless, there was much open criticism of the war against the South.

✪ Wartime Government in the South—In contrast with Northern prosperity, economic conditions grew progressively worse in the South as the war continued. The Confederacy was forced to finance the war mainly with paper money. As larger quantities were printed and the hopes of victory faded, goods grew scarce and prices soared. Excise and income taxes were levied.

The Confederate government was not as effective as it might have been. President Jefferson Davis quarreled with his subordinates; he continuously meddled in the conduct of the war to the great annoyance of his military commanders. Vice President Alexander Stephens, from Georgia, was a stickler for states' rights.

Toward the end of the war widespread draft evasion occurred. Because men might legally make a money payment to escape the draft, the disgruntled poor said it was a "rich man's war and a poor man's fight." With the disruption of transportation by invading Northern armies, the Southern economy collapsed completely. Many died of starvation.

✪ The Election of 1864—Lincoln ran under the National Union Party label with a War Democrat, Andrew Johnson of Tennessee, as his running mate.

The Democrats nominated General George B. McClellan who had been removed from his command by Lincoln. The party platform favored a negotiated peace with the South; however, McClellan himself favored preservation of the Union. The North was tired of the war and it seemed that Lincoln would be defeated in August 1864, but a succession of Union victories soon restored confidence in a timely victory. Lincoln won reelection by 212 electoral votes to only 21 for McClellan.

CHAPTER BOOK LIST

Boritt, Gabor S., ed., *Why the Confederacy Lost* (1992). Several conflicting interpretations of the questions.

Catton, Bruce, *America Goes to War* (Century).

Catton, Bruce, *Glory Road, the Bloody Route from Fredericksburg to Gettysburg* (Dolphin). Realistic account by a great writer.

Catton, Bruce, *Mr. Lincoln's Army* (Dolphin). Catton is a prolific writer on the Civil War.

Craven, Avery O., *The Coming of the Civil War* (2nd ed., rev., 1957).

Current, Richard N., *Lincoln and the First Shot* (1964).

Donald, David, ed., *Why the North Won the Civil War* (1960)

Fehrenbacher, Don E., *Lincoln in Text and Context* (1987). Aspects of Lincoln's leadership of the Union.

Foote, Shelby, *The Civil War: A Narrative* (1958–74). From the Southern point of view.

Franklin, John Hope, *The Emancipation Proclamation* (1960). Good, short account.

Glatthaar, Joseph T., *Forged in Battle: The Civil War Alliance of Black Soldiers and White Officers* (1991). Freedmen and other blacks in the Union army.

Hansen, Harry, *Civil War: A New One-Volume History* (Mentor).

Hyman, Harold M., *A More Perfect Union: The Impact of the Civil War and Reconstruction on the Constitution* (1973).

McElroy, John, *Andersonville: A Story of Rebel Military Prisons* (Premier). Horrors endured by Union prisoners of war.

McPherson, James M., ed., *The Negro in the Civil War* (1965).

Mitchell, Joseph, *Decisive Battles of The Civil War* (Premier). Maps, useful reference and guide book.

Oates, Stephen B., *With Malice Toward None: The Life of Abraham Lincoln* (1977). Excellent one-volume biography.

Parish, Peter J., *The American Civil War* (Holmes-Meier).

Randall, James G., and Donald, David, *The Civil War and Reconstruction* (Heath).

Wiley, B.I., *Life of Billy Yank* (Charter). Life of the soldier.

Wiley, B.I., *Life of Johnny Reb* (Charter). The Confederate soldier.

REVIEW QUESTIONS

MULTIPLE CHOICE

1. Which weapon or device was not employed in the Civil War? (1) The machine gun (2) observation balloons (3) the submarine (4) poison gas.

2. The first state to secede from the Union was (1) Mississippi (2) Alabama (3) South Carolina (4) Virginia.

3. In response to secession (1) the North stood solidly for preservation of the Union (2) the North had a large minority willing to let the South depart in peace (3) Buchanan favored action against the South (4) the border states joined the Confederacy.

4. The proposals embodied in the Crittenden Compromise were made up of (1) concessions to the South (2) concessions by both North and South (3) concessions to the North (4) limitations on the expansion of slavery.

5. The two greatest advantages of the North in the Civil War were (1) British friendship and large population (2) control of the navy and better trained army officers (3) control of the navy and diversified industry (4) control of the navy and united public opinion.

6. The earliest significant Union victories in the Civil War were won (1) by the Army of the Potomac (2) in Sherman's march (3) by the navy (4) in the West.

7. The two most decisive battles of the Civil War were (1) Bull Run and Chancellorsville (2) Shiloh and Vicksburg (3) Antietam and Gettysburg (4) Vicksburg and Seven Days.

8. The Emancipation Proclamation benefited the Northern victory most by (1) inciting slave insurrections (2) assuring the neutrality of Britain (3) winning loyalty of the border states (4) gaining support of abolitionists.

9. Who was not a Northern army commander in the Civil War? (1) Phil Sheridan (2) David Farragut (3) William T. Sherman (4) Irwin McDowell.

10. Who was *not* a leading Confederate general? (1) Robert E. Lee (2) Albert Sidney Johnston (3) Irwin McDowell (4) "Stonewall" Jackson.

11. Which was a Northern ship in the Civil War? (1) *Trent* (2) *Merrimac* (3) *Monitor* (4) *Alabama.*

12. The Union government was in error in seizing Mason and Slidell because (1) England had recognized the government of the Confederacy (2) they were diplomatic emissaries to governments that had recognized the Confederacy as a legal belligerent (3) they were aboard a British vessel when captured (4) they were citizens of a neutral country.

13. The greatest threat to Northern military victory after the Civil War began came from possible adverse action by (1) the border states (2) Britain (3) France (4) Copperheads.

14. Which means of war financing was *not* used by *both* the North and the South? (1) The issuance of irredeemable paper money (2) the sale of government bonds (3) the use of some kind of income tax (4) passage of a protective tariff.

15. Lincoln's attitude toward abolition during the Civil War was that (1) abolition was secondary to preservation of the Union (2) he opposed abolition but was driven to it only by international relations (3) he favored abolition above all war goals (4) he favored abolition in order to give the army a cause to fight for.

16. In procuring men for the army (1) both North and South depended on volunteers only (2) only the South used conscription (3) both the Union and the Confederacy conscripted men (4) only the North used the draft.

17. In 1864 what Democratic nominee opposed Lincoln for the Presidency? (1) Andrew Johnson (2) George McClellan (3) George Meade (4) Hamilton Fish.

TRUE-FALSE

18. Historians agree that it is superficial to attribute the causes of the Civil War to slavery.
19. The main war aim of the South was to continue its domination of the nation.
20. The South hoped by independence to renew the African slave trade and reduce the cost of labor.
21. Many Southerners hoped and expected secession to be peaceful.
22. Strong minorities in the Southern states opposed secession.
23. The strong, diversified economy of the North proved to be of more advantage to it than military ability did to the South.
24. The decisive battles of the Civil War were fought in the West.
25. The first battles of the Civil War made the North overconfident.
26. The most able Union commander in the West was General Sheridan.
27. At the beginning of the War the South forbade the export of cotton in the belief it would cause Britain and France to break the Northern blockade.
28. In England the upper classes favored the North and the lower classes the South.
29. The capture of Mason and Slidell actually was in violation of international law.
30. Lincoln's cabinet was made up of men representing divergent elements in his party.
31. Lincoln's order freeing the slaves applied only to slaves in the unoccupied parts of the South.
32. The Republican administration of Lincoln failed in most respects to enact legislation to carry out its campaign promises made to gain the support of various Northern elements.
33. The South may have been less democratic but the Confederate government was more concerned with preserving civil liberties and states' rights than the Union government.
34. Southern draftees in the army to the very last remained loyal to the Confederacy.
35. Military victories just before election won reelection for Lincoln in 1864.

COMPLETION

36. The President of the Confederacy was _____ , the capital was first located at _____ , later at _____ .

37. In the election of 1860 the South for the first time lost control of which branch of the national government? _____

38. All Southern grievances mentioned to justify secession were related to the question of _____ .

39. The first shots of the Civil War were fired at _____ in the harbor of _____ .

40. Radical Southerners who favored secession and were prepared to fight were called _____ .

41. "Peace Democrats" in the North were nicknamed _____ .

42. Other than Grant, the best known general at the head of the Army of the Potomac was _____ .

43. Opposing Lee at Gettysburg and supreme Union commander was General _____ .

44. Lee surrendered to Grant at _____ .

45. The last point to fall on the Mississippi River was _____ .

46. Sherman began his march through Georgia at _____ , Tennessee, and reached the sea at _____ . Sherman's campaign ended when he captured the Confederate commander, General _____ .

47. The United States increased tariff rates in the _____ Tariff.

48. _____ were the two Confederate emissaries captured aboard the British mailship named _____ . Secretary of State under Lincoln was _____ .

49. A uniform national currency was provided by the _____ Act of 1863.

50. Any possibility that Britain would intervene in the Civil War was prevented by the Union victory at the Battle of _____ after which slaves were freed by the _____ .

51. The author of the Land Grant College Act was named _____ .

MATCHING

52. Alexander H. Stephens   a. Attacked in First Battle of Bull Run

53. J.J. Crittenden   b. Lincoln's running mate in 1864

54. Winfield Scott   c. Vice-president of the Confederacy

55. Irwin McDowell   d. Union financial wizard of the Civil War

56. George C. McClellan   e. Tried to reconcile North and South

57. Jay Cooke   f. Confederate commander at Vicksburg

58. Andrew Johnson   g. Secretary of State of the Confederacy

                             h. Originated the Anaconda Plan

                             i. Twice removed from command of the
                                Army of the Potomac

THE RECONSTRUCTION PERIOD
1865–1877

CHRONOLOGY / CHAPTER 17

1863 Lincoln's plan of easy reconstruction announced.

1864 Wade-Davis Bill vetoed by Lincoln, a defeat for policy of harsh reconstruction.

1865 Andrew Johnson succeeded to Presidency after Lincoln's assassination.

Johnson proceeded to reconstruct South along lines of Lincoln's plan.

Black Codes passed by Southern states.

Sumner and Stevens control Joint Committee on Reconstruction and thwart Johnson's plan to reconstruct the South.

1866 Napoleon III's withdrawal of troops from Mexico vindicates Monroe Doctrine.

Johnson vetoed Freedmen's Bureau Bill.

Race riots in the South.

Civil Rights Bill passed over Johnson's veto.

Ku Klux Klan organized in South.

1867 Alaska purchased from Russia.

EARLY RECONSTRUCTION, 1865–1866

> The term "Reconstruction Period" designates the years following the surrender of Confederate military forces in April 1865, to the final withdrawal of Union occupation troops in the early part of 1877. During this time the North attempted to reshape Southern government and society according to goals determined by the victorious North.

THE PROBLEM OF RECONSTRUCTION

The word "reconstruction" was applied to Northern endeavors to restore the Southern states to the Union under certain stipulations set forth by the presidents and Congress. In its broader meaning the term takes in the whole process of attempting to rebuild and change the South along lines suitable to the North. Reconstruction ended without achieving its far-reaching goals of social and political reform.

✪ **Physical and Economic Ruin in the South After the War—**
The South, as the battlefield of the war, suffered much destruction. South Carolina, Georgia, and Virginia suffered most from the destruction of the campaigns and from the scorched earth policy of Sherman in Georgia and of Sheridan in the Shenandoah Valley of Virginia.

Cities were shelled and burned and farmhouses destroyed as the invading Union armies sought to destroy the war potential of the South. Systematic destruction of railroads and bridges and wartime wear and neglect left transportation severely crippled. River shipping, seaports, and country roads were destroyed or left in sad disrepair. Much private property in the South had been confiscated during the war. Confederate government property, including cotton in storage, naturally became property of the victors. Many dishonest individuals, either actual Treasury agents or thieves posing as Treasury agents, wrongfully confiscated private holdings of livestock, cotton, and other farm commodities from intimidated Southerners.

Individuals in the South suffered disastrous economic losses. Banks all closed their doors and individual accounts were lost. Confederate currency became only a collectors' item. Holders of war bonds lost their investment; the emancipation of slaves meant the loss of valuable property to their owners. Farm land lost most of its value as the result of the loss of the slaves and other economic disruption, and many plantations were foreclosed for taxes. The whole country faced the problem of physical rebuilding and of devising a new economic system under which the freed slaves might work. The South is the only section of the United States that has known poverty and defeat because of war.

Social Losses and Upheaval—About 250,000 Southern men died in uniform and others returned crippled while many civilians lost their lives as a consequence of the war. The emancipation of the slaves uprooted hundreds of thousands of them and brought sudden freedom they were unprepared for. Their labor was lost and they created a social problem for themselves and for the South as they wandered about looking for food and trying, like children, to enjoy their new freedom.

✪✪✪ **Lincoln's Plan of Reconstruction**—As the armies of the North occupied Southern territory, the North faced the problem of organizing loyal state governments. Lincoln held that the seceded states were out of a "proper practical relationship" with the rest of the Union and the only thing needed was to restore that relationship. Late in 1863 Lincoln formulated a simple and generous plan to achieve a speedy return of the conquered states. 1) Pardons were offered all residents of the South, except for higher political and military leaders, on condition they take an oath of allegiance to the United States. 2) As soon as ten percent of those who had voted in 1860 had taken the oath of allegiance to the federal government and to support the Thirteenth Amendment a state government could be organized and recognized by the president. Some congressional leaders thought this plan was too lenient and spoke of it derisively as the "ten percent plan." Under this plan governments in Tennessee, Louisiana, Arkansas, and Virginia were recognized by Lincoln.

✪✪ **Bases of Opposition to Moderate Reconstruction Policy**— From the beginning of the Lincoln administration there was a division of opinion within the Republican Party toward the South. While the moderate Republicans, like Lincoln, favored a lenient and understanding policy, the radical Republicans favored harsh policies and more extreme reforms in the South.

Differences between the Presidential and Radical plans may be explained as follows: 1) The Radicals feared that the supremacy of the Republican party, a newcomer to the political scene, might prove to be temporary if Northern and Southern Democrats should become united as they had been before the war. This was especially true as, with emancipation, the three-fifths ratio ceased to exist and the South's strength in the House of Representatives would increase when the former slaves were counted fully. 2) Conflict over the authority of the President was another cause of the opposition of Congress to Lincoln. Many congressmen were convinced that the President had exceeded his proper authority during the war and afterwards in assuming control over reconstruction of the Southern states. 3) There was disagreement with Lincoln regarding the legal status of the South. Lincoln held that the states of the South had never ceased to exist nor had they left the Union; they could not legally secede. This theory would limit the power of Congress to freely govern and reorganize the South as it might choose. 4) A strong desire among Northerners to punish the South asserted itself because of the sacrifice made to fight a long and costly war.

5) Behind most of the measures of political reconstruction in the South was the desire of Northern business interests to preserve and strengthen the Republican Party as the advocate of business interests. It was planned to keep the South impotent politically until the Republican Party had consolidated its gains and carried out its program. The control of the African American vote was a part of this plan. 6) Reformers in the North wished to promote social changes to humble and weaken the planter aristocracy of the South. They unwisely and revengefully sought to give full and immediate equality to the former slaves. The drastic measures they took were to embitter the South and cause hardship to the freedmen and make more difficult their adjustment to freedom and responsibility.

The Wade-Davis Bill (July 1864)—The Radical Republicans, the advocates of extreme reforms and punitive measures in the South, early challenged Lincoln's moderate measures. Under their leadership Congress passed the Wade-Davis Bill to give the Radicals control over the South. Lincoln gave the bill a pocket veto. Nevertheless, it demonstrated that Lincoln would have to deal with determined opposition in Congress from members of his own party. But Lincoln hoped to restore the Southern states to their former place in the Union before Congress could act.

✪ Johnson's Plan of Reconstruction—The assassination of Lincoln on April 15, 1865, threw the problem of reconstruction into the hands of the new President, Andrew Johnson. The Radicals assumed that Johnson would go along with their plans, since he had often railed against the planter aristocrats in favor of more political power for the common whites of the South. Johnson had remained in the Senate when his own state, Tennessee, seceded. However, as a Democrat and a Southerner Johnson favored a moderate policy. He wished to leave the Southern states free from federal intervention in what he considered internal affairs. He proceeded, therefore, to carry out a policy very similar to Lincoln's. Johnson's plan 1) called for the appointment of Southern civilians as provisional governors. 2) Next, constitutional conventions were to be called by the states and to be made up of delegates who had taken the oath of allegiance to the United States. 3) The conventions would next be expected to a) withdraw the ordinances of secession, b) abolish slavery, and c) cancel all Confederate war debts.

Having completed these steps, the states could resume their former places in the Union. The Southern states carried out this plan or were on their way to doing so when Congress convened in December, 1865. None of the states made provision to permit the freedmen to vote; Congress resented this and soon showed their unwillingness to recognize Johnson's plan. Congress refused to seat senators and representatives chosen by state governments under Johnson's plan.

POSTWAR DIPLOMACY UNDER JOHNSON

To President Johnson fell the task of expelling the French from Mexico and thereby upholding the Monroe Doctrine. Johnson and Seward handled this problem tactfully and secured French withdrawal during the time of the conflict with Congress over reconstruction policy. The purchase of Alaska originated with friendly wartime relations with Russia.

✪✪✪ **The French in Mexico**—French intervention began in 1862 when Archduke Maximilian of Austria, with the support of the French forces in collaboration with reactionary landowners and churchmen in Mexico, was enthroned as Emperor of Mexico. The French intervention was ordered by the Emperor Napoleon III. Mexico was only one of a half-dozen instances of Napoleon's aggression in search of an empire. The ambitious young couple, Maximilian and Carlota, were the unwitting dupes of Napoleon's scheme. Secretary of State Seward demanded the withdrawal of the French troops that upheld the French puppets against the will of the people of Mexico, but the Civil War precluded the use of American troops. In the fall of 1865 General Sheridan was sent to the Texas border at the Rio Grande by Johnson and Seward, and quiet demands invoking the Monroe Doctrine were made again for withdrawal; at the same time Benito Juarez, the revolutionary leader, was tacitly recognized. With growing problems of his own in Europe, Napoleon had no alternative and withdrew his troops in May 1866. Without foreign military support, Maximilian was captured and shot by a Mexican firing squad. The American course of action further reinforced the Monroe Doctrine.

✪✪ **Territorial Expansion, 1867**—Secretary of State Seward, an eager expansionist, was approached in December 1866 by the Russian minister in a move that resulted in the purchase of Alaska by the United States. The friendliness of the Russians in sending their fleet to New

York during the Civil War opened the way for these negotiations. The Russians wished to sell Alaska because its fur resources had now been well exhausted. Expecting that friction with Great Britain might lead to war and the capture of defenseless Alaska by the British, the Russians preferred to see it in American hands.

The United States bought "Seward's Folly" in 1867 chiefly through the energetic efforts of the Secretary of State. It was urged that the purchase would repay the Russians for their show of friendship during the Civil War. Rumors of its wealth of furs, fish, and gold along with a propaganda campaign helped to convince Congress of the wisdom of the purchase. It proved to be a profitable acquisition at a cost of $7,200,000.

In 1867 the United States also occupied the Midway Islands west of Hawaii; the United States had discovered them in 1859. Seward negotiated a treaty with Denmark for the purchase of the Virgin Islands but it failed to pass the Senate.

THE BEGINNINGS OF CONGRESSIONAL RECONSTRUCTION

In order to control and delay reconstruction of the conquered states the Radicals of both houses of Congress appointed a Joint Committee on Reconstruction.

✪✪✪**Leaders of Congressional Reconstruction**—The outstanding Radical congressional leader was Thaddeus Stevens, a Representative from Pennsylvania long noted for his advocacy of popular reforms, his hatred of the ruling class of the South, and his sincere sympathy for the African American. His theory of reconstruction held that the Southern states had become "conquered provinces," completely at the disposal of Congress. He maintained his domineering and vindictive leadership in Congress until 1868.

Charles Sumner, from Massachusetts, became the Senate Radical leader on the Joint Committee on Reconstruction. In bad health, avowedly due to the beating by Preston Brooks, his mind was obsessed with the single question of the African American. As an idealist and reformer he wished to enforce immediate racial equality. From cynical, selfish motives, the other Radicals permitted these misguided idealists to dominate Congress. Sumner reasoned, under his theory of "state suicide," that the Southern states had destroyed themselves by secession and were now as completely at the disposal of Congress as any territory.

✪**Mistakes of the South**—The Southern states chose many former high-ranking Confederate leaders to represent them in Congress upon the restoration of their state governments under Johnson's plan; this greatly irritated the North.

The "Black Codes" were passed by the Southern legislatures to settle the future status of the freedmen. These laws were supposedly meant to protect the freedmen, but they were actually designed to force them back to work under conditions that denied their legal, social, and economic rights.

Race riots occurred in the early part of 1866 in certain parts of the South with considerable loss of life, especially among the freedmen.

These events in the South played into the hands of the Radicals who now contended that the South was unwilling to accept the verdict of the war and that strong measures were necessary.

⊙ **The Freedmen's Bureau Bill**—The first direct clash between the President and Congress occurred in February, 1866, when Congress passed a bill to renew the Freedmen's Bureau. This agency, though basically a wartime relief organization of the national government, came to be used as a political device for making the African Americans loyal to the Republican Party. Because it represented federal action in an area which Johnson, with his states' rights views, believed should be left to the states, he vetoed the bill. The Radicals were unable to command enough votes to override the veto. As a consequence Johnson became overconfident and tactlessly denounced the Radicals and strongly criticized their leaders.

⊙ **The Civil Rights Bill**—Soon afterwards, in March, Congress passed the Civil Rights Bill. This law gave the African Americans citizenship and equal civil rights, including the right to vote. The bill was vetoed by Johnson but now repassed over his veto. The Radicals next passed a slightly modified Freedmen's Bureau Bill over the President's veto and thereby demonstrated that they now had the upper hand.

CHAPTER BOOK LISTS

Coulter, E.S., *The South During Reconstruction: 1865–1877* (1947). A general history.

Degler, Carl, *The Other South* (1974).

Donald, David, *The Politics of Reconstruction, 1863–1867* (1965). Relations between president and Congress.

Donald, Hendersen H., *The Negro Freedman: The Early Years After Emancipation* (1952).

DuBois, W.E.B., *Black Reconstruction in America, 1860–1880* (1935). By an early African American activist and scholar.

Franklin, John Hope, *Reconstruction After the Civil War* (University of Chicago)

Foner, Eric, *Emancipation and Its Legacy* (1983).

Foner, Eric, *Reconstruction: America's Unfinished Revolution* (1988). The best one-volume account.

Patrick, Rembert W., *The Reconstruction of the Nation* (1967).

Randall, J.G., *The Civil War and Reconstruction* (1961). Scholarly and readable.

REVIEW QUESTIONS

MULTIPLE CHOICE

1. Lincoln's and Johnson's reconstruction policies agreed in which way? (1) Both appointed military men as governors in the South (2) neither favored cancellation of Confederate war debts (3) both held that the Southern states had never been out of the Union (4) neither favored compensated emancipation.

2. Which necessitated the greatest economic readjustment in the South after the war? (1) Emancipation of slaves (2) confiscatory taxes (3) disruption of export markets (4) property damage.

3. Which motive was least apparent in Radical reconstruction plans for the South? (1) Consolidation of the Republican Party in the South (2) equality for the African American (3) hasty reconciliation of North and South (4) humiliation of ex-Confederates.

4. The Radicals hoped Johnson would acquiesce in their reconstruction plans because Johnson (1) had always been a Republican (2) favored equality for the African American (3) believed in states' rights (4) disliked the Southern aristocrats.

5. Congress early killed Johnson's reconstruction plans by (1) impeachment proceedings against him (2) refusing to seat congressmen from the South (3) early military occupation of the South (4) emancipation of all slaves.

6. The French intervention in Mexico was undertaken to (1) enlarge the French empire (2) aid the Confederacy (3) sustain the upper class in Mexico (4) forestall British intervention.

7. The negotiations for the purchase of Alaska began with an offer by (1) President Johnson (2) Secretary Seward (3) Russia (4) President Grant.

8. Which of these events did not occur in the South and convince the North that stronger measures were needed to reconstruct the South? (1) Refusal to ratify the Thirteenth Amendment (2) the "Black Codes" (3) race riots (4) election of former Confederates to Congress.

9. The Freedmen's Bureau was organized primarily to (1) provide relief and aid to freed slaves (2) organize the African American vote for the Republican Party (3) confiscate and redistribute plantation lands (4) intimidate Southern voters.

10. Which did *not* occur during the Reconstruction Period? (1) Congress dominated the Supreme Court (2) systematic, widespread redistribution of plantation lands was realized (3) the Radicals defied the office of the President (4) corruption in government was widespread.

TRUE-FALSE

11. Reconstruction was notably successful in achieving its goals.

12. Treasury agents rightfully confiscated cotton and other property belonging to the defeated Confederate government.

13. Individuals in the South escaped serious economic loss in the war.

14. Lincoln appointed Southern civilians as governors in the states under reconstruction.

15. Lincoln accepted several states as being "reconstructed" under his plan.

16. One of the strongest motives behind the harsh reconstruction policy of the Radicals was the desire to entrench the Republican Party in the South and to remain powerful as the spokesman of the victorious Northern business interests.

17. Many congressmen sincerely believed the presidents had exceeded their rightful authority in assuming control of reconstruction.

18. The policy of the Radicals was first proposed in the extremist Wade-Davis Bill.

19. Under his reconstruction plan Johnson appointed military commanders over the Southern states.

20. The Southern states all made plans to give the vote to the freedmen under Johnson's reconstruction plan.

21. Johnson vetoed the Freedmen's Bureau Bill because he felt it dealt with a type of activity that should be left to the states.

COMPLETION

22. The Reconstruction Period extended from _____ to _____ .

23. Lincoln's reconstruction plan was called the _____ .

24. President Johnson asserted the right of the United States under the _____ to expel the French from Mexico.

25. It was the emperor of France _____ who intervened in Mexico during the Civil War and made _____ emperor of Mexico.

26. Alaska was purchased in the year _____ ; about the same time a treaty with _____ for the purchase of the Virgin Islands failed to pass the Senate.

27. The leader of the Radical Republicans in the House was _____ and in the Senate was _____ . Their theories of reconstruction were called respectively the _____ theory and the _____ theory.

28. After the Civil War the South passed the _____ to regulate the behavior of the freedmen.

CHRONOLOGY / CHAPTER 18

1866   After February, Radicals gained enough adherents in
          Congress to override Johnson's vetoes.
          Johnson's supporters in Congress reduced by congressional
          elections.
          December, Radicals began to enact harsh measures to
          reconstruct the South.

1867   Reconstruction Act of 1867 applied main features of
          Congressional Reconstruction.
          Fourteenth Amendment passed by Congress.
          Tenure of Office Act passed over Johnson's veto.
          Impeachment proceedings against President Johnson begun.

1868   Attempt to remove Johnson from office failed by one vote.
          Fourteenth Amendment ratified.
          Grant (Rep.) elected President.

1869   Grant began first term as President.

1870   Fifteenth Amendment ratified.
          Reconstruction governments ended in most Southern states.
          First Enforcement Act passed to suppress Ku Klux Klan.

1872   Amnesty Act restored political rights to most former
          Confederates.

1876   Election results disputed but settled in 1877 in favor of Hayes
          (Rep.). Party leaders agree to withdraw federal troops from
          last of the Southern states.

1877   Reconstruction governments ended in all Southern states.
          Rule of the "Solid South" began.

18

THE CONGRESSIONAL RECONSTRUCTION PERIOD, 1866–1877

> After the Radicals in Congress had gained sufficient votes to carry their program against the President, they permitted few restraints to block their program. The authority of both the President and the Supreme Court were disregarded. After a few years Northern opinion revolted against the arbitrary policies and untimely reforms of the Radicals. Social and political reconstruction substantially failed to achieve its long-range goals in the South.

THE STRUGGLE BETWEEN CONGRESS AND THE PRESIDENT

Congress refused to seat members elected by the Southern states under Johnson's plan. After February 1866, the Radicals had enough adherents in Congress to override presidential vetoes. Congress next sought to nullify all interference by Johnson, even going so far as to attempt a political impeachment.

✪ **Johnson and the Elections of 1866**—The congressional elections of 1866 provided a popular referendum by which the North could endorse either Johnson's policies or those of Congress.

President Johnson campaigned vigorously for his congressional supporters, but this in itself was ill-advised, as presidents did not normally work publicly to secure passage of their proposals. Also, Johnson's East Tennessee style of political oratory was not thought equal to the dignity of the presidential office. The Radicals argued that a victory for Johnson would bring low tariffs and repudiation of the national war debt. Such events in the South as the election of ex-Confederates, the race riots, and the Black Codes convinced many Northern voters that the more strenuous program of the Radicals was needed. In the same election ten Southern states angered the North by rejecting the Fourteenth Amendment.

The Radicals won control of the House and Senate by margins that were sufficient to put their measures beyond the reach of the presidential veto.

❂❂❂**The Congressional Plan of Reconstruction**—When Congress reconvened in December, 1866, the Radicals enacted a series of laws that were vindictive and intended to assure the perpetuation of Radical Republican rule.

1) The Tenure of Office Act forbade the president from removing civil officers without the consent of the Senate; the purpose was to prevent Johnson from removing Radicals from office. 2) The Army Act was passed to make the military establishment almost free of presidential control.

3) The Reconstruction Act of March 2, 1867, a) rejected the new state governments in all the South except in Tennessee; b) the South was divided into five military districts, each under a high-ranking Northern army officer; c) in each district all voters were to be registered so as to enfranchise the freedmen and deny the vote to large numbers of white voters for disloyalty. This provision insured Radical control of state governments. d) Another provision required the states to provide for African American suffrage under newly drafted constitutions. e) The Fourteenth Amendment had to be ratified by state legislatures. f) Newly elected senators and representatives must be able to take the "ironclad oath" that they had never voluntarily aided the Confederacy. 4) Another act required that Congress convene on March 4, 1867. This was done to ensure that they would remain in session to dominate Reconstruction policies.

❂❂❂**The Fourteenth Amendment**—In the summer of 1866, the Radicals passed the Fourteenth Amendment to fix into law more firmly the provisions of the Civil Rights Bill. It was not ratified until 1868.

This "Omnibus Amendment" carried several other provisions to put the Radical program into effect and insure its success.

1) It gave citizenship with full rights to all persons born or naturalized in the country and forbade the states to pass any law to restrict such rights or deny equal protection. This same section forbade any state to deprive any person of life, liberty, or property without due process of law.

2) The next section, which was to become a dead letter, provided that to the extent that any state denied the vote to any of its male inhabitants, it would have its representation proportionately reduced in Congress and in the Electoral College.

3) The third section took from the president the traditional pardoning power by which ex-Confederates might be permitted to hold any state or federal offices.

4) The fourth section guaranteed the payment of the United States Civil War debt, but prohibited the payment of any debt or obligation incurred by the Confederacy and precluded any compensation for loss of slave property.

5) The power of enforcement of its provisions was vested in Congress, although traditionally the executive is the law-enforcing branch of government. The Radicals would not entrust its enforcement to President Johnson.

The Fourteenth Amendment went into effect in July 1868, after ratification by the Southern states while under carpetbag control.

✪✪✪ **The Impeachment of Johnson**—Although the Radicals had enough votes to override any presidential veto, they were determined to consolidate their strength further by removing Johnson from office by impeachment. Johnson ordinarily was careful to abide by the laws enacted by Congress. However, in August 1867, he asked for the resignation of Edwin M. Stanton, the two-faced Secretary of War, who acted as a spy for the Radicals in cabinet meetings. Johnson correctly believed the Tenure of Office Act to be unconstitutional and wished to bring a test case to the Supreme Court. But the Radicals in Congress welcomed Johnson's action since they could use his violation of an Act of Congress as the basis for impeachment.

In February 1868, the House of Representatives voted overwhelmingly to impeach Johnson; most of the charges were based on violations of the Tenure of Office Act. The Senate sat as a court to hear the case and judge the guilt of the accused. The President was ably defended, and the evidence against him was weak, but the Radicals, desperate to remove him, used all kinds of pressure on individual senators to force them to vote a verdict of guilty. Yet they could not muster the one additional vote needed to make good the charges by the necessary two-thirds vote. Seven independent Republican senators refused to join their colleagues in voting for removal. The trial demonstrated the extremes to which the Radical Congress would go to override the executive branch and dominate the government.

✪✪✪ **Radical Reconstruction in Effect in the South**—After the Radicals won control of the government, they proceeded in 1867 to enforce their extreme measures in the South. The South was organized into five military districts, each under a Union general whose authority was enforced by federal troops. The state governments were supplanted by military government—an unconstitutional peacetime military rule.

The control of the African American vote was the key to Republican political control of the Southern states. The African Americans were assured the vote by the Fourteenth Amendment and the presence of federal troops. The Union League, the Radical propaganda arm in the South, worked to cement the loyalty of the freedmen to the Republican Party and provided the effective Republican leadership in the South during Reconstruction. "Carpetbaggers," a term applied to Northerners who came South during Reconstruction, supplied leadership and encouragement to the freedmen and voted Republican themselves. The carpetbaggers were government officials, missionaries, politicians, and businessmen who came to work or to take advantage of the various opportunities in the South after the war.

Another Southern group supporting Radical reconstruction was the "Scalawags," Southern whites who hoped to win office or realize private advantage by collaborating with the Northerners. African American leaders among the freedmen also helped indoctrinate their fellows to loyalty to the Republican Party. These groups comprised the main elements of government in the South as long as federal troops were present to support them against the mass of Southern whites. The program of the Reconstruction governments called for enforcing civil, political, and social equality of African Americans with Southern whites. Many Southerners were denied the vote to enable the carpetbag governments to obtain power and keep it.

✪✪✪ Reconstruction Governments in the South—The Reconstruction governments have frequently been condemned for putting ignorant freedmen in office, for widespread graft and corruption, and for heavily increasing taxes. Although there were instances of these problems, few freedmen actually participated in government, as the presence of any African American, even an educated freeborn Northerner, was objectionable to the South. Corruption was not confined to the South; these were the days of Boss Tweed in New York and the Whiskey Ring in St. Louis. Finally, the higher taxes and debts frequently represented the cost of physical reconstruction and additional tasks, such as public education, previously shunned by Southern state governments.

Certain constructive results followed from the reforms instituted by the Reconstruction governments. 1) The new constitutions provided for more democracy by guaranteeing civil liberties and universal male suffrage. 2) Public works projects provided necessary roads, bridges, and public buildings. 3) A system of compulsory, free public education was started. Not only were the African Americans helped by the schools but the submerged whites benefited. 4) Taxes were redistributed in such a way as to levy the burden more equitably among different classes.

✪ Radical Defiance of the Supreme Court—After the Radicals had gained enough votes in Congress, they carried out their drastic program against both the executive and judicial branches of the federal government. Only the Supreme Court stood in the way of complete congressional domination after Johnson was outvoted in Congress. When Grant succeeded Johnson to the Presidency, that office offered no resistance to the Radicals.

Congress manipulated the Court first by raising the number of justices to ten during the war. In the decision *Ex Parte Milligan* (1866) the Court ruled that military trials were illegal where civilian courts were in operation. In retaliation for this decision Congress passed a law that new vacancies in the Court should not be filled until the number of justices should be reduced to seven. When Congress felt that new appointees under Grant would be friendly, the number was increased to nine. The Court lost much of its prestige in 1871 when, apparently under pressure from the Radicals, it reversed an earlier decision against the greenbacks. Thus, in the case of *Hepburn v. Griswold* the two new appointees of Grant joined in ruling that the greenbacks were legal tender for payment of all debts. The Supreme Court went out of the way to avoid giving offense to the Radical Congress. Not until national opinion had turned against the extremism of the Radicals did the Court assert itself to declare unconstitutional a number of the Reconstruction measures.

○ The Election of 1868—In 1868 the Republicans were practically assured of victory by their control of Southern state governments made effective by the presence of federal troops and the control over the registration of voters. The military hero Grant became the Republican nominee; he was completely acceptable to the Radicals and the business interests that had come to dominate the Party. The Democrats passed up Johnson for renomination and chose Horatio Seymour of New York. The Democrats supported the "Ohio Idea" for the payment of the national debt in greenbacks; this inflationary proposal frightened conservatives in the North. In spite of the factors favoring a Republican victory, Grant won by a lead of only 300,000 votes—a lead clearly due to Union League manipulation of the African American vote and army disenfranchisement of Southern whites.

○ The Fifteenth Amendment—Grant's slim victory convinced the Radicals that they needed the African American vote, both in the North and the South, in order to keep the Presidency. Even some Northern states, such as Connecticut, did not permit African Americans to vote. Accordingly, the Fifteenth Amendment was passed by Congress in 1869 and ratified by the states in 1870. It provided simply that no one could be denied the vote because of race, color, or having been a slave. African American leaders such as Frederic Douglass refused the request of women suffrage leaders to include sex in the amendment.

THE LAST YEARS OF RECONSTRUCTION

By 1868 the states of the South except Mississippi, Texas, Virginia, and Georgia had adopted new constitutions and otherwise had complied with provisions of the Reconstruction Acts and were readmitted to the Union. These four states were required to ratify the Fifteenth Amendment as a further condition for readmission; they ratified it by 1870.

○○ Restoration of Southern Control—After readmission the Southern whites gradually regained the upper hand. Northern opinion softened towards the South as the public turned against the more extreme Radical measures. The Reconstruction governments lost popularity because of high taxation, increases in indebtedness, and corruption. The native Southern whites united against outside control; the African Americans stopped voting. Opinion in the North, reacting against dishonesty among the Radicals and Northern Democrats, helped to soften the extremism of the Radicals.

In 1872 Congress passed the Amnesty Act which restored political rights to most of the former Confederates. The election of 1876, in reality a defeat for the Republicans, brought an end to the Reconstruction period in the next year. After this the reforms of Reconstruction were almost completely undone.

○ **The Ku Klux Klan**—The Klan was a secret vigilante organization in the South that had many imitators. The motive of these societies was to maintain native white rule and frustrate the program of political and social equality for the African American. While some freedmen did behave irresponsibly, even criminally, most of those terrorized by the Klan were asserting the rights guaranteed to them by the Constitution. The Klansmen resorted to the worst forms of intimidation and violence, especially against the African Americans. Unscrupulous and lawless elements joined or imitated the Klan to achieve their own selfish purposes. They all operated at night under masks and robes.

Congress and President Grant took drastic measures to suppress the Klan. The Enforcement Acts were passed in 1870 and 1871. The writ of *habeas corpus* was suspended and troops used to protect federal courts; these efforts sharply decreased Klan effectiveness. A Ku Klux Klan Committee in Congress investigated and exposed both the evils of the extralegal Klansmen and the problems the South faced. When the Klan was revived in the 1920s, Catholics, Jews, and recent immigrants, in addition to African Americans, were its primary targets.

○○ **Factors in the Economic Recovery of the South**—Of the various agencies and forces working for Southern economic recovery 1) the Freedmen's Bureau was one of the first to become effective. The national economic philosophy of rugged individualism prevalent in nineteenth century America did not call for government measures to revive the Southern economy. Yet the destitute condition of the freedmen called for a minimum of relief in the form of food, clothing, fuel, and medicine. Whites as well as African Americans were cared for by the Bureau's agents. 2) The federal troops stationed in the South after the war shared their food, clothing, and supplies with Southerners. Many African American troops stationed there shared with their own race. Money spent by the army and the troops indirectly helped bring recovery. 3) The War Department rebuilt Southern railroads where it needed them. 4) Northern churches carried on missionary activities among the African

Americans and built churches, schools, and gave relief to the needy. 5) Private philanthropy, such as that of George Peabody, provided some funds for schools. 6) The South promoted its own recovery by establishing new, small businesses in such industries as cotton milling, tobacco processing, and lumbering. 7) Cotton production was revived after a few years against the greatest handicaps.

✪✪✪ EFFECTS OF RECONSTRUCTION IN THE SOUTH

Reconstruction has often been condemned as more destructive to the South, especially in its long-range consequences, than the war itself, but critics have seldom pointed to a realistic alternative. Lincoln's generous policies would have quickly cemented back into power the antebellum political establishment and the freedmen may have ended up with none of the blessings of freedom and none of the presumed security of slavery. The Radicals did not truly attempt a social revolution as they did not try to give the freedmen the economic base needed to make their civil and political rights effective. Proposals of "forty acres and a mule," that is, giving each African American family a small farm and the means to work it, might have accomplished this, but the proposal involved more interference with property rights and expense than the nation was ready for. It also assumes good faith on the part of Southern whites, good faith that did not exist. Eventually, the nation abandoned the African American to the mercy of the Southern white establishment that kept its section solidly Democratic into the 1960s in order to keep the descendants of the slaves at the bottom of Southern society.

CHAPTER BOOK LIST

Benedict, Michael Les, *The Impeachment and Trial of Andrew Johnson* (1973). The best treatment of a very tangled episode.

Bentley, G.R., *A History of the Freedmen's Bureau* (1970).

Buck, P.H., *Road to Reunion, 1865–1900* (Vintage). About the South mainly.

Cruden, Robert, *The Negro in Reconstruction* (1969).

Current, Richard N., *Those Terrible Carpetbaggers: A Reinterpretation* (1989). A more positive account.

Dunning, W.A., *Reconstruction Political and Economic, 1865–1877* (Torchbooks). Takes conservative position; a standard one-volume history.

Quarles, Benjamin, *Frederick Douglass* (Associated Publishers).

Randall, J.G., and Donald, David, *The Civil War and Reconstruction* (1961).

Sharkey, Robert P., *Money, Class, and Party* (1959).

Stampp, Kenneth M., *The Era of Reconstruction 1865–1877* (Knopf).

Woodward, C. Vann, *Reunion and Reaction* (rev. ed., 1956) and *Origins of the New South, 1877–1913* (1951). Both cover the end of Reconstruction.

REVIEW QUESTIONS

MULTIPLE CHOICE

1. Johnson's influence while President (1) steadily increased (2) increased after 1866 (3) declined further after 1866 (4) greatly hindered the Radicals.

2. The Fourteenth Amendment did all *except* (1) give citizenship to the freedmen (2) cancel Confederate war debts (3) free the slaves (4) guarantee payment of the Union war debt.

3. The Fifteenth Amendment (1) denied the president power to pardon ex-Confederates (2) gave citizenship to African Americans (3) freed the slaves (4) sought to assure the African Americans' right to vote.

4. Johnson was impeached mainly on charges that he had (1) become an habitual drunkard (2) violated the Tenure of Office Act (3) opposed the vote for the freedmen (4) was a Democrat and not elected to his office.

5. The Union League (1) kept the African Americans from voting (2) worked to make the African Americans loyal to the Republican Party (3) provided food and clothing to the destitute in the South (4) elected Lincoln and Johnson in 1864.

6. Which was *not* a group supporting Radical reconstruction in the South (1) Freedmen (2) "Carpetbaggers" (3) "Scalawags" (4) Liberal Republicans.

7. A desirable outcome of Reconstruction was the (1) introduction of honesty in the Southern state governments (2) practice of economy in state government (3) restoration of educated leaders to public office (4) beginnings of free public schools.

8. Grant was elected in 1868 because (1) the Democratic Party had just split (2) the African American vote in the South was under the control of the Radicals (3) the Democratic candidate was unpopular in the South (4) the Democrats in the North had dissolved their party.

9. The Ku Klux Klan activities sharply declined after (1) Southern public opinion rejected the Klan (2) passage of the federal Enforcement Acts by Congress (3) their leaders were found guilty of misappropriation of funds (4) Cleveland became President.

10. An important proposal supported by the Democrats in the election of 1868 was (1) the "Ohio Idea" (2) termination of Reconstruction (3) the acquisition of Alaska (4) a transcontinental railroad.

TRUE-FALSE

11. President Johnson was formerly a Democrat and remained one as can be seen from his political policies during reconstruction.

12. The Reconstruction Act of 1867 embodied the most important essentials of the Radical reconstruction program; it divided the South into five military districts.

13. The Radicals required the Southern states to grant the suffrage to African Americans.

14. The Fourteenth Amendment guaranteed the payment of both the Union and Confederate war debts.

15. Johnson's impeachment trial was heard before the Supreme Court.

16. Several Republican Senators voted "not guilty" in the impeachment charges against Johnson.

17. Many Southerners were denied the vote in order to keep carpetbag governments in power.

18. Grant resisted the application of the vengeful Radical policies in the South.

19. The Supreme Court suffered considerable loss of prestige before and after the Civil War.

20. The "Ohio Idea" called for the payment of the Civil War debt in gold.

21. The Fifteenth Amendment provides that on no account may the African American be denied the right to vote.

22. After a time public opinion in the North rebelled at many of the extremist policies of the Radicals.

23. The Grant administration successfully suppressed the Klansmen in the South.

24. Southern economic recovery came about mainly from efforts within the South and from economic developments, unaided by government.

25. Southern social and political reconstruction by the North failed both because of a certain lack of sincerity and misguided idealism.

COMPLETION

26. To keep Johnson from removing Radicals from office Congress passed the _____ .

27. The _____ Amendment is the civil rights amendment.

28. Johnson was impeached in the year _____ ; presiding over the trial was _____ . One of the main charges against Johnson is that he had removed his Secretary of _____ named _____ from office. The impeachment failed by _____ vote (s).

29. In 1868, instead of renominating Johnson, the Democrats chose _____ as their Presidential candidate.

30. Political rights were restored to most of the former Confederates by the _____ Act in 1872.

31. The one-party politics of the South is referred to by the term _____ .

CHRONOLOGY / CHAPTER 19

1867 Farmers' Grange organized.

1868 "Ohio Idea" made a campaign issue, called for redemption of federal bonds with Greenbacks.
Cubans began ten-year war of revolt against Spain.
Burlingame Treaty drawn up with China.

1869 Grant inaugurated as President.
"Black Friday" gold conspiracy.
Attempt to annex Santo Domingo failed.

1870 Second Fenian invasion of Canada.

1871 Tweed Ring exposed in New York City.
Treaty of Washington signed and ended disputes with Great Britain, particularly the Alabama claims.

1872 Credit Mobilier scandal exposed in Congress.
Liberal Republicans revolted against Republican Party and nominated Horace Greeley as President but defeated by Grant.

1873 "Salary Grab" Act.
Panic of 1873.
"Crime of '73" demonetized silver.

1874 Sanborn Contract fraud revealed.

1875 Resumption Act provided for return to gold standard in 1879.
Greenback Party organized.

1876 Hayes-Tilden disputed election.

Chapter

19

THE ADMINISTRATION OF GRANT, 1869–1877

The moral climate of the times was more responsible for the scandals of his administration than Grant himself. Most of the scandals would have occurred no matter who was president. The conservative policies of the administration resulted from business control of the national government. The foreign policy of the administration was largely well managed and constructive.

THE PRESIDENCY OF GRANT

Although Grant was popular and was successful in his military career, his qualities of character and lack of political experience were not equal to the demands of the presidency.

✪ **The Rise of Grant**—Grant's rise from a typical Western family farm background to become the nation's leading military hero of the Civil War made him a logical candidate for the presidency. His career began when he graduated from West Point in 1843. He served creditably in the Mexican War and after that served in military outposts in California and Oregon. Bored with army life, he resigned in 1854, and in Missouri and Illinois engaged unsuccessfully in farming, real estate, and clerking in his father's store. With the opening of the Civil War he volunteered for the Illinois infantry and later was commissioned colonel. His notable victories at Forts Henry and Donelson, at Shiloh, Vicksburg, and Chattanooga brought him rapid promotion until he became supreme commander of the Union army. At the conclusion of the Civil War his magnanimous attitude toward the Confederate forces and his moderation, but willingness to cooperate with the Radical Republicans, made him attractive to various political elements. In personality he was quiet and unassuming but determined.

✪✪ **Grant's Imperfections**—His military experience in some ways proved a handicap in public office. He expected his political appointees to carry out orders as his military subordinates had done, but his trust proved misplaced. His lack of experience in public affairs often led to absurd decisions and the appointment of poorly qualified persons. Among numerous friends and relatives he appointed, there were several dozen of his wife's relatives. Grant was often petty and vindictive in his decisions and favored those who had contributed to funds raised to purchase three expensive houses and the large money contributions bestowed upon him by the wealthy and grateful. Having himself failed in business matters, he held high regard for those who had succeeded in piling up fortunes. He admired and listened to aggressive, selfish, and tricky businessmen who became his close friends. Not until Eisenhower did the nation choose another *professional* military man for the presidency.

⊙ The Moral Climate of the Postwar Period—Grant's administration with its scandals reflects the low moral climate of his time. The spending of vast amounts of money during the war had conditioned those responsible to a large degree of carelessness in handling public funds. The widespread corruption may be explained by the lust for power of cynical politicians, the aggressive greed for money by wartime profiteers, and the war-caused letdown in public morals. Both the North and the South suffered from cynicism and corruption during the Reconstruction period. A dog-eat-dog attitude prevailed in business life. Businessmen seemed to be living by the Darwinian idea of natural selection, translated by popularizers into "survival of the fittest." Businessmen survived and grew fat because they were ruthless, tricky, and by corruption gained special favors from government. In this environment Grant appeared as a callous, obtuse individual; unlike some of the reformers of the time, he was insensitive to what was going on around him. Although he received great contributions of wealth in the form of cash and property, he did not accept gifts as recompense for specific favors.

⊙⊙ Grant's Favoritism Toward Big Business—Under Grant big business interests of various sorts enjoyed more freedom from government interference and a more positively favorable political climate than ever before. The Civil War itself represented a victory for business interests centered in the Northeast, and the Radical Republicans saw to it that the gains they had won in war would not be lost in the political forums. Grant's administration favored business by maintaining high protective tariffs. The railroads received federal subsidies in land grants, loans, and exemption from tariff duties on imported steel. The creditor classes benefited from the deflationary return to the gold standard and a limited currency supply. Financiers and speculators benefited from inside information and from the favorable refinancing of the national bond issues.

SCANDALS OF GRANT'S ADMINISTRATION

Several prominent scandals occurring in Grant's administration illustrate the moral laxity of the times.

✪✪ **The "Black Friday" Gold Conspiracy**—Two notorious and unscrupulous speculators, Jim Fisk and Jay Gould, in September, 1869, engineered a plot to make millions in quick profit by cornering the nation's gold supply. Through a brother-in-law the President was convinced by a seemingly logical argument that a stoppage of the sale of gold by the Treasury would help farmers by causing a rise in the price of wheat. Grant's innocent complicity enabled these two speculators to buy much of the small supply of gold in the country and drive the price up fantastically. Businessmen who needed gold in legitimate transactions were driven to bankruptcy on "Black Friday" when the price was bid up madly. When Grant realized what was happening, he ordered the Treasury to sell gold and thereby broke the speculative bubble, but great harm had already been done to thousands of persons.

✪ **The Tweed Ring**—Representative of the extent to which corruption figured in even local political life, the Tweed Ring, led by William M. Tweed, was broken in 1871 by *The New York Times* and Samuel J. Tilden only when it went beyond what was usually tolerated while building a new city court house. Eventually, theft of $200 million was proven and the rule of Tammany Hall was temporarily broken in the city. As the following text will show, New York City was not unique.

✪✪ **The Credit Mobilier Scandal**—This scandal reflected badly upon the Republican majority in Congress in Grant's first term. The Credit Mobilier was the construction company organized by the insiders of the Union Pacific Railroad to skim off millions in profits paid to themselves for building the railroad. Oakes Ames, acting as the agent of the Credit Mobilier Company, bribed members of Congress to prevent any action to halt the profiteering made possible by the congressional subsidies for railroad building. Most of the wrong-doing occurred before Grant became President. The scandal, exposed in 1872 by congressional investigation, injured the reputation of many prominent members of Congress.

The Salary Grab Act—In 1873 Congress doubled the salary of the President and voted themselves a salary increase of 50 percent. The worst part of the Act was that it made the increase retroactive two years back. Public reaction gave the Democrats control of the next Congress and the law was repealed.

Sanborn Contract and Other Scandals—In the Sanborn Contract fraud, it was revealed in 1874 that a politician named Sanborn had been given a contract by the Treasury Department to collect

$427,000 in unpaid taxes. He was allowed a commission of 50 percent; the commission was used to finance Republican political activities.

The Whiskey Ring fraud was a conspiracy between distillers and treasury officials to defraud the federal government of revenue from the excise tax on liquor. Grant's personal secretary accepted favors in the plot and the President himself accepted gifts he should have suspected. Grant defended his secretary against the investigators. In still another scandal, Grant's Secretary of War, W. W. Belknap, accepted bribes from a post-trader in the Native American territory; Belknap would have been impeached had he not resigned.

FOREIGN RELATIONS UNDER GRANT

President Grant by fortunate choice made Hamilton Fish Secretary of State. Fish proved to be an unusually able diplomat who peacefully settled serious conflicts with Great Britain. In foreign relations the record of the Grant administration is considered quite constructive.

The Attempt to Annex Santo Domingo—Grant in 1869 fell in with a scheme of speculators to take over Santo Domingo. He submitted a treaty to the Senate, but there it was opposed by Charles Sumner who recognized the dishonesty involved. Grant persistently tried to secure Senate approval. Later Sumner was deposed from the chairmanship of the Senate Committee on Foreign Relations when Grant had his revenge.

The Fenians—A secret Irish-American brotherhood known as the Fenians organized in the 1850s to help achieve freedom for Ireland. After the Civil War they planned to use Union veterans of the Civil War to conquer Canada and exchange it to Britain for freedom for Ireland. In 1866 the Fenians invaded Canada from the United States at the Niagara River and fought a battle with the Canadian militia. After a second invasion in 1870 the United States arrested the Fenian leaders and took other steps to prevent other invasions of British Canada. The incidents may have made the British more willing to recognize their error in aiding the Confederacy.

✪✪✪ **The Treaty of Washington (1871)**—On behalf of the United States, Secretary of State Sumner made large claims against Great Britain for damage payments for the depredations of the *Alabama* and other British-built cruisers that had destroyed American shipping during the Civil War. Settlement was prevented for several years by the preposterous claims of Sumner and British reluctance to make any reasonable settlement. When Hamilton Fish became Secretary of State he quietly worked out a settlement in the Treaty of Washington in 1871. 1) In this treaty the British admitted their unneutral behavior and agreed to submit the claims to arbitration under conditions that assured the United

States an award. As a consequence the *Alabama* tribunal met at Geneva and awarded the United States $15,500,000 indemnity.

2) Another provision of the Treaty of Washington resulted in an award of $2,000,000 to Britain for property lost by her subjects in the Civil War. 3) Still another British claim against the United States over American fishing privileges resulted in an arbitration award of $5,500,000 to Britain. 4) A final provision led to settlement by arbitration of the exact boundary between the United States and British Columbia in the maze of islands in the Puget Sound. These awards constituted another landmark in the long record of peaceable settlement of serious disputes between the two countries and of victory for the principle of arbitration in international law.

○ **The Cuban Revolt**—A ten year long revolt of Cuba against Spain began in 1868; the United States, although sympathetic with the Cubans, adopted a policy of neutrality. In 1873 the Spaniards captured the *Virginius*, a ship illegally flying the American flag and proceeded with the execution of those aboard, including some Americans. Hostilities were avoided and Spain agreed to make damage payments to families of those executed.

○ **The Burlingame Treaty**—Anson Burlingame, the American Minister to China during the 1860s, drew up this agreement (1868) which permitted unrestricted Chinese immigration to the United States. Many Chinese immigrants were entering California, which vainly tried to reduce their numbers, on both racial and economic grounds.

○○ THE ELECTION OF 1872

The most notable feature of this presidential election year was the revolt of the Liberal Republicans; the liberals were tired of the vengeful Reconstruction policy, wished to promote honesty in government, and stood for various reforms. The regular Republicans renominated Grant; the liberals, foreseeing this, formed the Liberal Republican Party and chose Horace Greeley as their candidate. Greeley, the liberal and famous editor of the New York *Tribune*, had already been chosen by the Democratic Party as their presidential nominee. In the hard-fought campaign the Republicans waved the "Bloody Shirt" in an emotional appeal for their war hero; both sides engaged in false charges. The eccentric Greeley lost; the Republicans controlled enough African American votes in three states still unreconstructed to gain victory for Grant. The revolt of the liberals forced the Republicans to take steps for more honest government.

POSTWAR ECONOMIC PROBLEMS

Postwar adjustments in the economy to peacetime conditions brought sudden panic, and steps to resume the prewar convertibility of currency to gold brought sustained deflation and its consequent hardship to debtors and farmers.

✪✪ **The Panic of 1873**—The postwar depression struck in 1873 in America; it began as a panic precipitated by the failure of Jay Cooke and Company. The failure of this firm that had led in financing the Civil War shocked American businessmen. Causes of the panic and depression were the overexpansion in railroad building and in industry in the business boom following the Civil War. A panic in Vienna in 1873 initiated the financial troubles in America.

✪✪ **Money Controversy After the Civil War**—Farmers and other debtor groups suffered from falling prices due to the shrinkage in the nation's money supply following the Civil War. During the war large quantities of irredeemable paper money known as greenbacks were put into circulation by the federal treasury; this was necessary because of insufficient specie to meet the monetary needs of the country. The plentiful supply of cheap money caused prices to rise and made it easy for debtors to repay their obligations in the depreciated greenback currency.

At the end of the war the treasury ceased to issue greenbacks, in fact, withdrew them from circulation. The conservative business interests in the dominant Republican Party were beginning to take steps leading to eventual return to a specie basis; a reduction in the floating supply of greenbacks was necessary to accomplish this. Prices of agricultural commodities fell sharply and other prices less steeply but enough to create hardship for debtor groups. In 1868 the Democratic Party adopted the "Ohio Idea" in its platform; this urged the redemption of federal bonds with the greenbacks with which most of them were originally purchased, rather than in gold. It was not adopted.

In 1870 in the Legal Tender Cases the Supreme Court ruled that the greenbacks were not legal tender for debts created prior to issuance of the greenbacks in 1862. But Grant appointed two new justices who reversed this decision in 1871 by declaring the greenbacks constitutional—but this only recognized the validity of those already in circulation and did not relieve the money shortage.

✪✪ **The "Crime of '73"**—In 1873 Congress inadvertently restricted the money supply even further. The market price of silver had been far above its value as coin, and was therefore removed from the list of metals eligible for coin. Almost simultaneously, silver strikes in the West drove the market price below its coinage value and the metal was presented at mints. When it was refused, it seemed a deliberate plot to prevent silver from inflating the nation's money supply. This was referred to as the "Crime of '73" by advocates of the unlimited coinage of silver who began to agitate for its reinstatement on the coinage list at a ratio of sixteen to one with gold. This effort would reach its peak with the "free silver" campaign of William Jennings Bryan in 1896.

OO Resumption Act—In 1875 Congress yielded to financial interests to provide for a resumption of redeemability of the nation's paper money in gold. The Act went into effect in 1879. It created creditor confidence in the soundness of the American dollar but further increased the burden of the debtors.

OO Greenback Party—In 1875 the Greenback Party was organized to give expression to the debtors who demanded an increased money supply. In 1878 the disgruntled labor groups joined to form the Greenback Labor Party. Their platforms demanded the increased use of greenbacks and the free coinage of silver on a parity with gold. In 1878, at its peak, the Party elected 15 representatives to Congress and many state officials.

OO Farm Distress After the Civil War—The usual wartime prosperity of farmers came to an end soon after Appomattox. The world-wide depression beginning in 1873 brought a further drop in prices. In fact, the long term trend of farm prices tended downward until 1896. The shrinkage in the money supply only aggravated the more fundamental difficulty of overproduction. Railroads and improved oceanic transport were opening up new agricultural lands in western America, Canada, Argentina, Australia, and Russia. More than ever, American farmers were in a world market, one which they did not understand. They believed the difficulty was one of under consumption caused by high prices due to the additional charges of middlemen.

OO The Grangers—In 1867 Oliver H. Kelley, an employee in the Department of Agriculture, organized the Patrons of Husbandry, popularly known as the Grangers. This national organization began as a secret order, like the various lodges, to provide social life and educational meetings for farm families. After farm prices fell further in 1873 the Grangers became predominantly a political movement. The Grangers complained of various business interests whom they blamed for the poor economic status of the farmer. They opposed monopolistic sellers of the things farmers had to buy, especially machinery; they blamed the middleman for increasing the price of farm goods by the time they reached the consumer; they particularly blamed the railroads for multiple economic abuses.

By 1874 the Grangers had gained much political strength over the nation and in most states had sufficient influence to secure the passage of laws regulating the railroads and grain elevators. It was at this time that the railroad commissions were created as public utility regulatory bodies in the states.

In addition to social and political activity the Grangers established consumer and manufacturing cooperatives; these failed from lack of experience of their managers but much valuable experience brought later success to such ventures. The Granger movement reached its peak about 1879 but still operates as one of the leading farmers' organizations.

⊙⊙ THE ELECTION OF 1876

A third term movement for Grant was squelched and the way left open for the magnetic, moderate James G. Blaine. His candidacy for the nomination apparently would have succeeded except for the news of the favors he had accepted from a railroad for helping it secure a federal land grant in 1869. The liberal but colorless Civil War general and governor of Ohio, Rutherford B. Hayes, won the nomination. The Democrats appealed to the conservatism of the times and the desire for reform by choosing Samuel J. Tilden, Governor of New York and the dragon-slayer who had made himself nationally famous by bringing an end to the Tweed Ring in New York City.

The election returns produced the most disputed election in American history. Tilden won 264,000 more popular votes than Hayes but of the undisputed electoral votes Hayes had 165 to 184 for Tilden. Twenty electoral votes were disputed; 19 of these were in the three Southern states of Louisiana, South Carolina, and Florida. The Republicans would have to win every disputed elector to win the presidency. These states submitted two sets of election returns, one favoring each party, to Congress.

Congress had no law or precedent for settling such a dispute, but finally agreed to appoint an Electoral Commission of fifteen with five members from each—the House, the Senate, and the Supreme Court. The membership was made up of seven Republicans, seven Democrats, and one nonpartisan. When the nonpartisan member resigned from the Supreme Court he was necessarily replaced by a Republican since all remaining members of the Supreme Court were Republican. The strictly partisan vote gave every point in dispute to the Republicans. The dispute was decided just a few days before the new President was inaugurated. A political bargain between the two parties secured the assent of the Democrats to the decision of the Electoral Commission in return for the withdrawal of the remaining federal troops in Louisiana and South Carolina. Thus was military reconstruction terminated.

CHAPTER BOOK LIST

Carpenter, John A., *Ulysses Grant: A Biography* (1974). Excellent one-volume biography.

Hale, W.H., *Horace Greeley: Voice of the People* (Collier). Biography of a leader who reflected his time.

Hesseltine, William B., *Ulysses S. Grant* (1935). Useful, standard work.

Liddell-Hart, B.H., *Sherman—Soldier, Realist, American* (Praeger).

Nevins, Allan, *Hamilton Fish: The Inner History of the Grant Administration* (1936).

Randall, J.G., and Donald, David, *The Civil War and Reconstruction* (1961).

Rodman, Paul W., *The Far West and the Great Plains in Transition, 1859–1900* (1988). The last frontier for the farmer and miner.

Trelease, A.W., *White Terror: The Ku Klux Klan Conspiracy* (1971).

REVIEW QUESTIONS

MULTIPLE CHOICE

1. Before becoming President, Grant (1) spent much of his early life in Kentucky (2) became a successful businessman (3) promoted policies of harsh reconstruction (4) served creditably in the Mexican War but resigned the army several years later.

2. Grant's weaknesses as President included all *except* (1) the appointment of poorly qualified persons (2) lack of critical appraisal of his subordinates (3) permitting reckless currency inflation (4) taking advice from dishonest and self-seeking persons.

3. The two speculators who plotted the gold conspiracy were (1) Jay Gould and Jim Brady (2) Jim Fisk and Jay Gould (3) Tom Nast and Jim Fisk (4) Boss Tweed and Sam Tilden.

4. The wrongdoing in the Credit Mobilier scandal was (1) the wholesale bribery of members of Congress (2) the bribery of members of Grant's cabinet (3) the misappropriation of construction funds lent the railroads (4) the creation of a railroad monopoly.

5. Which of Grant's cabinet members resigned to avoid impeachment for accepting bribes? (1) Hamilton Fish (2) W. W. Belknap (3) Zachary Chandler (4) Schuyler Colfax.

6. The Fenians (1) wanted to annex Canada to the United States (2) were encouraged by Grant's administration (3) wanted to take Canada and exchange it for freedom for Ireland (4) sought to force Britain to settle the Alabama claims.

7. The Treaty of Washington did all of these *except* (1) settle the fisheries dispute once again (2) give the British a favorable settlement in the Alabama claims (3) set an early example of successful arbitration (4) finally provide for settlement of the boundary between the United States and Canada.

8. The Burlingame Treaty (1) provided for the importation of Chinese contract labor to the United States (2) created a loose alliance of America and China (3) permitted unrestricted Chinese immigration to the United States (4) stopped Chinese immigration to the United States.

9. The most significant development in the election of 1872 was the (1) split in the Democratic Party (2) reelection of Grant (3) creation of a special commission to determine the victor (4) split in the Republican Party.

10. The "Crime of '73" is a term given to the (1) resumption of the gold standard (2) Supreme Court decision declaring greenbacks legal tender (3) demonetization of silver (4) dishonesty in treasury bond refunding operations.

11. The Grangers main achievement was the (1) founding of farmer's marketing cooperatives (2) passage of state laws against trade monopolies (3) founding of farmer's consumer cooperatives (4) establishment of railroad commissions in the states.

12. The election of 1876 was unique at its time because of all *except* which one? (1) Republican interference in the election in some Southern states (2) the means adopted to settle the disputed election (3) an agreement to withdraw federal troops from the South (4) the election of a liberal Republican.

TRUE-FALSE

13. The moral climate of the post-Civil War period accounts for much of the corruption of Grant's administration.

14. The Grant administration expected business to uphold high ethical standards such as Grant himself lived by.

15. The postwar period experienced continued inflation which hurt the debtor classes.

16. Oakes Ames acted as an agent for the Credit Mobilier in its bribery of Congressmen.

17. In 1873 Congress voted itself a 100 percent salary increase.

18. Overexpansion in railroad building was an important cause of the Panic of 1873.

19. Silver was demonetized in 1873 because it had become relatively scarce but immediately thereafter it became more plentiful.

20. Debtor farmers for decades after the Civil War suffered from a long-term decline in prices.

21. The Farmers' Grange was organized originally as a political agency but by 1875 concentrated upon social and educational activities.

22. In the 1880s the Grange died out completely.

23. The election of 1876 was actually settled by a political compromise rather than by a fair election.

COMPLETION

24. The corner on gold which caused great losses to many businessmen in 1869 was called the _____ gold conspiracy.

25. The _____ was a notoriously corrupt group of politicians operating in New York City before 1871. They were exposed through the efforts of _____ and _____ .

26. The _____ was a railroad construction company guilty of wholesale bribery of members of Congress.

27. The _____ during Grant's term was guilty of defrauding the government of excise taxes on liquor.

28. It was _____ who prevented an attempt to dishonestly annex Santo Domingo. Grant's able Secretary of State was _____ .

29. The Democratic nominee in the election of 1872 was _____ who was also nominated by the _____ but was defeated by _____ .

30. The Panic of 1873 began with the failure of _____ , a great investment banking firm.

31. In the Legal Tender Cases the Supreme Court finally ruled that _____ were legal tender.

32. The redemption of all money in gold was provided for by the _____ of 1785. Opposing the gold standard, there arose a new political party called the _____ Party.

33. The Patrons of Husbandry was founded by _____ .

34. The Democratic presidential candidate in 1876 was _____ and the Republican _____ . _____ received the most popular votes but _____ was elected when the dispute was settled by _____ .

ANSWERS TO CHAPTER REVIEW QUESTIONS

REVIEW QUESTIONS TO CHAPTER 1—Pages 13–15

1. 3	12. 2	23. T	34. c
2. 2	13. 3	24. T	35. k
3. 4	14. 2	25. T	36. j
4. 2	15. T	26. F	37. d
5. 3	16. F	27. F	38. g
6. 2	17. F	28. T	39. f
7. 1	18. T	29. F	
8. 1	19. F	30. b	
9. 1	20. F	31. h	
10. 2	21. F	32. e	
11. 4	22. T	33. a	

REVIEW QUESTIONS TO CHAPTER 2—Pages 27–32

1. 4	25. F	49. St. Mary's
2. 1	26. T	50. Quit-rent
3. 3	27. F	51. Lords Proprietors
4. 1	28. T	52. Holy Experiment
5. 3	29. T	53. Quakers
6. 3	30. T	54. Swedes
7. 1	31. F	55. b
8. 4	32. F	56. f
9. 2	33. F	57. e
10. 2	34. T	58. h
11. 3	35. T	59. a
12. 1	36. F	60. i
13. 3	37. T	61. d
14. 2	38. Armada	62. k
15. 4	39. "Sea Dogs"	63. g
16. 4	40. Enclosure	64. j
17. 2	41. Joint-stock	65. c
18. 4	42. Nathaniel Bacon	66. b
19. 2	43. Pilgrims	67. f
20. T	44. John Calvin	68. a
21. T	45. Freemen	69. e
22. F	46. Baptists	70. d
23. F	47. Thomas Hooker	
24. T	48. Massachusetts	

REVIEW QUESTIONS TO CHAPTER 3—Pages 42–45

1. 1	16. F	31. Navigation
2. 2	17. F	32. Enumerated
3. 3	18. F	33. Writs of Assistance
4. 4	19. F	34. Indigo
5. 2	20. T	35. Sea Island
6. 1	21. F	36. Headright
7. 2	22. F	37. Naval Stores
8. 3	23. F	38. Wool
9. 3	24. F	39. Triangular
10. 3	25. F	40. Redemptioners
11. 2	26. Property	
12. 4	27. Common	
13. F	28. County	
14. T	29. Sheriff	
15. T	30. Balance of Trade	

REVIEW QUESTIONS TO CHAPTER 4—Pages 54–57

1. 3	17. T	33. h
2. 2	18. F	34. d
3. 1	19. T	35. f
4. 3	20. T	36. g
5. 2	21. F	37. e
6. 2	22. F	38. a
7. 4	23. T	39. i
8. 3	24. Presbyterian	40. j
9. 2	25. Huguenot	41. b
10. 1	26. "Blue-Laws"	
11. 4	27. Salem	
12. T	28. Harvard	
13. F	29. Philadelphia	
14. F	30. Copernicus	
15. T	31. Franklin	
16. T	32. Deism	

REVIEW QUESTIONS TO CHAPTER 5—Pages 76–81

1. 1	18. 4	35. T	52. Committees of Correspondence
2. 1	19. 3	36. F	53. Paxton Boys
3. 1	20. 4	37. F	54. Intolerable Acts
4. 2	21. 3	38. King Philip's	55. 1774
5. 3	22. 2	39. William of Orange	56. Galloway
6. 1	23. T	40. Utrecht	57. Lexington
7. 2	24. T	41. Fort Necessity	58. Olive Branch
8. 2	25. F	42. Franklin	59. *Common Sense*
9. 4	26. T	43. Wolfe	60. Tory
10. 2	27. T	44. Florida	61. e
11. 3	28. F	45. George III	62. f
12. 4	29. T	46. Parson's Cause	63. c
13. 4	30. T	47. Pontiac's	64. a
14. 3	31. T	48. Blue Grass	65. h
15. 3	32. T	49. Sons of Liberty	66. b
16. 3	33. T	50. Virtual	67. d
17. 2	34. F	51. "Liberty Boys"	68. i

REVIEW QUESTIONS TO CHAPTER 6—Pages 91–94

1. 1	16. T	31. Gibraltar
2. 2	17. F	32. Rhode Island
3. 3	18. T	33. Maryland
4. 3	19. F	34. Tithes
5. 3	20. F	35. i
6. 4	21. T	36. f
7. 3	22. F	37. j
8. 4	23. F	38. h
9. 1	24. Armed Neutrality	39. a
10. 3	25. Spain	40. i
11. 2	26. Hessians	41. d
12. 3	27. St. Leger	42. c
13. 4	28. Saratoga	43. e
14. T	29. Commercial	44. g
15. F	30. Benedict Arnold	

REVIEW QUESTIONS TO CHAPTER 7—Pages 103–106

1. 2	16. F	30. Daniel Shays
2. 2	17. F	31. Mount Vernon
3. 4	18. F	Annapolis
4. 4	19. T	32. 1781, 1787, 1790
5. 1	20. T	33. Washington and Franklin
6. 4	21. F	34. Patrick Henry
7. 1	22. F	35. France
8. 1	23. F	36. Two Thirds
9. 4	24. T	37. Judicial Review
10. 4	25. F	38. Federalists
11. 1	26. Virginia	39. Rhode Island
12. 4	North Carolina	
13. 3	27. Yazoo Strip	
14. 2	28. 60,000	
15. T	29. James Wilkinson	

REVIEW QUESTIONS TO CHAPTER 8—Pages 119–123

1. 3	16. F	31. Jefferson	44. John Adams
2. 1	17. F	32. 1791	45. Privateers
3. 2	18. T	33. Jefferson	46. Sedition
4. 4	19. T	Strict	47. Jefferson
5. 3	20. T	34. Implied Powers	48. Twelfth
6. 3	21. F	35. Excise	49. b
7. 1	22. T	36. Britain	50. e
8. 2	23. F	37. Vermont	51. g
9. 3	24. F	Kentucky	52. f
10. 2	25. T	Tennessee	53. c
11. 1	26. F	38. 1789	54. h
12. 3	27. T	39. Citizen Genet	55. a
13. 4	28. New York City	40. Rule of 1756	56. d
14. 4	29. Bill of Rights	41. Contraband	
15. F	30. Alexander	42. Paper	
	Hamilton	43. Pinckney	

REVIEW QUESTIONS TO CHAPTER 9—Pages 138–142

1. 2	20. F	39. Whiskey	53. New England
2. 2	21. T	40. Mosquito	54. Tecumseh
3. 4	22. F	41. Decatur	55. War Hawks
4. 2	23. F	42. Midnight	56. Harrison
5. 1	24. T	43. *Marbury v. Madison*	57. New Orleans
6. 1	25. F	44. Chase	58. Hartford Convention
7. 3	26. T	45. 320, 160	59. Nationalism
8. 2	27. F	46. Eleventh	60. f
9. 3	28. T	47. San Ildefonso	61. g
10. 1	29. F	48. Lewis and Clark	62. a
11. 4	30. T	49. Aaron Burr	63. h
12. 3	31. T	General Wilkinson	64. k
13. 3	32. F	50. Impressment	65. c
14. 3	33. T	51. Berlin	66. i
15. 1	34. F	Milan	67. b
16. 1	35. T	Orders-in-Council	68. d
17. 2	36. F	52. Embargo	69. j
18. 3	37. F	Nonintercourse	
19. T	38. Monticello		

REVIEW QUESTIONS TO CHAPTER 10—Pages 158–163

1. 4	23. 1	45. T	Maine
2. 2	24. T	46. T	61. Fort Ross
3. 1	25. F	47. 1816	62. Holy Alliance
4. 4	26. T	Twenty	Austria, Russia, and
5. 1	27. F	48. Panic of 1819	Prussia
6. 2	28. T	49. 1816	63. 1823
7. 3	29. T	50. Erie Canal	J.Q. Adams
8. 3	30. F	51. Cumberland	64. J.Q. Adams
9. 4	31. T	National	Corrupt Bargain
10. 1	32. T	Cumberland Wilderness	65. Panama Congress
11. 3	33. F	52. 1793	66. Exposition and Protest
12. 1	34. T	53. Lancaster	67. Anti-Masonic
13. 3	35. T	54. Erie	68. c
14. 1	36. F	55. Rush-Bagot	69. i
15. 1	37. F	Convention of 1818	70. f
16. 3	38. T	Joint Occupation	71. a
17. 2	39. F	56. Adams-Onis	72. k
18. 1	40. T	1819	73. b
19. 3	41. F	57. *Fletcher v. Peck*	74. e
20. 4	42. T	58. *McCulloch v. Maryland*	75. h
21. 1	43. F	59. *Gibbons v. Ogden*	76. i
22. 2	44. F	60. Tallmadge	77. d

REVIEW QUESTIONS TO CHAPTER 11—Pages 177–181

1. 3	21. F	39. Jefferson	49. Harrison
2. 4	22. F	40. *Worcester*	Whig
3. 2	23. T	*v. Georgia*	50. Preemption
4. 4	24. F	41. Maysville	51. Caroline
5. 1	25. T	42. Thomas Hart	Creole
6. 3	26. F	Benton	Webster-Ashburton
7. 3	27. F	43. "Squatters"	1842
8. 4	28. T	44. Nullification	52. d
9. 2	29. T	Ordinance	53. h
10. 1	30. F	Nullification	54. g
11. 3	31. T	Proclamation	55. a
12. 2	32. T	Force Bill	56. e
13. 1	33. T	Tariff of 1832	57. b
14. 3	34. T	45. Henry Clay	58. k
15. 1	35. T	Bank	59. c
16. 2	36. Caucus	46. "Wild-cat"	60. i
17. 4	Conventions	"Pet"	61. f
18. 4	37. 1829, 1837	47. Specie Circular	
19. 4	38. Eaton	48. 1836	
20. T	Peggy O'Neill	San Jacinto	
	Calhoun		

REVIEW QUESTIONS TO CHAPTER 12—Pages 193–196

1. 2	16. T	28. 1845	34. Mountain
2. 1	17. T	Joint Resolution	Jedediah Smith
3. 4	18. F	Five	35. Thomas O. Larkin
4. 1	19. T	29. Hudson's Bay	John Sutter
5. 2	20. F	John McLoughlin	Jones
6. 4	21. T	John Jacob Astor	36. John Slidell
7. 4	22. F	30. Jason Lee	37. Taylor
8. 3	23. F	Marcus Whitman	Rio Grande
9. 1	24. F	Pierre De Smet	Buena Vista
10. 3	25. T	31. Independence	Kearny
11. 1	26. Manifest	South Pass	38. Joseph Smith
12. 3	Destiny	32. 1846	Brigham Young
13. 1	27. Clay	49th Parallel	
14. F	Polk	33. Independence	
15. T	Liberty	Arkansas	

REVIEW QUESTIONS TO CHAPTER 13—Pages 203–205

1. 4	11. T	21. J. I. Case
2. 1	12. T	22. Illinois Central
3. 4	13. F	23. Samuel Slater
4. 3	14. T	24. Samuel F. B. Morse
5. 2	15. F	Elias Howe
6. 3	16. T	Isaac Singer
7. 1	17. F	
8. 2	18. Louisiana	
9. 3	19. Cincinnati	
10. 1	20. John Deere	

REVIEW QUESTIONS TO CHAPTER 14—Pages 211–213

1. 3	12. Liberia	23. h
2. 2	13. "Gag Rule"	24. i
3. 2	14. "Underground Railroad"	25. c
4. 1	15. Elijah Lovejoy	26. f
5. F	16. Thomas R. Dew	27. a
6. F	17. "Teetotallers"	28. k
7. F	18. New Harmony	29. e
8. T	19. Amana	30. g
9. T	20. Lyceum	31. d
10. F	21. Oberlin	
11. T	22. b	

REVIEW QUESTIONS TO CHAPTER 15—Pages 229–233

1. 4	16. 2	31. F	45. Personal Liberty
2. 3	17. 4	32. T	46. Pierce
3. 2	18. 1	33. F	Democratic
4. 3	19. 3	34. T	47. Perry Expedition
5. 2	20. 3	35. F	48. Gadsden Purchase
6. 2	21. 4	36. T	49. Yeomen
7. 4	22. 1	37. T	50. Republican
8. 3	23. 1	38. T	51. Harriet Beecher Stowe
9. 4	24. T	39. T	52. Lawrence and Topeka
10. 4	25. T	40. F	53. Pottawatomie Massacre
11. 1	26. T	41. Wilmot Proviso	54. Buchanan
12. 4	27. F	42. Minnesota	55. 1854
13. 2	28. F	Oregon	56. Taney
14. 3	29. T	43. 1848	57. Crimean
15. 1	30. T	44. Taylor	58. Harper's Ferry

59. John C. Breckinridge   63. f   67. d
60. e   64. b   68. g
61. c   65. a   69. j
62. h   66. k

REVIEW QUESTIONS TO CHAPTER 16—Pages 246–250

1. 4   22. T   40. "Fire-Eaters"   49. National Banking
2. 3   23. T   41. Copperheads   50. Antietam
3. 2   24. F   42. McClellan   Emancipation
4. 1   25. F   43. Meade   Proclamation
5. 3   26. F   44. Appomattox Courthouse   51. Morrill
6. 4   27. T   45. Vicksburg   52. c
7. 3   28. F   46. Chattanooga   53. e
8. 2   29. T   Savannah   54. h
9. 2   30. T   Albert Sidney Johnston   55. a
10. 3   31. T   47. Morrill   56. i
11. 3   32. F   48. Mason and Slidell   57. d
12. 2   33. T   Trent   58. b
13. 2   34. F   Seward
14. 4   35. T
15. 1   36. Jefferson Davis
16. 3   Montgomery, Alabama
17. 2   Richmond, Virginia
18. F   37. Executive
19. F   38. Slavery
20. T   39. Fort Sumter
21. T   Charleston, South Carolina

REVIEW QUESTIONS TO CHAPTER 17—PAGES 260–262

1. 3   13. F   25. Napoleon III
2. 1   14. F   Maximilian
3. 3   15. T   26. 1867
4. 4   16. T   Denmark
5. 2   17. T   27. Thaddeus Stevens
6. 1   18. T   Charles Sumner
7. 3   19. F   "Conquered Provinces"
8. 1   20. F   "State Suicide"
9. 1   21. T   28. "Black Codes"
10. 2   22. 1865, 1877
11. F   23. "Ten Percent Plan"
12. T   24. Monroe Doctrine

REVIEW QUESTIONS TO CHAPTER 18—Pages 271-273

1. 3	13. T	25. T
2. 3	14. F	26. Tenure of Office Act
3. 4	15. F	27. Fourteenth
4. 2	16. T	28. 1867
5. 2	17. T	Chief Justice Chase
6. 4	18. F	War
7. 4	19. T	Stanton
8. 2	20. F	One
9. 2	21. F	29. Horace Seymour
10. 1	22. T	30. Amnesty
11. T	23. T	31. Solid South
12. T	24. T	

REVIEW QUESTIONS TO CHAPTER 19—Pages 283-285

1. 4	16. T	Hamilton Fish
2. 3	17. F	29. Horace Greeley
3. 2	18. T	Liberal Republicans
4. 1	19. T	Grant
5. 2	20. T	30. Jay Cooke and Company
6. 3	21. F	31. Greenbacks
7. 2	22. F	32. Resumption Act
8. 3	23. T	Greenback
9. 4	24. Black Friday	33. Oliver H. Kelley
10. 3	25. Tweed Ring	34. Tilden
11. 4	Samuel J. Tilden	Hayes
12. 1	*The New York Times*	Tilden
13. T	26. Credit Mobilier	Hayes
14. F	27. Whiskey Ring	An Electoral Commission
15. F	28. Charles Sumner	

APPENDICES

REVIEW QUESTIONS FOR ESSAY-TYPE EXAMINATIONS

1. What factors culminated in the discovery of America?

2. What was the significance of Spanish, French, and Dutch colonization within the present bounds of the United States?

3. Outline the leading motives of English colonization in America. How do you account for the success of the English?

4. What factors conspired to promote self-government in colonial times?

5. Write a discussion of the meaning of mercantilism. How did England attempt to execute the philosophy of mercantilism in America?

6. Discuss the growth of democracy in colonial times. What influences promoted democracy?

7. What were the main influences and persons promoting religious toleration in colonial times?

8. Discuss the political, economic, and social causes of the American Revolution.

9. What territories in America did England acquire in her several imperial wars in colonial times?

10. Write an essay on the Declaration of Independence as a reflection of the causes and philosophy of the American Revolution.

11. Specifically what aid did France give America in the Revolution?

12. Compare the advantages of the British and Americans in the Revolutionary War.

13. Discuss political and social changes in America arising from the Revolution.

14. Why was the United States weak in foreign relations during the Confederation Period?

15. State the various compromises reached in the Constitutional Convention.

16. Contrast the political views of Hamilton and Jefferson in various issues.

17. State the nature of the various federal financial problems dealt with in Washington's administration.

18. In a brief essay evaluate the Presidency of John Adams.

19. What presidential leadership in domestic affairs best reflected Jefferson's political views?

20. What rights of neutrals did the United States try to uphold during the French Revolution and Napoleonic Wars? How successful was the United States?

21. State the main places of conflict of American and British forces in the War of 1812.

22. What were the consequences of the War of 1812?

23. What decisions did the Supreme Court reach in five leading decisions before 1820?

24. To what extent did the Republicans after 1800 adopt Federalist ideas?

25. State the effect of the leading developments in transportation before the Civil War. Do the same for the leading inventions (outside of changes affecting transportation).

26. Explain the origins of the Monroe Doctrine. What were its main pronouncements?

27. What similarities and differences do you see between Jacksonian Democracy and Jeffersonial Democracy?

28. State the leading legislative goals of the three sections during the 1820s and 1830s.

29. What are the important political changes associated with Jacksonian Democracy that increased the political power of the common man?

30. How were the various disputes between Britain and America settled in the Webster-Ashburton Treaty?

31. Write a criticism of both sides in their conduct with regard to the question of the Second Bank of the United States.

32. Evaluate the Presidencies of Van Buren and Tyler.

33. Who were the leaders of the three main campaigns of the Mexican War? What were the main consequences of the War?

34. Trace the history of the Oregon question to its settlement.

35. Contrast factors that brought about the American migration to Oregon, Texas, and California.

36. In what ways did the Mexican War exhibit the spirit of Manifest Destiny?

37. Describe the economy of the South before the Civil War and its relation to politics.

38. What were the causes of the growth of industry before 1860?

39. Name the leading reform movements of the period 1830 to 1850 and tell what success they achieved.

40. Explain the historical and constitutional basis of the three main views as to how the slavery question ought to be settled in the territories. What leaders represented each view?

41. What attempts did some leaders make in the early 1850s to divert national attention from the slavery controversy?

42. Discuss the motives and consequences of the Kansas-Nebraska Act.

43. List leading events in the North-South confrontation from 1850 to 1861.

44. What continuity is there in the political philosophy and legislative goals of the Federalists, Whigs, and Republicans?

45. Compare advantages of the North and the South in the Civil War.

46. State the objectives of Northern offensives in the four main areas of conflict in the Civil War.

47. Why was British policy such a crucial factor in the Civil War?

48. How did Republican legislation under Lincoln represent the attempt to fulfill its platform commitments to various economic groups?

49. Sketch the political, social and economic changes the Civil War brought to the South.

50. Why did Andrew Johnson have so much trouble with Congress? Write a short essay upholding Johnson's views.

51. Evaluate the combination of cynical and idealistic motives of the Radicals.

52. Name and explain the provisions of the three Civil War amendments to the Constitution.

53. Evaluate the consequences of the carpetbag governments in the Southern states.

54. Why did the North eventually abandon Reconstruction in the South?

55. What were Grant's shortcomings as President?

56. Explain the leading political repercussions of the economic depression in the 1870s.

57. Explain the disputed election of 1876 and how it was settled.

GENERAL OR SURVEY FINAL EXAMINATION REVIEW QUESTIONS

1. Briefly sketch the history of the Democratic Party up to the Civil War by naming great leaders, predecessor parties, and important election victories. Do the same for the Republican Party.

2. State the leading events in the history of the controversy over states' rights from 1798 to 1850. In each event show how a minority defended itself under the doctrine of states' rights.

3. What were the goals of the third party movements before the Civil War?

4. Trace the difference in attitudes in the North and South toward slavery from colonial times to the Civil War.

5. Summarize main trends in land legislation from 1785 to 1862.

6. List American territorial acquisitions from the Revolution to 1853.

7. What were the four most significant presidential elections before the Civil War? Explain your choices.

8. Excluding presidents, name the four most significant statesmen before 1860 and explain your choices.

9. Name leading tariff measures before 1865. What change did each make?

THE DECLARATION OF INDEPENDENCE[†]

In Congress, July 4, 1776

THE UNANIMOUS DECLARATION OF
THE THIRTEEN UNITED STATES OF AMERICA

When, in the Course of human events, it becomes necessary for one people to dissolve the political bands which have connected them with another, and to assume among the powers of the earth, the separate and equal station to which the Laws of Nature and of Nature's God entitle them, a decent respect to the opinions of mankind requires that they should declare the causes which impel them to the separation.

We hold these truths to be self-evident, that all men are created equal, that they are endowed by their Creator with certain unalienable Rights, that among these, are Life, Liberty, and the pursuit of Happiness. That, to secure these rights, Governments are instituted among Men, deriving their just powers from the consent of the governed, that, whenever any Form of Government becomes destructive of these ends, it is the Right of the People to alter or to abolish it, and to institute new Government, laying its foundation on such principles, and organizing its powers in such form, as to them shall seem likely to effect their Safety and Happiness. Prudence, indeed, will dictate that Governments long established, should not be changed for light and transient causes; and, accordingly, all experience hath shewn, that mankind are more disposed to suffer, while evils are sufferable, than to right themselves by abolishing the forms to which they are accustomed. But, when a long train of abuses and usurpations, pursuing invariably the same Object, evinces a design to reduce them under absolute Despotism, it is their right, it is their duty, to throw off such Government and to provide new Guards for their future security.—Such has been the patient sufferance of these Colonies; and such is now the necessity which constrains them to alter their former Systems of Government. The history of the present King of Great Britain is a history of repeated injuries and usurpations, all having in direct object the establishment of an absolute Tyranny over these States. To prove this, let Facts be submitted to a candid world.—

He has refused his Assent to Laws the most wholesome and necessary for the public good.

He has forbidden his Governors to pass Laws of immediate and pressing importance, unless suspended in their operation till his Assent should be obtained; and when so suspended, he has utterly neglected to attend to them.

---

† Spelling and capitalization follow the parchment copy.

He has refused to pass other laws for the accommodation of large districts of people, unless those people would relinquish the right of Representation in the Legislature; a right inestimable to them and formidable to tyrants only.

He has called together legislative bodies at places unusual, uncomfortable, and distant from the depository of their public Records, for the sole purpose of fatiguing them into compliance with his measures.

He has dissolved Representative Houses repeatedly, for opposing with manly firmness his invasions on the rights of the people.

He has refused for a long time, after such dissolutions, to cause others to be elected; whereby the Legislative powers, incapable of Annihilation, have returned to the People at large for their exercise; the State remaining, in the meantime, exposed to all the dangers of invasion from without, and convulsions within.

He has endeavored to prevent the population of these States; for that purpose, obstructing the Laws for Naturalization of Foreigners; refusing to pass others to encourage their migrations hither, and raising the conditions of new Appropriations of Lands.

He has obstructed the Administration of Justice, by refusing his Assent to Laws for establishing Judiciary powers.

He has made Judges dependent on his Will alone, for the tenure of their offices, and the amount and payment of their salaries.

He has erected a multitude of New Offices, and sent hither swarms of Officers to harass our people, and eat out their substance.

He has kept among us, in times of peace, Standing Armies, without the Consent of our legislatures.

He has affected to render the Military independent of, and superior to, the Civil power.

He has combined, with others, to subject us to a jurisdiction foreign to our constitution, and unacknowledged by our laws; giving his Assent to their Acts of pretended Legislation:

For quartering large bodies of armed troops among us:

For protecting them by a mock Trial, from punishment, for any Murders which they should commit on the Inhabitants of these States:

For cutting off our Trade with all parts of the world:

For imposing Taxes on us without our Consent:

For depriving us, in many cases, of the benefits of Trial by Jury:

For transporting us beyond Seas to be tried for pretended offenses:

For abolishing the free System of English Laws in a neighboring Province, establishing therein an Arbitrary government, and enlarging its

Boundaries, so as to render it at once an example and fit instrument for introducing the same absolute rule into these Colonies:

For taking away our Charters, abolishing our most valuable Laws, and altering, fundamentally, the Forms of our Governments:

For suspending our own Legislatures, and declaring themselves invested with power to legislate for us in all cases whatsoever.

He has abdicated Government here, by declaring us out of his Protection, and waging War against us.

He has plundered our seas, ravaged our Coasts, burnt our towns, and destroyed the lives of our people.

He is, at this time, transporting large Armies of foreign Mercenaries to compleat the works of death, desolation, and tyranny, already begun with circumstances of Cruelty & perfidy scarcely paralleled in the most barbarous ages, and totally unworthy the Head of a civilized nation.

He has constrained our fellow Citizens, taken Captive on the high Seas, to bear Arms against their Country, to become the executioners of their friends and Brethren, or to fall themselves by their Hands.

He has excited domestic insurrections amongst us, and has endeavored to bring on the inhabitants of our frontiers, the merciless Indian Savages, whose known rule of warfare, is, an undistinguished destruction of all ages, sexes and conditions.

In every stage of these Oppressions, We have Petitioned for Redress, in the most humble terms; our repeated Petitions have been answered only by repeated injury. A Prince, whose character is thus marked by every act which may define a Tyrant, is unfit to be the ruler of a free people.

Nor have we been wanting in attentions to our British brethren. We have warned them, from time to time, of attempts made by their legislature to extend an unwarrantable jurisdiction over us. We have reminded them of the circumstances of our emigration and settlement here. We have appealed to their native justice and magnanimity, and we have conjured them by the ties of our common kindred to disavow these usurpations, which would inevitably interrupt our connections and correspondence. They too have been deaf to the voice of justice and of consanguinity. We must, therefore, acquiesce in the necessity, which denounces our Separation, and hold them, as we hold the rest of mankind, Enemies in War, in Peace Friends.

We, therefore, the Representatives of the united States of America, in General Congress, Assembled, appealing to the Supreme Judge of the world for the rectitude of our intentions, do, in the Name, and by Authority of the good People of these Colonies, solemnly publish and declare, That these United Colonies are, and of Right ought to be, Free and Independent States; that they are Absolved from all Allegiance to the British Crown, and that all political connection between them and the State of Great Britain is, and ought to be, totally dissolved: and that, as Free and Independent States, they have full Power to levy War, conclude Peace, contract Alliances, establish Commerce, and to do all other Acts and Things which Independent States may of right do. And, for the support of this Declaration, with a firm reliance on the protection of divine Providence, we mutually pledge to each other our Lives, our Fortunes, and our sacred Honor.

The foregoing Declaration was, by order of Congress, engrossed, and signed by the following members:

John Hancock

NEW HAMPSHIRE
Josiah Bartlett
William Whipple
Matthew Thornton

MASSACHUSETTS BAY
Samuel Adams
John Adams
Robert Treat Paine
Elbridge Gerry

RHODE ISLAND
Stephen Hopkins
William Ellery

CONNECTICUT
Roger Sherman
Samuel Huntington
William Williams
Oliver Wolcott

NEW YORK
William Floyd
Philip Livingston
Francis Lewis
Lewis Morris

NEW JERSEY
Richard Stockton
John Witherspoon
Francis Hopkinson
John Hart
Abraham Clark

PENNSYLVANIA
Robert Morris
Benjamin Rush
Benjamin Franklin
John Morton
George Clymer
James Smith
George Taylor
James Wilson
George Ross

DELAWARE
Caesar Rodney
George Read
Thomas M'Kean

MARYLAND
Samuel Chase
William Paca
Thomas Stone
Charles Carroll,
of Carrollton

VIRGINIA
George Wythe
Richard Henry Lee
Thomas Jefferson
Benjamin Harrison
Thomas Nelson, Jr.
Francis Lightfoot Lee
Carter Braxton

NORTH CAROLINA
William Hooper
Joseph Hewes
John Penn

SOUTH CAROLINA
Edward Rutledge
Thomas Heyward, Jr.
Thomas Lynch, Jr.
Arthur Middleton

GEORGIA
Button Gwinnett
Lyman Hall
George Walton

RESOLVED, That copies of the Declaration be sent to the several assemblies, conventions, and committees, or councils of safety, and to the several commanding officers of the continental troops; that it be proclaimed in each of the united States, at the head of the army.

THE CONSTITUTION OF THE UNITED STATES†

General objectives
of the Constitution

WE THE PEOPLE of the United States, in Order to form a more perfect Union, establish Justice, insure domestic Tranquility, provide for the common defence, promote the general Welfare, and secure the Blessings of Liberty to ourselves and our Posterity, do ordain and establish this Constitution for the United States of America.

ARTICLE I • LEGISLATIVE DEPARTMENT

A bicameral
Congress

SECTION 1.   All legislative Powers herein granted shall be vested in a Congress of the United States, which shall consist of a Senate and House of Representatives.

Selection and term
of Representatives

SECTION 2.   [1]The House of Representatives shall be composed of Members chosen every second Year by the People of the several States, and the Electors in each State shall have the Qualifications requisite for Electors of the most numerous Branch of the State Legislature.

Qualifications of
Representatives

[2]No person shall be a representative who shall not have attained to the Age of twenty five Years, and been seven Years a Citizen of the United States, and who shall not, when elected, be an Inhabitant of that State in which he shall be chosen.

Apportionment of
Representatives
among states—see
Section 2 of
Fourteenth
Amendment: a
decennial census;
maximum and
minimum size
of House

[3][Representatives and direct Taxes shall be apportioned among the several States which may be included within this Union, according to their respective Numbers, which shall be determined by adding to the whole Number of free Persons, including those bound to Service for a Term of Years, and excluding Indians not taxed, three fifths of all other Persons.].* The actual Enumeration shall be made within three Years after the first Meeting of the Congress of the United States, and within every subsequent Term of ten Years, in such Manner as they shall by Law direct. The Number of Representa-tives shall not exceed one for every thirty Thousand, but each State shall have at Least one Representative; and until such enumeration shall be made, the State of New Hampshire shall be entitled to chuse three, Massachusetts eight, Rhode-Island and Providence Plantations one, Connecticut five, New-York six, New Jersey four, Pennsylvania eight, Delaware one,

† Note:—This text of the Constitution follows the engrossed copy signed by Gen. Washington and the deputies from 12 States. The superior number preceding the paragraphs designates the number of the clause; it was not in the original.

* The part included in brackets was changed by Section 2 of the Fourteenth Amendment.

Maryland six, Virginia ten, North Carolina five, South Carolina five, and Georgia three.

Filling of vacancies

⁴When vacancies happen in the Representation from any State, the Executive Authority thereof shall issue Writs of Election to fill such Vacancies.

Choice of Speaker and other officers; sole power of impeachment

⁵The House of Representatives shall chuse their Speaker and other Officers; and shall have the sole Power of Impeachment.

Composition of Senate; see Seventeenth Amendment for selection of Senators.

SECTION 3. The Senate of the United States shall be composed of two Senators from each State, [chosen by the Legislature thereof,]* for six Years; and each Senator shall have one Vote.

Terms of Senator— overlapping

²Immediately after they shall be assembled in Consequence of the first Election, they shall be divided as equally as may be into three Classes. The Seats of the Senators of the first Class shall be vacated at the Expiration of the second Year, of the second Class at the Expiration of the fourth Year, and of the third Class at the Expiration of the sixth Year, so that one third may be cho-

Vacancies—see Seventeenth Amendment

sen every second Year; [and if Vacancies happen by Resignation, or otherwise, during the Recess of the Legislature of any State, the Executive thereof may make temporary Appointments until the next Meeting of the Legislature, which shall then fill such Vacancies].**

Qualifications

³No Person shall be a Senator who shall not have attained to the Age of thirty Years, and been nine Years a Citizen of the United States, and who shall not, when elected, be an Inhabitant of that State for which he shall be chosen.

Vice President to preside; choice of other officers

⁴The Vice President of the United States shall be President of the Senate, but shall have no Vote, unless they be equally divided.

⁵The Senate shall chuse their other Officers, and also a President pro tempore, in the Absence of the Vice President, or when he shall exercise the Office of President of the United States.

---

* The part included in brackets was changed by Section 1 of the Seventeenth Amendment.
** The part included in brackets was changed by Clause 2 of the Seventeenth Amendment.

Trial of impeach-
ments by Senate;
penalties if
impeached and
convicted

[6]The Senate shall have the sole Power to try all Impeachments. When sitting for that Purpose, they shall be on Oath or Affirmation. When the President of the United States is tried, the Chief Justice shall preside: And no Person shall be convicted without the Concurrence of two thirds of the Members present.

[7]Judgment in Cases of Impeachment shall not extend further than to removal from Office, and disqualification to hold and enjoy any Office of honor, Trust or Profit under the United States: but the Party convicted shall nevertheless be liable and subject to Indictment, Trial, Judgment and Punishment, according to Law.

Times, places and
manner of holding
Congressional
elections

SECTION 4. [1]The Times, Places and Manner of holding Elections for Senators and Representatives, shall be prescribed in each State by the Legislature thereof; but the Congress may at any time by Law make or alter such Regulations, except as to the Places of chusing Senators.

Congressional
sessions—see
Twentieth
Amendment

[2]The Congress shall assemble at least once in every Year, and such Meeting shall [be on the first Monday in December,]* unless they shall by Law appoint a different Day.

Judging elections
and qualifications;
size of a quorum;
expulsion of
members of
Congress

SECTION 5. [1]Each House shall be the Judge of the Elections, Returns and Qualifications of its own Members, and a Majority of each shall constitute a Quorum to do Business; but a smaller Number may adjourn from day to day, and may be authorized to compel the Attendance of absent Members, in such Manner, and under such Penalties as each House may provide.

Rules of proceeding
and keeping of
journal

[2]Each House may determine the Rules of its Proceedings, punish its Members for disorderly Behavior, and, with the Concurrence of two thirds, expel a Member.

[3]Each House shall keep a Journal of its Proceedings, and from time to time publish the same, excepting such Parts as may in their Judgment require Secrecy; and the Yeas and Nays of the Members of either House on any question shall, at the Desire of one fifth of those Present, be entered on the Journal.

Adjournment

[4]Neither House, during the Session of Congress, shall, without the Consent of the other, adjourn for more than three days, nor to any other Place than that in which the two Houses shall be sitting.

---

* The part included in brackets was changed by Section 2 of the Twentieth Amendment.

SECTION 6. [1]The Senators and Representatives shall receive a Compensation for their Services, to be ascertained by Law, and paid out of the Treasury of the United States. They shall in all Cases, except Treason, Felony and Breach of the Peace, be privileged from Arrest during their Attendance at the Session of their respective Houses, and in going to and returning from the same; and for any Speech or Debate in either House, they shall not be questioned in any other Place.

Compensation and immunities of members of Congress

[2]No Senator or Representative shall, during the Time for which he was elected, be appointed to any civil Office under the Authority of the United States, which shall have been created, or the Emoluments whereof shall have been increased during such time; and no Person holding any Office under the United States, shall be a Member of either House during his Continuance in Office.

Limitations on appointment of members of Congress to civil offices; no national office-holder to be a member of Congress

SECTION 7. [1]All Bills for raising Revenue shall originate in the House of Representatives; but the Senate may propose or concur with Amendments as on other Bills.

Origin of revenue bills

[2]Every Bill which shall have passed the House of Representatives and the Senate, shall, before it becomes a Law, be presented to the President of the United States; If he approve he shall sign it, but if not he shall return it, with his Objections to that House in which it shall have originated, who shall enter the Objections at large on their Journal, and proceed to reconsider it. If after such Reconsideration two thirds of that House shall agree to pass the Bill, it shall be sent, together with the Objections, to the other House, by which it shall likewise be reconsidered, and if approved by two thirds of that House, it shall become a Law. But in all such Cases the Votes of both Houses shall be determined by Yeas and Nays, and the Names of the Persons voting for and against the Bill shall be entered on the Journal of each House respectively. If any Bill shall not be returned by the President within ten days (Sundays excepted) after it shall have been presented to him, the Same shall be a Law, in like Manner as if he had signed it, unless the Congress by their Adjournment prevent its Return, in which Case it shall not be a Law.

Veto power of President: overriding of veto

[3]Every Order, Resolution, or Vote to which the Concurrence of the Senate and House of Representatives may be necessary (except on a question of Adjournment) shall be presented to the President of the United States; and before the Same shall take Effect, shall be approved by him, or being disapproved by him, shall be repassed by two thirds of the Senate and House of Representatives, according to the Rules and Limitations prescribed in the Case of a Bill.

Enumerated powers of Congress: Taxation

SECTION 8. [1]The Congress shall have Power To lay and collect Taxes, Duties, Imposts and Excises, to pay the Debts and provide for the common Defence and general Welfare of the United States; but all Duties, Imposts and Excises shall be uniform throughout the United States;

Borrowing of money

[2]To borrow Money on the credit of the United States;

Regulation of commerce

[3]To regulate Commerce with foreign Nations, and among the several States, and with the Indian Tribes;

Naturalization and bankruptcy

[4]To establish an uniform Rule of Naturalization, and uniform Laws on the subject of Bankruptcies throughout the United States;

Coining of money; weights and measures

[5]To coin Money, regulate the Value thereof, and of foreign Coin, and fix the Standard of Weights and Measures;

Punishment of counterfeiting

[6]To provide for the Punishment of counterfeiting the Securities and current Coin of the United States;

Postal service

[7]To establish Post Offices and post Roads;

Patents and copyrights

[8]To promote the Progress of Science and useful Arts, by securing for limited Times to Authors and Inventors the exclusive Right to their respective Writings and Discoveries;

Creation of courts

[9]To constitute Tribunals inferior to the supreme Court;

Piracies and high seas felonies

[10]To define and punish Piracies and Felonies committed on the high Seas, and Offences against the Law of Nations;

Declaration of War

[11]To declare War, grant Letters of Marque and Reprisal, and make Rules concerning Captures on Land and Water;

Provide armed forces and for calling forth and organizing the militia

¹²To raise and support Armies, but no Appropriation of Money to that Use shall be for a longer Term than two Years;

¹³To provide and maintain a Navy;

¹⁴To make Rules for the Government and Regulation of the land and naval Forces;

¹⁵To provide for calling forth the Militia to execute the Laws of the Union, suppress Insurrections and repel Invasions;

¹⁶To provide for organizing, arming, and disciplining the Militia and for governing such Part of them as may be employed in the Service of the United States, reserving to the States respectively, the Appointment of the Officers, and the Authority of training the Militia according to the discipline prescribed by Congress;

Congress to govern the District of Columbia and other places owned by national government

¹⁷To exercise exclusive Legislation in all Cases whatsoever, over such District (not exceeding ten Miles square) as may, by Cession of particular States, and the Acceptance of Congress, become the Seat of the Government of the United States, and to exercise like Authority over all Places purchased by the Consent of the Legislature of the State in which the Same shall be, for the Erection of Forts, Magazines, Arsenals, dock-Yards, and other needful Buildings;—And

Necessary and proper (elastic) clause

¹⁸To make all Laws which shall be necessary and proper for carrying into Execution the foregoing Powers, and all other Powers vested by this Constitution in the Government of the United States, or in any Department or Officer thereof.

Express limitations on national government— Congress in particular

SECTION 9. ¹The Migration or Importation of such Persons as any of the States now existing shall think proper to admit, shall not be prohibited by the Congress prior to the Year one thousand eight hundred and eight, but a Tax or duty may be imposed on such Importation, not exceeding ten dollars for each Person.

²The Privilege of the Writ of Habeas Corpus shall not be suspended, unless when in Cases of Rebellion or Invasion the public Safety may require it.

³No Bill of Attainder or ex post facto Law shall be passed.

*⁴No Capitation, or other direct, Tax shall be laid, unless in Proportion to the Census or Enumeration herein before directed to be taken.

* See also the Sixteenth Amendment.

[5]No Tax or Duty shall be laid on Articles exported from any State.

[6]No Preference shall be given by any Regulation of Commerce or Revenue to the Ports of one State over those of another: nor shall Vessels bound to, or from, one State be obliged to enter, clear, or pay Duties in another.

[7]No Money shall be drawn from the Treasury, but in Consequence of Appropriations made by Law; and a regular Statement and Account of the Receipts and Expenditures of all public Money shall be published from time to time.

[8]No Title of Nobility shall be granted by the United States: And no Person holding any Office of Profit or Trust under them, shall, without the Consent of the Congress, accept of any present, Emolument, Office, or Title, of any kind of whatever, from any King, Prince, or foreign State.

Express limitations on states **SECTION 10.** [1]No State shall enter into any Treaty, Alliance, or Confederation; grant Letters of Marque and Reprisal, coin Money, emit Bills of Credit; make any Thing but gold and silver Coin a Tender in Payment of Debts; pass any Bill of Attainder, ex post facto Law, or Law impairing the Obligation of Contracts, or grant any Title of Nobility.

[2]No State shall, without the Consent of the Congress, lay any Imposts or Duties on Imports or Exports, except what may be absolutely necessary for executing it's inspection Laws: and the net Produce of all Duties and Imposts, laid by any State on Imports or Exports, shall be for the Use of the Treasury of the United States; and all such Laws shall be subject to the Revision and Controul of the Congress.

[3]No State shall, without the Consent of Congress, lay any Duty of Tonnage, keep Troops, or Ships of War in time of Peace, enter into any Agreement or Compact with another State, or with a foreign Power, or engage in War, unless actually invaded, or in such imminent Danger as will not admit of delay.

ARTICLE II • EXECUTIVE DEPARTMENT

Executive power vested in President; term of office—see Twenty-second Amendment **SECTION 1.** [1]The executive Power shall be vested in a President of the United States of America. He shall hold his Office during the Term of four Years, and, together with the Vice President, chosen for the same Term, be elected as follows

Selection
of Presidential
electors and
number per state
[2]Each State shall appoint, in such Manner as the Legislature thereof may direct, a Number of Electors, equal to the whole Number of Senators and Representatives to which the State may be entitled in the Congress: but no Senator or Representative, or Person holding an Office of Trust or Profit under the United States, shall be appointed an Elector.

Replaced by
Twelfth Amendment
[The Electors shall meet in their respective States, and vote by Ballot for two Persons, of whom one at least shall not be an Inhabitant of the same State with themselves. And they shall make a List of all the Persons voted for, and of the Number of Votes for each; which List they shall sign and certify, and transmit sealed to the Seat of the Government of the United States, directed to the President of the Senate. The President of the Senate shall, in the Presence of the Senate and House of Representatives, open all the Certificates, and the Votes shall then be counted. The Person having the greatest Number of Votes shall be the President, if such Number be a Majority of the whole Number of Electors appointed; and if there be more than one who have such Majority, and have an equal Number of Votes, then the House of Representatives shall immediately chuse by Ballot one of them for President; and if no Person have a Majority, then from the five highest on the List the said House shall in like Manner chuse the President. But in chusing the President, the Votes shall be taken by States, the Representation from each State having one Vote; A quorum for this Purpose shall consist of a Member or Members from two thirds of the States, and a Majority of all the States shall be necessary to a Choice. In every Case, after the Choice of the President, the Person having the greatest Number of Votes of the Electors shall be the Vice President. But if there should remain two or more who have equal Votes, the Senate shall chuse from them by Ballot the Vice President.]*

Congress to
determine the time
of choosing
electors and
the casting of
electoral votes
[3]The Congress may determine the Time of chusing the Electors, and the Day on which they shall give their Votes; which Day shall be the same throughout the United States.

---

* This paragraph has been superseded by the Twelfth Amendment.

[4]No Person except a natural born Citizen, or a Citizen of the United States, at the time of the Adoption of this Constitution, shall be eligible to the Office of President; neither shall any Person be eligible to that Office who shall not have attained to the Age of thirty five Years, and been fourteen Years a Resident within the United States.

[5]In Case of the Removal of the President from Office, or of his Death, Resignation, or Inability to discharge the Powers and Duties of the said Office, the Same shall devolve on the Vice President, and the Congress may by law provide for the Case of Removal, Death, Resignation or Inability, both of the President and Vice President declaring what Officer shall then act as President, and such Officer shall act accordingly, until the Disability be removed, or a President shall be elected.

[6]The President shall, at stated Times, receive for his Services, a Compensation, which shall neither be encreased nor diminished during the Period for which he shall have been elected, and he shall not receive within that Period any other Emolument from the United States, or any of them.

[7]Before he enter on the Execution of his Office, he shall take the following Oath or Affirmation:—"I do solemnly swear (or affirm) that I will faithfully execute the Office of President of the United States, and will to the best of my Ability, preserve, protect and defend the Constitution of the United States."

SECTION 2. [1]The President shall be Commander in Chief of the Army and Navy of the United States, and of the Militia of the several States, when called into the actual Service of the United States; he may require the Opinion, in writing, of the principal Officer in each of the executive Departments, upon any Subject relating to the Duties of their respective Offices, and he shall have Power to grant Reprieves and Pardons for Offenses against the United States, except in Cases of Impeachment.

<table>
</table>

Treaty-making with advice and consent of Senate

Appointment of officials with advice and consent of Senate; appointment of inferior officers by President alone if Congress so provides

^{2}He shall have Power, by and with the Advice and Consent of the Senate, to make Treaties, provided two thirds of the Senators present concur; and he shall nominate and by and with the Advice and Consent of the Senate, shall appoint Ambassadors, other public Ministers and Consuls, Judges of the supreme Court, and all other Officers of the United States, whose Appoint-ments are not herein otherwise provided for, and which shall be established by Law: but the Congress may by Law vest the Appointment of such inferior Officers, as they think proper, in the President alone, in the Courts of Law, or in the Heads of Departments.

Temporary filling of vacancies

^{3}The President shall have Power to fill up all Vacancies that may happen during the Recess of the Senate, by granting Commissions which shall expire at the End of their next Session.

Make recommendations to Congress and provide information

Call special sessions of Congress

Receive ambassadors and other public ministers

Enforce the laws

SECTION 3.   He shall from time to time give to the Congress Information of the State of the Union, and recommend to their Consideration such Measures as he shall judge necessary and expedient; he may, on extraordinary Occasions, convene both Houses, or either of them, and in Case of Disagreement between them, with Respect to the Time of Adjournment, he may adjourn them to such Time as he shall think proper; he shall receive Ambassadors and other public Ministers; he shall take Care that the Laws be faithfully executed, and shall Commission all the Officers of the United States.

Civil officers, including President and Vice President, to be removed from office if impeached and convicted

SECTION 4.   The President, Vice President and all civil Officers of the United States, shall be removed from Office on Impeachment for, and Conviction of, Treason, Bribery, or other high Crimes and Misdemeanors.

ARTICLE III • JUDICIAL DEPARTMENT

Structure of national judiciary

Tenure and compensation of judges

SECTION 1.   The judicial Power of the United States, shall be vested in one supreme Court, and in such inferior Courts as the Congress may from time to time ordain and establish. The Judges, both of the supreme and inferior Courts, shall hold their Offices during good Behaviour, and shall, at stated Times, receive for their Services a Compensation, which shall not be diminished during their Continuance in Office.

Jurisdiction of the national judiciary

SECTION 2. [1]The judicial Power shall extend to all Cases, in Law and Equity, arising under this Constitution, the Laws of the United States, and Treaties made, or which shall be made, under their Authority;—to all Cases affecting Ambassadors, other public Ministers and Consuls;—to all Cases of admiralty and maritime Jurisdiction;—to Controversies to which the United States shall be a Party;—to Controversies between two or more States;—between a State and Citizens of another State;*—between Citizens of different States,—between Citizens of the same State claiming Lands under Grants of different States, and between a State, or the Citizens thereof, and foreign States, Citizens or Subjects.

Original and appellate jurisdiction of the Supreme Court

[2]In all Cases affecting Ambassadors, other public Ministers and Consuls, and those in which a State shall be Party, the supreme Court shall have original Jurisdiction. In all the other Cases before mentioned, the supreme Court shall have appellate Jurisdiction, both as to Law and Fact, with such Exceptions, and under such Regulations as the Congress shall make.

Jury trial in criminal cases other than impeachment

[3]The Trial of all Crimes, except in Cases of Impeachment shall be by Jury; and such Trial shall be held in the State where the said Crimes shall have been committed; but when not committed within any State, the Trial shall be at such Place or Places as the Congress may by Law have directed.

Definition of treason and requisites for conviction

SECTION 3. [1]Treason against the United States, shall consist only in levying War against them, or in adhering to their Enemies, giving them Aid and Comfort. No Person shall be convicted of Treason unless on the Testimony of two Witnesses to the same overt Act, or on Confession in open Court.

Punishment for treason

[2]The Congress shall have Power to declare the Punishment of Treason, but no Attainder of Treason shall work Corruption of Blood, or Forfeiture except during the Life of the Person attainted.

---

* This clause has been affected by the Eleventh Amendment.

ARTICLE IV • RELATION OF THE STATES TO EACH OTHER

Interstate obligations; full faith and credit, privileges and immunities of citizens, rendition of fugitives from justice

SECTION 1. Full Faith and Credit shall be given in each State to the public Acts, Records, and judicial Proceedings of every other State. And the Congress may by general Laws prescribe the Manner in which such Acts, Records and Proceedings shall be proved, and the Effect thereof.

SECTION 2. ^{1}The Citizens of each State shall be entitled to all Privileges and Immunities of Citizens in the several States.

^{2}A Person charged in any State with Treason, Felony, or other Crime, who shall flee from Justice, and be found in another State, shall on Demand of the executive Authority of the State from which he fled, be delivered up, to be removed to the State having Jurisdiction of the Crime.

Obsolete

^{3}[No Person held to Service or Labour in one State, under the Laws thereof, escaping into another, shall, in Consequence of any Law or Regulation therein, be discharged from such Service or Labour but shall be delivered up on Claim of the Party to whom such Service or Labour may be due.]*

Admission of new states

SECTION 3. ^{1}New States may be admitted by Congress into this Union; but no new State shall be formed or erected within the Jurisdiction of any other State; nor any State be formed by the Junction of two or more States, or Parts of States, without the Consent of the Legislatures of the States concerned as well as the Congress.

Government of territories

^{2}The Congress shall have Power to dispose of and make all needful Rules and Regulations respecting the Territory or other Property belonging to the United States; and nothing in this Constitution shall be so construed as to Prejudice any Claims of the United States, or of any particular State.

Guarantee of republican form of government and protection against invasion and domestic violence

SECTION 4. The United States shall guarantee to every State in this Union a Republican Form of Government, and shall protect each of them against Invasion; and on Application of the Legislature, or of the Executive (when the Legislature cannot be convened) against domestic Violence.

---

* This paragraph has been superseded by the Thirteenth Amendment.

ARTICLE V • AMENDMENTS

Proposal and
ratification of
amendments

The Congress, whenever two thirds of both Houses shall deem it necessary, shall propose Amendments to this Constitution, or, on the Application of the Legislatures of two thirds of the several States, shall call a Convention for proposing Amendments, which, in either Case, shall be valid to all Intents and Purposes, as Part of this Constitution, when ratified by the Legislatures of three fourths of the several States, or by Conventions in three fourths thereof, as the one or the other Mode of Ratification may be proposed by the Congress: Provided, [that no Amendment which may be made prior to the Year One thousand eight hundred and eight shall in any Manner affect the first and fourth Clauses in the Ninth Section of the first Article; and]* that no State, without its Consent, shall be deprived of its equal Suffrage in the Senate.

ARTICLE VI • GENERAL PROVISIONS

Validity of debts
contracted prior to
adoption of the
Constitution

[1]All Debts contracted and Engagements entered into, before the Adoption of this Constitution shall be as valid against the United States under this Constitution, as under the Confederation.

Supremacy of
the national
constitution, laws,
and treaties

[2]This Constitution, and the Laws of the United States which shall be made in Pursuance thereof; and all Treaties made, or which shall be made, under the Authority of the United States, shall be the supreme Law of the Land; and the Judges in every State shall be bound thereby, any Thing in the Constitution or Laws of any State to the Contrary notwithstanding.

Oath of office to
support Constitution:
required of all
officials, national
and state;
no religious
qualification

[3]The Senators and Representatives before mentioned, and the Members of the several State Legislatures, and all executive and judicial Officers, both of the United States and of the several States, shall be bound by Oath or Affirmation, to support this Constitution; but no religious Test shall ever be required as a Qualification to any Office or public Trust under the United States.

* Obsolete.

ARTICLE VII • RATIFICATION OF THE CONSTITUTION

Schedule   The Ratification of the Conventions of nine States, shall be sufficient for the Establishment of this Constitution between the States so ratifying the Same.

DONE in convention by the Unanimous Consent of the States present the Seventeenth Day of September in the Year of our Lord one thousand seven hundred and Eighty seven and of the Independence of the United States of America the Twelfth IN WITNESS whereof We have hereto subscribed our Names,

George Washington
President and Deputy from Virginia

[Signed also by the deputies of twelve States.]

NEW HAMPSHIRE
John Langdon
Nicholas Gilman

MASSACHUSETTS
Nathaniel Gorham
Rufus King

CONNECTICUT
William Samuel
Johnson
Roger Sherman

NEW YORK
Alexander Hamilton

NEW JERSEY
William Livingston
David Brearley
William Paterson
Jonathan Dayton

PENNSYLVANIA
Benjamin Franklin
Robert Morris
Thomas FitzSimons
James Wilson
Thomas Mifflin
George Clymer
Jared Ingersoll
Gouverneur Morris

DELAWARE
George Read
John Dickinson
Jacob Broom
Gunning Bedford, Jr.
Richard Bassett

MARYLAND
James McHenry
Daniel Carroll
Dan of St. Thomas
Jenifer

VIRGINIA
John Blair
James Madison, Jr.

NORTH CAROLINA
William Blount
Hugh Williamson
Richard Dobbs Spaight

SOUTH CAROLINA
John Rutledge
Charles Pinckney
Charles Cotesworth
Pinckney
Pierce Butler

GEORGIA
William Few
Abraham Baldwin

Attest: *William Jackson,*
Secretary

RATIFICATION OF THE CONSTITUTION

The Constitution was adopted by a convention of the States on September 17, 1787, and was subsequently ratified by the several States, on the following dates: Delaware, December 7, 1787; Pennsylvania, December 12, 1787; New Jersey, December 18, 1787; Georgia, January 2, 1788; Connecticut, January 9, 1788; Massachusetts, February 6, 1788; Maryland, April 28, 1788; South Carolina, May 23, 1788; New Hampshire, June 21, 1788; Virginia, June 25, 1788; New York, July 26, 1788; North Carolina, November 21, 1789; Rhode Island, May 29, 1790.

ARTICLES IN ADDITION TO, AND AMENDMENT OF, THE CONSTITU- TION OF THE UNITED STATES OF AMERICA, PROPOSED BY CONGRESS, AND RATIFIED BY THE LEGISLATURES OF THE SEVERAL STATES PUR- SUANT TO THE FIFTH ARTICLE OF THE ORIGINAL CONSTITUTION

ARTICLE I*

Freedom of religion, speech, and assembly

Congress shall make no law respecting an establish- ment of religion, or prohibiting the free exercise thereof; or abridging the freedom of speech, or of the press; or the right of the people peaceably to assemble, and to petition the Government for a redress of grievances.

ARTICLE II

Militia and the right to bear arms

A well regulated Militia, being necessary to the securi- ty of a free State, the right of the people to keep and bear Arms, shall not be infringed.

ARTICLE III

Quartering of soldiers

No Soldier shall, in time of peace be quartered in any house, without the consent of the Owner, nor in time of war, but in a manner to be prescribed by law.

ARTICLE IV

Unreasonable searches and seizures prohibited

The right of the people to be secure in their persons, houses, papers, and effects, against unreasonable search- es and seizures, shall not be violated, and no Warrants

---

* Only the 13th, 14th, 15th, and 16th articles of amendment had numbers assigned to them at the time of ratification.

shall issue, but upon probable cause, supported by Oath or affirmation, and particularly describing the place to be searched, and the persons or things to be seized.

ARTICLE V

Indictment by grand jury; no double jeopardy; due process of law; no self-incrimination; compensation for taking property

No person shall be held to answer for a capital, or otherwise infamous crime, unless on a presentment or indictment of a Grand Jury, except in cases arising in the land or naval forces, or in the Militia, when in actual service in time of War or public danger; nor shall any person be subject for the same offence to be twice put in jeopardy of life or limb, nor shall be compelled in any criminal case to be a witness against himself, nor be deprived of life, liberty, or property, without due process of law; nor shall private property be taken for public use without just compensation.

ARTICLE VI

Guarantee of basic procedural rights in criminal prosecutions, e.g., jury trial, confrontation of witnesses

In all criminal prosecutions, the accused shall enjoy the right to a speedy and public trial, by an impartial jury of the State and district wherein the crime shall have been committed; which district shall have been previously ascertained by law, and to be informed of the nature and cause of the accusation; to be confronted with the witnesses against him; to have compulsory process for obtaining Witnesses in his favor, and to have the Assistance of Counsel for his defence.

ARTICLE VII

Jury trial in common law suits

In Suits at common law, where the value in controversy shall exceed twenty dollars, the right of trial by jury shall be preserved, and no fact tried by a jury shall be otherwise reexamined in any Court of the United States, than according to the rules of the common law.

ARTICLE VIII

Excessive bail or fines, cruel and unusual punishments prohibited

Excessive bail shall not be required, nor excessive fines imposed, nor cruel and unusual punishments inflicted.

ARTICLE IX

Retention of rights
by the people

The enumeration in the Constitution, of certain rights, shall not be construed to deny or disparage others retained by the people.

ARTICLE X

Reserved powers
of the states

The powers not delegated to the United States by the Constitution nor prohibited by it to the States, are reserved to the States respectively, or to the people.

ARTICLE XI

Immunity of states
from suits by
citizens or aliens in
national courts

The Judicial power of the United States shall not be construed to extend to any suit in law or equity, commenced or prosecuted against one of the United States by Citizens of another State, or by Citizens or Subjects of any Foreign State.

ARTICLE XII

Replaces third
paragraph of
Section 1, Article II.
Principal provision
requires separate
ballots for President
and Vice President
and a majority
electoral vote.
Procedure to be
followed if no
candidate obtains
a majority

The electors shall meet in their respective states and vote by ballot for President and Vice-President, one of whom, at least, shall not be an inhabitant of the same state with themselves; they shall name in their ballots the person voted for as President, and in distinct ballots the person voted for as Vice-President, and they shall make distinct lists of all persons voted for as President, and of all persons voted for as Vice-President, and of the number of votes for each, which lists they shall sign and certify, and transmit sealed to the seat of the government of the United States, directed to the President of the Senate;—The President of the Senate shall, in presence of the Senate and House of Representatives, open all the certificates and the votes shall then be counted;—The person having the greatest number of votes for President, shall be the President, if such number be a majority of the whole number of Electors appointed; and if no person have such majority, then from the persons having the highest numbers not exceeding three on the list of those voted for as President, the House of Representatives shall choose immediately, by ballot, the President. But in choosing the President, the votes shall be taken by states, the representation from each state having one vote; a quorum for this purpose shall consist of a member or members from two-thirds of the states, and a majority of all the states shall be necessary to a choice. [And if the House of Representatives shall not choose a President whenever the right of choice shall devolve upon them, before the fourth day of March next following, then the Vice-President shall act as President, as in the case of the death or other constitutional disability of the President.]* The person having the greatest number of votes as Vice-President, shall be the Vice-President, if such number be a majority of the whole number of Electors appointed, and if no person have a majority, then from the two highest numbers on the list, the Senate shall choose the Vice-President; a quorum for the purpose shall consist of two-thirds of the whole number of Senators, and a majority of the whole number shall be necessary to a choice. But no person constitutionally ineligible to the office of President shall be eligible to that of Vice-President of the United States.

ARTICLE XIII

Slavery and involuntary servitude prohibited

SECTION 1. Neither slavery nor involuntary servitude, except as a punishment for crime whereof the party shall have been duly convicted, shall exist within the United States, or any place subject to their jurisdiction.

SECTION 2. Congress shall have power to enforce this article by appropriate legislation.

ARTICLE XIV

Definition of United States and state citizenship; no state abridgement of privileges and immunities of United States citizens; no state denial of due process of law or equal protection of the laws to any person

SECTION 1. All persons born or naturalized in the United States, and subject to the jurisdiction thereof, are citizens of the United States and the State wherein they reside. No State shall make or enforce any law which shall abridge the privileges or immunities of citizens of the United States; nor shall any State deprive any person of life, liberty, or property, without due process of law; nor deny to any person within its jurisdiction the equal protection of the laws.

---

* The part included in brackets has been superseded by Section 3 of the Twentieth Amendment.

Apportionment of
Representatives
among the states
according to popu-
lation, excluding
untaxed Indians.
Provision for
reduction of
representation
under specified
circumstances

SECTION 2. Representatives shall be apportioned among the several States according to their respective numbers, counting the whole number of persons in each State, excluding Indians not taxed. But when the right to vote at any election for the choice of electors for President and Vice President of the United States, Representatives in Congress, the Executive and Judicial officers of a State, or the members of the Legislature thereof, is denied to any of the male inhabitants of such State, being twenty-one years of age, and citizens of the United States, or in any way abridged, except for participation in rebellion, or other crime, the basis of representation therein shall be reduced in the proportion which the number of such male citizens shall bear to the whole number of male citizens twenty-one years of age in such State.

Disqualification
from office-holding
by officials who,
having taken an
oath to support the
Constitution,
engage in rebellion
against the United
States

SECTION 3. No person shall be a Senator or Representative in Congress, or elector of President and Vice President, or hold any office, civil or military, under the United States, or under any State, who, having previously taken an oath, as a member of Congress, or as an officer of the United States, or as a member of any State legislature, or as an executive or judicial officer of any State, to support the Constitution of the United States, shall have engaged in insurrection or rebellion against the same, or given aid or comfort to the enemies thereof. But Congress may by a vote of two-thirds of each House, remove such disability.

Validity of public
debt incurred for
suppressing rebel-
lion not to be ques-
tioned. All indebt-
edness incurred in
support of rebellion
illegal and void

SECTION 4. The validity of the public debt of the United States, authorized by law, including debts incurred for payment of pensions and bounties for services in suppressing insurrection or rebellion, shall not be questioned. But neither the United States nor any State shall assume or pay any debt or obligation incurred in aid of insurrection or rebellion against the United States, or any claim for the loss of emancipation of any slave; but all such debts, obligations and claims shall be held illegal and void.

SECTION 5. The Congress shall have power to enforce, by appropriate legislation, the provisions of this article.

ARTICLE XV

SECTION 1. The right of citizens of the United States to vote shall not be denied or abridged by the United States or by any State on account of race, color, or previous condition of servitude.

SECTION 2. The Congress shall have power to enforce this article by appropriate legislation.

ARTICLE XVI

The Congress shall have power to lay and collect taxes on incomes, from whatever source derived, without apportionment among the several States, and without regard to any census or enumeration.

ARTICLE XVII

The Senate of the United States shall be composed of two Senators from each state, elected by the people thereof, for six years; and each Senator shall have one vote. The electors in each State shall have the qualifications requisite for electors of the most numerous branch of the State legislatures.

When vacancies happen in the representation of any State in the Senate, the executive authority of such State shall issue writs of election to fill such vacancies: *Provided,* That the legislature of any State may empower the executive thereof to make temporary appointments until the people fill the vacancies by election as the legislature may direct.

This amendment shall not be so construed as to affect the election or term of any Senator chosen before it becomes valid as part of the Constitution.

ARTICLE XVIII

SECTION 1. After one year from the ratification of this article the manufacture, sale, or transportation of intoxicating liquors within, the importation thereof into, or the exportation thereof from the United States and all territory subject to the jurisdiction thereof for beverage purposes is hereby prohibited.

Section 2. The Congress and the several States shall have concurrent power to enforce this article by appropriate legislation.

Section 3. This article shall be inoperative unless it shall have been ratified as an amendment to the Constitution by the legislatures of the several States, as provided in the Constitution, within seven years from the date of the submission hereof to the States by the Congress.*

ARTICLE XIX

Right of citizens to vote not to be denied because of sex.

The right of citizens of the United States to vote shall not be denied or abridged by the United States or by any State on account of sex.

Congress shall have power to enforce this article by appropriate legislation.

ARTICLE XX

Ending of terms of President, Vice President, Senators, and Representatives

Section 1. The terms of the President and Vice President shall end at noon on the 20th day of January, and the terms of Senators and Representatives at noon on the 3d day of January, of the years in which such terms would have ended if this article had not been ratified; and the terms of their successors shall then begin.

Beginning of required annual Congressional sessions

Section 2. The Congress shall assemble at least once in every year, and such meeting shall begin at noon on the 3d day of January, unless they shall by law appoint a different day.

Procedure to be followed if President elect has died or no President has been chosen or qualified by beginning of the Presidential term. This amendment also deals with other contingencies

Section 3. If, at the time fixed for the beginning of the term of the President, the President elect shall have died, the Vice President elect shall become President. If a President shall not have been chosen before the time fixed for the beginning of his term, or if the President elect shall have failed to qualify, then the Vice President elect shall act as President until a President shall have qualified; and the Congress may by law provide for the case wherein neither a President elect nor a Vice President elect shall have qualified, declaring who shall then act as President, or the manner in which one who is to act shall be selected, and such person shall act accordingly until a President or Vice President shall have qualified.

---

* Repealed by Section 1 of the Twenty-first Amendment.

SECTION 4. The Congress may by law provide for the case of the death of any of the persons from whom the House of Representatives may choose a President whenever the right of choice shall have devolved upon them, and for the case of the death of any of the persons from whom the Senate may choose a Vice President whenever the right of choice shall have devolved upon them.

SECTION 5. Sections 1 and 2 shall take effect on the 15th day of October following the ratification of this article.

SECTION 6. This article shall be inoperative unless it shall have been ratified as an amendment to the Constitution by the legislatures of three-fourths of the several States within seven years from the date of its submission.

ARTICLE XXI

The Eighteenth Amendment establishing prohibition repealed

SECTION 1. The eighteenth article of amendment to the Constitution of the United States is hereby repealed.

SECTION 2. The transportation or importation into any State, Territory, or possession of the United States for delivery or use therein of intoxicating liquors, in violation of the laws thereof, is hereby prohibited.

SECTION 3. This article shall be inoperative unless it shall have been ratified as an amendment to the Constitution by conventions in the several States, as provided in the Constitution, within seven years from the date of the submission hereof to the States by the Congress.

ARTICLE XXII

No person may be elected to Presidency for more than two terms

SECTION 1. No person shall be elected to the office of the President more than twice and no person who has held the office of President, or acted as President, for more than two years of a term to which some other person was elected President shall be elected to the office of the President more than once. But this article shall not apply to any person holding the office of President when this Article was proposed by the Congress, and shall not prevent any person who may be holding the office of President, or acting as President, during the term within which this Article becomes operative from holding the office of President or acting as President during the remainder of such term.

Section 2. This article shall be inoperative unless it shall have been ratified as an amendment to the Constitution by the legislatures of three-fourths of the several States within seven years from the date of its submission to the States by the Congress.

ARTICLE XXIII

Allocation of presidential electors to District of Columbia

Section 1. The District constituting the seat of Government of the United States shall appoint in such manner as the Congress may direct:

A number of electors of President and Vice President equal to the whole number of Senators and Representatives in Congress to which the District would be entitled if it were a State, but in no event more than the least populous State; they shall be in addition to those appointed by the States, but they shall be considered, for the purposes of the election of President and Vice President, to be electors appointed by a State; and they shall meet in the District and perform such duties as provided by the twelfth article of amendment.

Section 2. The Congress shall have power to enforce this article by appropriate legislation.

ARTICLE XXIV

Right of citizens to vote in national elections not be denied because of failure to pay taxes

Section 1. The right of citizens of the United States to vote in any primary or other election for President or Vice President, for electors for President or Vice President, or for Senator or Representative in Congress, shall not be denied or abridged by the United States or any State by reason of failure to pay any poll tax or other tax.

Section 2. The Congress shall have power to enforce this article by appropriate legislation.

ARTICLE XXV

Succession to the Presidency and Vice Presidency in case of vacancies

Section 1. In case of the removal of the President from office or of his death or resignation, the Vice President shall become President.

Section 2. Whenever there is a vacancy in the office of the Vice President, the President shall nominate a Vice President who shall take office upon confirmation by a majority vote of both Houses of Congress.

SECTION 3. Whenever the President transmits to the President pro tempore of the Senate and the Speaker of the House of Representatives his written declaration that he is unable to discharge the powers and duties of his office, and until he transmits to them a written declaration to the contrary, such powers and duties shall be discharged by the Vice President as Acting President.

Presidential disability: procedure for determining when and for how long disability exists. Vice President to act as President for duration of disability

SECTION 4. Whenever the Vice President and a majority of either the principal officers of the executive departments or of such other body as Congress may by law provide, transmit to the President pro tempore of the Senate and the Speaker of the House of Representatives their written declaration that the President is unable to discharge the powers and duties of his office, the Vice President shall immediately assume the powers and duties of the office as Acting President.

Thereafter, when the President transmits to the President pro tempore of the Senate and the Speaker of the House of Representatives his written declaration that no inability exists, he shall resume the powers and duties of his office unless the Vice President and a majority of either the principal officers of the executive department or of such other body as Congress may by law provide, transmit within four days to the President pro tempore of the Senate and the Speaker of the House of Representatives their written declaration that the President is unable to discharge the powers and duties of his office. Thereupon Congress shall decide the issue, assembling within forty-eight hours for that purpose if not in session. If the Congress, within twenty-one days after receipt of the latter written declaration, or, if Congress is not in session, within twenty-one days after Congress is required to assemble, determines by two-thirds vote of both Houses that the President is unable to discharge the powers and duties of his office, the Vice President shall continue to discharge the same as Acting President; otherwise, the President shall resume the powers and duties of his office.

ARTICLE XXVI

Citizens eighteen years or older not be denied suffrage because of age

SECTION 1. The right of citizens of the United States, who are eighteen years of age or older, to vote shall not be denied or abridged by the United States or by any State on account of age.

Section 2. The Congress shall have power to enforce this article by appropriate legislation.

ARTICLE XXVII

Congressional pay   No law varying the compensation for the services of the Senators and Representatives, shall take effect until an election of Representatives shall have intervened.

ARTICLE XXVIII — PROPOSED

Equal legal rights for men and women   **Section 1.** Equality of rights under the law shall not be denied or abridged by the United States or by any State on account of sex.

Section 2. The Congress shall have the power to enforce this article by appropriate legislation.

STATES OF THE UNION

Original Thirteen States in Capitals

State	Capital	First Permanent Settlement	Date Entered Union[1]	Area in Square Miles
Alabama	Montgomery	1702	Dec. 14, 1819	51,609
Alaska	Juneau	1790	Jan. 3, 1959	590,884
Arizona	Phoenix	1848	Feb. 14, 1912	113,909
Arkansas	Little Rock	1785	June 15, 1836	53,104
California	Sacramento	1769	Sept. 9, 1850	158,693
Colorado	Denver	1858	Aug. 1, 1876	104,247
CONNECTICUT	Hartford	1635	Jan. 9, 1788	5,009
DELAWARE	Dover	1638	Dec. 7, 1787	2,057
Florida	Tallahassee	1565	Mar. 3, 1845	58,560
GEORGIA	Atlanta	1733	Jan. 2, 1788	58,876
Hawaii	Honolulu	—	Aug. 21, 1959	6,449
Idaho	Boise	1842	July 3, 1890	83,557
Illinois	Springfield	1720	Dec. 3, 1818	56,400
Indiana	Indianapolis	1733	Dec. 11, 1816	36,291
Iowa	Des Moines	1788	Dec. 28, 1846	56,290
Kansas	Topeka	1727	Jan. 29, 1861	82,276
Kentucky	Frankfort	1774	June 1, 1792	40,395
Louisiana	Baton Rouge	1699	Apr. 30, 1812	48,523
Maine	Augusta	1624	Mar. 15, 1820	33,215
MARYLAND	Annapolis	1634	Apr. 28, 1788	10,577
MASSACHUSETTS	Boston	1620	Feb. 6, 1788	8,257
Michigan	Lansing	1668	Jan. 26, 1837	58,216
Minnesota	St. Paul	1805	May 11, 1858	84,068
Mississippi	Jackson	1699	Dec. 10, 1817	47,716
Missouri	Jefferson City	1764	Aug. 10, 1821	69,674
Montana	Helena	1809	Nov. 8, 1889	147,138
Nebraska	Lincoln	1847	Mar. 1, 1867	77,227
Nevada	Carson City	1850	Oct. 31, 1864	110,540
NEW HAMPSHIRE	Concord	1623	June 21, 1788	9,304
NEW JERSEY	Trenton	1664	Dec. 18, 1787	7,836

[1]Date ratified Constitution, or date of admission to Union.

New Mexico	Santa Fe	1605	Jan. 6, 1912	121,666
NEW YORK	Albany	1614	July 26, 1788	49,576
NORTH CAROLINA	Raleigh	1650	Nov. 21, 1789	52,712
North Dakota	Bismarck	1766	Nov. 2, 1889	70,665
Ohio	Columbus	1788	Mar. 1, 1803	41,222
Oklahoma	Oklahoma City	1889	Nov. 16, 1907	69,919
Oregon	Salem	1811	Feb. 14, 1859	96,981
PENNSYLVANIA	Harrisburg	1682	Dec. 12, 1787	45,333
RHODE ISLAND	Providence	1636	May 29, 1790	1,214
SOUTH CAROLINA	Columbia	1670	May 23, 1788	31,055
South Dakota	Pierre	1856	Nov. 2, 1889	77,047
Tennessee	Nashville	1757	June 1, 1796	42,244
Texas	Austin	1691	Dec. 29, 1845	267,339
Utah	Salt Lake City	1847	Jan. 4, 1896	84,916
Vermont	Montpelier	1724	Mar. 4, 1791	9,609
VIRGINIA	Richmond	1607	June 26, 1788	40,815
Washington	Olympia	1811	Nov. 11, 1889	68,192
West Virginia	Charleston	1727	June 20, 1863	24,181
Wisconsin	Madison	1766	May 29, 1848	56,154
Wyoming	Cheyenne	1824	July 10, 1890	97,914

POPULATION OF THE UNITED STATES, 1790–1990

1790 3,929,214	1870 38,558,371
1800 5,308,483	1880 50,155,783
1810 7,239,881	1890 62,947,714
1820 9,638,453	1900 75,994,575
1830 12,860,692	1910 91,972,266
1840 17,063,353	1920 105,710,620
1850 23,191,876	1930 122,775,046
1860 31,443,321	1940 131,669,275

1950 150,697,361
1960 179,323,175
1970 203,302,031
1980 226,504,825
1990 248,709,873

PRESIDENTS AND VICE PRESIDENTS

Term	President	Vice President
1789–1793	George Washington	John Adams
1793–1797	George Washington	John Adams
1797–1801	John Adams	Thomas Jefferson
1801–1805	Thomas Jefferson	Aaron Burr
1805–1809	Thomas Jefferson	George Clinton
1809–1813	James Madison	George Clinton (d. 1812)
1813–1817	James Madison	Elbridge Gerry (d. 1814)
1817–1821	James Monroe	Daniel D. Tompkins
1821–1825	James Monroe	Daniel D. Tompkins
1825–1829	John Quincy Adams	John C. Calhoun
1829–1833	Andrew Jackson	John C. Calhoun (resigned 1832)
1833–1837	Andrew Jackson	Martin Van Buren
1837–1841	Martin Van Buren	Richard M. Johnson
1841–1845	William H. Harrison (d. 1841) John Tyler	John Tyler
1845–1849	James K. Polk	George M. Dallas
1849–1853	Zachary Taylor (d. 1850) Millard Fillmore	Millard Fillmore
1853–1857	Franklin Pierce	William R. D. King (d. 1853)
1857–1861	James Buchanan	John C. Breckinridge
1861–1865	Abraham Lincoln	Hannibal Hamlin
1865–1869	Abraham Lincoln (d. 1865) Andrew Johnson	Andrew Johnson
1869–1873	Ulysses S. Grant	Schuyler Colfax
1873–1877	Ulysses S. Grant	Henry Wilson (d. 1875)
1877–1881	Rutherford B. Hayes	William A. Wheeler
1881–1885	James A. Garfield (d. 1881) Chester A. Arthur	Chester A. Arthur
1885–1889	Grover Cleveland	Thomas A. Hendricks (d. 1885)
1889–1893	Benjamin Harrison	Levi P. Morton

1893–1897	Grover Cleveland	Adlai E. Stevenson
1897–1901	William McKinley	Garret A. Hobart (d. 1899)
1901–1905	William McKinley (d. 1901) Theodore Roosevelt	Theodore Roosevelt
1905–1909	Theodore Roosevelt	Charles W. Fairbanks
1909–1913	William H. Taft	James S. Sherman (d. 1912)
1913–1917	Woodrow Wilson	Thomas R. Marshall
1917–1921	Woodrow Wilson	Thomas R. Marshall
1921–1925	Warren G. Harding (d. 1923) Calvin Coolidge	Calvin Coolidge
1925–1929	Calvin Coolidge	Charles G. Dawes
1929–1933	Herbert C. Hoover	Charles Curtis
1933–1937	Franklin D. Roosevelt	John N. Garner
1937–1941	Franklin D. Roosevelt	John N. Garner
1941–1945	Franklin D. Roosevelt	Henry A. Wallace
1945–1949	Franklin D. Roosevelt (d. 1945) Harry S. Truman	Harry S. Truman
1949–1953	Harry S. Truman	Alben W. Barkley
1953–1957	Dwight D. Eisenhower	Richard M. Nixon
1957–1961	Dwight D. Eisenhower	Richard M. Nixon
1961–1963	John F. Kennedy (d. 1963) Lyndon B. Johnson	Lyndon B. Johnson
1963–1969	Lyndon B. Johnson	Hubert Humphrey
1969–1973	Richard M. Nixon	Spiro T. Agnew
1973–1974	Richard M. Nixon	Gerald R. Ford
1974–1977	Gerald R. Ford	Nelson Rockefeller
1977–1981	James E. Carter	Walter Mondale
1981–1985	Ronald W. Reagan	George H.W. Bush
1985–1989	Ronald W. Reagan	George H.W. Bush
1989–1993	George H.W. Bush	J. Danforth Quayle
1993–	William J.B. Clinton	Albert Gore

CHIEF JUSTICES OF THE SUPREME COURT

John Jay, New York	1789–1795
John Rutledge, South Carolina	1795
Oliver Ellsworth, Connecticut	1795–1799
John Marshall, Virginia	1801–1835
Roger B. Taney, Maryland	1836–1864
Salmon P. Chase, Ohio	1864–1873
Morrison R. Waite, Ohio	1874–1888
Melville W. Fuller, Illinois	1888–1910
Edward D. White, Louisiana	1910–1921
William H. Taft, Ohio	1921–1930
Charles E. Hughes, New York	1930–1941
Harlan F. Stone, New York	1941–1946
Fred M. Vinson, Kentucky	1946–1953
Earl Warren, California	1953–1969
Warren E. Burger, Virginia	1969–1986
William H. Rehnquist, Arizona	1986–

COMPREHENSIVE BOOKS IN AMERICAN HISTORY

Works listed in this bibliography have been carefully selected from writings generally recognized for reliability and readability. The reader interested in a reliable listing of paperback books should check Bowker's *Paperbound Books in Print,* printed in quarterly editions and available in most libraries. Annotated and more extensive bibliographies may be found in standard American history textbooks. Students who need a still more extensive, classified bibliography should consult the **Harvard Guide to American History.**

CONSTITUTIONAL AND JUDICIAL

Corwin, E.S., *The Constitution and What It Means Today* (1971).
Hall, Kermit L., *The Magic Mirror: Law in American History* (1987). Interpretative study of the development of American law.
Kelley, A.H., and Harbison, W.A., *The American Constitution* (1963).
Lieberman, Jethro, *Understanding Our Constitution* (1967).
Schwartz, Bernard, *American Constitutional Law* (1955).
Swisher, C., *The Supreme Court in Modern Role* (1965).

ECONOMIC

Brownlee, W. Elliot, *Dynamics of Ascent; A History of the American Economy* (1988).
Bruchey, Stuart W., *Enterprise: The Dynamic Economy of a Free People* (1990).
Cochran, Thomas C., and Miller, William, *The Age of Enterprise: A Social History of Industrial America* (1942).
Faulkner, H.U., *American Economic History* (8th ed. 1960).
Fogel, Robert W., *Railroads and American Economic Growth* (1964).
Galbraith, John, *The New Industrial State* (1967).
Groner, A., *American Heritage History of American Business and Industry* (1972).

FOREIGN RELATIONS

Bailey, T.A., *A Diplomatic History of the American People* (1975).
Ferrell, R., *American Diplomacy* (1969).
Lens, S., *Forging of the American Empire* (1971).
Merk, Frederick, *Manifest Destiny and Mission in American History* (1963).
Merli, F., *Makers of American Diplomacy.* (2 vols. 1974).
Perkins, Dexter, *Hands Off: A History of the Monroe Doctrine* (1941).
Weinberg, Albert K., *Manifest Destiny: A Study of National Expansion in American History* (1935).

FRONTIER

Billington, R.A., *Westward Expansion* (3rd ed. 1967).
Clark, T.D., *Frontier America* (1959).

Fite, Gilbert C., *The Farmer's Frontier, 1865–1900* (1966).
Merk, Frederick, *History of the Westward Movement* (1978).
Riegel, R.E., *America Moves West* (3rd ed. 1956).
Webb, W.P., *The Great Plains* (1931).

IMMIGRATION, NATIONALITY, AND RACE
Davis, David B., *The Problem of Slavery in Western Culture* (1966).
Dinnerstein, L., *Ethnic Americans* (1975).
Farrell, J., *Give Us Your Poor* (1976).
Higham, J., *Strangers in the Land* (1963).
Huthmacher, J.J., *Nation of Newcomers* (1967).
Jones, Maldwyn Allen, *American Immigration* (1960).
Jordan, Winthrop D., *White Over Black: American Attitudes Toward the Negro* (1968).
Pitt, Leonard, *The Decline of the Californios: A Social History of Spanish-Speaking Californians* (1966).
Takaki, Ronald, *Strangers from a Different Shore: A History of Asian Americans* (1990).
Taylor, Philip, *The Distant Magnet: European Immigration to the United States of America* (1971).
Thornton, Russell, *American Indian Holocaust and Survival: A Population History Since 1492* (1987).
Washburn, Wilcomb E., *The Indian in American History* (1975).

INTELLECTUAL
Barker, C., *American Convictions, 1600–1850* (1970).
Curti, Merle, *The Growth of American Thought* (1951).
Grob, G., *Ideas in America* (1970).
Green, T., *America's Heroes* (1970).
Miller, P., *Life of the Mind in America* (1965).
Parrington, V.L., *Main Currents in American Thought* (3 vols. 1958).
Strout, Cushing, *Intellectual History in America* (1968).

INTERPRETATIVE
Bryce, James, *The American Commonwealth*. (2 vols. 1888).
De Tocqueville, Alexis, *Democracy in America*. (2 vols. 1835). Available in several paperback editions.
Parkes, H.B., *The American Experience* (1953).
Robertson, James Oliver, *American Myth, American Reality* (1980).
Thistlewaite, Frank, *The Great Experiment*. Cambridge University Press.

LABOR
Dulles, F.R., *Labor in America* (1960).
Peterson, Florence, *American Labor Unions* (1963).

Rayback, J.G., *A History of American Labor* (1959).
Reynolds, L.G., *Labor Economics and Labor Relations* (1964).

MILITARY
Leckie, Robert, *Wars of America* (1968).
Walton, R., *Beyond Diplomacy* (1970).
Weigley, Russell, *American Way of War* (1973).

POLITICAL
Borden, Morton, ed., *America's Eleven Greatest Presidents*. Rand McNally.
Brock, W., *Evolution of American Democracy* (1970).
Hesseltine, W., *Third Party Movements in America* (1962).
Mayer, George, *The Republican Party, 1854–1966* (1967).
Polakoff, Keith I., *Political Parties in American History* (1981).
Roseboom, Eugene, *A History of Presidential Elections* (1970).
Rutland, Robert A., *The Democrats: From Jefferson to Carter* (1979).
Schlesinger, Albert M., Jr., ed., *History of United States Political Parties* (4 vols. 1973).
Warren, Sidney, *Battles for the Presidency* (1968).

REFERENCE
Adams, J.T., and Coleman, R.V., *Dictionary of American History* (6 vols. 1940).
Handlin, Oscar, et al., *The Harvard Guide to American History* (1972).
Johnson, Allen, and Malone, Dumas, *The Dictionary of American Biography* (21 vols. 1928–1944).
Klein, Bernard, and Icolari, Daniel, eds., *Reference Encyclopedia of the American Indian* (1967).
Morris, R.B., and Commager, H.S., *The Encyclopedia of American History* (1970).
Statistical Abstract of the United States (1965).

RELIGION
Ahistrom, S., *Religious History of the American People* (1972).
Herberg, W., *Protestant, Catholic, Jew* (1961).
Hudson, W., *Religion in America* (1973).
Richey, R., *American Civil Religion* (1974).
Rosten, L., *Religions in America* (1975).
Weiss, B., *God in American History* (1966).

TECHNOLOGY
Allen, F.R., *Technology and Social Change* (1957).
Fortune, *Great American Scientists* (1961).
Jaffe, Bernard, *Men of Science in America* (1958).
Oliver, J.W., *History of American Technology* (1956).

DICTIONARY OF IMPORTANT AND DIFFICULT TERMS

Adams-Onis Treaty, 1819—Also known as the Florida Treaty, since it completed the annexation of Florida by the United States.

Albany Congress, 1754—A meeting of delegates from seven colonies that drew up the Albany Plan providing a grant of important powers to a colonial Congress. The Plan was not adopted by the colonies but it set a precedent for united action in the Continental Congresses.

Alien and Sedition Acts, 1798—Restrictive legislation passed by the Federalists to weaken their opposition, the Republicans.

American System—A nationalist economic program originated by Henry Clay and favored by the Whigs; it called for protective tariffs, a national bank, internal improvements through federal aid, and the sale of public lands to produce revenue.

Amnesty Act, 1872—By this law Congress pardoned and restored the political rights of former Confederates.

Anarchism—A political philosophy opposed to organized government which it considers an instrument of oppression used by the ruling classes. Some anarchists advocated various forms of violence to achieve their goals.

Armada—A Spanish fleet of about 800 ships gathered for the conquest of England in 1588; its defeat in the Battle of the Armada marks the beginning of English naval supremacy in the Atlantic.

Bacon's Rebellion, 1676—Frontier rebellion led by Nathaniel Bacon against the Governor of Virginia, Sir William Berkeley, in protest of grievances against the ruling clique at Jamestown.

balance of payments—The difference in the value of goods and services bought and those sold by a nation. An unfavorable balance represents payments in excess of receipts and ultimately may have to be settled by payments of gold.

"Barnburners"—An antislavery faction that split the Democratic Party in New York in 1848 and caused the Whigs to elect General Taylor as President. The loyal Democrats in this election were nicknamed the "Hunkers."

Bessemer Process—A method of producing steel cheaply; developed contemporaneously by Henry Bessemer in England and William Kelley in America during the 1850s.

bill of attainder—Punishment of an individual by legislative process used formerly in England for political reasons and used in the place of judicial processes requiring evidence of guilt; the Constitution denies this power to Congress.

bimetallism—The use of both gold and silver as standards of value in a monetary system; under bimetallism the standard unit of money, as the dollar, is defined as equal to fixed weights of both gold and silver.

"Black Codes"—Laws passed by the Southern states immediately after the Civil War to regulate behavior of the former slaves.

"Black Friday"—Stock and gold market crisis, September 24, 1869, caused by attempt of the speculators Jay Gould and Jim Fisk to corner the national gold supply.

blacklist—A list of names or firms with which one refuses to do business; a weapon formerly used by management to prevent the employment of union organizers and members.

blockade—The isolation of an enemy by military force, usually naval patrols, to cut off commerce with the rest of the world; a "paper blockade" is one not actually in effect in the vicinity of the enemy coastline.

"blue laws"—Legislation to regulate individual conduct and morals, such as compulsory observance of the Sabbath and prohibition of certain kinds of recreation; enacted by colonial Puritans.

Bonus Bill, 1817—A measure passed by Congress providing that the bonus paid to the federal government by the Second Bank of the United States would be spent for internal improvements; the bill was vetoed by President Madison.

"Boomers"—Homeseekers who defied federal authorities and occupied land in Oklahoma during the 1880s. The term is also applied to those who made the "runs" legally to take up land. See "Sooners."

boondoggling—Practice of spending public funds to create unneeded jobs; term has implications of political motives.

boycott—A concerted movement, as of labor or consumers, to refuse to buy, sell, or use certain goods.

Burlingame Treaty, 1868—American treaty of friendship with China that permitted unrestricted immigration of Chinese to the United States.

Calvinism—The religious teachings of John Calvin; the most prominent feature was the doctrine of predestination which held that most persons, except for a few "elect," were predestined to eternal damnation.

carpetbaggers—Derogatory term applied to Northern politicians, businessmen, and others who migrated to the South during Reconstruction to take advantage of opportunities to advance their own fortunes.

caucus—An informal political meeting; until 1824 caucuses of members of Congress nominated presidential candidates.

Chesapeake and Leopard Affair, 1807—The attack of the British warship *Leopard* upon the American warship *Chesapeake* for the purpose of impressing seamen.

Clayton-Bulwer Treaty, 1850—A compromise between the United States and Great Britain by which it was agreed that neither power would take exclusive control over any isthmian canal.

Coercive Acts, 1774—Known as the Intolerable Acts in the colonies; four Parliamentary acts designed to punish and discipline Massachusetts following the Boston Tea Party.

Commercial Revolution—The rise of extensive commerce in Europe in the late middle ages and the introduction of modern business methods; included large-scale merchandising and the use of money.

common law—The unwritten law of England based on ancient customs and handed down in court decisions which became precedents for the settlement of similar, subsequent cases; differs from Roman law and statutory law.

Common Sense—Pamphlet published by Thomas Paine in January, 1776, pleading in plain language the cause of independence.

compact theory—A term used to designate both John Locke's theory of government and the states' rights theory of the relationship of the states to the federal government.

Continental Congress, First and Second—The First Continental Congress met in September, 1774, and united the colonies in certain measures of defense against the British; the Second met in May, 1775, and later declared independence and constituted the central American government during the Revolution.

"Copperheads"—Northern Democrats, also called Peace Democrats, who opposed the Lincoln administration in its war efforts against the seceded Southern states.

Credit Mobilier—A scandal, exposed in 1872, named after the Credit Mobilier, the construction company of the Union Pacific Railroad. Wholesale bribery was practiced.

"Crime of '73"—Name given to an Act of Congress discontinuing the coinage and use of silver as money.

Crittenden Compromise, 1861—Proposals made by Senator Crittenden of Kentucky to bring the seceded states back into the Union by protecting their interests in slavery by "permanent amendments" to the Constitution.

Crusades—A series of seven successive religious wars from 1095–1291 waged by Europe against the Moslems in regions bordering the eastern Mediterranean.

Cumberland Road—Another name for the National Road beginning at Cumberland, Maryland, and extending westward; not to be confused with the Cumberland Gap across the Appalachians and leading to the Wilderness Road into central Kentucky.

Currency Act, 1764—Law enacted by Parliament that prohibited issues of legal-tender paper money by colonial assemblies; the law was much resented by the colonists who were suffering from a money shortage following the French and Indian War.

Dawes Act, 1887—Act of Congress providing for distribution of Native American tribal lands to individual ownership and conferring citizenship upon those who renounced tribal allegiance.

Declaratory Act, 1766—After repeal of the Stamp Act, Parliament passed this Act to assert the right to legislate for the colonies "in all cases whatsoever."

Deism—A religion or philosophy of free thinkers; flourished during the period of the American Revolution; denied the minute intervention of God in the lives of individuals.

Demarcation Line—Global boundary drawn by the Pope in 1492 and changed in 1493 in the Treaty of Tordesillas; the Line separated Spanish and Portuguese spheres of trade and colonization.

distribution—A policy, advocated by the Whigs, of distributing among the states the revenues from land sales.

Dominion of New England, 1685–1688—A union of New England, New York, and New Jersey formed by James II who appointed Sir Edmund Andros as royal governor over the Dominion.

Dred Scott Case, 1857—A decision of the Supreme Court favorable to the South; it legalized slavery in the territories and declared the Missouri Compromise unconstitutional.

Dust Bowl—A semiarid high plains area subject to serious wind erosion in years of drought; the area straddles parts of Texas, Oklahoma, Colorado, and Kansas.

embargo—Any government restriction of commerce; somewhat similar to boycott.

Embargo Act, 1807—An extreme measure by Jefferson to secure a recognition of American commercial rights; it stopped all foreign trade of America.

entail—A legal means to prevent an heir from disposing of land; the purpose was to assure that an estate be kept intact.

enumerated powers—The principle that a government may exercise only those powers granted to it by its founders, as in the American Constitution.

Era of Good Feeling—The period of strong nationalism from 1816 into the 1820s during which there was an absence of strife between political parties.

established churches—Official, or government, churches in the colonies; tithes were collected from all citizens for their support during this time of union of church and state; the disestablishment of the churches brought the separation of church and state.

European Cooperation Administration—See Marshall Plan.

excise—An internal revenue tax; term usually applied to a sales tax upon selected commodities as distinguished from a general sales tax.

ex post facto—Any law or measure providing a penalty for an act not made illegal before it was committed. Such laws are forbidden by the Constitution.

Exposition and Protest, 1828—South Carolina's protest against protective tariffs which it declared to be unconstitutional.

Farmers' Alliances—National and local farmers' organizations prominent in the 1880s; they took over the leadership of the farmers' protest movement begun by the Grangers. The Alliances disappeared as they were absorbed by the Populist Party in the early 1890s.

Federalist Papers—Political essays written by Hamilton, Jay, and Madison to win support for the Constitution during the campaign for ratification.

Fenians—A secret organization of Irish-Americans during the Civil War period; invaded Canada in 1866 in a plan to exchange Canada for Irish independence.

filibuster—This term has two distinct meanings: (1) an unauthorized military expedition of adventurers against another country in time of peace; (2) obstructive parliamentary tactics employed by a minority to prevent passage of unwanted legislation, usually takes form of long pointless speechmaking.

"Fire-eaters"—Southern extremists who favored secession in the decade preceding the Civil War.

franchise—Any special right granted by a governing body, such as the individual right to vote or the right of a corporation to operate a public utility.

Freedmen's Bureau—Controversial federal agency that provided relief for distressed freedmen in the South after the Civil War.

freemen—In colonial times those possessing the right to vote.

Freeport Doctrine—The position taken by Douglas in his debate with Lincoln at Freeport, Illinois, that, if the people of a territory wish, they could exclude slavery by failing to enact local regulations for its protection. He said this could he done in spite of the Dred Scott decision which held that it was legal to take slaves into the territories.

fundamentalism—The term is applied primarily to orthodox religious beliefs upholding the literal interpretation of the Bible—opposed to the modernists who accept the findings of science.

Fundamental Orders of Connecticut—This first written constitution in America was drawn up to provide an instrument of government and to unite several towns in the Connecticut valley.

Gadsden Purchase, 1853—The purchase from Mexico of a strip of territory south of the Gila River in the present states of Arizona and New Mexico. James Gadsden of South Carolina made the purchase to obtain the best route for the construction of a transcontinental railroad.

"gag rule"—Rules adopted in both houses of Congress, beginning in 1837, to dispose of abolitionist petitions without taking action on them.

GAR, Grand Army of the Republic—Organized in 1865 among the Union veterans of the Civil War.

Geographic Revolution—The widening knowledge of other lands among Europeans in the late middle ages and the shift in the center of the Western world from the Mediterranean to the Atlantic.

gerrymander—To organize legislative and congressional districts in such a way as to secure the greatest number of districts with a majority of voters favorable to the party doing the redistricting.

GOP—Grand Old Party, nickname of the Republican Party.

graduation—The policy of land sales, advocated by Benton and other Western Democrats, providing for reduction according to a schedule of the price of unsold land.

"grandfather clauses"—Laws passed in Southern states to prevent African Americans from voting. So-called because they qualified persons to vote whose ancestors had voted before 1867 or other dates that excluded African Americans.

Granger Laws—State laws enacted under the influence of the Farmers' Grange during the 1870s to provide for the regulation of public utilities, especially the railroads.

Grangers—Popular name for the post-Civil War farmers organization officially known as the Patrons of Husbandry.

Great Awakening—An evangelical religious crusade in the later colonial period; began with Jonathan Edwards in New England but was most influential in the frontier regions.

"Great Compromise"—The compromise made in the Constitutional Convention on the issue of representation in Congress between the large state plan of Virginia and the small state plan of New Jersey.

Great Migration—This term is applied primarily to the large-scale migration of Puritans from England to America from 1620 to 1640; it is also used in reference to the great westward movement following the War of 1812.

"greenbacks"—legal-tender paper money used to help finance the Civil War in the North.

habeas corpus—A legal writ by which an arrested person may demand his freedom unless sufficient cause can be shown to justify holding him for trial.

"Half-Breeds"—A nickname given to Liberal Republicans by their "Stalwart" opponents about 1880. "Half-Breeds" included Hayes, Blaine, and Garfield; "Stalwarts" included Conkling, Platt, and Arthur.

Hartford Convention, 1814—Meeting of delegates from the New England states to express opposition to the War of 1812; demanded constitutional amendments to protect the interests of New England.

headright—A land grant in colonial Virginia given originally to those who paid the passage of an immigrant; usually 50 acres.

Hispaniola—Spanish name for the West Indian island often referred to as Haiti today and the site of the first Spanish colony in America.

holding company—A corporation owning sufficient shares in other corporations to effectively control them; frequently used as a monopoly device.

"Holy Experiment"—Name given by William Penn to his colony of Pennsylvania; refers to idealistic religious, social, and political innovations he sought to realize there.

implied powers—Powers of Congress not directly granted by the Constitution but permitted by the elastic clause which gives Congress the power "To make all laws...necessary and proper" for executing the powers expressly granted.

impressment—The practice of forcing individuals into military or other service.

indentured servants—Immigrants in colonial times who voluntarily or involuntarily entered into contracts to sell their labor for a period of years in return for payment of their ship passage to America.

Independent Treasury—Also called Sub-Treasury system. The practice of depositing federal revenues in government offices in lieu of banks of any kind. In government offices the money could not be lent or used by bankers as reserves upon which paper money could be issued.

indigo—A plant grown in the colonial South from which was extracted a blue dye used in clothing.

initiative and referendum—Processes by which voters may directly vote upon laws; intended to give law-making power to the voters since state and local legislative bodies are not always fully responsive to the popular will.

injunction—A court order forbidding some action; frequently used as a weapon against organized labor except as outlawed. Violation of an injunction may result in assessment of heavy penalties for "contempt of court."

joint-stock company—Trading companies, forerunners of present-day corporations, organized for single trading ventures by selling stock to members; used in founding the early colonies in America.

Kentucky and Virginia Resolutions, 1798—Resolutions passed by these two Republican-dominated state legislatures condemning and denying the constitutionality of the Alien and Sedition Acts; these resolutions were the first formal statement of the doctrines of states-rights and nullification.

"King Cotton"—Term expressing the economic importance of cotton to the South.

"Kitchen Cabinet"—An informal group of advisers, not members of the President's cabinet, consulted by Andrew Jackson. Leaders among them were newspaper editors.

Know-Nothing Party—A nationalist third party movement in the 1850s that appealed to those born in the United States against recent immigrants and their influence.

laissez-faire—Almost literally, "Let them do as they please"; economic philosophy associated with Adam Smith in his *Wealth of Nations;* calls for an economy free of government controls; the free enterprise system.

Lecompton Constitution, 1857—Proslavery constitution for Kansas statehood; it never was accepted by Kansas.

Liberal Republicans—A faction which left the Republican Party in 1872 to support the Democratic nominee Horace Greeley.

Liberty Party—An antislavery, third party that nominated a presidential candidate in 1840.

lobbying—Practice of individuals and pressure groups of seeking by various means to influence the vote of members of governmental bodies.

Locofocos—A hard money faction that sprang up in the Democratic Party in the late 1830s; they opposed banks and paper money and favored the Independent Treasury system.

log-rolling—A practice of vote-trading by legislators in support of each other's favorite laws.

Macon's Bill No. 2, 1810—Reopened trade with Britain and France and offered to place an embargo against the enemy of whichever country that first recognized American commercial rights.

mandamus—A written order of a court ordering that a specific thing be done.

Manifest Destiny—A widely held belief among Americans that the United States was clearly destined to occupy all of North America.

***Marbury v. Madison*, 1803**—The case in which the Supreme Court first asserted the right of judicial review.

Mayflower Compact—An agreement signed aboard the ship *Mayflower* in 1620 by the Pilgrim settlers at Plymouth; it pledged colonists to abide by the democratic principle of majority rule.

mercantilism—The prevailing economic theory applied in Europe during colonial times; called for the exercise of numerous economic powers and controls by the state; contrasts with later economic philosophy of laissez-faire or free enterprise.

merit system—The civil service system by which public employees are chosen upon a basis of qualifications rather than by political influence.

Molasses Act, 1733—Levied prohibitive duties on molasses imported from the French and Spanish West Indies, but the law was not enforced.

Molly Maguires—A secret, criminal labor organization operating in the anthracite coal fields of Pennsylvania in the 1870s; eventually suppressed.

moratorium—A provision for delaying the repayment of debt.

National Labor Union—The first national labor organization, founded in 1866 and lasted until 1871; it was a federation of other unions instead of being a single great union.

Nat Turner Rebellion, 1831—Slave revolt in Virginia led by an African American preacher. Fifty-seven whites were killed and twice as many African Americans, including those executed after being tried.

Navigation Acts—Laws enacted by the British Parliament to implement the mercantilist theory of government control over economic relations between mother country and colonies.

New England Confederation—A union of Massachusetts, Plymouth, Connecticut, and New Haven organized in 1643 by its members. This league was the first formed among the American colonies. The members organized for defense against the Native Americans and Dutch and for cooperation in other common problems.

Nonintercourse Act, 1809—An American embargo against Britain and France; included a provision that trade would be reopened with either nation if it would repeal restrictions against American shipping.

Nullification Ordinance, 1832—South Carolina's attempt to carry out its theory of the right of a state to nullify any act of the Federal Congress judged unconstitutional by a state; the ordinance nullified the Tariffs of 1828 and 1832.

"Ohio Idea"—An inflationary proposal of paper money advocates to pay the Union Civil War debt with greenbacks instead of in gold.

Ostend Manifesto, 1854—An unofficial statement by American ministers that Spain ought to sell Cuba to the United States and if Spain refused the United States would be justified in taking it by force.

Parson's Cause—Court case in colonial Virginia in which a jury defied the British government by awarding minimum damages to Anglican ministers who sued for back pay under a British law.

paternalism—The practice by a nation or employer of controlling and caring for people as dependents in the manner of a father toward his children.

patroon—Dutch colonizers awarded large land grants in New Netherland in return for bringing settlers to America; settlers became tenants of the patroons.

Pendleton Act, 1883—Act of Congress that created the Federal Civil Service Commission and instituted the merit system for federal employees.

plurality—The votes polled by the leading candidate, not necessarily a majority of all votes cast.

pool—A monopoly device adopted in the 1860s; agreements to avoid competition by dividing markets geographically or by percentage or by the payment of profits to a common treasury to be divided according to agreement.

"popular sovereignty"—The solution offered by Douglas to the controversy over slavery in the territories; it proposed to leave the decision regarding slavery to the residents of a territory.

Populism—A reform third party of the 1890s, especially active among farmers in the West and South; protested against big business domination of American economic and political life.

"Pottawatomie Massacre," 1856—The murder of five pro-slavery men in "Bleeding Kansas" by John Brown in retaliation for the burning of the free state capital at Lawrence.

Preemption Act, 1841—Federal law that gave squatters an option to buy land they had settled.

primogeniture—Laws of inheritance providing descent of land to the oldest son.

Prince Henry—Portuguese founder of the school of navigation at Sagres where the sciences of navigation, geography, and seamanship were taught.

privateering—Waging war by privately-owned armed vessels commissioned to capture enemy ships; a kind of legalized piracy outlawed by international agreement since 1856.

Proclamation of 1763—An attempt by the British government to settle problems with Native Americans by regulating entry into the Native American reserve west of the Allegheny divide.

proprietors—English individuals or groups awarded land for settling colonists on it; the proprietor became the landlord and the settlers his tenants.

Quartering Act, 1765—Required colonial assemblies to provide barracks and provisions for British troops.

Quebec Act, 1774—British law providing for government of the province of Quebec; its several provisions greatly antagonized Protestants in the thirteen colonies.

"Quids"—Name given to extreme advocates of states' rights who, led by John Randolph of Virginia, strongly opposed Jefferson's policy of conciliating the Federalists.

quit rents—Annual payments, usually small, required of tenants by proprietary landlords in acknowledgment of the lord's ownership of the land; provided an income for the landlords but detested by the tenants.

reciprocity—Mutual concessions to reduce tariff rates, trade agreements between two countries.

redemptioners—Also called "free-willers"; voluntary immigrants to America who became indentured servants of a better class than the involuntary indentured servants who were often of the criminal classes.

referendum—A form of direct legislation whereby certain measures are required to be submitted to the decision of voters, usually because of a failure to act by a legislative body.

refunding—The settlement of a debt by substitution of a new issue of bonds for an earlier issue.

reparations—Payments assessed usually against a defeated nation held responsible for war damage.

Resumption Act, 1875—An Act of Congress providing for the resumption of specie payment beginning January 1, 1879: it made greenbacks redeemable in gold and practically placed the nation on the gold standard.

right of deposit—The right of American shippers to store goods in New Orleans free of customs duties while awaiting reloading for shipment on ocean-going vessels.

Rule of 1756—A British-enforced rule of international law that held that a roundabout, or "broken," shipment of goods to evade a wartime blockade was the same as a direct shipment and therefore illegal.

"salutary neglect"—Describes the economic freedom the English colonies were allowed by the failure to enforce mercantilist controls.

sanctions—The application of economic or other measures against a nation to force it to obey international law.

"Scalawags"—Southern whites who cooperated during Reconstruction with the Northern carpetbag rule.

"Sea-dogs"—English sea captains under Queen Elizabeth acting as legalized pirates in conducting trade and raiding Spanish towns and ships in America and Europe.

Separatists—A group of Puritans who favored complete separation from the Church of England and the independence of each congregation. The colony of Plymouth was founded by the Separatist Pilgrims in 1620.

Shays' Rebellion, 1886—Insurrection of farmer-debtors in western Massachusetts led by the Revolutionary War veteran Daniel Shays against the hard money policies of the governing class; an important cause for calling the Constitutional Convention in 1787.

Slidell Mission—Polk's appointment of John Slidell to go to Mexico to bargain for the cession of New Mexico, California, and the disputed boundary of Texas in return for American assumption of debt claims against Mexico and a large payment of cash. The Mexican government refused to enter into discussion with Slidell.

social contract—Theory of government formulated by the English philosopher John Locke; became the philosophical basis of the American Revolution.

"Solid South"—Term applied to the one-party (Democratic) system of the South following the Civil War; followed to preserve white supremacy.

Sons of Liberty—Secret groups organized in colonial towns to prevent enforcement of the Stamp Act; they forced all stamp agents in the colonies to resign.

"Sooners"—Term applied to landseekers around 1890 who tried to enter Oklahoma sooner than the deadline for the "runs" to begin.

"Stalwarts"—Nickname applied to the spoilsmen and conservatives in the Republican Party around 1880. See "Half-Breeds."

sovereignty—Supreme and independent authority of a government.

Specie Circular—A printed letter issued by President Jackson to land offices instructing federal land agents to accept only specie in payment for land, in effect, to refuse paper money.

"spoils system"—The practice of victorious political parties of removing officeholders of the opposition party and giving their jobs to supporters of the ruling party.

squatter—A settler who appropriates land for himself without first securing title.

"squatter sovereignty"—A solution proposed by Lewis Cass to the controversy over slavery in the territories; it proposed to allow residents of a territory to decide whether it would be slave or free.

Stamp Act, 1765—Parliamentary Act passed to collect direct taxes from the American colonists for the support of an army in the colonies; resented as a direct tax and for other reasons.

Sugar Act, 1764—A revenue measure that took the place of the Molasses Act of 1733 and reduced duties on molasses by one half; attempts to enforce the Act led to serious friction between the colonies and England.

syndicalism—Radical trade union movement and philosophy advocating use of violent, direct action such as sabotage and general strikes.

Tallmadge Amendment—An amendment to the Missouri statehood bill to prohibit the introduction of slaves into Missouri and providing for emancipation of slaves born after the admission of Missouri; intended to make Missouri a free state but failed to pass.

"Tariff of Abominations," 1828—Nickname given to the Tariff of 1828 by its opponents because of its high protective rates. It evoked Calhoun's *Exposition and Protest* which was adopted by the legislature of South Carolina.

Tea Act, 1773—A Parliamentary Act that gave the British East India Company a virtual monopoly over the sale of tea in America; resented both because it was a precedent for British monopolies in America and because it retained an import duty on tea bought by the Americans.

theocracy—Rule by religious leaders, as in early Massachusetts.

Townshend Acts, 1767—Parliamentary revenue measures passed under the leadership of Charles Townshend; duties were levied on colonial imports; superseded the Stamp Act.

transcendentalism—An optimistic, liberal philosophy of Emerson and other New England intellectuals before the Civil War; emphasized the dignity of the common man; held that intuition transcended experience.

Trent Affair, 1861—Diplomatic crisis between the United States and Great Britain precipitated by American removal of two Confederate diplomats, Mason and Slidell, from the British mailship.

triangular trade—The predominant patterns of foreign trade by the thirteen colonies with Europe, Africa, and the West Indies.

trust—A device used to create business monopolies. Under it competing corporations surrender voting stock to a board of trustees in return for trust certificates. The trustees then operate the separate companies as a unit for purposes of price-fixing and other policies.

Tweed Ring—A grossly corrupt political machine in New York City around 1870, led by "Boss" Tweed.

Underground Railroad—Systems of stations organized in the Northern states to aid runaway slaves escape from the South and gain their freedom in Canada.

Union League—A propaganda agency of the Radical Republicans in the South worked to assure the loyalty of the Freedmen to the Republican Party.

"virtual" representation—English theory of Parliamentary representation as opposed to the American theory of "actual" representation. England held that the actual election by the Americans of a quota of representatives to Parliament was unnecessary since Parliament theoretically represented the interests of the whole Empire regardless of who elected them.

Wade-Davis Bill, 1864—Reconstruction program introduced by the Radical Republicans but pocket-vetoed by Lincoln.

watered stock—Stock issued with a nominal value in excess of capital actually invested in earning assets of an operating corporation.

wildcat banks—State-chartered banks that followed unsound banking practices by issuing paper money not sufficiently backed up by reserves of specie.

Wilmot Proviso—An amendment offered repeatedly in Congress to bills relating to the Mexican War; the Proviso sought to exclude slavery from any soil won from Mexico.

Womens Christian Temperance Union (WCTU)—Founded 1874 to curb liquor consumption and promote prohibition laws.

writs of assistance—General search warrants; used by British colonial customs officials to enable them to search in all places for smuggled goods; upheld by the colonial courts but public opinion considered them illegal.

Yazoo Strip—A strip of land parallel to the northern boundary of Florida extending from western Georgia to the Mississippi; American claim to it conceded by Spain in the Pinckney Treaty.

"yellow-dog" contract—An agreement required by employers that an employee promise not to join any union during his employment.

"yellow" journalism—Newspapers made sensational to attract readers; associated originally with the use of yellow ink, particularly in the first comic strip, "The Yellow Kid."

Zenger Trial—An unsuccessful attempt in New York in 1735 to convict John Peter Zenger, newspaper publisher, on a charge of libel; important landmark in establishing freedom of the press.

See index for persons or terms not listed above.

INDEX